D1597577

"Proving that continuing to apply logic to the thinking process (yes, the principles dating back to Aristotle that were adapted and advanced by Eliyahu M. Goldratt in our modern age) can improve it substantially, H. William Dettmer's new edition of his landmark book, *Goldratt's Theory of Constraints*, reflects the evolution of the thinking process to its current level: the *Logical* Thinking Process. Make no mistake: the majority of heavy lifting to elevate the thinking process has been done by Dettmer himself. Goldratt once told me that he did not write anything of depth about the thinking process (TP). Instead, he left it to the few brave and uniquely qualified educators, of whom Dettmer has risen to the forefront. This new edition teaches how leaders can face down real-life issues by employing the rigorous deductive logic he's honed to perfection by repeated application: how a better quality Current Reality Tree (CRT) can be created in less time. New material includes a chapter on changing the status quo. If there's one Dettmer book to own ahead of all others, it is *The Logical Thinking Process.*"

Jeff "SKI" Kinsey, Jonah
Throughput Press
Hilton Head Island, SC

"Where would the logical approach to problem solving espoused by TOC proponents be without Bill Dettmer? Is logical thinking so simple that a cave man might be able to do it? Is it common sense, that we need not overthink it? I would argue neither. *The Logical Thinking Process* clearly demonstrates that a thorough, logical approach can be used not only to identify complex problems and find potential solutions, but also to generate buy-in among those individuals who must bring about improvement in the organization as well as provide support for the process of planning and implementing effective solutions. Bill's dedication, experience, and motivation to develop the necessary tools for this problem-solving approach have been invaluable to both practitioners and academicians. He goes about it in such a thoughtful, unrelenting, and disciplined way that his work has effectively defined the field of study."

J. Wayne Patterson, Ph.D.
Professor of Operations Management
Clemson University

"After years of thinking, applying, re-thinking, and modifying, we have now Bill Dettmer's most recent update, documenting those years of experience with verbalizing intuition into clear logic and applying it to business. This process facilitates clarification of thoughts, the challenge of hidden assumptions, identification of real root causes, and rational prediction of what could happen in the future. This is all based on logic and common sense; there is no 'believe me— it works.' All managers who use this book will find themselves better prepared to think logically, without losing any of their own intuition. Is there anything more important for managers to be doing? Read this book carefully— it could be very important to you."

Eli Schragenheim
Elyakim Management Systems, Ltd.

"Don't buy this book if you believe that 'gut feel' is the perfect tool for leaders to use in deciding what they should do and what their people should do. However, if you are looking for a box of logical decision-making tools to use in setting goals, deciding how they should be achieved, and leading the execution of your plan, then this book must be on the top of your desk daily. It is *the* reference for the tools of constraint management—the leadership discipline that focuses on finding and resolving system constraints."

Dieter Legat, Ph.D.
Managing Director
Delta Institute
Geneva, Switzerland

"Dettmer has made an important contribution to competitive strategy by writing what is, as far as I know, the first book to unify and demonstrate the power of both the Logical Thinking Process developed by Goldratt and the OODA loop (observe-orient-decide-act). Operating together, they will be very, very hard to beat."

Chet Richards, Ph.D.
Author of *Certain to Win* and an international expert on the philosophy of John Boyd

"When I started reading *The Logical Thinking Process*, I couldn't easily put it aside. There are a lot of new insights in this book, even for those who are already familiar with previous books on the Theory of Constraints. Bill does not simply tell the story of the logical thinking tools (as invented by someone else). He creates his own story of the thinking tools. He introduces a new tool, the Intermediate

Objectives Map, which brilliantly dissolves many difficulties that people might have had with the other tools. He merges the Prerequisite Tree and Transition Tree into a more useful Prerequisite Tree, and he dissects the 3-UDE Cloud.

He is at his best with this book, and you will feel the experience of decades of consulting and teaching. Working through the book is the next best thing to attending one of his thinking process classes in person. Get the book, take your time to read through it, be patient, and reap the benefits from your increased understanding and the streamlined method."

Christoph Steindl, Ph.D.
Managing Director, Catalysts GmbH
Linz, Austria

"*The Logical Thinking Process* is the most comprehensive, easy-to-follow, step-by-step guide to finding real solutions to problems I face in business every day. Dettmer has created the definitive guide for applying the Logical Thinking Process that Goldratt created. If you really want to find the key leverage points to fundamentally improve your business, *The Logical Thinking Process* will give you the tools to achieve your goal."

Christopher M. Zephro
Director, Supply Chain
Seagate Technology

"I find Bill to be the world's most articulate exponent of the thinking process tools of the *Theory of Constraints* and very much enjoy the experience and knowledge he brings to his writing style. This book manages to be precise without being pedantic, and entertaining without losing sight of the seriousness of the topic. The book works both as a grand overview of a systems approach to complex problem solving and as a practical chapter-by-chapter guide to the tools and techniques of rational thinking. If you're wondering how best to structure, test, and communicate your reasoning, then read Bill's book."

David V. Hodes, Managing Director
TOC Center of Australia (TOCCA)
Sydney, Australia

"This is a complete guide for the Logical Thinking Process (TP). It embodies the latest thinking about logical thinking. It covers all modes of TP application, from personal problem solving to strategic development, and from corporate problem solving to legal applications of the thinking process. In teaching this thinking process in Japan, I have personally witnessed phenomenal development of students' capabilities to solve problems and visualize the interactions of whole systems. This book is Bill Dettmer's gift for humanity."

Haruyuki Uchiyama, President
MoreThroughput.com
Japan

"The topics that are a must-read are the Intermediate Objectives Map and Current Reality Tree. There is a basic research in these areas that can be invaluable to the reader. The chapter on the Intermediate Objectives Map provides an excellent guide for understanding undesirable effects and selecting them effectively. This improves the quality of the Current Reality Tree significantly."

Sadashiv S Pandit
Executive Chairman
Fleetguard Filters Private Limited
India

"*The Logical Thinking Process* is a practical guide to improving any system's performance, from one of the clearest authors in the field of the Theory of Constraints. It quickly gets to the heart of major concepts and techniques, and updates prior readers of the literature with the latest developments.

Many standard tools for continuous improvement fail to achieve noteworthy results at a macro level. Why? Because too often, the problems to which the tools are applied are local in nature. The tools, and the problems to which they are applied, do not address the greatest constraints holding back the system as a whole. In *The Logical Thinking Process,* leaders and improvement teams are given a concrete method for creating the kind of major turnaround that today's crises so often demand.

The Logical Thinking Process is a must-have tool in the arsenal of any continuous improvement effort."

Paul H. Selden, Ph. D.
Founder and President, Performance Management, Inc.

The Logical Thinking Process

A Systems Approach to
Complex Problem Solving

Also available from ASQ Quality Press:

Breaking the Constraints to World-Class Performance
H. William Dettmer

Strategic Navigation: A Systems Approach to Business Strategy
H. William Dettmer

Enterprise Process Mapping: Integrating Systems for Compliance and Business Excellence
Charles G. Cobb

Root Cause Analysis: Simplified Tools and Techniques, Second Edition
Bjørn Andersen and Tom Fagerhaug

The Certified Quality Process Analyst Handbook
Eldon H. Christensen, Kathleen M. Coombes-Betz, and Marilyn S. Stein

Making Change Work: Practical Tools for Overcoming Human Resistance to Change
Brien Palmer

Business Process Improvement Toolbox, Second Edition
Bjørn Andersen

Business Performance through Lean Six Sigma: Linking the Knowledge Worker, the Twelve Pillars, and Baldrige
James T. Schutta

The Process-Focused Organization: A Transition Strategy for Success
Robert A. Gardner

Inside Knowledge: Rediscovering the Source of Performance Improvement
David Fearon & Steven A. Cavaleri

Decision Process Quality Management
William D. Mawby

Defining and Analyzing a Business Process: A Six Sigma Pocket Guide
Jeffrey N. Lowenthal

Avoiding the Corporate Death Spiral: Recognizing and Eliminating the Signs of Decline
Gregg Stocker

To request a complimentary catalog of ASQ Quality Press publications, call 800-248-1946, or visit our Web site at http://qualitypress.asq.org.

The Logical Thinking Process

A Systems Approach to Complex Problem Solving

H. William Dettmer

ASQ Quality Press
Milwaukee, Wisconsin

American Society for Quality, Quality Press, Milwaukee, WI 53203
© 2007 by H. William Dettmer
All rights reserved. Published 2007.
Printed in the United States of America.

13   12   11   10   09   08   07   5   4   3   2

Library of Congress Cataloging-in-Publication Data

Dettmer, H. William.
    The logical thinking process : a systems approach to complex problem solving /
H. William Dettmer.
    p. cm.
A total re-write, more than a second edition, of his Goldratt's Theory of Constraints, c1997.
Accompanied by a compact disk that contains a full-function, unrestricted copy of version 1.0 of
Transformation Logic Tree software.
ISBN 978-0-87389-723-5

1. Decision support systems. 2. Problem solving. 3. Theory of constraints (Management)
4. Decision trees--Computer programs. 5. Industrial management. I. Dettmer, H. William.
Goldratt's theory of constraints. II. Title. III. Title: Systems approach to complex problem solving.

HD30.213.D48 2007

658.4'03--dc22
                                    2007026109

Publisher: William A. Tony
Acquisitions Editor: Matt T. Meinholz
Project Editor: Paul O'Mara
Production Administrator: Randall Benson

ASQ Mission: The American Society for Quality advances individual, organizational, and
community excellence worldwide through learning, quality improvement, and knowledge
exchange.

Attention Bookstores, Wholesalers, Schools, and Corporations: ASQ Quality Press books,
videotapes, audiotapes, and software are available at quantity discounts with bulk purchases for
business, educational, or instructional use. For information, please contact ASQ Quality Press at
800-248-1946, or write to ASQ Quality Press, P.O. Box 3005, Milwaukee, WI 53201-3005.

To place orders or to request a free copy of the ASQ Quality Press Publications Catalog, including
ASQ membership information, call 800-248-1946. Visit our Web site at www.asq.org or
http://qualitypress.asq.org.

∞ Printed on acid-free paper

Quality Press
600 N. Plankinton Avenue
Milwaukee, Wisconsin 53203
Call toll free 800-248-1946
Fax 414-272-1734
www.asq.org
http://www.asq.org/quality-press
http://standardsgroup.asq.org
E-mail: authors@asq.org

ASQ
AMERICAN SOCIETY
FOR QUALITY

For Doris Herron, Jean Hardman, and Marjorie Ebeling.
All for one, and one for all.

Table of Contents

List of Illustrations

Preface

Books are snapshots in time. The previous edition of this book, *Goldratt's Theory of Constraints (GTOC)*, was a snapshot of "the state of the art" of the Thinking Process in 1996. But time passes, and people and things evolve. The Thinking Process is no exception.

Since 1996, I've applied the Thinking Process in commercial companies, government agencies, and not-for-profit organizations. And I've taught it to people throughout the United States, South America, Europe, Japan, Korea, and Australia. In each of these consulting and teaching engagements, *GTOC* was the basis of my work.

But over time I began to notice a developing tendency: I was diverging from the techniques and procedures I'd established in *GTOC*. In teaching, I found that I needed to modify the procedures for constructing the logic trees in order to overcome difficulties that some students had in learning to apply them. In my own applications, I found that the need to quickly develop more robust trees gradually drew me away from the procedures in the first edition.

This shouldn't be surprising. The Thinking Process was relatively new and still evolving when I wrote *GTOC*. Any new methodology can be improved. Yet *GTOC* still stood as a snapshot in time. In teaching Thinking Process courses, I began to supplement *GTOC* with a three-ring binder containing newer guidance and examples. By 2005, I had so transformed the way I taught the Thinking Process that *GTOC* became an adjunct to my courses, supporting the three-ring binder, rather than the other way around.

The transformation of the Thinking Process over the past ten years has been a good thing. In 1996, most people teaching the Thinking Process—including me—required ten days to cover it all. With some innovations, I found that I could include more material in six days than I originally could in ten, and still finish early. In 2006, I decided it was time to incorporate what I've learned about faster and better ways to teach and apply the Thinking Process into a new edition of *GTOC*.

But as I began to edit the original text of *GTOC*, I realized just how substantial the changes would be. It turned out to be far more than just an update of the 1996 version— it was a whole new approach to building and applying logic trees. For that reason alone, merely calling this book a second edition of *GTOC* would have been an inaccurate representation of the content, comparable to calling a 2006 Ford automobile "Model T, second edition."

Moreover, while the Thinking Process has its roots in the Theory of Constraints, it has since realized a much broader applicability in system analysis and systems thinking. Much as some trademarked brand names (e.g., Kleenex, Google, Post-it Notes, Scotch tape, and so on) enjoy a kind of evolution to generic usage over time, so too has the Thinking Process as a methodology become more of a generic logical analysis process. So it's appropriate to title this book in a way that conveys the broader applicability of the method—to characterize it as what it is: *the Logical Thinking Process, a systems-level approach to policy analysis.* At the risk of hyperbole, I would go so far as to say it's the most powerful such methodology yet created.

None of this alters the fact that this marvelous logical method was created and introduced by Eliyahu M. Goldratt as a means of identifying and breaking policy constraints. Though the principles of deductive logic date back to the days of Aristotle, it took Goldratt to make them more than just a topic of curiosity and academic interest. The Thinking Process is probably the first widely-used, practical tool for the application of deductive logic, and its users should not forget that Goldratt made this possible.

A major contribution of real value that this book offers users of the Thinking Process is software. Anyone who has used the Thinking Process for long knows what a challenge this is. When Goldratt first introduced the Thinking Process, computer-based graphics programs capable of rendering the logic trees were few, far between, and expensive. For the first several years, the only way to build and present Thinking Process trees involved using Post-it Notes connected by hand-drawn lines on flip-chart paper taped to walls. In the mid-1990s, a variety of drawing and flowcharting programs became available for both Macintosh computers and IBM PCs, but they were relatively expensive and they didn't lend themselves directly to Thinking Process applications. Icons needed to be created or modified, and standardization of symbols was consequently almost nonexistent.

In 2006, I was privileged to meet Dr. Mark Van Oyen, a professor of engineering at the University of Michigan, who had begun development of a unique graphical software application—one that was designed primarily to create Thinking Process logic trees, and only secondarily for other flowcharting uses. Dr. Van Oyen and I came to a meeting of the minds on incorporating that software, *Transformation Logic Tree*, with this book. The compact disk provided here contains a full-function, unrestricted copy of version 1.0 for new and experienced users of the Thinking Process alike to use in building their logic trees. Appendix J includes more information on how to install and use the software.

This book contains new examples of logic trees from a variety of real-world applications. Most of the diagrams and illustrations are new and improved. Explanations and procedures for constructing the logic trees are considerably simplified.

Yet notwithstanding all these improvements, the Thinking Process still requires concerted effort to learn and apply well. A book like this can't be all things to all people. Simply reading a book won't make you an expert in the Thinking Process. Only regular, repetitive practice can do that. And specialized training from someone who thoroughly understands (and has effective teaching skills) is advisable in order to realize maximum benefit. These can also compress the learning curve from months to days.

Even so, you're still likely to have questions that this book doesn't adequately address. I encourage readers to contact me directly with any such questions, as well as with comments, pro or con, about the book. How else can things improve?

H. William Dettmer
Port Angeles, Washington, USA
gsi@goalsys.com

Acknowledgments

Any book such as this is the culmination of effort by more people than just the author alone. I would be remiss if I failed to recognize those dedicated, consummate professionals who have helped me in a variety of ways to create the book you're reading now.

This help starts with ten years of feedback from Thinking Process students and practitioners who are too numerous to name—and I'd undoubtedly slight some by forgetting to mention them if I tried. For the review of parts or all of the manuscript of this book, I'm indebted to (in reverse alphabetical order), Christopher Zephro, Haruyuki Uchiyama, Christoph Steindel, Paul Selden, Timothy Sellan, Chet Richards, Wayne Patterson, Sadashiv Pandit, Dieter Legat, Larry Leach, David Hodes, and Jerry Harvey.

I am also indebted to Stephen F. Kaufman, hanshi 10th dan, who graciously shared with me his understanding of the Way of the Warrior as expressed in the writings and life of Miyamoto Musashi, the prototypical samurai.

The high-quality production of this book would not have been possible without the initiating efforts of Matt Meinholz and Paul O'Mara at Quality Press; Janet Sorensen, who created this layout and superbly rendered my initial drawings into the crisp, clean illustrations you find here; and Linda Presto, whose eagle-eye copyediting and superlative skill in constructing the indispensable, invaluable index helped deliver the truly professional result you hold in your hand.

Mark Van Oyen earns my deep appreciation for contributing the *Transformation Logic Tree* software to the efforts of aspiring Thinking Process practitioners, and for his willingness to see it included with this book.

Finally, none of us would have the Thinking Process at all if not for the creativity of Eli Goldratt.

Introduction

What's really new in this book that warrants a change in the title? First, I've learned how to streamline the process of constructing the logic trees while simultaneously ensuring that the results are more logically sound and closer representations of reality than ever before. Whereas Current Reality Trees (CRT) once took several days to complete, a better-quality tree is now possible in a matter of several hours. When used as part of an integrated Thinking Process, all of the trees are now more precisely and seamlessly aligned with one another.

This better integration is possible because of a new application of an old (and little used) tree: the Intermediate Objectives (IO) Map. An hour or less spent perfecting an IO Map at the beginning shaves days off completion of the rest of the process, and the results are much more robust. So, with this book, the IO Map takes its place as the first step in the Thinking Process.

A second major change is in the relationship between the Evaporating Cloud and the Current Reality Tree. As Goldratt originally conceived the Thinking Process, these two trees enjoyed a close logical relationship, but it was frequently a difficult transition. Sometime in the late 1990s, a number of Thinking Process practitioners began using an approach to analyzing problems called "the 3-UDE Cloud."* The 3-UDE Cloud was then used to create something called a "communication current reality tree." This combination of the Evaporating Cloud and the Current Reality Tree certainly streamlined the process of creating these two trees in many situations, but this process is logically flawed (and often myopic). I found the results of this process to be incomplete, too narrowly focused, and not really representative of a system's larger issues. It certainly did offer some efficiencies and economies over the Thinking Process as originally described in *GTOC*— though at the expense of logical quality and robustness. This book explains the deficiencies of the "3-UDE Cloud to communication CRT" approach in Appendix E. Chapter 5 explains an easier, more logically sound way to integrate the Current Reality Tree with the Evaporating Cloud.

A third major change is a reorientation of solution implementation. In the original incarnation of the Thinking Process, injections (ideas for solutions) from the Future Reality Tree went through two subsequent steps: a Prerequisite Tree to help identify and overcome obstacles, and a Transition Tree to "flesh out" the step-by-step implementation plan. One of the phenomena I noticed over the past decade was the tendency for students

---

* UDE is an acronym for undesirable effect.

learning the Thinking Process to incorporate much more detail into the Prerequisite Tree than it was originally intended to have. And at the same time, there was less patience with the often mind-numbing detail of the Transition Tree.

As an experiment in one Thinking Process course, I suggested that students dispense with the Transition Tree altogether and instead incorporate more detail into their Prerequisite Trees. Not only did implementations become faster and easier, but there was no deterioration in their quality. And everyone preferred this approach because of its speed. Because almost without exception the people I work with are competent professionals, it's no problem for them to execute change from comprehensive Prerequisite Trees alone. The Transition Tree became superfluous.

Yet there was still an opportunity to realize some synergy among tools in change execution. The Theory of Constraints offers the best improvement to project scheduling and management methods conceived in the past 50 years: critical chain. Since the new Prerequisite Tree identifies all the activities needed to execute a change as intermediate objectives, it's a natural next step to use it to create a project activity network. These activities can be implemented using Critical Chain Project Management. So, this version of the Thinking Process "retires" the Transition Tree in favor of the marriage of a more detailed Prerequisite Tree and Critical Chain Project Management.

There's another "elephant in the parlor" that attends any system improvement methodology, including (but not limited to) the Thinking Process: *change management.* The challenge of changing existing ways of doing things, which is really what the Thinking Process is designed to facilitate, goes far beyond logic. It's necessary, but not sufficient, to create technically and economically sound solutions to problems. But even so, some estimates of failure run as high as 80 percent. There's a reason why many major systemic changes fail to realize expectations fully, or fail outright. The missing sufficiency is the failure of most methods, including the Thinking Process, to inherently address the psychology of change. Theory of Constraints philosophy has touched on this challenge before, but only in a superficial way (that is, the so-called layers of resistance). Most methods, such as Six Sigma and lean, don't address it at all.

Yet with potentially valuable solutions falling by the wayside because system improvers fail to consider the psychology of change, it's somewhat surprising that more methods don't aggressively deal with this problem. I've tried to start that process in Chapter 8, "Changing the Status Quo." But it's only a start. The psychology of change is a field unto itself. All I can do in this book is to point you in the right direction and provide a "push start."

There are two components to this push. The first is the concept of the executive summary tree, a tool for reducing complete, complex Thinking Process analysis to a streamlined version that can be presented succinctly to an executive in a limited period of time, without compromising the logical soundness of the analysis. The second is a six-stage model for handling the psychology of change. Executive summary trees are described in detail in Appendix B. The behavioral change model is introduced in Chapter 8.

This book is organized to take you from the general to the specific, following a tried-and-true scientific systems analysis approach developed at the Rand Corporation in the 1950s by E. S. Quade. The approach begins with a determination of the desired system outcome, defines the problem, creates alternatives, tests those alternatives, and determines the best alternative according to a predetermined decision rule. However, the traditional systems analysis approach stops short of implementation. This book goes the extra mile. It's divided into three major parts.

Part I, "The Destination," sets the stage, the ground rules, and the expected outcome. In Chapter 1, we start with an overview of systems thinking and constraint management in particular, including the principles of constraint theory and its major tools. Chapter 2 begins our more detailed examination of the Thinking Process with an explanation of the Categories of Legitimate Reservation—the logical "rules of the game." After all, we can't excel at the game if we don't know the rules.

Chapter 3 starts our comprehensive exploration of the Thinking Process itself. Following Quade's scientific systems analysis approach, we learn how the Intermediate Objectives Map is used to establish the standard for desired performance of our system: the goal, critical success factors, and supporting necessary conditions.

Part II, "Gap Analysis and Correction," defines the magnitude of the divide between the existing system and the aforementioned expected outcome. In Chapter 4, we learn how to construct a Current Reality Tree to express the gap as undesirable effects (UDEs) and logically trace the path back to critical root causes for these UDEs. Chapter 5 describes the resolution of conflict associated with changing the critical root causes, and Chapter 6 lays out proposed solutions for logical testing and "bulletproofing" (consideration of the law of unintended consequences).

Part III, "Executing Change," addresses the implementation of the new direction that was logically tested in Chapter 6. Construction of the Prerequisite Tree, Chapter 7, provides the framework of an execution plan and shows how Critical Chain Project Management can help with the technical aspects of implementation. However, as Will Rogers once observed, "Plans get you into things, but you've got to work your own way out." Chapter 8 emphasizes the importance of a concerted effort to accommodate the human element in change. The Thinking Process may be necessary, but it's not sufficient alone. And while Chapter 8 can't provide more than a survey of change management techniques, it does offer an introduction to some human-oriented aids to consider.

Finally, nine appendices provide real-world examples, exercises, and deeper insight into the Logical Thinking Process. And the tenth appendix introduces the *Transformation Logic Tree* software included with this book.

It's difficult for any book to be all things to all people. This one is as comprehensive as I can make it. It can supplement formal training, facilitate self-study, and be a continuing desk reference. Or it can be a dandy doorstop. Which it will be for you is for you alone to determine.

> *Without the assistance of a teacher many roads become open to a practitioner, some on the correct path and some on the incorrect path. It is not for everyone to be without guidance—only a few, and they are exceptional, can make a journey to wisdom without a teacher. You must have extraordinary passion, patience, and self-discipline to make a journey alone. The goals must be understood, and no diversion can be acknowledged or permitted if you are to attain enlightenment within the sphere of a chosen art. This is a very difficult road to travel and not many are made for it. It is frustrating, confusing, very lonely, certainly frightening, and it will sometimes make you think you do not have much sanity left to deal with the everyday surroundings of your world. Also, there is no guarantee that you will attain perfection. It must all come from inside you without any preconceived notions on your part.*
>
> *And so we begin...*
>
> — Miaymoto Musashi (1643)
> (*The Book of Five Rings*, translated by
> Stephen F. Kaufman, hanshi 10th dan)

Part I
The Destination

1

Introduction to the Theory of Constraints

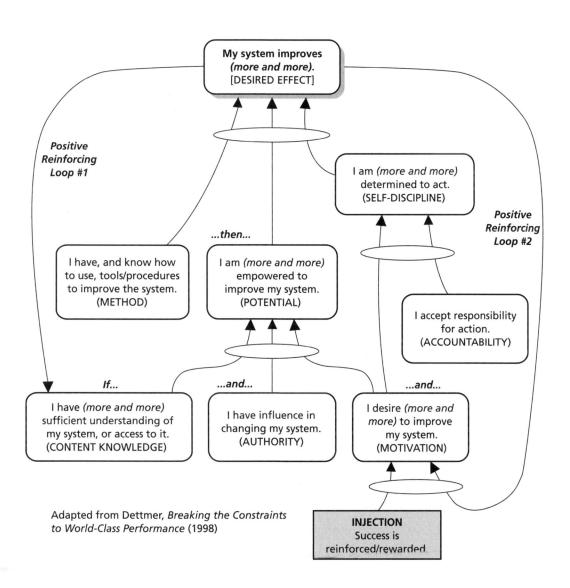

My system improves
(more and more).
[DESIRED EFFECT]

Positive Reinforcing Loop #1

I am *(more and more)*
determined to act.
(SELF-DISCIPLINE)

Positive Reinforcing Loop #2

...then...

I have, and know how
to use, tools/procedures
to improve the system.
(METHOD)

I am *(more and more)*
empowered to
improve my system.
(POTENTIAL)

I accept responsibility
for action.
(ACCOUNTABILITY)

If...

I have *(more and more)*
sufficient understanding of
my system, or access to it.
(CONTENT KNOWLEDGE)

...and...

I have influence in
changing my system.
(AUTHORITY)

...and...

I desire *(more and
more)* to improve
my system.
(MOTIVATION)

Adapted from Dettmer, *Breaking the Constraints
to World-Class Performance* (1998)

INJECTION
Success is
reinforced/rewarded

3

> *Profound knowledge must come from outside the system, and by invitation.*
>
> —W. Edwards Deming

SYSTEMS AND "PROFOUND KNOWLEDGE"

W. Edwards Deming maintained that real quality improvement isn't possible without profound knowledge.[7:94-98] According to Deming, profound knowledge comes from:

- An understanding of the theory of knowledge

- Knowledge of variation

- An understanding of psychology

- Appreciation for systems

"Appreciation for systems"—what does that mean? A system might be generally defined as a collection of interrelated, interdependent components or processes that act in concert to turn inputs into some kind of outputs in pursuit of some goal (see Figure 1.1). Systems influence—and are influenced by—their external environment. Obviously, quality (or lack of it) doesn't exist in a vacuum. It can only be considered in the context of the system in which it resides. So, to follow Deming's line of reasoning, it's not possible to improve quality without a thorough understanding of how that system works. Moreover, the Logical Thinking Process that is the subject of this book also provides a solid foundation of understanding of the theory of knowledge: how we know what we know.

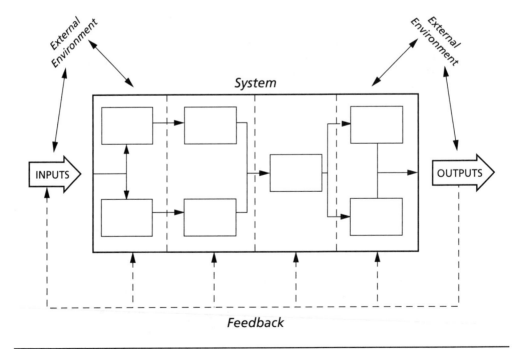

Figure 1.1   A basic system and its environment.

THE SYSTEM'S GOAL

Let's look at systems from a broader perspective. Why do systems exist? In the most basic sense, the answer is, "To achieve a goal." If a system's purpose is to achieve some goal, who gets to decide what that goal should be? Obviously, in natural systems the answer to this question is often beyond the scope of human understanding. But in human organizational systems, which are the primary focus of this book, the goal setter ought to be the system's owner—or owners. If you or I paid for the system, we'd expect to be the one to decide what that system's goal should be. Privately held companies respond to the directions of their owners. Publicly held corporations work toward the goals of their stockholders—or at least they're supposed to. Government agencies are essentially "owned" by the taxpayers and should be doing what the taxpayers expect them to do.

> *The essence of management is recognizing the need for change, then initiating, controlling, and directing it, and solving the problems along the way. If it were not so, managers wouldn't be needed—only babysitters.*

THE MANAGER'S ROLE

In most complex systems, the responsibility for satisfying the owners' goals rests with the managers of the system—from the chief executive officer down to the frontline supervisor. In a general sense, the Theory of Constraints (TOC) is about management.

> *1. Anyone can make a decision, given enough facts.*
> *2. A good manager can make a decision without enough facts.*
> *3. A perfect manager can operate in perfect ignorance.*
>
> —Spencer's Laws of Data

Who Is a Manager?

Inevitably, some readers will respond, "But I'm not a manager. Why would the Theory of Constraints be important to me?" The truth is, we're all managers. Everyone is a manager of something—in different arenas, perhaps, but a manager nonetheless. Whether you're in charge of a large corporation, a department, or a small team, you're a manager. Even if you're "none of the above," you're still a manager. Under ideal circumstances, all individuals manage their lives and careers, though sometimes they don't do a very effective job of it.

Some of us have more than one management role. Basically, we differ only in our span of control and the size of our sphere of influence. At the very least you manage (or possibly fail to manage) your personal activities, your time, and perhaps your finances. For example, a homemaker manages a household; a lawyer manages legal case preparation and litigation; a student manages time and effort.

One of the hallmarks of effective managers is that they deal less with the present and more with the future. In other words, they concentrate on "fire prevention" rather than "fire fighting." If you're more focused on the present than the future, you'll always be in a time lag, chasing changes in your environment—a reactive rather than a proactive mode.

> *Have you seen them? Which way did they go? I must be after them,*
> *for I am their leader!*

What Is the Goal?

The Theory of Constraints rests on the admittedly somewhat rash assumption that managers and/or organizations know what their real purpose is, what goal they're trying to achieve. Unfortunately, this isn't always the case. No manager can hope to succeed without knowing four things:

- What the ultimate goal is
- What the critical success factors are in reaching that goal
- Where he or she currently stands in relation to that goal
- The magnitude and direction of the change needed to move from the status quo to where he or she wants to be (the goal)

This might be considered "management by vector analysis." But in fact that's really what managers do: They determine the difference between what is and what should be, and they change things to eliminate that deviation.

> *Average managers are concerned with methods, opinions, and*
> *precedents. Good managers are concerned with solving problems.*
>
> —Unknown

Goal, Critical Success Factor, or Necessary Condition?

If you're a manager, how do you know what the system's goal is? Frequently a system's managers—and perhaps even the owners—have different ideas about the system's goal. In a commercial enterprise, the stockholders (owners) usually consider the system's goal to be "to make more money." The underlying assumption here is that a system making money pays dividends to stockholders who, in turn, make more money.

The managers in a system might see the goal a little differently. While they acknowledge the need to make money for the stockholders, they also realize that other things are important—things like competitive advantage; market share; customer satisfaction; a satisfied, secure workforce; or first-time quality of product or service. Factors like these often show up as goals in strategic or operating plans. But are they really goals or are they necessary conditions?

For the purposes of this book, a goal is defined as *the result or achievement toward which effort is directed.*[19] But in complex systems we normally can't jump directly to desired outcomes without satisfying some necessary conditions. A necessary condition is *a circumstance indispensable to some result, or that upon which everything is contingent.*[18] Inherent in these definitions is a *prerequisite relationship:* you must satisfy the necessary conditions in order to attain the goal.

How many necessary conditions does it take to realize a goal? The answer is, "It depends"—on how detailed you want to be. Stephen Covey recommends beginning "with the end in mind."[4:95] That's obviously the goal itself, as we've defined it.

But if we conceive of the process of goal attainment as a journey rather than a destination, there are clearly some intermediate progress milestones along the way—some "show-stoppers" without which we won't be able to reach the goal. Normally there aren't too many of these. I submit that there are no more than three to five, and perhaps fewer than three.

We could call these *critical success factors* (CSF). They are definitely necessary conditions for goal attainment, but because they're major milestones, there won't be very many. Most of what people might consider necessary conditions actually support (are required to satisfy) these critical success factors. As we'll see in Chapter 3, "The Intermediate Objectives Map," the goal, critical success factors, and subordinate necessary conditions can be configured as a hierarchy.

Goldratt suggested that the relationship is actually interdependent, at least at the goal-CSF level. In other words, if the system's owner decides to change the goal—say, to one of the critical success factors—the original goal can't be ignored. But it will most likely revert to the CSF position vacated by the new goal. Because of this interdependency, the goal is really no more than one of the system's "constellation" of critical success factors that has been arbitrarily designated for primacy.

For example, your stockholders (represented by the board of directors) might decide that "increased profitability" is the company's goal (see Figure 1.2). In this case, "customer satisfaction," "technology leadership," "competitive advantage," and "improved market share" might all be necessary conditions that you can't ignore without the risk of not attaining the profitability goal. But you might just as easily consider the goal to be "customer satisfaction," as many quality-oriented companies do these days. In this instance, "profitability" becomes a necessary condition without which you can't satisfy customers. Why? Because unprofitable companies don't stay in business very long, and if they're not in business, they can't very well satisfy customers.

> *The major difference between rats and people is that rats learn from experience.*
>
> —B. F. Skinner

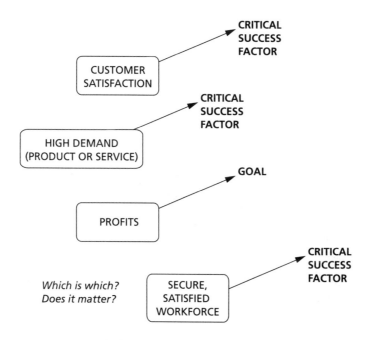

Figure 1.2 Goal or critical success factor?

THE CONCEPT OF SYSTEM CONSTRAINTS

Let's assume for the moment that you, the manager, have decided what your system's goal is and what the CSF and necessary conditions are for attaining it. Are you attaining that goal right now? Most people would agree that they could be doing a better job of progressing toward it.

What keeps your system from doing better? Would it be fair to say that something is constraining your system—keeping it from realizing its maximum potential? If so, what do you think that constraining factor might be? The chances are that everybody in your organization has an opinion about it. But who's right? And how would you know if they're right? If you can successfully answer that question, you probably have a bright future ahead of you. Let's see if we can help you find that answer. To do this, we'll go back to the concept of a system.

Systems as Chains

Goldratt likens systems to chains, or to networks of chains. Let's consider the chain in Figure 1.3 a simple system. Its goal is to transmit force from one end to the other. If you accept the idea that all systems are constrained in some way, how many constraints do you think this chain has?

The "Weakest Link"

Let's say you keep increasing the force you apply to this chain. Can you do this indefinitely? Of course not. If you do, eventually the chain will break. But where will it break—at what point? The chain will fail at its weakest link (see Figure 1.3). How many "weakest links" does a chain like this have? One—only one. There may be another link or two that are very close in "weakness," but there is only one weakest link. The chain will fail first at only one point, and that weakest link is the constraint that prevents the chain (system) from doing any better at achieving its goal (transmission of force).

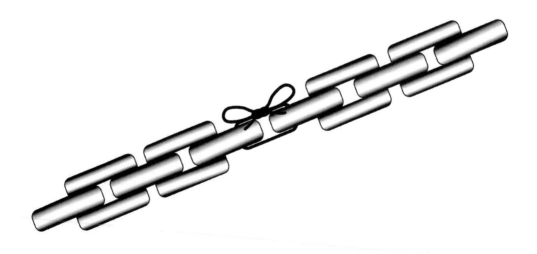

Figure 1.3   A system: the "chain" concept.

Constraints and Non-constraints

So we can conclude that our chain has only one link constraining its current performance. How many non-constraints does it have? An indeterminate number, but equal to the number of remaining links in the chain. Goldratt contended that there is usually only one constraint in a system at any given time. Like the narrow neck of an hourglass, that one constraint limits the output of the entire system. Everything else in the system, at that exact time, is a non-constraint.

Let's say we want to strengthen this chain (improve the system). Where would be the most logical place to focus our efforts? Right—the weakest link. Would it do us any good to strengthen anything except the weakest link (that is, a non-constraint)? Of course not. The chain would still break at the weakest link, no matter how strong we made the others. In other words, efforts on non-constraints—nearly all of a system—will *not* produce immediate, measurable improvement in system capability.

Now let's assume we're smart enough to figure out which link is the weakest, and let's say we double its strength. It's not the weakest link anymore. What has happened to the chain? It has become stronger, but is it twice as strong? No. Some other link is now the weakest, and the chain's capability is now limited by the strength of that link. It's stronger than it was, but still not as strong as it could be. The system is still constrained, but the constraint has migrated to a different component.

A Production Example

Here's a different look at the chain concept (see Figure 1.4). This is a simple production system that takes raw materials, runs them through five component processes, and turns them into finished products. Each process constitutes a link in the production chain. The system's goal is to make as much money as possible from the sale of its products. Each of the component processes has a daily capacity as indicated. The market demand is 15 units per day.

Where is the constraint in this chain, and why? The answer is Step C, because it can never produce more than six units per day, no matter how many the rest of the components produce. Where are the non-constraints? Everywhere else.

What happens if we improve the C process so that its daily capacity is now tripled, to 18 units per day? What constrains the system now, and why? The answer is Step D, because it can produce only eight units per day. Where are the non-constraints? Everywhere else.

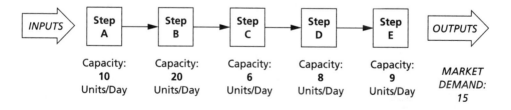

- *What is the maximum system output per day?*
- *Where is the weakest link? Why?*

Figure 1.4 A production example.

Let's continue this improvement process, until Steps D, E, and A are all much better than before. Look at this new version of the production diagram (see Figure 1.5).

Where's the system's constraint now? It's in the marketplace, which is only accepting 15 units per day. We've finally removed the constraint, haven't we? Well, not really. All we've done is eliminate internal constraints. That which keeps our system from doing better in relation to its goal is now outside the system, but it's a constraint nonetheless. If we're going to attack this constraint, however, we'll need a different set of task skills and knowledge.

RELATION OF CONSTRAINTS
TO QUALITY IMPROVEMENT

Deming developed 14 points that he offered as a kind of "road map to quality."[5] Most other approaches to continuous improvement have comparable prescriptions for success. Deming's 14th point is, "Take action to accomplish the transformation." He amplifies this by urging organizations to get everyone involved, train everybody in the new philosophy, convert a "critical mass" of people, and form process improvement teams.[6:86-92]

Management in most organizations interprets this point quite literally: Get everyone involved. Employee involvement is a very important element of Deming's theory, and of most other total quality philosophies, and for good reason: Success is inherently a cooperative effort. Most organizations having formal improvement efforts include employees, in the process usually in teams.

Let's assume that these improvement teams are working on things that "everybody knows" need improving. If we accept Goldratt's contentions about constraints and non-constraints, how many of these team efforts are likely to be working on non-constraints? Answer: probably all but one (see Figure 1.6). How many of us know for sure exactly where in our organizations the constraint lies? If our management isn't thinking in terms of system constraints, yet they're putting everybody to work on the transformation, how much effort do you think might actually be unproductive?

"Wait a minute," you're probably thinking. "Continuous improvement is a long-term process; it can take years to produce results. We have to be patient and persevere. We'll need all of these improvements someday."

That's true. The way most organizations approach it, continuous improvement *is* a long-term process that may take years to show results. Limited time, energy, and resources are spread across the entire system, instead of focused on the one part of it that has the potential to produce immediate system improvement: the constraint. Impatience, lack of perseverance, and failure to see progress quickly enough are all reasons why many organizations give up on methods such as TQM and Six Sigma. People—including managers—soon get

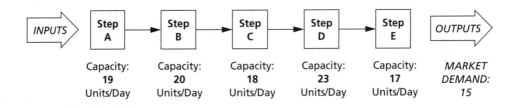

- *Now what's the maximum system output per day?*
- *Now where's the weakest link? Why?*

Figure 1.5   Another version of the production example.

"Put Everybody to Work..."
Process Improvement Teams

Figure 1.6   Who is working on a non-constraint?

discouraged when they see no tangible system results from the dedicated efforts they've put into process improvement. So interest, motivation, and eventually commitment to continuous improvement die from a lack of *intrinsic reinforcement*. Everybody might be working diligently, but only a few have the potential to really make a difference quickly. For most organizations, the real question is: Will our business environment allow us the luxury of time? Can we wait for the long term to see results?

Does it have to be this way? No. Goldratt developed the approach to continuous improvement called the Theory of Constraints. He even wrote a book describing this theory, called *The Goal.*[11] Another, entitled *It's Not Luck,*[10] demonstrates how the logical tools of the theory might be applied. The Theory of Constraints (TOC) is a prescriptive theory, which means it tells you not only what's holding your system back, but also what to do about it and how to do it. A lot of theories answer the first question—what's wrong. Some even tell you what to do about it, but those that do usually focus on processes rather than the system as a whole. And they're completely oblivious to the concept of system constraints.

> *There is no such thing as staying the same. You are either striving to make yourself better or allowing yourself to get worse.*
>
> —Unknown

CHANGE AND THE THEORY OF CONSTRAINTS

Deming talks about "transformation," which is another way of saying "change." Goldratt's Theory of Constraints is essentially about change. Applying its principles and tools answers the four basic questions about change that every manager needs to know:

- What's the desired standard of performance?
- What must be changed? (Where is the constraint?)
- What is the appropriate change? (What should we do with the constraint?)
- How is the change best accomplished? (How do we implement the change?)

Remember that these are system-level questions, not process-level. The answers to these questions undoubtedly have an impact on individual processes, but they're designed to focus efforts in system improvement. Processes are important, but our organizations ultimately succeed or fail as complete systems. What a shame it would be to win the battle on the process level, only to lose the war at the system level!

Why is the distinction between system and process so important? The answer lies in one of the fundamental assumptions of systems theory: the whole is *not* equal to the sum of its parts. The assumption that it is originates in a basic algebraic axiom. Unfortunately, however, complex systems are anything but mathematically precise. The improper allocation of this algebraic axiom to the management of organizations would sound like this:

> *If we break down our system into its components, maximize the efficiency of each one, then reassemble the components, we'll have the most efficient whole system.*

It's been said that elegant theories are often slain by ugly, inconvenient facts. That's the case here. The mathematical, or analytical, approach to system improvement is one of those victims. It's also been said that "the devil is in the details." Where complex systems are concerned, those details make up many of the aforementioned ugly, inconvenient facts. And they are often in the *linkages* between system components, not in the components (links) themselves. Yet organizations continue to blithely polish the efficiency of these links, blissfully ignorant of the real location of the most vexing contributors to less-than-desirable system performance: the interfaces among components.[3:3-4]

Most continuous improvement (CI) methods never adequately address how best to channel improvement efforts for maximum immediate effect. In other words, by using TOC in addition to CI methods such as Six Sigma, the problem of taking a long time to show results goes away. Effectively applying TOC in concert with CI, you're likely to find that CI and significant short-term results need not be mutually exclusive. So don't think about throwing away your CI toolbox. If anything, the traditional CI tools become more productive than ever, because TOC can suggest when and how to employ each one to best effect: on the current (and sometime future) system constraint.

> *It is not necessary to change; survival is not mandatory.*
>
> —W. Edwards Deming

TOC PRINCIPLES

Theories are usually classified as either descriptive or prescriptive. Descriptive theories, such as the law of gravity, tell us why things happen, but they don't help us to do anything about them. Prescriptive theories both explain why and offer guidance on what to do. TOC is a prescriptive theory, but we'll look at the descriptive part first.

Several principles converge to make the environment particularly fertile ground for the prescriptive part of Goldratt's theory. The accompanying chart (see Figure 1.7) lists most of these principles, but a few of them are worth emphasizing because of their striking impact on reality.

Systems as Chains

This is crucial to TOC. If systems function as chains, weakest links can be found and strengthened.

Local vs. System Optima

Because of the interdependence of system components and the effects of entropy, the optimum performance of the entire system is not equivalent to the sum of all the

- Systems thinking is preferable to analytical thinking in managing change and solving problems.
- An optimal solution deteriorates over time as the system's environment changes. A process of ongoing improvement is required to update and maintain the effectiveness of a solution—or replace it if it becomes irrelevant.
- If a system is performing as well as it can, not more than one of its component parts will be performing as well as they can. If all parts are performing as well as they can, the system as a whole will not be. The system optimum is not the sum of the local optima.
- Systems are analogous to chains. Each system has a "weakest link" (constraint) that ultimately limits the success of the entire system.
- Strengthening any link in a chain other than the weakest one does nothing to improve the performance of the whole chain.
- Knowing what to change requires a thorough understanding of the system's current reality, its goal, and the magnitude and direction of the difference between the two.
- Most of the undesirable effects within a system are caused by a few critical root causes.
- Root causes are almost never superficially apparent. They manifest themselves through a number of undesirable effects (UDEs) linked by a network of cause and effect.
- Elimination of individual UDEs gives a false sense of security while ignoring the underlying critical root causes. Solutions that do this are likely to be short-lived. Eliminating a critical root cause simultaneously eliminates all resulting UDEs.
- Root causes are often perpetuated by a hidden or underlying conflict. Eliminating root causes requires challenging the assumptions underlying the conflict and invalidating at least one.
- System constraints can either be physical or policy. Physical constraints are relatively easy to identify and simple to eliminate. Policy constraints are usually more difficult to identify and eliminate, but removing them normally results in a larger degree of system improvement than elimination of a physical constraint.
- Inertia is the worst enemy of a process of ongoing improvement. Solutions tend to assume a mass of their own that resists further change.
- Ideas are not solutions.

Figure 1.7   Partial list of TOC principles.

component optima. We saw this in the production example earlier. If all the components of a system are performing at their maximum level, the system as whole will not be performing at its best.

Cause and Effect

All systems operate in an environment of cause and effect. Something causes something else to happen. This cause-and-effect phenomenon can be very complicated, especially in complex systems.

Undesirable Effects and Critical Root Causes

Nearly all of what we see in our systems that we don't like are not *problems*, but *indicators*. They are the resultant effects of underlying causes. Treating an undesirable effect alone is like putting a bandage on an infected wound: It does nothing about the underlying infection, so its remedial benefit is only temporary. Eventually the indication resurfaces, because the underlying problem causing the indication never really went away. Eliminating undesirable effects gives a false sense of security. Identifying and eliminating a critical root cause not only eliminates all the undesirable effects that issue from it, but also prevents them from returning.

Solution Deterioration

An optimal solution deteriorates over time as the system's environment changes. Goldratt once said, "Yesterday's solution becomes today's historical curiosity." ("Isn't that interesting?! Why do you suppose they ever did that?") A process of ongoing improvement is essential for updating and maintaining the efficiency (and effectiveness) of a solution. Inertia is the worst enemy of a process of ongoing improvement. The attitude that, "We've solved that problem—no need to revisit it" hurts continuous improvement efforts.

Physical vs. Policy Constraints

Most of the constraints we face in our systems originate from policies—how we deliberately choose to operate—not physical things. Physical constraints are relatively easy to identify and break. Policy constraints are much more difficult, but they normally result in a much larger degree of system improvement than does the elimination of a physical constraint.

> *An organization must have some means of combating the process by which people become prisoners of their procedures. The rule book becomes fatter as the ideas become fewer. Almost every well-established organization is a coral reef of procedures that were laid down to achieve some long-forgotten objective.*
>
> —John W. Gardner

Ideas Are *Not* Solutions

The best ideas in the world never realize their potential unless they're implemented. And most great ideas fail in the implementation stage.

THE FIVE FOCUSING STEPS OF TOC

This is the beginning of the prescriptive part of the Theory of Constraints. Goldratt developed five sequential steps to concentrate improvement efforts on the component that is capable of producing the most positive impact on the system.[11:300-308]

1. Identify the System Constraint

What part of the system constitutes the weakest link? If it's a physical constraint, what policy is driving it?

2. Decide How to Exploit the Constraint

By "exploit," Goldratt means we should wring every bit of capability out of the constraining component as it currently exists. In other words, "What can we do to get the most out of this constraint without committing to potentially expensive changes or upgrades?"

NOTE: The constraint, if physical, is the one place in the chain where efficiency or productivity is paramount.

3. Subordinate Everything Else

After we've identified the constraint (Step 1) and decided what to do about it (Step 2), we adjust the rest of the system to a "setting" that will enable the constraint to operate at maximum effectiveness. We may have to "de-tune" some parts of the system, while "revving up" others. Inevitably, this means sacrificing the individual efficiencies of non-constraints to some extent. However, care must be taken to assure that deliberate "detuning" of a non-constraint doesn't actually turn it into the system constraint.

Once we've subordinated non-constraints, we must evaluate the results of our actions: Is the constraint still constraining the system's performance? If not, we've eliminated this particular constraint, and we skip ahead to Step 5. If it is, we still have the same constraint—and we continue with Step 4.

4. Elevate the Constraint

If we're doing Step 4, it means that Steps 2 and 3 weren't sufficient to eliminate the constraint. We have to do something more. It's not until this step that we entertain the idea of major changes to the existing system—reorganization, divestiture, capital improvements, or other substantial system modifications. This step can involve considerable investment in time, energy, money, or other resources, so we must be sure we aren't able to break the constraint in the first three steps.

It's not uncommon for organizations that are not cognizant of constraint theory to jump straight from Step 1 (Identify) to Step 4 (Elevate). The net effect is that more costs are incurred, usually unnecessarily, and that opportunities to wring better performance from the system at no additional cost are ignored or overlooked.

"Elevating" the constraint means that we take whatever action is required to eliminate the constraint. When this step is completed, the initial constraint is broken, but some new factor, within the system or outside of it, becomes the new system constraint.

5. Go Back to Step 1, But Beware of "Inertia"

If a constraint is broken at Steps 3 or 4 we must go back to Step 1 and begin the cycle again, looking for the next thing constraining our performance. If you'll recall the production example (see Figure 1.5), this is exactly what we did. After we broke the constraint at process Step C, we went back and found D, then E, then A, and, finally, the marketplace.

The caution about inertia reminds us that we must not become complacent; the cycle never ends. We keep on looking for constraints, and we keep breaking them. And we never forget that because of interdependency and variation, each subsequent change we make to our system will have new effects on those constraints we've already broken. We may have to revisit and update those solutions, too.

The Five Focusing Steps have a direct relationship with the four management questions pertaining to change: What's the standard, what to change, what to change to, and how to cause change? They tell us how to answer those questions.

To determine what to change, we look for the constraint. To determine what to change *to*, we decide how to exploit the constraint and subordinate the rest of the system to that decision. If that doesn't do the complete job, we elevate the constraint. The subordinate and elevate steps also address the question "how to cause the change."

"This is all well and good," you're probably saying, "but how do we convert these abstract steps into concrete actions we can take? And how do we know when we've had a positive impact on the system?" These are two key questions. Let's look at the second one first.

THROUGHPUT, INVENTORY, AND OPERATING EXPENSE

A burning question we must address is, "How do we know whether our constraint-breaking has had a positive effect on our overall system?" Another way of asking this same question is, "How do we measure the effects of local decisions on the global system?" Organizations have struggled with this question for years. The Theory of Constraints is particularly useful in this arena.

Part of the answer to the question lies in the TOC emphasis on fixing the weakest link (constraint) and ignoring, at least temporarily, the non-constraints. Most effective laboratory research involves quantifying the effect of a change in one variable by holding all the others constant—or as nearly so as possible. This is *sensitivity analysis*, and it's particularly useful in determining how much of an outcome is attributable to a particular cause.

By doing essentially the same thing in our organizations (that is, working only on the constraint), we achieve two benefits: (1) we realize the maximum system improvement from the least investment in resources, and (2) we learn exactly how much effect improving a specific system component has on overall system performance. I suspect Deming would consider this "appreciation for a system"[7:96] of the highest order.

Goldratt conceived a simple relationship for determining the effect that any local action has on progress toward the system's goal. Every action is assessed by its effect on three system-level dimensions: Throughput, Inventory, and Operating Expense.[11:58-62] Goldratt provides precise definitions of these terms (see Figure 1.8).

The concept of Throughput, Inventory/Investment, and Operating Expense has been referred to by several names: throughput accounting, constraints accounting, and cash flow accounting. Each of these terms is, in some way, descriptive of the desired function of these metrics. Unfortunately, a detailed examination of this approach is beyond the scope of this book. Readers are strongly encouraged to educate themselves about this crucial topic. The two best of several sources for doing so are *Management Dynamics* by John A. Caspari and Pamela Caspari[2] and *Throughput Accounting* by Steven M. Bragg.[1]

Throughput (T)

Throughput is the rate at which the entire system generates money through sales.[11:58-62] Another definition of Throughput is "all the money coming into the system." In for-profit companies, Throughput is equivalent to marginal contribution to profit. In a not-for-profit organization or a government agency, the concept of "sales" may not apply. In cases where an organization's Throughput may not be easily expressed in dollars, it might be defined in terms of the delivery of a product or service to a customer. Another way of thinking about Throughput is…

> *The world is not interested in the storms you encountered, but did you bring in the ship?*
>
> —William McFee

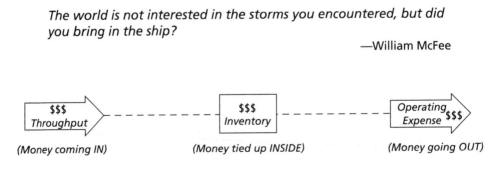

Figure 1.8   Definitions of Throughput, Inventory and Operating Expense.

Inventory/Investment (I)

Inventory and Investment are all the money the system invests in things it intends to sell, or all the money tied up within the system.[12:58-62] Inventory includes the acquisition cost of raw materials, unfinished goods, purchased parts, and other "hard" items intended for sale to a customer. Investment includes the expenditures an organization makes in equipment and facilities. Eventually, obsolescent equipment and facilities will be sold, too, even if only at their scrap value. As these assets depreciate, their depreciated value remains in the "I" column, but the depreciation is added to Operating Expense (see the next section).

Operating Expense (OE)

Operating Expense is all the money the system spends turning Inventory into Throughput. In other words, it's the money going out of the system.[12:58-62] Direct and indirect labor, utilities, interest, and the like are examples of operating expenses. Depreciation of assets is also considered an Operating Expense, because it constitutes the value of a fixed asset expended, or "used up," in turning Inventory into Throughput.

Goldratt contended that these dimensions are interdependent. That is, a change in one will usually automatically result in a change in one or both of the other two. Let's consider that for a minute. If you increase Throughput by increasing sales, Inventory and Operating Expense will also increase. Why? Because you're likely to need more physical inventory to support increased sales, and you're likely to spend more, in variable costs, to produce more. It's also possible to make more money (if that's your goal) without increasing sales. How? If you can produce the same sales revenues with less physical inventory, and spend less on Operating Expense doing it, you get to keep more of the money coming into the company (net profit).

So what would you, as a manager, try to do to improve your system? Obviously, you would increase Throughput while decreasing Inventory and Operating Expense. And here we have the key to relating local decisions to the performance of the entire system. As you decide what action to take, ask yourself these questions:

- Will it increase Throughput? If so, how?
- Will it decrease Inventory? If so, how?
- Will it decrease Operating Expense? If so, how?

If the answer to any of these questions is "yes," go ahead with your decision (as long as doing so doesn't compromise one or more of the other two), confident that the overall system will benefit from it. If you're not sure, perhaps you'd better re-evaluate. The bottom line is that if it doesn't eventually result in increased Throughput, you're wasting your time—and probably your money.

Which Is Most Important: T, I, or OE?

To improve your system, where should you focus your efforts? On T, I, or OE? Consider the example in Figure 1.9. The choices are to focus on decreasing OE, decreasing I, or increasing T.

As you look at the graph, note that the theoretical limit in reducing OE and I is zero. A system can't produce output with no physical inventory and no Operating Expense, so the practical limits of I and OE are somewhat above zero. Theoretically, there's no upper limit to how high you can increase T, but from a practical standpoint there is a limit to the size of your market. But still, it's highly probable that the potential for increasing T will always be much higher than the potential for decreasing I and OE. Consequently, it makes

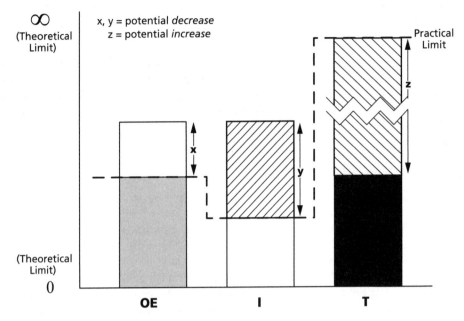

- *Decreasing OE and I reaches a practical limit LONG before the limit of increased T*
- *Decreasing OE and I below practical limits degrades ability to generate T*

Figure 1.9 Limits to T, I, and OE.

sense to expend as much effort as possible on activities that tend to increase T, and make reduction of I and OE a secondary priority (see Figure 1.10).

But what's the normal priority of most companies in a competitive environment? Cut costs (Operating Expense) first. Then, maybe, reduce physical inventory (often without considering how far it can be reduced without hurting Throughput). And finally, try to increase throughput directly.

T, I, and OE: An Example

A classic example is the American aerospace defense industry. Traditionally, these companies have depended on huge government contracts to keep them going. As the defense budget dramatically declined in the early 1990s, fewer contracts were awarded, and for much smaller production runs. In most cases, the remaining defense business of these companies was not enough to keep the organization, as originally structured, afloat. So what was the response of these companies? Most took the traditional approach to some extent: cut fixed costs (Operating Expense). They laid off thousands of workers. Some

Figure 1.10 Management priorities with T, I, and OE.

even reduced Investment by selling off plants, warehouses, or other physical assets. But even that wasn't enough for certain companies, so they merged with others to "strengthen" their capacity to bid for whatever defense business remained. A few companies, however, have seen the handwriting on the wall. With the bottom not yet in sight, they couldn't continue to cut physical inventory or Operating Expense, so they opted to do what they probably should have done in the first place: look for ways to increase Throughput.

How? By finding new market segments for their core competencies, markets that don't depend on government contracts. One satellite builder found a market for its data technology in credit reporting and for its electronic technology in the automotive industry. Another defense electronics firm diversified into consumer communications: home satellite television and data communication. In both cases, the companies found new ways to increase Throughput, rather than just reducing Operating Expense and Inventory.*

T, I, and OE in Not-for-Profit Organizations

A common question often asked is, "What about organizations in which 'making more money, now and in the future' isn't the goal—as with charitable foundations, government agencies, and some hospitals? How do T, I, and OE apply to them?"

It's true that Goldratt conceived of Throughput, Inventory (or Investment), and Operating Expense as ways to measure an organization's progress toward its goal. However, when he created these measures, he was focusing exclusively on for-profit companies. In such organizations, money is an effective surrogate measure for almost all critical aspects of system-level performance, especially those pertaining to the organization's goal.

But it's clearly different in the case of a not-for-profit or government agency. Since that kind of organization's goal is *not* to "make more money, now and in the future," the financial expression of Throughput loses significance. So, how can we measure progress toward our goal if we're a not-for-profit organization?

A variety of alternatives has been suggested to modify expressions of T, and the variable elements of I, so that they accurately reflect progress toward a non-monetary goal. The problem with almost all of these alternatives is that they're contrived—an attempt to fit not-for-profits into a "metrics box" they were never intended to occupy.

Goldratt himself has offered what may be the best solution to the problem of assessing the progress of not-for-profits toward their goals. In July of 1995 he made the following observations.[18] Figure 1.11 illustrates his concept.

Universal Measures of Value

In recorded history, money has been the closest thing to a universal measure of value that humankind has ever created. Where it applies completely, it's very effective. But because it's not always a valid measure of value, and since no other universal non-monetary measure of value has been invented, a different scheme for not-for-profits should be employed.

Goldratt suggested a dual approach. Operating Expense is still measurable in monetary terms; inventory, only partially so; and Throughput, not at all. Inventory, he proposed, should be differentiated as either "passive" or "active."

---

* A more detailed treatment of T, I, and OE can be found in three other sources: *The Haystack Syndrome*[12] by Goldratt and *Management Dynamics*[2] by the Casparis and *Throughput Accounting*[1] by Bragg. (1990, 2004, and 2007 respectively).

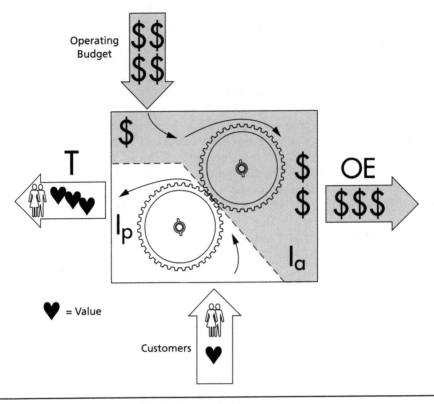

Figure 1.11 T, I, and OE in a not-for-profit organization.

Passive Inventory

Passive inventory, as the name implies, is acted upon. In the manufacturing model, passive inventory would be the raw materials that are converted into Throughput. But in a not-for-profit (a hospital, for example), passive inventory isn't measurable in monetary terms because the "raw materials" are often people. Figure 1.11 shows customers (patients) going through the non-monetary side of the system and becoming "Throughput": well people.

Active Inventory (Investment)

Active inventory might actually be better defined as *investment*. It *is* measurable in monetary terms, because it constitutes the facilities, equipment, and tangible assets that act upon the passive inventory. This part of the inventory is shown in the upper right portion of the system in Figure 1.11.

So how should managers of not-for-profits adjust their focus? In principle, the emphasis remains the same: increase Throughput, limit Investment, and decrease Operating Expense—in that order. In practice, Investment and Operating Expense—both expressed in monetary terms—are managed the same way they are in for-profit companies. The difference arises in how we should manage Throughput and passive inventory.

Managing T Through Undesirable Effects

Without a universal non-monetary measure of value, Goldratt maintained that measuring T and passive I in not-for-profits isn't ever likely to be practical. So, he says, don't bother trying to do it. Instead, work on eliminating the undesirable effects (UDE) associated with

Throughput. (Refer to Chapter 4, "Current Reality Trees," for a thorough discussion of undesirable effects and their relationship to root causes.) Use UDEs as your indicators of progress. As you eliminate them, progress toward the organization's goal can be assumed.

In summary, a not-for-profit should search out and correct the causes of UDEs affecting Throughput, while keeping the costs of Investment and Operating Expense down (refer to Figure 1.11). But the primary emphasis should always be on the former, not the latter.

> **NOTE:** Many people will inevitably ask, "What about the operating budget of a not-for-profit? Where does that fit into the T, I, and OE formulation?" It isn't in Throughput, because production efforts aren't aimed at increasing it. And it isn't really an Operating Expense alone, because some part of it is spent on capital improvements, which are really Inventory (Investment). The answer, according to Goldratt, is that the annual operating budget should be considered a *necessary condition*. Efforts to reduce active Inventory and Operating Expense will naturally have a beneficial effect on the annual budget. But the budget is the means to an end—a necessary condition—not the goal.

THE TOC PARADIGM

The Theory of Constraints is considerably more than just a theory. In effect, it's a paradigm, a pattern or model that includes not only concepts, guiding principles, and prescriptions, but tools and applications as well.

We've seen its concepts (systems as chains; T, I, and OE) and its principles (cause and effect, local vs. system optima, and so on). We've examined its prescriptions (the Five Focusing Steps; what to change, what to change to, how to change). To complete the picture, we'll consider its applications and tools.

Applications and Tools

Each application of TOC starts out being unique. As the theory is applied in a new situation, it creates a distinctive solution. Often, however, such solutions can be generalized to a variety of other circumstances.

Drum-Buffer-Rope

For example, in *The Goal*, Goldratt describes a TOC solution to a production control problem in a specific plant of a fictitious company. This solution became the basis for a generic solution applicable to similar production situations in other industries. Goldratt called this production control solution "drum-buffer-rope."[5,13,17] Many companies have applied this solution, originally developed to solve one company's problem, with great success. Consequently, drum-buffer-rope, which began as an application of TOC principles, has become a tool in the TOC paradigm.

Critical Chain Project Management

A natural extension of the drum-buffer-rope concept to project management is called critical chain.[9,14,15,16] Whereas production is repetitive, projects are usually one-time deliveries; some of the elements of drum-buffer-rope required modification before they could be applied to managing projects. But the basics are similar. Critical chain, perhaps to an even greater extent than drum-buffer-rope, has become a widespread way of ensuring shorter project durations and a higher probability of delivering them on time.

Replenishment and Distribution

Just as the drum-buffer-rope concept was extended to project management, so too has it been applied to manufacturers' raw material acquisition management and finished goods distribution. Combined with drum-buffer-rope, the TOC replenishment and distribution tool can make for a fast, streamlined supply chain. As of this writing, there is not much formally published about it beyond a few conference papers.

Throughput Accounting

Another tool is called Throughput accounting. This is a direct outcome of the use of Throughput, Inventory, and Operating Expense as management decision tools, as opposed to traditional management cost accounting.[1,2] Throughput accounting basically refutes the commonly used concept of allocating fixed costs to units of a product or service. While the summary financial figures remain essentially the same, the absence of allocated fixed costs promotes very different management decisions concerning pricing and marketing for competitive advantage. In other words, Throughput accounting is a much more robust approach for supporting good operational decisions than standard cost accounting. As with drum-buffer-rope production control, throughput accounting began as a specific solution to one company's system performance measurement problem and ended up applicable to any company's measurement problems.

The Logical Thinking Process

The Thinking Process Goldratt developed to apply TOC is logical by nature. The drum-buffer-rope, critical chain project management, supply chain, and throughput accounting tools all have foundations in the logic of cause and effect. But that logic isn't necessarily intuitive, and it certainly doesn't spring fully formed, like Pegasus from the head of Medusa. Rather, this logic finds its expression in another TOC tool—the most universal of them all—the Logical Thinking Process.

The Thinking Process comprises six* distinct logic trees and the "rules of logic" that govern their construction. The trees include the Intermediate Objectives Map, the Current Reality Tree, the Evaporating Cloud, the Future Reality Tree, the Prerequisite Tree, and the Transition Tree. The rules are called the Categories of Legitimate Reservation. These trees, the Categories of Legitimate Reservation, and how to use them, are the subject of this book.

THE INTERMEDIATE OBJECTIVES MAP

The Intermediate Objectives (IO) Map is a "destination finder." Stephen R. Covey contends that one should always begin any endeavor with the end in mind.[4:95] The IO Map (see Figure 1.12) helps problem solvers to do that.

---

* Originally, Goldratt conceived of only five tools. In the mid-1990s, he briefly dabbled with the idea of another logical aid he referred to as an Intermediate Objectives (IO) Map, but he never continued with a concerted effort to develop and use it. In my strategy development work, I found the IO Map to be not just useful, but critical to success. (See Dettmer, *Strategic Navigation*, Quality Press, 2003.)[8] It became apparent that it was equally useful for the kind of system problem solving for which the Thinking Process was originally conceived. The IO Map concept is fully developed, explained, and illustrated in this edition for the first time.

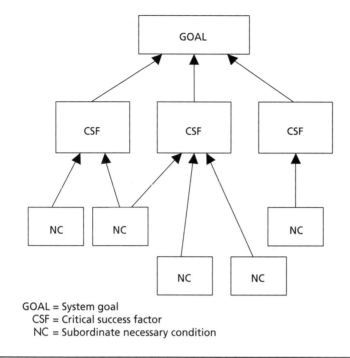

GOAL = System goal
CSF = Critical success factor
NC = Subordinate necessary condition

Figure 1.12   The Intermediate Objectives Map.

It begins with a clear, unequivocal goal statement and the few critical success factors that are required to realize it. It then provides a level or two of detailed necessary conditions for achieving those critical success factors.

These elements are structured in a tree that represents the normative situation for the system—what *should* be happening, or what we want to be happening. The IO Map provides the benchmark for determining how big the deviation is between what is happening in the system and what should be happening. Chapter 3 describes the IO Map in detail and provides comprehensive instructions for constructing one.

THE CURRENT REALITY TREE

The Current Reality Tree (CRT) is a gap-analysis tool (see Figure 1.13). It helps us examine the cause-and-effect logic behind our current situation and determines why that situation is different from the state we'd prefer to be in, as expressed in the IO Map.

The CRT begins with the undesirable effects we see around us—direct comparisons between existing reality and the terminal outcomes expressed in the IO Map. It helps us work back to identify a few critical root causes that originate all the undesirable effects we're experiencing. These critical root causes inevitably include the constraint we're trying to identify in the Five Focusing Steps.

The CRT tells us *what* to change—the one simplest change to make that will have the greatest positive effect on our system. Chapter 4 describes the Current Reality Tree in detail and provides comprehensive instructions and examples on how to construct one.

THE EVAPORATING CLOUD:
A CONFLICT RESOLUTION DIAGRAM

Goldratt designed the Evaporating Cloud (EC), which amounts to a conflict resolution diagram, to resolve hidden conflicts that usually perpetuate chronic problems (see Figure 1.14). The EC is predicated on the idea that most core problems exist because some underlying tug-of-war, or conflict, prevents straightforward solution of the problem; otherwise, the problem would have been solved long ago. The EC can also be a "creative engine," an idea generator that allows us to invent new, "breakthrough" solutions to such nagging problems. Consequently, the EC answers the first part of the question, what to change to. Chapter 5 describes the Evaporating Cloud in detail.

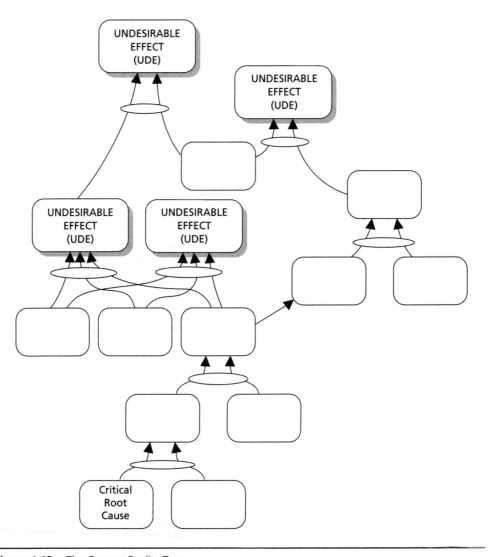

Figure 1.13   The Current Reality Tree.

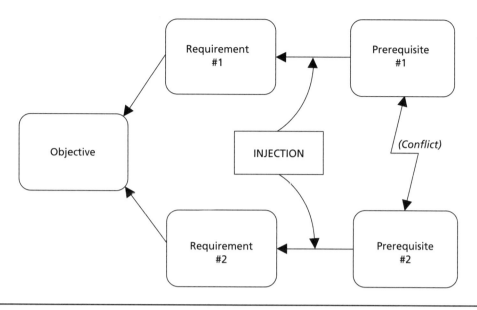

Figure 1.14   The Evaporating Cloud (conflict resolution diagram).

THE FUTURE REALITY TREE

The Future Reality Tree (FRT) serves two purposes (see Figure 1.15). First, it allows us to verify that an action we'd like to take will, in fact, produce the ultimate results we desire. Second, it enables us to identify any unfavorable new consequences our contemplated action might have, and to nip them in the bud.

These functions provide two important benefits. We can logically "test" the effectiveness of our proposed course of action before investing much time, energy, or resources in it, and we can avoid making the situation worse than when we started.

This tool answers the second part of the question—what to change to—by validating our new system configuration. The FRT can also be an invaluable strategic planning tool. Chapter 6 describes the Future Reality Tree in detail, providing examples and comprehensive instructions on how to create one.

THE PREREQUISITE TREE

Once we've decided on a course of action, the Prerequisite Tree (PRT) helps implement that decision (see Figure 1.16). It tells us in what sequence we need to complete the discrete activities in implementing our decision. It also identifies implementation obstacles and suggests the best ways to overcome those obstacles. The PRT provides the first part of the answer to the last question, how to change. Chapter 7 describes the Prerequisite Tree in detail and provides both examples and comprehensive procedures for constructing one.

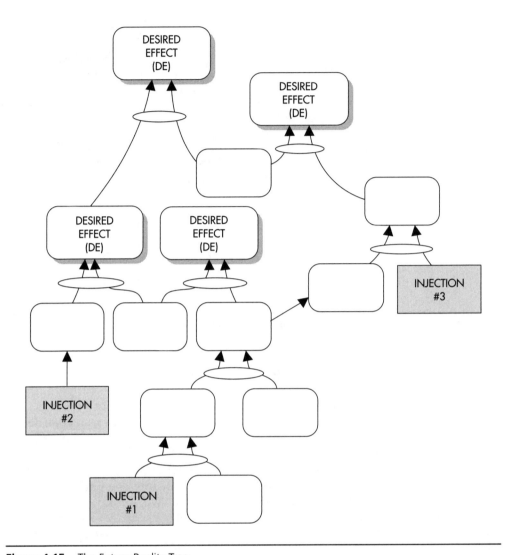

Figure 1.15 The Future Reality Tree.

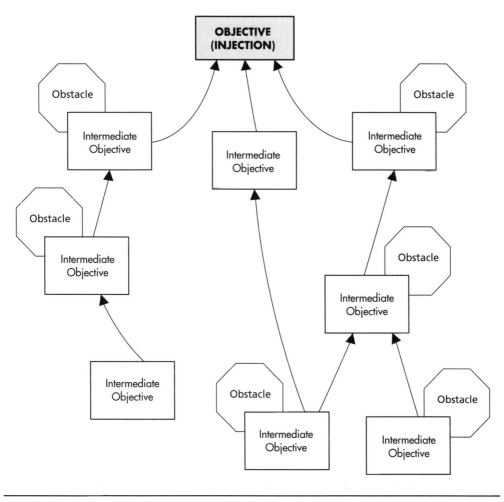

Figure 1.16   The Prerequisite Tree.

THE TRANSITION TREE

The last of the six logical tools is the Transition Tree (TT) (see Figure 1.17). The TT was designed to provide detailed step-by-step instructions for implementing a course of action. It provides both the steps to take (in sequence) and the rationale for each step. The TT could be considered a detailed road map to our objective. It answers the second part of the question, how to change. Chapter 7 also describes the Transition Tree.

> **NOTE:** With this edition, a comprehensive examination of the Transition Tree and instructions for constructing it are omitted. A historical perspective for doing so is provided in Chapter 7. Instead of a Transition Tree, a three-phase project management approach to implementing policy changes is introduced.

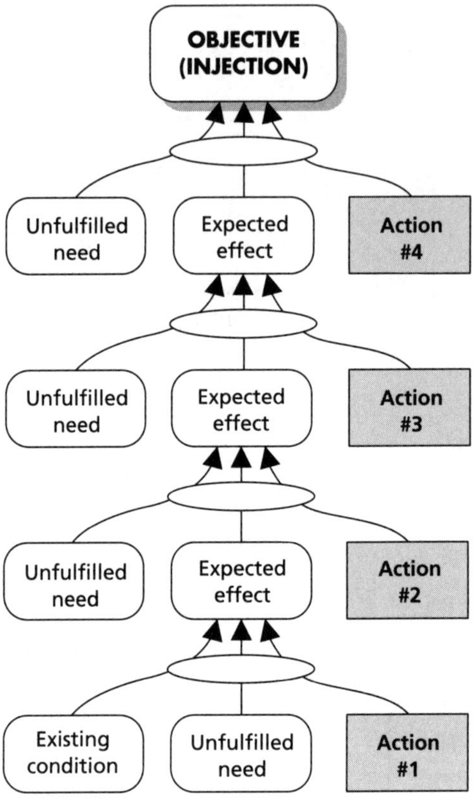

Figure 1.17   The Transition Tree.

THE CATEGORIES OF LEGITIMATE RESERVATION

The Categories of Legitimate Reservation (CLR) are the "logical glue" that holds the trees together. Essentially, they are eight rules, or tests, of logic that govern the construction and review of the trees. To be logically sound, a tree must be able to pass the first seven of these tests. The eight CLR include:

1. Clarity

2. Entity existence

3. Causality existence

4. Cause sufficiency

5. Additional cause

6. Cause-effect reversal

7. Predicted effect existence

8. Tautology (circular logic)

We use the CLR as we construct our trees to ensure that our initial relationships are sound. We use the CLR after the tree is built to review it as a whole. We use the CLR to scrutinize and improve the trees of others (and they to review ours). And, most important, we use the CLR to communicate disagreement with others in a non-threatening way, which promotes better understanding rather than animosity. Chapter 2 describes the CLR in detail, gives examples of their application, and provides instructions on how to scrutinize your own trees as, or after, you build them.

THE LOGICAL TOOLS AS A COMPLETE "THINKING PROCESS"

Each of the six logical tools can be used individually or they can be used in concert, as an integrated "thinking process." Recall that earlier we discussed TOC as a methodology for managing change. The four basic questions a manager must answer about change (what is the standard, what to change, what to change to, and how to cause the change) can be answered using the logical tools as an integrated package. Figure 1.18 shows the relationship of the logical tools to the four management questions about change.

State of Change	Applicable Logic Tree
What's the desired *standard?*	Intermediate Objectives Map
What to change?	Current Reality Tree
What to change *to?*	Evaporating Cloud, Future Reality Tree
How to cause the change?	Prerequisite Tree, Transition Tree

Figure 1.18 How the logic trees relate to four management questions about change.

Figure 1.19 shows a general overview of how each tool fits together with the others to produce an integrated thinking process. Non-quantifiable problems of broad scope and complexity are particularly prime candidates for a complete thinking process analysis. The rest of this book is devoted to explaining how the six logic trees and the Categories of Legitimate Reservation are used.

It is wise to keep in mind that no success or failure is necessarily final.

—Unknown

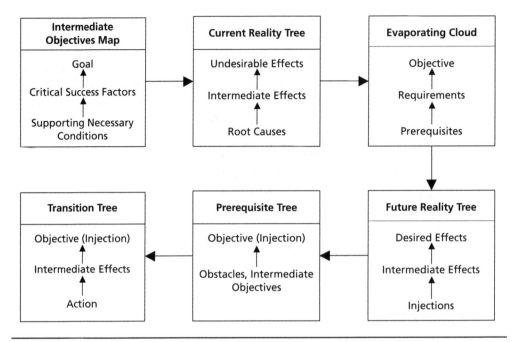

Figure 1.19   The six logical tools as an integrated thinking process.

ENDNOTES

1. Bragg, Steven M. *Throughput Accounting: A Guide to Constraint Management.* Hoboken, NJ: John Wiley and Sons, 2007.
2. Caspari, John A., and Pamela Caspari. *Management Dynamics: Merging Constraints Accounting to Drive Improvement.* Hoboken, NJ: John Wiley and Sons, 2004.
3. Cilliers, Paul. *Complexity and Postmodernism: Understanding Complex Systems.* NY: Routledge (Taylor and Francis Group), 1998.
4. Covey, Stephen R. *The Seven Habits of Highly Effective People: Powerful Lessons in Personal Change.* NY: Simon and Schuster, 1989.
5. Cox, James F., III, and Michael S. Spencer. *The Constraints Management Handbook,* Boca Raton, FL: The St. Lucie Press, 1998.
6. Deming, W. Edwards. *Out of the Crisis.* Cambridge, Mass.: MIT Center for Advanced Engineering Study, 1986.
7. _____. *The New Economics for Industry, Government, Education.* Cambridge, Mass.: MIT Center for Advanced Engineering Study, 1993.
8. Dettmer, H. William. *Strategic Navigation: A Systems Approach to Business Strategy.* Milwaukee, WI: ASQ Quality Press, 2003.
9. Goldratt, Eliyahu M. *Critical Chain,* Great Barrington, MA: North River Press, 1997.
10. _____. *It's Not Luck,* Great Barrington, MA: North River Press, 1994.
11. _____. *The Goal,* 2nd ed. Great Barrington, MA: North River Press, 1992.
12. _____. *The Haystack Syndrome,* Croton-on-Hudson, NY: North River Press, 1990.
13. _____ and Robert E. Fox. *The Race,* Croton-on-Hudson, NY: North River Press, 1987.
14. Leach, Lawrence P. *Critical Chain Project Management,* Boston, MA: Artech House, 2000.
15. _____. *Lean Project Management: Eight Principles for Success.* Boise, ID: Advanced Projects Institute, 2005.
16. Newbold, Robert C. *Project Management in the Fast Lane,* Boca Raton, FL: St. Lucie Press,
17. Schragenheim, Eli, and H. William Dettmer. *Manufacturing at Warp Speed,* Boca Raton, FL: The St. Lucie Press, 2000.
18. Source: Message posted to the TOC-L Internet Discussion List, July 19, 1995, SUBJ: "T, I, and OE in Not-For-Profit Organizations," summarizing a conversation between Dr. Eliyahu M. Goldratt and the author on July 16, 1995, and posted at Dr. Goldratt's request.
19. http://dictionary.reference.com/browse/goal

2

Categories of Legitimate Reservation

```
1. CLARITY

2. ENTITY EXISTENCE

3. CAUSALITY EXISTENCE

4. CAUSE INSUFFICIENCY

5. ADDITIONAL CAUSE

6. CAUSE-EFFECT REVERSAL

7. PREDICTED EFFECT EXISTENCE

8. TAUTOLOGY
```

When both logic and intuition agree, you are always right.

—Unknown

The Logical Thinking Process is composed of logical tools. The emphasis here is on the word "logic" for a good reason. A lot of problem-analysis tools use graphical representations. Flowcharts, "fishbone" diagrams, and tree and affinity diagrams are typical examples. But none of these diagrams are, strictly speaking, logic tools, because they don't incorporate any rigorous criteria for validating the connections between one element and another. In most cases, they're somebody's perception of the relationship.

The most significant difference between the Logical Thinking Process and traditional problem-analysis tools is a series of rules that govern the acceptability of the connections in each of the trees. These rules of logic are called the Categories of Legitimate Reservation—often abbreviated as CLR. The CLR are what differentiate somebody's perception from an accurate representation of existing reality.

A thorough understanding of these logical rules is absolutely essential to your success in using the logic trees. While the rules are not difficult to understand, there are eight of them, and it requires some study and practice to keep them straight in your mind and to know when each one applies. So what, exactly, are these Categories of Legitimate Reservation?

DEFINITION

The CLR constitute a framework of eight specific tests, or proofs, used to verify cause-and-effect logic. The eight proofs consist of:

1. Clarity

2. Entity existence

3. Causality existence

4. Cause insufficiency

5. Additional cause

6. Cause-effect reversal

7. Predicted effect existence

8. Tautology

PURPOSE

The Categories of Legitimate Reservation are the foundation upon which logic in general, and the Logical Thinking Process in particular, are built. The CLR can be used for a number of purposes. Although they were designed to verify the validity of cause-and-effect logic trees, they can be applied in other ways, too. Some of these applications include:

- Use by a *tree builder* to initially construct the six structures of the Logical Thinking Process (Intermediate Objectives Map, Current Reality Tree, Evaporating Cloud, Future Reality Tree, Prerequisite Tree, and Transition Tree).

- Use by a *tree builder* to self-check the tree after construction.

- Use by a *scrutinizer* with subject matter knowledge to review and evaluate a tree *built* and *presented* by someone else.

- Use by a *facilitator* in a group setting to ensure that both scrutinizers and presenters adhere to the rules of logic.

- Use by a *scrutinizer* or *facilitator* to communicate disagreement with the cause-and-effect logic of a presenter's tree in a way that fosters consensus and discourages confrontation.

- Use by anyone in interactive discussion, not associated with logic trees, to evaluate and challenge or accept the validity of logic in the statements of others without offending or generating animosity.

- Use by anyone in evaluating the validity of logic in written text (books, magazines or journals, newspapers, advertising, and the like).

NOTE: It would be appropriate here to define some new terms we just introduced. A *tree builder* is one who uses the procedures of the Logical Thinking Process to construct one of the six trees described at the end of Chapter 1. A *scrutinizer* is one who did not participate in the construction of the logic tree, but who has content knowledge of the subject matter addressed in the tree and who has been enlisted to critique the work of the tree builder. A scrutinizer does not necessarily need to understand the CLR to provide critique of the content or logical connections, but it helps. A *facilitator* is one who has been enlisted by a tree builder to ensure that scrutiny is conducted in accordance with the CLR. The facilitator does not necessarily need to have content knowledge of the subject matter of the tree, but must be knowledgeable in the CLR to facilitate scrutiny effectively.

ASSUMPTIONS

The effectiveness of the Categories of Legitimate Reservation in fulfilling their intended purpose is based on the following assumptions:

1. Tree builders want to construct logically sound trees

2. Tree builders, at some point, will also present their trees to others to communicate and elicit action

3. Tree builders/presenters naturally develop an emotional attachment to their own trees ("pride of the inventor")

4. Tree builders/presenters often express cause-and-effect connections that are intuitive to themselves but not to others (that is, intermediate steps appear to be missing)

5. Tree builders/presenters don't want to be embarrassed by presenting logically weak trees

6. Presenters look for affirmation as well as constructive advice on their trees

7. Presenters are sensitive to criticism of their work

8. Presenters can accept, even welcome, constructive advice when they solicit it, and if it is offered in a non-threatening way (that is, not "You against me," but "You and I against the system")

9. Scrutinizers are truly interested in helping presenters to improve their trees and in contributing to the analysis of the subject

10. Scrutinizers are not interested in humiliating presenters or in bolstering their own egos by their scrutiny

11. Scrutinizers have substantial intuition in the area of the tree's subject matter

12. Facilitators concern themselves exclusively with the logical process and not with subject matter content

HOW TO USE THIS CHAPTER

This chapter is composed of text with accompanying illustrations. Figure 2.36 at the end of the chapter is designed to be used as a checklist, or for quick reference, after the entire chapter has been read.

- Read all of Chapter 2 and the accompanying examples to understand the circumstances in which each applies.

- Review Figure 2.36, "Categories of Legitimate Reservation: Self-Scrutiny Checklist," which provides a concise checklist that you can use for constructing and scrutinizing your own cause-effect trees.

> *The weaker the argument, the stronger the words.*
>
> —Unknown

DESCRIPTION OF THE CATEGORIES OF LEGITIMATE RESERVATION

> *I know you think you understand what you think I said, but I'm not sure you realize that what you heard is not what I meant.*
>
> —Unknown

1. Clarity

Clarity is always the first reservation one should consider when questioning the logic of cause and effect. Clarity is not, strictly speaking, a logic-based reservation. Its roots are in communication.

Why Clarity Comes First

Clarity is raised first so that any misunderstandings resulting from inaccurate or incomplete communication of an idea are eliminated before the logic is examined. Most conflict in any situation involves communication breakdown to some extent. The clarity reservation helps defuse potential conflict between speaker and listener early in the scrutiny process and helps keep it on a professional rather than a personal level.

Raising the clarity reservation first establishes the protocol for the use of all the other categories. Stated briefly, in the words of Stephen R. Covey *(The Seven Habits of Highly Effective People)*, that protocol is:[1:236-260]

> Seek to *understand* before seeking *to be understood.*

By following this protocol we ensure that ineffective communication doesn't compromise logic.

What Clarity Means

A clarity reservation means that a listener doesn't comprehend the speaker. Since the clarity reservation is the first step in a check of logical validity, be sure that you and the speaker agree on the meaning of the speaker's statement. Whether the listener agrees with the *content* of the speaker's statement is not at issue in a clarity reservation—just the *meaning*. Validity of logic is not addressed until *mutual understanding* is achieved. Some indications or examples of a breakdown in communication:

- The listener doesn't understand the *meaning* of the speaker's statement.

- The listener doesn't see the *significance* of the speaker's statement.

- The listener doesn't understand the *meaning* or *context* of specific words or phrases in the speaker's statement.

- The listener doesn't recognize a reasonable connection between a stated cause and a stated effect.

- The listener doesn't see some intermediate steps implied by the speaker but not explicitly stated. (In cause-effect trees, this is sometimes referred to as a "long arrow.")

Up to this point, we've spoken of clarity as though we were referring to conversation among two or more people. Like the other categories, clarity is certainly useful in this respect. However, the primary focus of this chapter is on using the Categories of Legitimate Reservation in constructing, validating, and streamlining logic trees. As we proceed into more details on logic trees, what we've called "statements" by speakers (or writers, for that matter) will be referred to as entities in logic trees. "Entities," as used this way, are defined in the next section. Figure 2.1 presents an abbreviated test and example of the clarity reservation.

The greatest tragedy of science is that you often slay a beautiful hypothesis with an ugly fact.

—Thomas Huxley

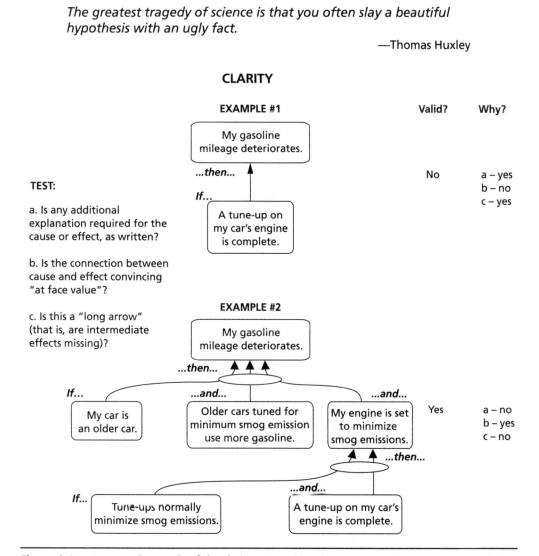

Figure 2.1   A test and example of the clarity reservation.

2. Entity Existence

For the purposes of logical examination, an *entity* is a complete idea expressed as a statement. Most often this idea is a cause or an effect represented in a logic tree, but in a broader application of the rules of logic it can also be a statement made in conversation, discussion, lecture, or writing. *Entity existence* is a reservation raised by a listener when he or she detects one of three conditions affecting the statement:

- The statement is an incomplete idea. Normally, this means the statement is not expressed in a grammatically correct sentence.
- The statement is not structurally sound; that is, it expresses multiple ideas in a single entity, or it contains an embedded "if–then" statement within it.
- The statement, at face value, does not seem valid to the listener.

Completeness

A complete idea is normally communicated using a grammatically correct sentence. In building logic trees, complete sentences are essential. At a minimum, there must be a *subject* and a *verb*; frequently there is an *object* as well. Impersonal pronouns (for example, "it," "this," and "those") are not acceptable (see Figure 2.2).

For example, the phrase "economic recession" can't stand alone as an idea. It raises the inevitable question, "What *about* economic recession?" To be effective in a logic tree, the entity must make sense when read with "if" or "then" preceding it. "Economic recession occurs" would be an acceptable entity from the standpoint of completeness.

Structure

An entity existence reservation based on structure is concerned exclusively with the mechanics of the sentence. Adherence to structural rules for entities is necessary to preclude confusion, ensure simplicity of depiction, and achieve logically tight or "dry" trees. The two structural rules for entities are:

- No compound entities (see Figure 2.3). A single entity must not contain more than one idea. For example, "The sky is falling" is an entity that contains only one idea.

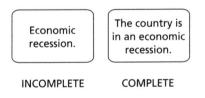

INCOMPLETE   COMPLETE

Figure 2.2   Completeness.

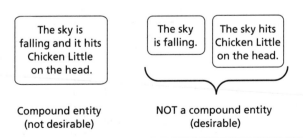

Compound entity   NOT a compound entity
(not desirable)   (desirable)

Figure 2.3   Structure: compound entity.

A sentence reading, "The sky is falling and it hits Chicken Little on the head," would be a *compound entity*. Two different ideas are expressed here, and each merits its own entity statement.

- No embedded "if–then" statements (see Figure 2.4). It's very hard to isolate causes and effects when the two are wrapped together in a single statement. It would seem easy to avoid this trap: Just make sure the words "if" and "then" don't appear in your entity statements. But there is an insidious form of "if–then" that is indicated by the phrases "in order to . . ." or ". . . because. . . ." Since "if" or "then" aren't there, it may seem acceptable, but it wouldn't be.

Let's look at two examples. The entity reads, "We park the car in the garage *in order* to avoid damage from the elements." No "if" or "then" appears in this sentence anywhere. But the phrase "in order to" alerts us to the fact that the idea can be conveyed another way: "*If* we park the car in the garage, *then* we avoid damage from the elements." This is an "if–then" expression in disguise. Similarly, a ". . . because . . ." statement may be nothing more than an "if–then" statement reversed. For example, an entity that reads, "He insults me *because* he doesn't like me" could just as easily read, "*If* he doesn't like me, *then* he insults me."

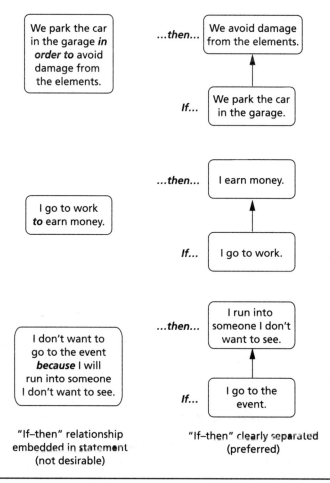

Figure 2.4   Structure: embedded "if-then."

NOTE: As a general rule, the more simply you can state your entities, the better off you'll be when building logic trees.

Validity

Once an idea has passed the clarity, completeness, and structure hurdles (that is, do I understand the presenter, and is it a complete, properly constructed statement?), the next test of entity existence is *validity* (see Figure 2.5). For our purposes, validity means that the content of the statement is sound, or well founded. It must have real meaning in the experience of the listener, or it must be a conclusion that the listener can reasonably accept.

Validity is normally established by evidence. Logic tree quality is improved dramatically if documented evidence of cause and/or effect can be produced. This helps avoid unfounded speculation or invalid assumptions about causality.

For example, "The sky is falling" doesn't exist in most people's reality. Moreover, it's impossible to find evidence for it. So even though it might be a clear, complete, structurally sound statement, it could nevertheless be questioned based on entity existence. On the other hand, "Most grass is green" is complete, structurally correct, and a valid statement.

NOTE: The validity test normally applies only to conditions of reality, not actions. For example, a condition of reality might be, "The sun is overhead at noon." An action might be, "I drive my car." In Future Reality and Transition Trees, the completeness and structure of action statements may be challenged, but not their validity, because future actions and their effects don't yet exist. However, the same action ("I drive my car.") in a Current Reality Tree is a statement of common practice and thus verifiable.

INVALID   VALID

Figure 2.5 Validity.

Figure 2.6 presents an abbreviated test and example of the entity existence reservation.

> *Beware of half-truths; you may have gotten the wrong half.*
>
> —Unknown

3. Causality Existence

A listener with a causality existence reservation has some doubts about whether the stated cause does, in fact, lead to the stated effect. Where entity existence focuses on the validity of the statements themselves, causality existence challenges the validity of the arrows, or connections, between entities. Causality existence addresses the following concerns:

- **Does the cause really result in the effect?** Does an "if–then" connection really exist? Verbalizing the arrow often helps to clarify any doubts about the causality: "If [cause], then we must have [effect]." The cause-effect relationship must make sense when read aloud exactly using "if–then" (see Figure 2.7).

ENTITY EXISTENCE

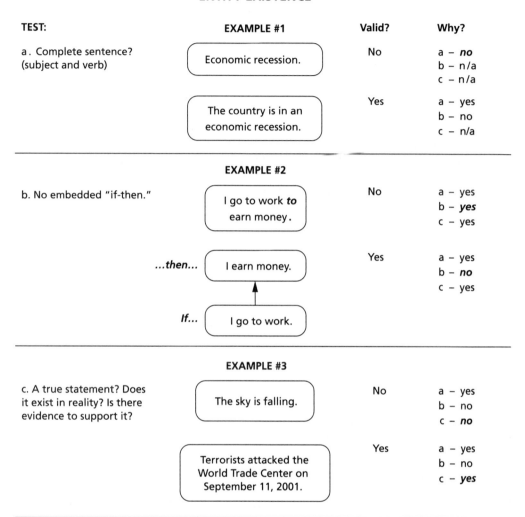

TEST:	EXAMPLE #1	Valid?	Why?
a. Complete sentence? (subject and verb)	Economic recession.	No	a – *no* b – n/a c – n/a
	The country is in an economic recession.	Yes	a – yes b – no c – n/a

	EXAMPLE #2		
b. No embedded "if-then."	I go to work **to** earn money.	No	a – yes b – *yes* c – yes
...then... I earn money. If... I go to work.		Yes	a – yes b – *no* c – yes

	EXAMPLE #3		
c. A true statement? Does it exist in reality? Is there evidence to support it?	The sky is falling.	No	a – yes b – no c – *no*
	Terrorists attacked the World Trade Center on September 11, 2001.	Yes	a – yes b – no c – *yes*

Figure 2.6   A test and example of the entity existence reservation.

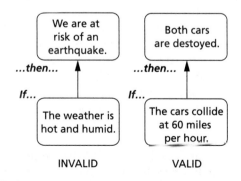

INVALID   VALID

Figure 2.7   Causality existence.

Caution: Scrutinizers and other listeners must be careful to read or hear only what is written or said, not what they read into it. Raising the clarity reservation should preclude this problem most of the time.

- **Is the cause intangible?** To be "tangible," a cause must be measurable or observable. Frequently an effect may be directly measurable or observable, but the cause is not (see Figure 2.8). For example, "My boss is dissatisfied with me" is not really observable in and of itself (unless the boss happens to tell you so). But "I stop watering the lawn" is observable. In both cases, the effects are measurable or observable, but in the first case, the cause is not. Verifying the cause-effect relationship in this instance requires identifying the presence of at least one other directly measurable effect attributable to the same cause. Discussion of the CLR "predicted effect existence," later in this chapter, contains a more detailed discussion of this technique of verification. Figure 2.9 presents an abbreviated test and example of the causality existence reservation.

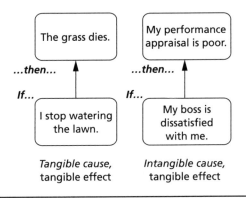

Figure 2.8   Tangible vs. intangible causes.

4. Cause Insufficiency

Because the world is a network of intricate, complex systems, cause insufficiency is the most common deficiency found in logic trees or human dialogue. In complex interactions, relatively few effects are likely to have a single, unequivocal cause. Most of the time, a given effect will have either multiple dependent factors causing it, or perhaps more than one completely independent cause. In this section, we see how several dependent factors combine to produce cause sufficiency, and how to know when there is a cause insufficiency. Additional cause is discussed in the next section.

The cause insufficiency reservation is raised when a listener believes that a presenter's stated cause is not enough, by itself, to produce the stated effect. As with causality existence, cause insufficiency focuses more attention on the *arrow* than on the entity. With a cause insufficiency reservation, the listener is tacitly saying, "I agree that your stated cause is an element of causality, but it isn't sufficient to create your effect without including some other factor that you haven't stated."

The Ellipse

How are multiple dependent causes expressed in a logic tree? In portraying such a relationship, contributing entities are linked to their resulting effect with arrows passing through an ellipse (see Figure 2.10). Sometimes this ellipse is described as an "AND" gate, or, because of its shape, a lens or a "banana." Whatever you choose to call it, the ellipse's

CAUSALITY EXISTENCE

TEST:	EXAMPLE #1	Valid?	Why?

a. Does the cause, in fact, result in the effect? (that is, does an "if-then" connection *really* exist?)

EXAMPLE #1

We can expect an earthquake.

...then...

If... The weather is hot and humid.

No

a – *no*
b – *no*
c – *no*

EXAMPLE #2

b. Does it make sense when read aloud *exactly* using "if-then"?

My performance appraisal is poor.

...then...

If... I did not complete my work.

Yes

a – *yes*
b – *yes*
c – *yes*

EXAMPLE #3

c. Is the cause intangible? (If so, an additional predicted effect should be identified.)

(Observed tangible effect)   *(Additional predicted effect)*

Sales are down.   A competitor's sales of a similar product increase.

Customers don't like our product.
(Intangible cause)

Yes

a – *yes*
b – *yes*
c – *yes*

Figure 2.9   A test and example of the causality existence reservation.

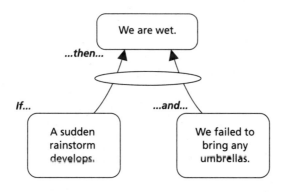

We are wet.

...then...

If...   ...and...

A sudden rainstorm develops.   We failed to bring any umbrellas.

Figure 2.10   Indicating cause sufficiency with an ellipse.

function is to identify and enclose the major contributing causes that are *sufficient in concert but not alone* to produce the effect.

Relative Magnitude of Dependent Causes
The idea of relative magnitude in a true dependency has no real meaning. Both (or all) causes are needed to produce the effect, and removing any one eliminates the effect. So we might say that any one of these causes accounts for all of the effect. But they all need each other, too. The sidebar entitled "Complex Causality," following the section "Additional Cause," discusses some important aspects of causality.

How Many Arrows?
Theoretically, there is no limit to how many arrows can pass through an ellipse. But there is a practical limit. At some point it becomes extremely difficult to depict and keep track of an expanding number of component causes. Also, at some point the number of contributors becomes so large that the effect of any one may be considered negligible.

How many arrows should you include in the ellipse? This is an individual judgment call. Only you can determine the break point between having enough weight of causes to produce the effect or not. As a rule of thumb, however, try to limit the number of contributing causes to three if possible, or four at most (see Figure 2.11). Beyond four, the relative influence of each contributor becomes so low that it might not be considered "major." Your objective should be to include only those causes without which the effect would either cease to exist or be of such limited magnitude that it would not be consequential to the larger system relationship.

Realistically, most effects are likely to have only a few major causes. If you have to exceed three contributing causes, take a closer look at all the causes. One or more might be an independent, or *additional*, cause. (The following section discusses additional cause.)

The Concept of "Oxygen"
One of the most common points of contention concerning cause insufficiency is the exclusion of some cause factor that is so basic to the situation that it is "transparent" to the presenter—but maybe not to the listener or scrutinizer. The best way to illustrate this issue is with an example. Consider the following cause-and-effect statement (see Figure 2.12):

"If we have fuel and a sufficient heat source, then we have a fire."

Is there something missing? A physicist might say, "You forgot something very important—oxygen. You can't have combustion without it." So in this case, a cause insufficiency reservation might be raised about the example statement.

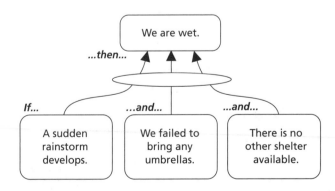

Figure 2.11 How many contributing causes?

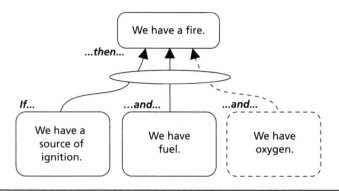

Figure 2.12 The concept of "oxygen."

But a presenter might respond, "True, but since oxygen is always present in the situation where my fire might occur, I consider it a constant that doesn't have to be shown." So the concept of "oxygen" connotes a factor that is accepted as present-but-transparent by anyone with intuitive knowledge of the system under examination.

As a presenter, however, you should be prepared for scrutinizers to raise one of two concerns:

- The cause factor you omitted is not obvious ("oxygen") to the audience of a presentation.

- The cause factor cannot really be assumed, but rather is a significant variable factor that is neither transparent nor constant in the situation.

In either case, presenters must be prepared to re-examine their cause-effect relationship. Figure 2.13 presents an abbreviated test and example of the cause insufficiency reservation.

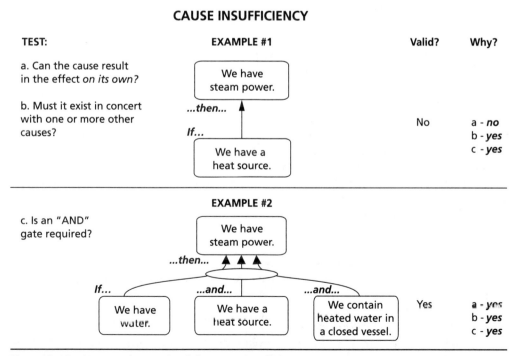

Figure 2.13 A test and example of the cause insufficiency reservation.

5. Additional Cause

Sometimes more than one completely independent cause can produce a similar effect. A listener who recognizes this situation might raise an additional cause reservation. For example, an above-normal human body temperature can result from either an internal infection or physical exertion on a hot summer day. Neither depends on the presence of the other. The key words are "either" and "or." Whereas a cause insufficiency reservation challenges an incomplete "and" condition, an additional cause reservation signifies a missing "or" condition.

With an additional cause reservation, the listener or scrutinizer is not contesting the presenter's stated cause. He or she is only suggesting that there is something else that, by itself, might generate the same effect (see Figure 2.14).

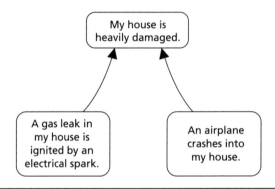

Figure 2.14   Additional cause.

Magnitude

In order for the additional cause reservation to be valid, the suggested additional cause must produce the stated effect in *at least as much magnitude* as the presenter's originally stated cause. For example, everyone's sales may drop 10 percent in a declining economy, but if your sales declined 20 percent, there may be an additional cause accounting for the other 10 percent. If the effect produced by the suggested additional cause is relatively small when compared with the original stated cause, it shouldn't be considered an additional cause. As with the cause insufficiency reservation, magnitude of effect is a personal judgment call.

A magnitudinal causality implies addition. In the preceding example about decreasing sales, more than one independent cause produced an effect that increased in magnitude as each was added to the causality. Each cause independently accounted for some degree of the effect, but in combination they produced a greater total effect.

Because a magnitudinal cause is a unique variation of a basic additional cause, it requires a distinctive depiction. For this, we'll use a "bowtie" symbol with the letters "MAG" inside it (see Figure 2.20).

Test

The quickest test for an additional cause condition is to ask the question, "If I eliminate the stated cause, is there any other circumstance under which the same degree of effect would occur?"

A Unique Variation of Additional Cause

It is possible, even common, to have multiple independent (additional) causes that are themselves made up of contributing factors. Under some circumstances, three contributing entities with arrows passing through an ellipse to an effect may be considered one independent cause, if that effect can also be caused by something else. That "something else" may, itself, be composed of multiple causes joined by an ellipse (see Figure 2.15). In such cases, each ellipsed group is considered an additional cause, but cause sufficiency rules still apply within the ellipse.

Figure 2.16 presents an abbreviated test and example of the additional cause reservation.

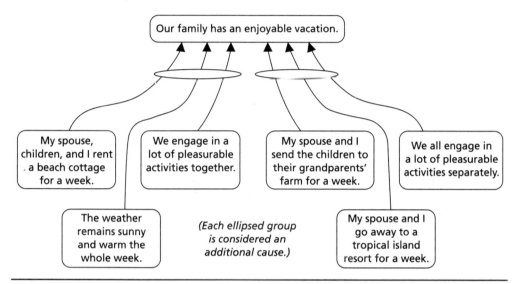

Figure 2.15 Variation of additional cause.

ADDITIONAL CAUSE

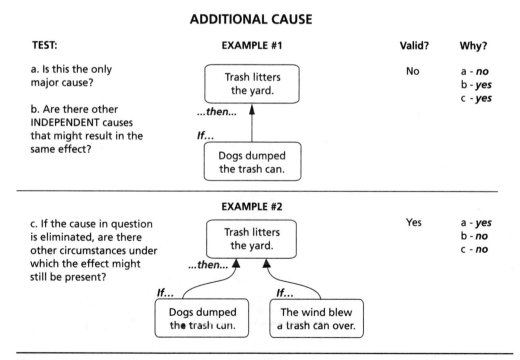

Figure 2.16 A test and example of the additional cause reservation.

COMPLEX CAUSALITY

What Is It?

"It's not as simple as that . . ." How many of us have heard that phrase at least once? It's an audible indication that complex causality might be involved. Simply stated, *complex causality* is a situation in which a given effect might have more than one cause. Maybe these causes are somehow related to one another, or maybe not. In any case, it's helpful to realize that complex causality is more likely to be the rule than the exception. If you accept this as a basic assumption about reality, wouldn't it be nice to know how to handle complex causality when you're building a tree? And wouldn't it make you feel more confident about the logical soundness of a tree when you read it?

Simple causality is represented in a logic tree by a single arrow connecting a single cause with a single effect (see Figure 2.17). It implies that the stated cause alone is enough to produce all of the indicated effect. Complex causality, on the other hand, implies that more than one cause is involved in producing the same effect.

Complex causality occurs two different ways. One is inherent in the Category of Legitimate Reservation known as additional cause, and another in cause sufficiency.

Cause Sufficiency

As we've seen, cause sufficiency (or insufficiency, as used in the Categories of Legitimate Reservation) describes a situation in which two or more causes relate to one another in order to produce an effect. Cause sufficiency comes in two variations.

Conceptual "AND"

This is the cause sufficiency situation we see most often. It's represented by arrows from several causes passing through an ellipse to the effect (see Figure 2.18). Each cause is needed, but it can't produce the effect without the help of the other(s). Removal of any one cause completely eliminates the effect. Thus, each cause could be said to be 100 percent responsible for the effect. But unlike the additional cause scenario, the causes *need each other.* They're interdependent.

Additional Cause

The additional cause postulates that several independent causes can produce the same effect. In fact, each cause can account for 100 percent of the effect *by itself* (see Figure 2.19). We show this relationship by drawing separate single arrows from each cause to the same effect.

What does this mean to you? Basically, if you want to get rid of the effect, you have to eliminate all the causes. Removing only one or two might not do any good, because any remaining cause can still produce the effect by itself.

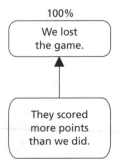

Figure 2.17 Simple causality.

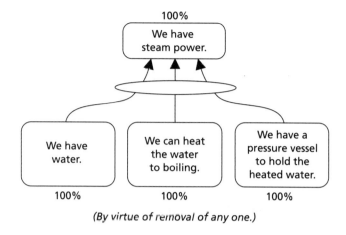

Figure 2.18 Conceptual "AND."

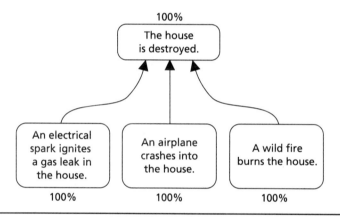

Figure 2.19 Additional cause.

Magnitudinal "AND"

This additional cause situation is fairly common. In a magnitudinal "and" condition, each cause contributes to the effect in an *additive* way. In other words, each cause adds progressively more to the effect. Conversely, removing one cause neither leaves the effect completely intact nor completely eliminates it. The effect is proportionately reduced (see Figure 2.20).

Exclusive "OR"

There's another variation on additional cause—the *exclusive "or."* This is a condition in which there are two possible independent causes (or outcomes), but they're mutually exclusive. In other words, if one of the causes is active, the other won't be; or if one of the effects happens, the other won't, and vice-versa. The exclusive "or" condition is not rare, but it's not an everyday occurrence, either.

For example, my house may be destroyed by a tornado or by an electrical fire. But if one causes the destruction, the other won't. The causes are not additive like the magnitudinal cause—the effect is a "zero-or-one" condition. Nor would alternative effects both be present. One happens, or the other, but not both. But both causality paths must be reflected in the logical depiction so as to account for either eventuality (see Figure 2.21).

Symbols

Because the causes in a magnitudinal "and" situation aren't completely independent (that is, any one cause producing all of the effect) or completely dependent (that is, removal of any one eliminates the effect), we have a problem graphically representing the magnitudinal "and." Goldratt established an ellipse to indicate a conceptual "and" (complete dependency). Not using an inclusive symbol at all indicates an additional cause (complete independence).

But the independent arrows of the additional cause don't accurately represent the magnitudinal relationship. Neither does the ellipse of cause sufficiency.

So there's a need for a new symbol to signify that unusual condition—the Magnitudinal "AND." In this book, we'll use a "bow-tie" shape to reflect a magnitudinal "and" (refer to Figure 2.20). If we don't differentiate between the conceptual "and" and magnitudinal "and" somehow, sooner or later we're likely to have a logic problem with a tree.

Like the magnitudinal cause condition, the exclusive "or" is a unique situation requiring a distinctive notation. We'll do this with a capital "OR" inside two pointed brackets (<OR>) placed between the exclusive cause or effect branches (refer to Figure 2.21).

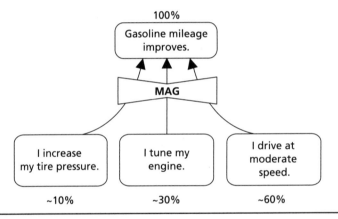

Figure 2.20   Magnitudinal "AND."

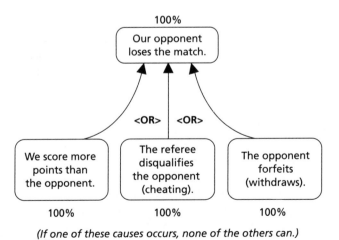

Figure 2.21   Exclusive "OR."

6. Cause-Effect Reversal

The cause-effect reversal reservation is based on a subtle distinction: *why* an effect exists versus *how we know* it exists. Sometimes this distinction is lost when a cause-effect relationship is written down or graphically depicted. Another way of verbalizing this concern is to ask the question, "Is the stated cause the source of the effect, or is the effect really the source of the cause?" It seems as if this should be an obvious error to detect, but that's not always the case.

The "Fishing Is Good" Example

To clarify the difference between why something happens and how we know it happens, consider the following two cause-effect relationships (see Figure 2.22):

   #1:   "*If* many fishermen are fishing from the river bank, *and* the fishermen's stringers are full of fish, *then* fishing is good."

   #2   "*If* the river was stocked with fish yesterday, *and* fishing season opens today, *then* fishing is good."

   Which of these statements makes more sense? Was the good fishing caused by the fishermen fishing or the stringers full of fish? Or were these the *indications* that led us to conclude that fishing was good? In actuality, the two cause-effect relationships should be combined, with some modification, to present a much more accurate picture of the situation in Figure 2.23

The Statistical Example

"*If* standardized test scores are at or below the 50th percentile, *then* the academic qualifications of new students are poor." Are the low test scores the cause of poor qualifications, or are they the reason we know those qualifications are poor? In other words, did the low scores cause the poor qualifications, or are they just an indicator of them?

   Remember, in reading or hearing an *if-then* statement, the part associated with "If…" is the cause; the part following "…then…" is the effect.

The Medical Example

"*If* my body temperature is higher than normal, *and* I have a pain in my lower abdomen, *then* I have appendicitis." Did the fever and the pain cause the appendicitis, or was it the other way around? As you can see, it's east to go astray on cause-effect reversal.

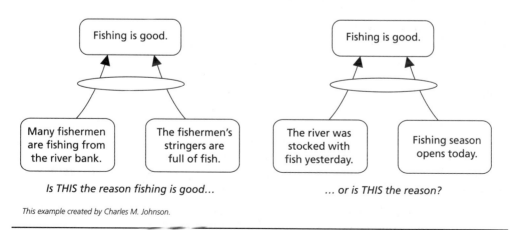

Is THIS the reason fishing is good...   *... or is THIS the reason?*

This example created by Charles M. Johnson.

Figure 2.22 The "fishing is good" example.

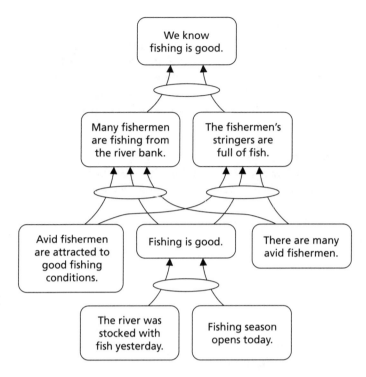

A more complete, accurate expression of the situation...that makes logical sense

This example created by Charles M. Johnson

Figure 2.23 Combined "fishing is good" example.

Test

There are two ways to detect a cause-effect reversal:

- Does it seem that the arrow between cause and effect is pointing in the wrong direction? This is most likely to be a "gut feeling" and the first inkling you have that something is not quite right.

- Could the stated cause really be an indicator, rather than a source?

Figure 2.24 presents an abbreviated test and example of the cause-effect reversal reservation.

7. Predicted Effect Existence

Predicted effect existence means that if a proposed cause-effect relationship is valid, some other unstated effect would also be expected. For example, "I have appendicitis" might be offered as the cause of the effect "I have a pain in my abdomen." But if the cause is really valid, we might also expect to see a couple of other effects: "I have a fever" and "My white cell count is elevated."

The predicted effect existence reservation does not stand alone. It is always invoked to substantiate a reservation for causality existence. Predicted effect existence becomes the proof that the causality existence reservation is—or is not—valid. Consequently, the predicted effect existence reservation can be used either by a presenter to *support* causality, or by a scrutinizer to *refute* causality. Here are a couple of examples:

PRESENTER: "If appendicitis is really causing the pain in my abdomen, we should also expect to see an elevated white blood cell count and perhaps a fever. Since we *do* see these additional predicted effects, I conclude that appendicitis *is* a valid cause."

SCRUTINIZER: "If appendicitis is really the cause of the pain in your abdomen, we should also expect to see an elevated white blood cell count and maybe a fever. But since neither of these additional predicted effects is present, we must conclude that appendicitis is not a valid cause."

Conflict or Differences in Magnitude?

The predicted effect existence reservation recognizes the complex nature of most systems. Most causes in the "real world" result in more than one effect. Even if only one effect is stated or germane to a given situation, if you look hard enough, in most cases additional effects can be identified. Three characteristics of predicted effects make them especially useful in validating or refuting proposed effects:

- *Expectation.* ("Is it there?") Given the proposed effect, one expects to see another related effect; or, one expects *not* to see a certain effect. It's either there or it isn't, and its presence or absence will either support or refute the proposed cause-effect relationship.

- *Coexistence.* ("Is it there at the same time?") If the predicted effect is present, proposed effects and predicted effects must be able to coexist. If a case can be made that the two effects can't exist at the same time (or that the cause can't produce both effects), then the proposed cause-effect relationship is suspect. Or, if the proposed cause can be shown to produce the same effect to differing degrees under the same circumstances, the cause-effect relationship is also called into question. For example, the same cause, under the same circumstances, can't simultaneously cause a profit and a loss. If you can show that it does, the original cause-effect relationship is refuted.

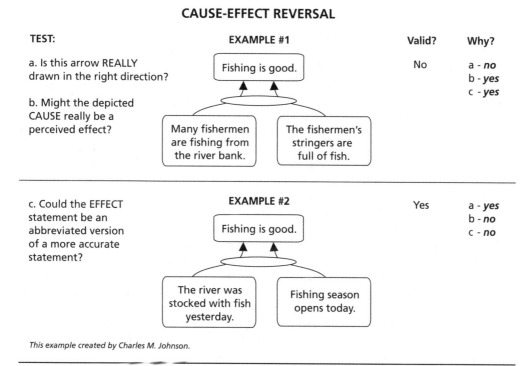

CAUSE-EFFECT REVERSAL

TEST:

a. Is this arrow REALLY drawn in the right direction?

b. Might the depicted CAUSE really be a perceived effect?

c. Could the EFFECT statement be an abbreviated version of a more accurate statement?

EXAMPLE #1

Fishing is good.

Many fishermen are fishing from the river bank.

The fishermen's stringers are full of fish.

Valid? No

Why?
a - *no*
b - *yes*
c - *yes*

EXAMPLE #2

Fishing is good.

The river was stocked with fish yesterday.

Fishing season opens today.

Valid? Yes

Why?
a - *yes*
b - *no*
c - *no*

This example created by Charles M. Johnson.

Figure 2.24 A test and example of the cause-effect reversal reservation.

- *Magnitude.* ("Is it all there?") If the predicted effect is present and it can coexist with the proposed effect, the predicted effect may also be expected to exist at a specific magnitude. If the actual magnitude is significantly greater or less than expected, the proposed cause may be refuted as either invalid or insufficient. If the actual magnitude approximates the expected magnitude, the cause-effect relationship is validated.

To determine whether a predicted effect supports or refutes a cause-effect relationship, test it with the following proofs:

	Support	Refute
1. The effect is *there*, but *shouldn't* be.		X
2. The effect is *not* there, but *should* be.		X
3. The effect *is* there, and *should* be.	X	
4. The effect can coexist with the predicted effect.	X	
5. The predicted and proposed effects are mutually exclusive.		X
6. The predicted effect is more or less than expected.		X
7. The predicted effect is about the same degree as expected.	X	

Figure 2.25 includes several examples showing how the predicted effect existence reservation is used to support or refute causality.

Tangible or Intangible?

As previously mentioned in "Causality Existence" earlier in this chapter, predicted effect existence can be used to verify the existence of an intangible cause. It can also be used when the cause is tangible. In the latter case, however, the cause doesn't need verification; it's already tangible. The causal connection, or arrow, does.

A scrutinizer taking issue with the existence of an intangible cause would use predicted effect existence to show that another expected effect of the same cause is absent. For example, let's assume the presenter says, "If customers don't like our product, then sales are down." A scrutinizer could challenge the causality existence of this relationship by pointing out the absence of just one other expected effect of that intangible cause. Figure 2.26 illustrates two such possible collateral effects.

If either of these predicted effects doesn't exist, then the originally stated cause is invalid, and the scrutinizer's reservation is valid. However, if the presenter can demonstrate that both of those collateral effects do exist, then predicted effect existence supports the original cause-effect relationship.

What if the cause *is* tangible? Predicted effect existence can also be used to support or refute the logical connection, or arrow, between cause and effect. For example, "Quality has deteriorated" may be a quantitatively verifiable fact (see Figure 2.27). "Sales are going down" may also be substantiated by numbers. But has deteriorated quality necessarily caused decreased sales? One additional predicted effect of poor quality might be "Customers' complaints increase." Does this quantitatively verifiable effect exist? If so, the causality relationship between poor quality and decreased sales is likely to be valid. If not, decreased sales may have another cause—perhaps a general economic downturn— but decreased quality may not be the cause. In fact, if there is no alternative product or service, it isn't likely to be the cause.

Situation	Proposed Cause and Effect	Predicted Effect	Actual Condition

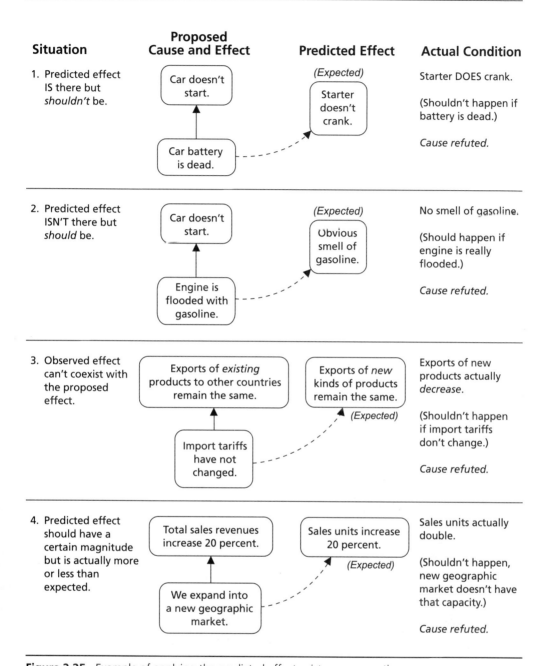

1. Predicted effect IS there but *shouldn't* be.

Car doesn't start.

Car battery is dead.

(Expected)

Starter doesn't crank.

Starter DOES crank.

(Shouldn't happen if battery is dead.)

Cause refuted.

2. Predicted effect ISN'T there but *should* be.

Car doesn't start.

Engine is flooded with gasoline.

(Expected)

Obvious smell of gasoline.

No smell of gasoline.

(Should happen if engine is really flooded.)

Cause refuted.

3. Observed effect can't coexist with the proposed effect.

Exports of *existing* products to other countries remain the same.

Import tariffs have not changed.

Exports of *new* kinds of products remain the same.

(Expected)

Exports of new products actually *decrease*.

(Shouldn't happen if import tariffs don't change.)

Cause refuted.

4. Predicted effect should have a certain magnitude but is actually more or less than expected.

Total sales revenues increase 20 percent.

We expand into a new geographic market.

Sales units increase 20 percent.

(Expected)

Sales units actually double.

(Shouldn't happen, new geographic market doesn't have that capacity.)

Cause refuted.

Figure 2.25 Example of applying the predicted effect existence reservation.

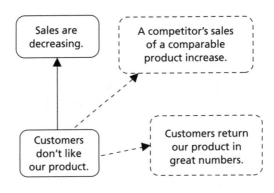

Figure 2.26 Predicted effect: verifying an *intangible* cause.

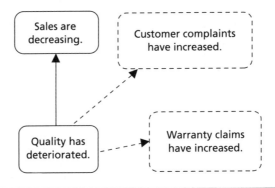

Figure 2.27 Another predicted effect: verifying a *tangible* cause.

Verbalizing Predicted Effect Existence

To avoid confusion, verbalize a predicted effect existence reservation this way:

> "If we accept that [CAUSE] is the reason for [ORIGINAL EFFECT], then it must also lead to [PREDICTED EFFECT(S)], which [do / do not] exist."

Figure 2.28 provides an abbreviated test and example of the predicted effect existence reservation.

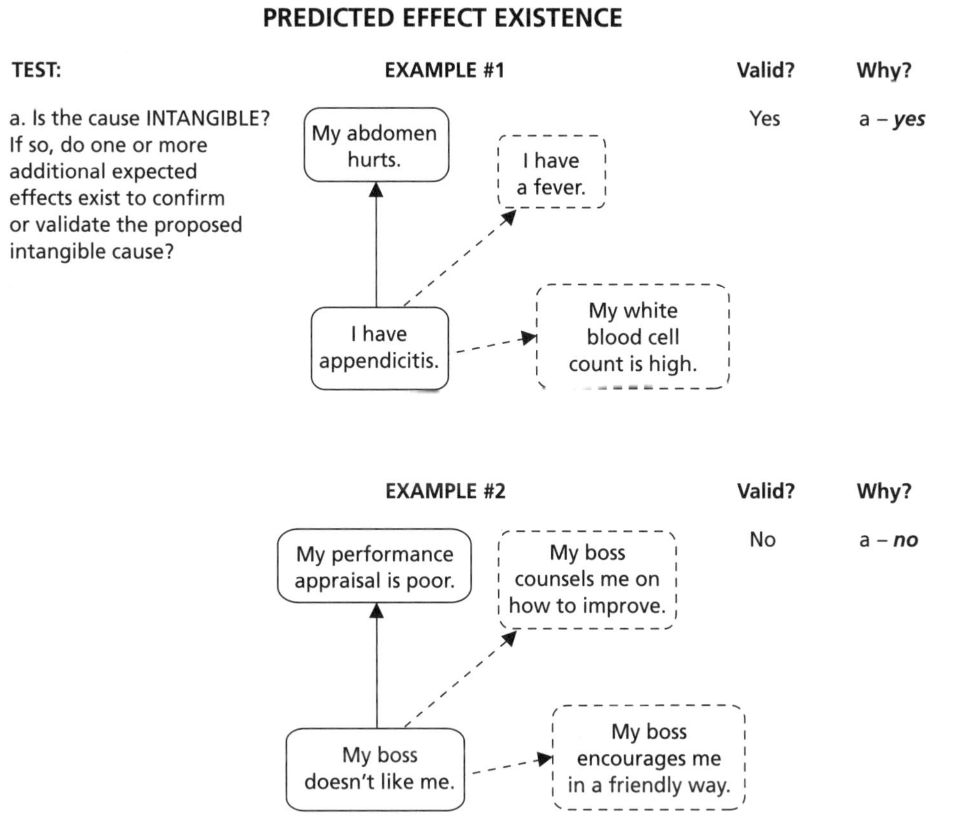

PREDICTED EFFECT EXISTENCE

TEST:	EXAMPLE #1	Valid?	Why?

a. Is the cause INTANGIBLE? If so, do one or more additional expected effects exist to confirm or validate the proposed intangible cause?

Yes   a – *yes*

```
┌──────────┐        ┌─────────┐
│My abdomen│        │ I have  │
│  hurts.  │        │ a fever.│
└──────────┘        └─────────┘
      ▲
      │              ┌──────────────┐
┌──────────┐         │   My white   │
│  I have  │ ──────▶ │  blood cell  │
│appendicitis.│      │ count is high.│
└──────────┘         └──────────────┘
```

EXAMPLE #2	Valid?	Why?

No   a – *no*

```
┌──────────────┐      ┌──────────────┐
│My performance│      │   My boss    │
│appraisal is poor.│  │ counsels me on│
└──────────────┘      │ how to improve.│
      ▲               └──────────────┘
      │
┌──────────────┐      ┌──────────────┐
│  My boss     │ ───▶ │   My boss    │
│doesn't like me.│    │ encourages me │
└──────────────┘      │ in a friendly way.│
                      └──────────────┘
```

Figure 2.28   A test and example of the predicted effect existence reservation.

8. Tautology (Circular Logic)

Tautology is another name for *circular logic*: The effect is offered as a rationale for the existence of the cause. Since causality must be questioned before the issue of tautology can be raised, tautology, like predicted effect existence, can never stand alone. It must be preceded by another causality reservation—usually causality existence. Consequently, like predicted effect existence, a tautology reservation is not really observable by a scrutinizer until *after* a causal relationship has been verbalized by the tree builder and the causality of one of the connections is questioned. Tautology becomes obvious when the reason for the causation has been challenged.

Tautology is most likely to surface when causality existence is questioned and the cause is intangible. If no additional predicted effect is offered, other than the stated one, to substantiate the intangible cause, it becomes easy to forsake a more rigorous examination of the causality and let the effect provide the rationale for the cause.

Baseball Example

This example, while not presented in "if–then" format, is typical of tautologies common in the electronic and print media (see Figure 2.29).

> STATEMENT: "The Dodgers lost the game because they played poorly."
>
> CHALLENGE: *What makes you think they played poorly?*
>
> RATIONALE: "They lost the game, didn't they?"

In this example, the effect is clearly offered as a rationale for the existence of the cause. Since causality was not more intensively investigated, additional predicted effects such as number of errors, bases on balls, extra-base hits, and so forth were not offered to substantiate the intangible cause. And totally ignored is the fact that the Dodger pitcher may have had a no-hitter going into the 10th inning when he gave up a solo home run.

Vampire Example

Figure 2.30 is an example in an "if–then" format.

> PROPOSED CAUSE: "I wear garlic around my neck and sleep with a cross."
>
> PROPOSED EFFECT: "Vampires stay away."
>
> CHALLENGE: *How do you know that the garlic and cross really work?*
>
> RATIONALE: "You don't see any vampires, do you?"

Test

To avoid the tautology trap, ask the following questions:

- Is the cause intangible?

- Is the effect offered as a rationale for the existence of the cause?

- Are there any additional predicted effects that could substantiate the intangible cause?

Figure 2.31 presents an abbreviated test and example of the tautology reservation.

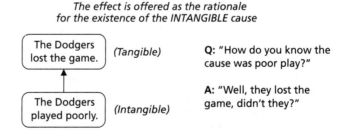

Figure 2.29 Tautology (circular logic).

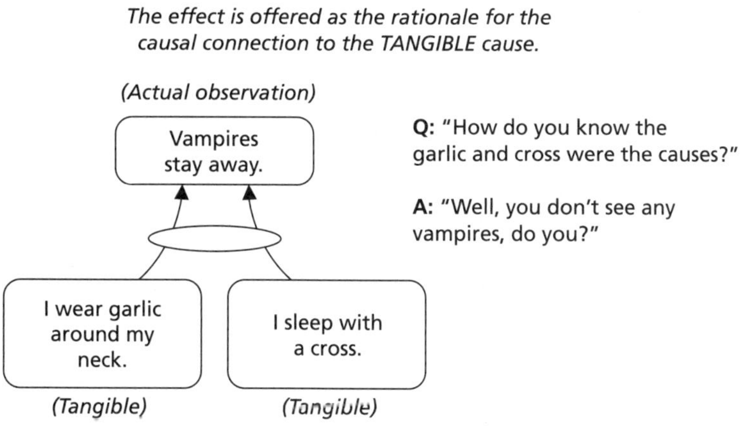

The effect is offered as the rationale for the causal connection to the TANGIBLE cause.

(Actual observation)

Vampires
stay away.

Q: "How do you know the garlic and cross were the causes?"

A: "Well, you don't see any vampires, do you?"

I wear garlic
around my
neck.

(Tangible)

I sleep with
a cross.

(Tangible)

Figure 2.30　Circular logic (tangible cause).

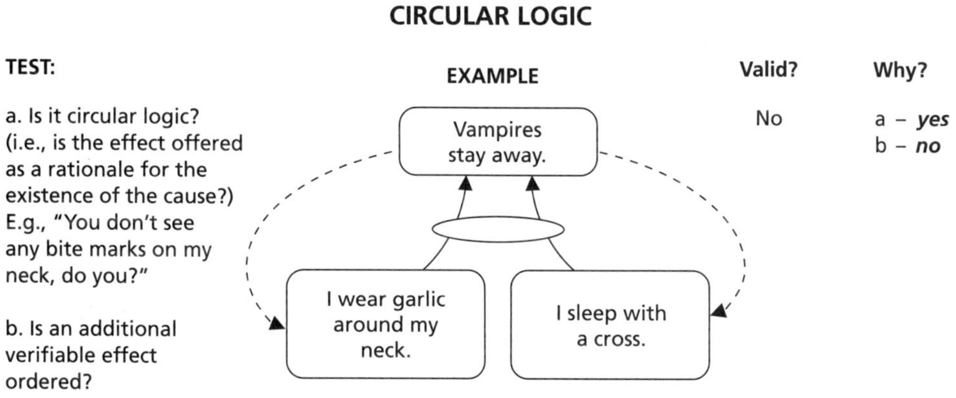

CIRCULAR LOGIC

TEST:	**EXAMPLE**	**Valid?**	**Why?**

a. Is it circular logic? (i.e., is the effect offered as a rationale for the existence of the cause?) E.g., "You don't see any bite marks on my neck, do you?"

b. Is an additional verifiable effect ordered?

Vampires
stay away.

I wear garlic
around my
neck.

I sleep with
a cross.

No

a – *yes*
b – *no*

Figure 2.31　A test and example of the circular logic reservation.

It's a wonderful feeling when you discover some logic to substantiate your beliefs.

　　　　　　　　　　　　　　　　　—Unknown

USING THE CLR IN A GROUP

Earlier, we discussed the use of the Categories of Legitimate Reservation by tree builders to validate their own work as they're actually constructing the logic trees. This is usually a solitary application. But more commonly the CLR are used in groups of two or more to scrutinize the logic of trees that have been constructed by others—in other words, review of first or second drafts.

When two or more people use the CLR as a group, one of two situations applies:

- All (or most) of the parties understand the eight CLR and what they mean.

- Only one person (often the one who constructed the tree) really understands the CLR and how to use them.

CLR Known by All

When the CLR are understood by all participants, logical scrutiny *can* proceed very quickly, provided that not too many are participating. The value in having everyone thoroughly conversant with the CLR is that critiques can be communicated in a kind of verbal shorthand, by reference to the CLR title alone. A scrutinizer can merely say, "I have a causality existence reservation about the connection between entities 104 and 105." The tree builder will know exactly what the scrutinizer means without any explanation being required.

On the other hand, if you want to see the scrutiny process grind to a near-halt, invite four or more scrutinizers conversant in the CLR to participate. In the immortal words of George Washington:

> *My observation is that whenever one person is found adequate to the discharge of a duty by close application thereto, it is worse executed by two persons, and scarcely done at all if three or more are employed therein.*

This often happens because people knowledgeable in the CLR tend to "nit-pick" every little deficiency they find.

CLR Known Only by the Tree Builder

More often than not, the availability of scrutinizers knowledgeable in the CLR is limited. In some organizations, perhaps nobody but the tree builder really understands the CLR.

This need not be a problem. In fact, it could be a definite advantage. In most cases, the logic trees are being prepared for an audience that is unfamiliar with the CLR anyway. So scrutinizers who aren't conversant with the CLR can be extremely helpful, for two reasons. First, they'll be inclined to explain their concerns about the logic in the same terms as the eventual intended audience. Second, they'll be better focused on the content of the subject matter and their intuition about what causes what. They'll be less distracted by trying to categorize their concerns according to a preconceived eight-category taxonomy.

Gaining effective scrutiny from people who don't really know much (if anything) about the CLR puts a larger burden on the tree builder. The person who prepares the logic trees must have such a thorough understanding of the CLR that he or she will instantly know what category of reservation applies, even though the scrutinizer is "talking through it"—in other words, explaining the nature of the deficiency instead of naming it directly.

For example, a scrutinizer without knowledge of the CLR might say:

"John's absence from work isn't enough to keep the engineering review from happening. There would have to be nobody else who could do it, too."

What an experienced tree builder, knowledgeable in the CLR, hears in this statement (even though it's not explicitly stated this way) is:

"I have a cause insufficiency reservation. An ellipse with another entity is required. That new entity reads 'Nobody else can do the engineering review.'"

Scrutiny of logic trees does not require people knowledgeable in the CLR. You don't have to teach them the eight categories as long as you yourself know them frontward and backward. It does require people who are highly knowledgeable in the subject matter that is the topic of the tree they're scrutinizing.

SUFFICIENCY-BASED VS. NECESSITY-BASED LOGIC TREES

As we proceed through the six trees of the Logical Thinking Process, you'll notice that three of these trees—the Intermediate Objectives Map, the Evaporating Cloud, and the Prerequisite Tree—are expressed differently from the Current Reality Tree, Future Reality Tree, and Transition Tree. That's because their foundations are a little different.

The Current Reality Tree, Future Reality Tree, and Transition Tree are considered *sufficiency* trees. They're read in an "if–then" form. The validity of their cause-effect relationships depends on sufficiency. To determine sufficiency, we ask questions such as, "Is *this* enough (or sufficient) to cause *that*?"

The Intermediate Objectives Map, the Evaporating Cloud, and the Prerequisite Tree are considered *necessity* trees. They're read in an "In order to . . . we must . . . because . . ." format. The validity of their cause-effect relationships depends on meeting *minimum necessary requirements.*

A sufficiency tree implies that the causes are enough to actually *produce* the effect. A necessity tree implies that you can't *realize* the resulting entity *without* the preceding one. The distinction between *producing* and *enabling* is a subtle one.

The Categories of Legitimate Reservation were designed to apply primarily to sufficiency trees, but they do have some applicability to necessity trees as well. These distinctions will be explained in more detail in Chapter 3, "Intermediate Objectives Map," and Chapter 7, "Prerequisite and Transition Trees."

SYMBOLS AND LOGIC TREE CONVENTIONS

When Goldratt originally conceived the Thinking Process, he used a simple graphics program—*Mac Flow*—to construct and print or display the early logic trees. His selection of various symbols to represent different entities (causes, effects, injections, obstacles, sufficiency, and so on) was probably somewhat arbitrary and constrained by the available symbols in that early version of the program. (Remember, this took place well before the sophisticated graphics and charting programs we have available today.) For the first several years after the Thinking Process was introduced, it was common practice to use Goldratt's original symbology.

Sometime in the late 1990s, however, as the practice and teaching of the Thinking Process became more widespread and various flowcharting and computer-aided design programs became more widely available, some users began to diverge from the conventions Goldratt had originally established. There was no deliberate effort by any Theory of Constraints practitioner to establish a standard set of symbols or conventions for drawing trees. A kind of "free-for-all, do-your-own-thing" situation prevailed. The variety of conventions and symbols is easy to see in the many published papers and books available in the public domain. This is unfortunate.

Three Reasons to Standardize

My experience in the last ten years of teaching and applying the Thinking Process persuades me that there are three compelling reasons for using a standard symbol set and standard logical connection conventions.

Credibility

The first has to do with credibility. A methodology without standard, commonly accepted symbols and conventions for using them has a hard time commanding the respect of non-users. Rightly or wrongly, non-users perceive the method to lack rigorous discipline (especially when combined with lax application of the Categories of Legitimate Reservation). As anyone who has tried to implement organizational change in a complex environment can tell you, credibility of method is critical. Ultimate success in applying the Thinking Process—and sustaining continued use of the logic trees—depends on establishing credibility and acceptance among non-users, particularly influential ones such as executive decision makers. For this reason alone, standard symbols and conventions make sense.

Ergonomics

The second reason is purely ergonomic. The ergonomic issue is human sensory overload and the resulting confusion. The symbol set and connection conventions Goldratt originally used are elegantly simple. Certain advances in graphic display since then have contributed refinements that make them "easy on the eye" as well. Where visual absorption and comprehension are concerned, "round and smooth" beats "sharp and abrupt" every time. Moreover, with different people using different symbols to mean the same thing, exchange or sharing of trees can be tedious, since a *tree reader* using one set of conventions must mentally translate the work of a *tree builder* using a different set.

Miscommunication of Logic

Another problem I've observed in the last decade is that many people, especially those with engineering backgrounds, like to think of logic trees (and express them) as flow charts. *Logic trees are not flowcharts.* The arrows that connect text boxes in logic trees convey much more than a mere circuit-flow connection. It does a disservice to both the methodology and to the user when tree builders and tree readers think of them that way.

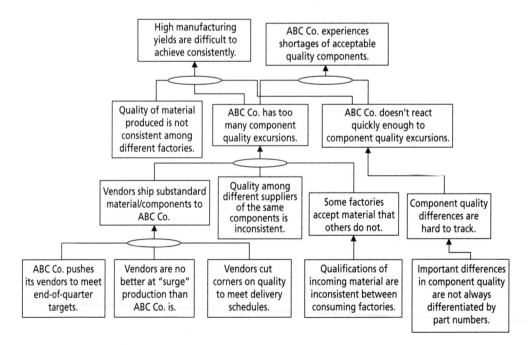

Figure 2.32a Thinking Process as an engineering flowchart.

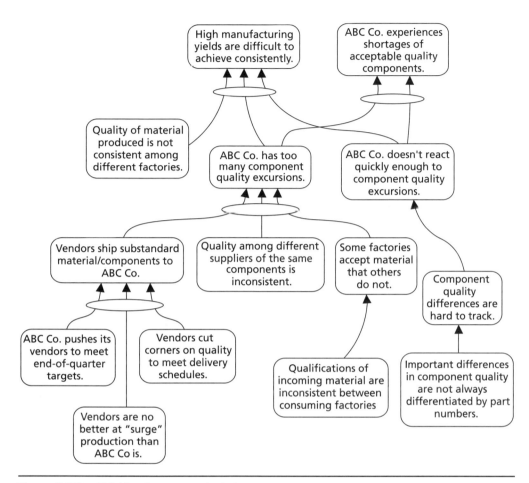

Figure 2.32b   Thinking Process as a logic tree.

Here's a simple comparison that demonstrates the importance of a clean, uncluttered, "easy-on-the-eye" look to logic trees. (Figures 2.32a and 2.32b) The first is a typical example of a tree formatted somewhat like an engineering flow chart. The second adheres more to Goldratt's original conventions. The only exception is the curved causality arrows, which weren't available until the more recent generation of graphics applications became common. Notice, too, that the boxes aren't rectangularly aligned, either.

Both of these excerpts from a complex-process Current Reality Tree contain exactly the same content. The only differences are in the use of symbols and connection conventions. Which of these do you think is easier to read and absorb quickly? (Don't worry about the details of the content; just decide which format is easier to follow and comprehend.)

A Standard Symbol Set

To facilitate common understanding and communication, I submit the symbology in Figure 2.33 as a standard. The only change from Goldratt's original symbols is the substitution of an octagon in place of a hexagon to represent obstacles in a Prerequisite Tree, about which more in a moment.

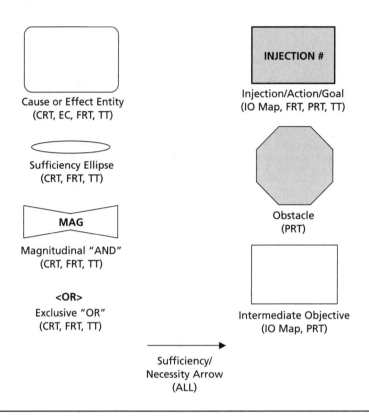

Figure 2.33 Standard logic tree symbols.

A Standard Convention for Logical Connections

One of the characteristics that makes flow-chart-format logic trees difficult to read is the 90-degree corner. When the human eye is following the path of an arrow connecting two boxes, turning these corners demands full attention. Another characteristic is the merging of multiple connecting arrows into one coming out of an ellipse. The most vexing problem with merging several arrows into one becomes more obvious when several causes simultaneously produce two or more effects. The top two layers of Figure 2.32a illustrate this configuration. It requires extraordinary effort for the reader's eye to absorb and mind to comprehend the causal relationship.

Figure 2.34 shows the preferred convention for connecting entities in a logic tree. Notice that in addition to avoiding arrows with 90-degree corners, it also arranges entities in ways that conserve page space (a common challenge in building logic trees for presentation) without cramming too many into a small space. Combining these conventions with the round corners of most entities creates a total effect that is much easier on the eye and on the brain. The use of sharp-cornered boxes should be limited to injections and intermediate objectives.

---

* I'm indebted to Dr. Paul Selden for suggesting the use of the octagon—a "stop" sign shape—to indicate an obstacle.

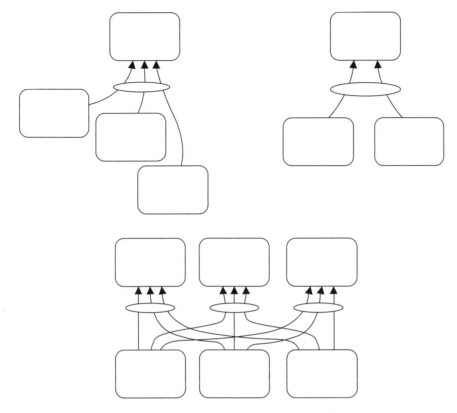

(Three causes combining to produce three effects.
Imagine trying to depict this with flow chart conventions.)

Figure 2.34 Standard logical connection conventions.

The one liberty that I've taken with Goldratt's original symbol set is a minor change to the prerequisite tree. Goldratt originally used hexagons to depict obstacles. I offer octagons instead. In many parts of the world, "STOP" signs are octagonal, making the octagon a fitting symbol for an obstacle that stops progress. But the more important reason for using octagons is that they consume less space on a page because word-wrapping is rectangular within them.

Using the octagon facilitates another minor improvement: elimination of superfluous, confusing arrows. Goldratt originally configured the prerequisite tree to look like the example in the left side of Figure 2.35. Arrows were drawn from the hexagon to the midpoint of the arrow connecting two intermediate objectives. The surfeit of arrows was confusing to those new to the Thinking Process. The important thing is to assure that an obstacle is effectively associated with the intermediate objective that overcomes it. Using an octagon allows the tree builder to conveniently overlay the intermediate objective on a corner of the obstacle, conveying the idea that the obstacle is "overcome" and closely associating the two entities without the need for additional, confusing arrows. The example in the right side of Figure 2.35 shows how this is done.

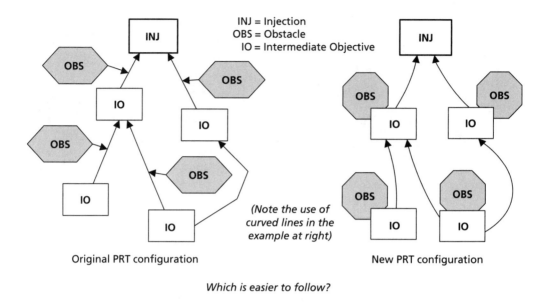

Figure 2.35   Two versions of a prerequisite tree.

SUMMARY

The Categories of Legitimate Reservation are used to ensure that the cause-and-effect trees we build are logically sound. We've seen how to use them to scrutinize the logic trees of others. They can also be used in the course of normal interpersonal interaction to evaluate what people say, even if the speakers are not expressing themselves with logic trees. We've also been introduced to some standard symbols and conventions for using them. Next, we'll start using the CLR and these conventions to build a tree.

> *There is a mighty big difference between good, sound reasons and reasons that sound good.*
>
> —Burton Hillis

1. **CLARITY** *(seeking to understand)*
   - Would I add any verbal explanation if reading the tree to someone else?
   - Is the meaning/context of words unambiguous?
   - Is the connection between cause and effect convincing "at face value"?
   - Are intermediate steps missing?

2. **ENTITY EXISTENCE** *(complete, properly structured, valid statements of cause or effect)*
   - Is it a complete sentence?
   - Does it make sense?
   - Is it free of embedded "if-then" statements? (Look for "...because..." and "...in order to....")
   - Does it convey only one idea? (not a compound entity)
   - Does it exist in my (or someone's) reality?
   - Can it be documented with evidence?

3. **CAUSALITY EXISTENCE** *(logical connection between cause and effect)*
   - Does an "if-then" connection really exist?
   - Does the proposed cause, in fact, result in the stated effect?
   - Does it make sense when read aloud exactly as written?
   - Is the cause intangible? (If so, look for a confirming additional predicted effect)

4. **CAUSE INSUFFICIENCY** *(a non-trivial dependent element missing)*
   - Can the cause, as stated, result in the effect on its own?
   - Are any significant causal factors missing?
   - Is/are the written cause(s) sufficient to justify all parts of the effect(s)?
   - Is an ellipse required?
   - Are any causes that are not really dependent included?

5. **ADDITIONAL CAUSE** *(a separate, independent cause producing the same effect)*
   - Is there anything else that might cause the same effect on its own?
   - If the stated cause is eliminated, will the effect be (almost completely) eliminated?

6. **CAUSE-EFFECT REVERSAL** *(effect misstated as the cause; arrow pointing in the wrong direction.)*
   - Is the stated effect really the cause, and the stated cause really the effect?
   - Is the stated cause really a reason why, or just how we know the effect exists?

7. **PREDICTED EFFECT EXISTENCE** *(additional corroborating effect resulting from the cause)*
   - Is the cause intangible?
   - Do other unavoidable outcomes of the proposed cause exist besides the stated effect?

8. **TAUTOLOGY** *(circular logic)*
   - Is the cause intangible?
   - Is the effect offered as the rationale for the existence of the cause? (for example, "What else could it be?")
   - Are other unavoidable outcomes identifiable besides the proposed effect?

Figure 2.36 Categories of legitimate reservation: self-scrutiny checklist.

ENDNOTES

1. Covey, Stephen R. *The Seven Habits of Highly Effective People: Powerful Lessons in Personal Change.* NY: Simon and Schuster, 1989.

3

Intermediate Objectives Map

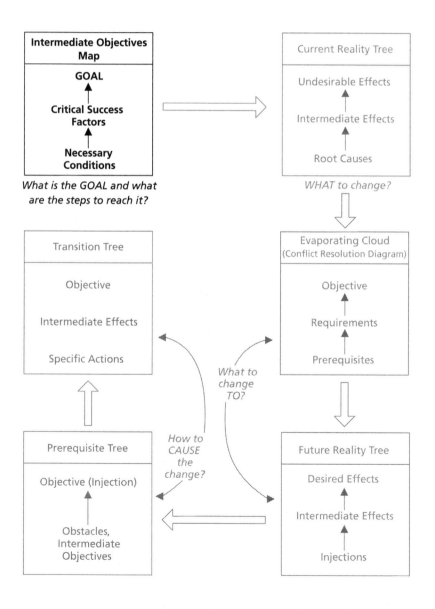

> *It is more important to know where you are going than to get there quickly. Do not mistake activity for achievement.*
>
> —Mabel Newcomber

INTRODUCTION

The most insidious contributor to the failure of continuous improvement effort is what might be called the "Nero syndrome"—fiddling while Rome burns, or rearranging deck chairs on the Titanic. In other words, focusing on the inconsequential instead of the critical. In Theory of Constraints terms, this is known as working on a non-constraint.

As we saw in Chapter 1, by trying to improve everything everywhere, we risk not improving anything that really counts. Why? Because if only a few key leverage points in any system influence overall system performance at any given time, trying to improve most of the system will be counterproductive. It will consume more resources than the value of the improvement it produces. Only resources applied to the real leverage points will pay for themselves. This is the "anchor" holding back continuous improvement programs such as Six Sigma.

DEFINITION

An Intermediate Objectives (IO) Map is a graphical representation of a system's goal, critical success factors (CSFs), and the necessary conditions (NC) for achieving them. These elements are arrayed in a logically connected hierarchy, with the goal at the top, the CSFs immediately below it, and the supporting NCs below them. Each of the entities in the IO Map exists in a necessity-based relationship (see Chapter 2) with the entities below it. The CSFs could be considered major milestones, or terminal outcomes, on the journey to the goal. NCs represent the conclusion of significant activities required to complete the CSFs.

PURPOSE

The IO Map is intended to fix in time and space a firm baseline or standard for what should be happening if a system is to succeed. Its collective depiction of goal, CSFs, and NCs constitute the system's benchmark of desired performance—the destination toward which all system improvement efforts should be directed. In other words, before you can decide *how well* you're doing, you must have a clear understanding of *what* you *should be doing*. A well-constructed IO Map presents a rational, unemotional representation of the non-negotiable requirements a system must satisfy in its quest to achieve its stated goal. These are not things you'd *like* to do, but rather things you *must* do if the goal is to be achieved. Without such a frame of reference, the determination of what should be changed within the system is merely a matter of opinion and speculation.

ASSUMPTIONS

- All systems have a goal and critical success factors that must be satisfied if the goal is to be achieved.

- The goal and CSFs exist in an interdependent, hierarchical structure.

- The goal will be unique to each system.

- Critical success factors and their interrelationships will be unique to each system and the environment in which the system functions or competes.

- CSFs and NCs are related to each other in a necessity-based configuration that reflects the rule set governing the system's competitive/functional environment.

- The Goal, CSFs, and NCs can be determined by people within or outside of a system.

- A robust IO Map will present an accurate picture of a system's goal, CSFs, and their supporting NCs.

HOW TO USE THIS CHAPTER

- Read "System Boundaries, Span of Control, and Sphere of Influence," "Doing the Right Things Versus Doing Things Right," and "Description of the Intermediate Objectives Map"

- Read "How to Construct an Intermediate Objectives Map"

- Review Figures 3.14, "How to Construct an Intermediate Objectives Map," and 3.15, "Example of a Real-World Intermediate Objectives Map"

- Review Appendix A

- Practice creating your own Intermediate Objectives Map

SYSTEM BOUNDARIES, SPAN OF CONTROL, AND SPHERE OF INFLUENCE

We've been talking about systems since Chapter 1. By now it should be clear that the Logical Thinking Process is a system-level problem-solving tool. But one person's system can be another person's process, and vice-versa. For example, a production manager might see his operation as a system, but the chief executive officer of the same company might see it as a process that's only a part—albeit an interdependent part—of the larger company system. The company itself is part of a larger system that might be called the national industrial base, which, in turn, is part of a still larger system called the nation's society. You can see that this concept can be extended to many successively higher (or lower) levels.

We'll discuss this hierarchical nature of systems in more detail shortly, but for now this concept is important because it helps us keep from losing control of our problem-solving process. We must be able to define precisely what system (and level) we're addressing. In other words, we need to be able to define a *boundary* for the system we're trying to improve, or we risk "wandering in the wilderness for forty years."

In some cases, this can be as easy as drawing a dotted line around specific boxes on an organization chart. When the system is less structured than that, it may be necessary to create a mental picture of it. Defining a system boundary makes it easier to determine which elements of our problem lie within the system and which reside in the external environment.

Being able to differentiate internal elements from external makes it easier to identify which ones may lie within our span of control, which might be within our sphere of influence, and which ones are beyond our influence altogether. Issues that are within our span of control are relatively easy to resolve. Those within our sphere of influence will likely be more difficult to address. And we might have no impact at all on those beyond our influence altogether.

Span of Control

Simply put, our span of control includes all of those things in our system over which we have unilateral change authority. In other words, we can decide to change those things on our own. Span of control varies for each individual, but it has one common characteristic for everybody: it's extremely limited. It doesn't matter if you're the President of the United States or a company employee—most of what you must deal with on a daily basis is beyond your unilateral control.

Sphere of Influence

Sphere of influence is an arbitrary perimeter enclosing those aspects of our lives that we can influence to some degree, even if we can't exercise unilateral control over them. The sphere of influence obviously is substantially larger than the span of control.*

The External Environment

The external environment is composed of some elements over which we have a degree of influence, and many more elements over which we have no influence at all. Knowing which external elements we can influence gives us clues about how difficult influencing them will be and what must be done to improve our situation. Knowing which elements we can't influence immediately identifies obstacles we'll have to work around.

Control vs. Influence

The distinction between span of control and sphere of influence is important, because the latter is not fixed or absolute. In the systems in which we operate, we can influence far more than we can control, and we can influence far more than most of us realize that we can. As we'll see, the Logical Thinking Process provides a way to extend our spheres of influence to include things we never thought possible. So, before we begin problem solving, it's a good idea to have a sense of "our place in the universe"—where our boundaries lie, what we can control, what we can influence and what we can't. Figure 3.1 illustrates the concept of system boundary, span of control, and sphere of influence.

DOING THE *RIGHT THINGS* vs. DOING THINGS *RIGHT*

How can we be sure of applying efforts where they'll do the most good? Goldratt would say, "Use the Five Focusing Steps" (see Chapter 1) to find and manage the system's leverage points. Fine, but specifically how is that done? Obviously, no two organizations are exactly alike, even within the same industry. By their very natures, different systems will be constrained in different ways. Warren Bennis and Burt Nanus have equated management with *efficiency*—doing things *right*—and leadership with *effectiveness*—doing the *right things*.[1:21] If you subscribe to this characterization, then defining what needs changing is an expression of effectiveness. So, how can leader find those right things to do—the few critical things that need changing?

The Goal

Determining what needs changing requires that we first know what we're trying to achieve—where we want to be when all is said and done. Or, as Stephen Covey suggests, "Begin with the end in mind."[2:95] There's a simple reason for doing this. The desire to

---

* In fact, for some people sphere of influence is all they have. They may not even have unilateral decision authority over something as basic as the television remote control!

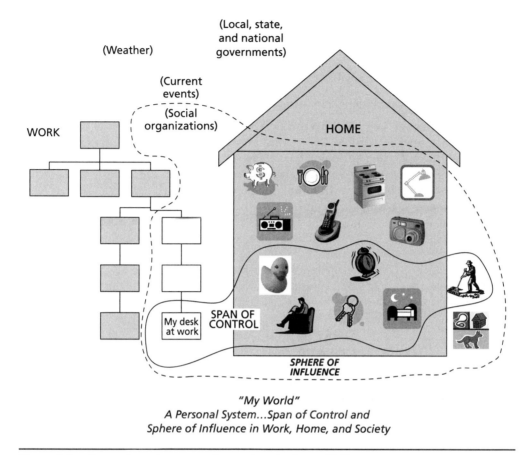

(Weather)

(Local, state, and national governments)

(Current events)

(Social organizations)

WORK

HOME

My desk at work

SPAN OF CONTROL

SPHERE OF INFLUENCE

"My World"
A Personal System...Span of Control and
Sphere of Influence in Work, Home, and Society

Figure 3.1   System boundary, span of control, and sphere of influence.

change something stems from dissatisfaction with the current situation. Dissatisfaction, in turn, grows from the perception of a gap between what *is* and what *should be*. Before we can legitimately criticize what is, it's essential for us to have a clear impression of what *should be*—in other words, our system's goal.

An unequivocal goal statement is the basic starting point. By definition, a goal is an end to which a system's collective efforts are directed.[6] To that extent, it might be considered a destination of sorts. A destination naturally implies a journey across the aforementioned gap between where we are and where we want to be. In order to determine the size of the gap and the direction of the correction needed, agreement on the system's goal is essential.

Who Sets the Goal?

Often there are diverse opinions about what the goal is or should be, or what it can or can't be. Everybody is entitled to an opinion, but when it comes to deciding what the goal is, only one opinion counts: *that of the system's owner.*

For a privately held company, the owner is sometimes a single individual. This is especially common in family-owned companies. Some private and all public companies are collectively owned, with ownership represented by a board of directors. Not-for-profit organizations may not have an owner, *per se*, but they're usually governed by a board of trustees. Government agencies are ultimately "owned" by the citizens whose taxes fund them.* Regardless of whether ownership is solitary or collective, the system's owners are the only ones with the authority to determine what the goal will be. If someone other than the owner establishes the goal, it's incumbent upon that person to define a goal with which the owner (or board) would agree.

Critical Success Factors and Necessary Conditions

In striving for a goal, inevitably we find certain high-level requirements or necessary conditions that must be satisfied. These conditions qualify as "show-stoppers"—if *all* are not satisfied, the goal can't be attained.

There are normally no more than about three to five of these *critical success factors* (CSFs), and they are high level from the perspective of the whole system. In fact, they might be considered terminal outcomes in attaining the goal.

Each CSF usually has some number of *necessary conditions* (NC) that are prerequisites to its accomplishment. The only real difference between a CSF and a NC is their degree of specificity.

Picture NCs and CSFs arranged in a vertical hierarchy (see Figure 3.2). Before the CSFs can be achieved, the subordinate necessary conditions must be satisfied. But these necessary conditions may themselves have supporting necessary conditions (see Figure 3.3).

DESCRIPTION OF THE
INTERMEDIATE OBJECTIVES (IO) MAP

The relationship among the ultimate system goal, the critical success factors, and their supporting necessary condition hierarchy can be represented in a single logic tree called an Intermediate Objectives (IO) Map (see Figure 3.4). The IO Map is a cascading structure of requirements, from general at the upper level to more specific at the lower level. In its entirety, it represents what ought to be happening—the system's destination, mentioned earlier. Notice, too, that the CSFs in Figure 3.4 are terminal outcomes and that the subordinate NCs are more narrowly focused, detailed efforts.

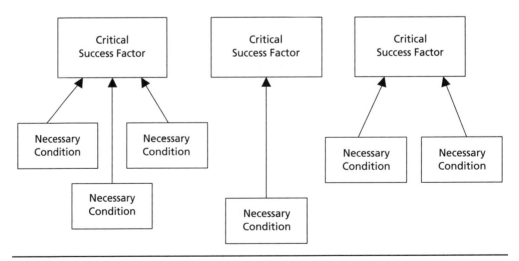

Figure 3.2   Necessary conditions: prerequisites to critical success factors.

---

* I know, I know...when it comes to government agencies, they often seem more like civil masters than civil servants, but it's not supposed to be that way!

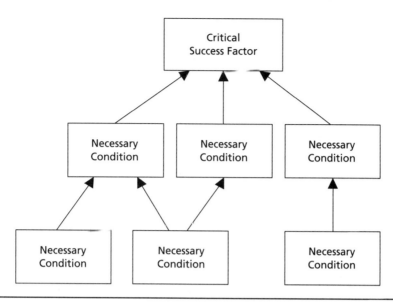

Figure 3.3   Necessary conditions: a vertical hierarchy.

Strategic Application

As Covey says, beginning with the end in mind is essential in any problem-solving process. Whether you're solving problems at a process level or at some higher system level, a standard of desired performance must be commonly accepted, or you risk fragmented, uncoordinated, ineffective efforts.

This danger is even more pronounced at the highest system levels—the strategic. The broader and more sweeping system changes are, the greater the risk of failure and the higher the price tag in wasted resources. Consequently, the need to define a goal, critical success factors, and necessary conditions is even more compelling at the strategic or highest organizational level.

The concept of a Strategic Intermediate Objectives Map is addressed in more detail in *Strategic Navigation: A Systems Approach to Business Strategy.*[4]

A Hierarchy of Systems

There's a little poem that illustrates the nature of complex systems:

> *Big fleas have little fleas upon their backs to bite 'em.*
> *Little fleas have lesser fleas, and so on, ad infinitum.*[5]

What this couplet says about systems is that they are essentially "nested" in hierarchies. The tool and die department of a company is itself a small-scale system. But it's also a key component of a somewhat larger system called the production process. The production process, in turn, is part of a larger system called operations, which includes engineering. The operations system is part of yet a larger system: the business division. The business division is part of an even larger system called the corporation.

Each of these system levels could be said to have a goal, critical success factors, and necessary conditions of its own—in other words, its own Intermediate Objectives Map. At the top of each IO Map is a goal. But because of the "nested" nature of these systems (and their respective IO Maps), each lower level's goal constitutes a necessary condition—or perhaps a critical success factor—of the next higher level. This concept continues in a

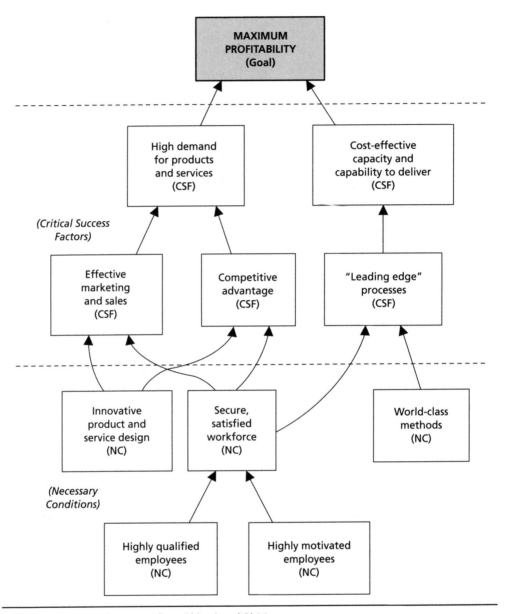

Figure 3.4 Strategic Intermediate Objectives (IO) Map.

repeating fashion until the consensus boundary of the largest system is reached: the corporation; the municipal, state, or national government; or some other generally accepted delineation between what's considered "internal" and "external." Figure 3.5 illustrates this hierarchical concept of systems and IO Maps.

IO Maps Are Unique

An Intermediate Objectives Map for a particular system will be unique to that system and the environment in which it operates. This should not be surprising, since it represents the set of interdependent conditions that any given system must satisfy in order to achieve its goal. That set will differ for Boeing, Microsoft, Archer Daniels Midland, the Los Angeles

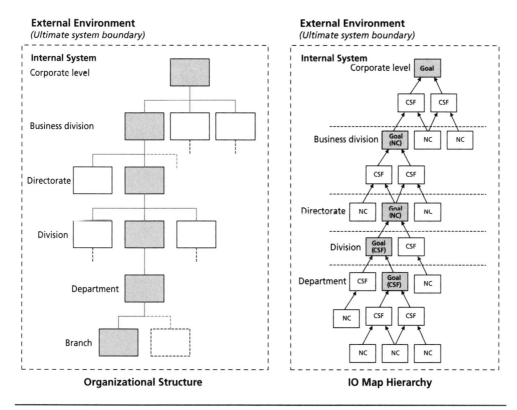

Figure 3.5   The "nested" hierarchy.

Unified School District, the United Way, the U.S. Department of the Interior, Swain's General Store, the Yankee Candle Company...you get the idea.

None of these systems will have the same IO Map as any other. Though there may be common elements among them, each system's IO Map will reflect the unique, interconnected elements necessary for that system to succeed—to achieve its goal—in its chosen mission and the environment in which it operates. Whether the system in question is a government, a multinational corporation, an army, a family, an individual, or even a plant in a garden, there will be a specific, unique IO Map that identifies the hierarchy of requirements the system must meet in order to realize its goal. Two identical systems operating in the same environment might be the only possible exceptions.

Characteristics of the IO Map

Though unique in their content, all IO Maps have some common basic characteristics:

- They terminate in the system goal at the top.

- A limited number of critical success factors—usually no more than three to five— are the immediately preceding prerequisites to achieving the goal. Normally, these are high-level outcomes of supporting (subordinate) requirements or necessary conditions.

- A limited number of necessary conditions—milestones—must be attained, sometimes in combination, in order to satisfy each critical success factor.

- Each successive descending layer of necessary conditions is somewhat more specific or detailed than the layer above it. There should not be more than about two layers of necessary conditions below the level of critical success factors.

- As a whole, the IO Map represents the destination and key intermediate milestones the system is striving for.

CSFs and NCs are not a matter of choice or wishful thinking; their existence and necessity is a matter of logic that is governed by the choice of the system mission, the environment in which it functions, and its stated goal.

Examples of Strategic Intermediate Objectives Maps

Nothing conveys a message as effectively as a good example. Here are two examples of Intermediate Objectives Maps. One is the IO Map of a commercial company. The second represents a not-for-profit foundation.

Process-Level IO Map

Figure 3.6 shows a notional IO Map for a production process. Keep in mind that because the focus of this IO Map is process rather than a higher level system, the goal and the CSFs are more limited in scope than one would expect for the company-level map of the same organization. Notice, too, that the goal is likely to be a necessary condition or critical success factor of that higher level company IO Map.

System-Level IO Map

Figure 3.7 shows a real IO Map for a not-for-profit educational foundation.* Notice that the goal is that of the whole organization, not just a process or part. The CSFs are decidedly functionally oriented, and the NCs address specific activities.

HOW TO CONSTRUCT AN INTERMEDIATE OBJECTIVES (IO) MAP

An Intermediate Objectives Map can easily be constructed by one person, often in as little as 15 minutes or less. But if the system it represents is larger than the span of control of the person constructing the IO Map, external scrutiny of the finished IO Map and its components is more than just advisable—it's necessary in order to prevent starting down the wrong path. Here's the procedure for constructing an IO Map.

1. Define the System

The first step is to determine the boundary of the system under consideration, your span of control, and your sphere of influence in it. Can you define the system as an organizational entity with clearly established functional limits?

Keep in mind that while geography can play a part, the important factors in any system are functional, regardless of where they're located. A grocery store chain, for example, has clearly definable organizational boundaries, even though it may have a headquarters, many distribution warehouses, and hundreds of retail stores spread out over a wide geographic area.

---

* The Sam Spady Foundation is dedicated to educating young people, parents, and teachers on the dangers of binge drinking and alcohol poisoning. For more information, visit: www.samspadyfoundation.org

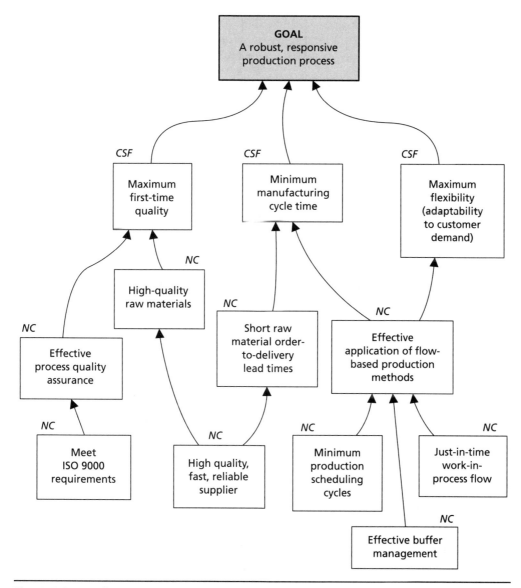

Figure 3.6   Production process IO Map.

An easy way to determine the boundaries of an organizational system is to ask, "Who's this system analysis for? Who's the ultimate decision maker in this system or subsystem?" The answers to these questions tell you what the boundaries of the organizational unit will be.

Taking this first important step helps us determine what's within the system—directly within our span of control or sphere of influence. In other words, the components or factors we may be able to work on directly. Determining our span of control and sphere of influence tells us the degree to which we'll need the assistance of others to effect changes that we ourselves don't have the authority to make alone. In other words, who else's "horsepower" must we bring to bear on the situation? Knowing the answer to this question gives us a preliminary sense for the scope of the persuasion task ahead of us.

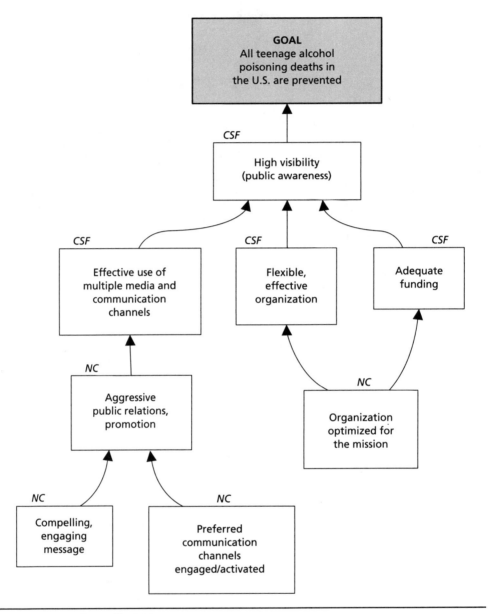

Figure 3.7   Not-for-profit IO Map.

2. Determine the System Goal

Once we know the boundaries of the system we're working with, the next step is to articulate its goal. If we personally aren't the ultimate decision makers for the system, we'd be well advised to find that person and ask what the goal is. Alternatively, we could formulate our best guess about the goal of the system and present it as a "straw man" for the decision maker to accept or modify. However we decide to do it, we should try to put ourselves in the shoes of the real owners of the system and come up with a goal statement they would agree with.

Remember that the underlying purpose of the IO Map is to identify a destination that we're trying to reach—a benchmark against which we can assess what's actually happening within the system. This means that the goal statement should reflect *outcomes*, not continuing activities. For example, in the fifth of his famous 14 points, W. Edwards Deming said:

> *"Improve constantly and forever the system of production and service, to improve quality and productivity, and thus constantly decrease costs."*[3:23]

Certainly admirable, and a means to a goal (an activity), but not a goal in itself. Whenever we find ourselves tempted to list an activity as the goal, we should ask ourselves, "Why are we doing this? What's the higher purpose toward which this activity is directed? What would the owner(s) expect to result from this?" Figure 3.8 shows generic examples of typical goal statements for a commercial for-profit company and a not-for-profit charitable foundation.

Notice that in both cases, the goal is stated as a condition—an outcome of activity—not as an action or activity itself.

> **NOTE:** The goal statement is obviously not a complete sentence. This would seem to be a violation of the Entity Existence reservation (see Chapter 2). However, keep in mind that the Categories of Legitimate Reservation (CLR) were designed to verify sufficiency statements (if-then). The logic trees that use sufficiency statements are Current Reality, Future Reality, and Transition. The IO Map, the Evaporating Cloud, and the Prerequisite Tree are necessary condition trees—they indicate minimum essential requirements, not all elements sufficient to produce the result. These trees may be expressed as short phrases rather than as complete sentences.

3. Determine the Critical Success Factors

Once the goal is agreed upon, we must unearth the major critical success factors (CSFs) without which the goal can't be achieved. Normally, there aren't more than three to five of these, and there may be fewer. The common characteristic of CSFs is that they're high-level terminal events or milestones. Their satisfaction is usually the culmination of more specific, detailed efforts, usually in different functional areas. We might call these major functional outcomes.

Remember that this is a complex system we're talking about, so each of the major system components is likely to be represented in the critical success factors in some way. Also keep in mind that critical success factors, by definition, are high-level "show-stoppers." If they don't happen, we don't reach our goal. Figure 3.9 shows typical CSFs for the goals indicated in Figure 3.8.

GOAL
Increasing profitability, now and in the future.

(Typical goal for a commercial for-profit company)

GOAL
Cost-effective improvement of the overall health of the community.

(Typical goal for a not-for-profit medical center)

Figure 3.8 Goal statements (examples).

NOTE: At this stage, the important thing is to brainstorm all the critical success factors and, eventually, the necessary conditions that precede them. But it's not necessary to start doing so in a tree format, although you could if you chose to. It would be sufficient to list the CSFs on a piece of paper. Then, beside each one, list the necessary conditions that must be satisfied to achieve the CSFs. This list can be converted into the entities of an IO Map later.

4. Determine Key Necessary Conditions

The critical success factors can't stand alone. They're high-level outcomes, only slightly less abstract than the goal itself. Their distinguishing characteristic is that they are related to the functional activity of some component of the system. For the commercial company illustrated in Figure 3.9, these functions are revenue generation, cost control, and inventory control. In the case of the medical center, they're the cost-effective prevention of illness or injury and the remediation of such illness or injury as does occur. Notice that in both cases, the CSFs are functional subsets of the goal they're supporting, but they're not "actionable" in and of themselves. In other words, the discrete activities needed to make the CSFs happen lie below the level of the CSFs themselves.

These activities are *necessary conditions* for the satisfaction of the CSFs. We might call them "building blocks." The CSFs rest on the foundation of these necessary conditions (NCs). The NCs may be quantifiable, measurable outcomes of specific activities, or they may be qualitative outcomes—"yes" or "no" conditions. Their common characteristics are that they are functionally related to the CSFs they support and that they are more specific in their content.

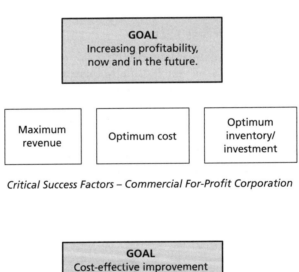

GOAL
Increasing profitability, now and in the future.

| Maximum revenue | Optimum cost | Optimum inventory/ investment |

Critical Success Factors – Commercial For-Profit Corporation

GOAL
Cost-effective improvement of the overall health of the community.

| Prevent illness/ injury affordably | Cure illness/injury affordably in minimum time |

Critical Success Factors, Not-for-Profit Medical Center

Figure 3.9   Critical success factors (examples).

As we saw earlier, NCs are hierarchical, too, just like the goal and the CSFs. Theoretically, we could build such a vertical hierarchy from the goal of an organization all the way down to the day-to-day functions of the lowest-level employee. But for the purposes of establishing an overall destination, that would be far too much detail to include in an IO Map. Let's not lose sight of the purpose of the IO Map: *to define a clearly identifiable benchmark for success of the overall system.*

Of necessity, then, we can't allow this IO Map to become too detailed. It's not likely that any CSFs will need more than three to five NCs. Because these NCs themselves are hierarchical, there could be more than one layer of them below the CSFs, but as an arbitrary rule of thumb, we'll try to limit the NC to no more than *two layers,* if possible. Figure 3.10 shows the NCs for the two sets of goals and CSFs from Figures 3.8 and 3.9.

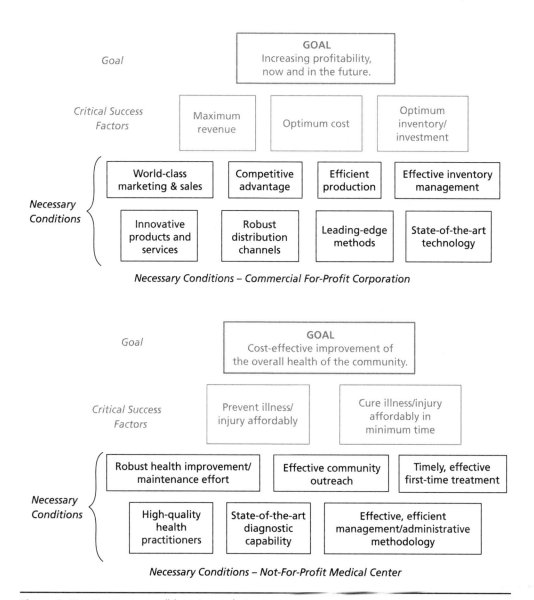

Figure 3.10   Necessary conditions (examples).

5. Arrange the IO Map Components

Now it's time to start constructing the IO Map itself. If you captured your CSFs and NCs as a list on a single sheet of paper (see Figure 3.11), it's time to convert them to entities for the IO Map. If you created your list of CSFs and NCs on Post-it Notes, you can begin arranging them immediately.

Transcribe the goal, CSFs, and NCs onto Post-it Notes or enter them into a computer application that can generate logic tree entities. Then, either on Post-it Notes or in the computer, arrange the logic tree entities in a rough pyramid, with the goal at the top, the CSFs in the middle, and the supporting NCs near the bottom. Figure 3.12 shows the entities listed in Figure 3.11 converted to both forms.

6. Connect the Goal, Critical Success Factors, and Necessary Conditions

The tree is formed when the goal, CSFs and NC are connected in a necessity-logic relationship.

Connect each of the CSFs to the goal. If one or more CSFs actually precede and lead to another CSF, rearrange the entities and connect them with single arrows, as required.

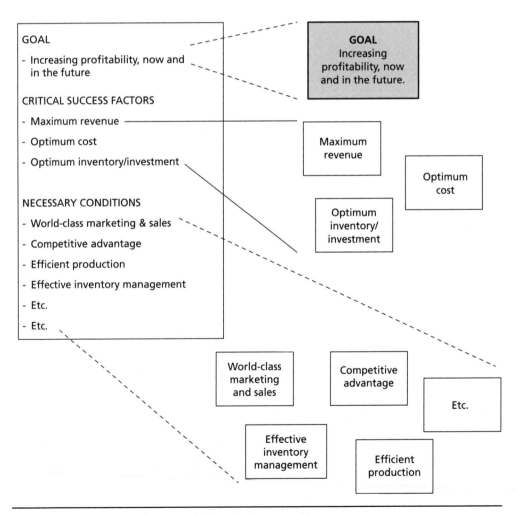

Figure 3.11   Convert goal, CSF, and NCs to logic tree entities.

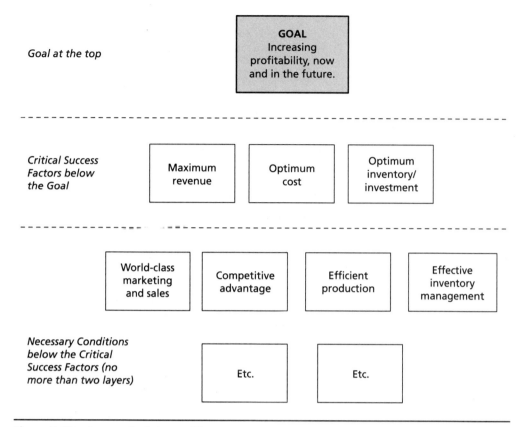

Goal at the top

GOAL
Increasing profitability, now and in the future.

Critical Success Factors below the Goal

Maximum revenue

Optimum cost

Optimum inventory/investment

World-class marketing and sales

Competitive advantage

Efficient production

Effective inventory management

Necessary Conditions below the Critical Success Factors (no more than two layers)

Etc.

Etc.

Figure 3.12 Arrange logic tree entities.

Connect the NCs to the appropriate CSFs using single arrows. You identified most of these relationships when the NCs were articulated, so connection should be just a formality. Create a second layer of NCs if the situation dictates.

> **NOTE:** Try to limit yourself to two layers of NCs or you risk making the IO Map too detailed. Remember: this is meant to be a high-level tree. The details will emerge in Future Reality Trees and Prerequisite Trees.

Almost all your connections will be oriented vertically—that is, from a lower layer to the one above it. But some connections may be lateral as well. In other words, look carefully to identify any NC that is required for more than one CSF, and add connections as required. Likewise, NCs on a second level may support more than one NC on the level above them. Figure 3.13 shows what the final IO Map should look like. Notice that in both cases a single NC supports more than one CSF.

7. Verify the Connections

Remember, this is not a sufficiency-logic tree, so not all the Categories of Legitimate Reservation apply the way they would to a Current Reality, Future Reality, or Transition Tree. Even though this is a necessity-logic tree, you can check for some of the same logical elements that you find in the CLR.

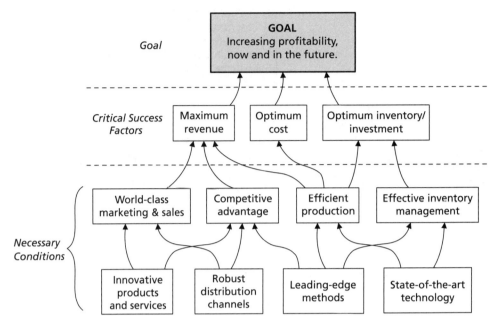

Necessary Conditions – Commercial For-Profit Corporation

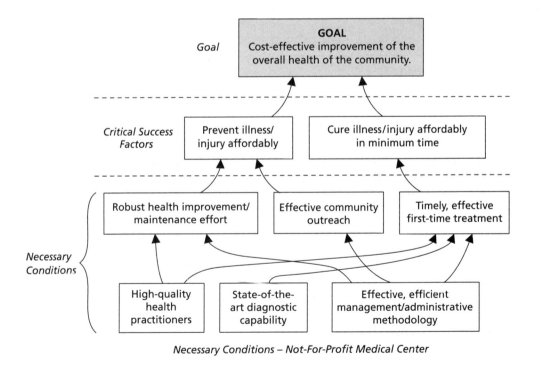

Necessary Conditions – Not-For-Profit Medical Center

Figure 3.13 Strategic-level IO Maps (examples).

- Consider the CSFs, for example. Are they really indispensable to realizing the goal? If a particular CSF were absent, could the goal still be achieved? If so, then it wasn't a legitimate CSF in the first place. If it *must* be there, you can be sure that it's a legitimate CSF. Repeat this process for each of your proposed CSFs.

- Is the proposed CSF the last thing that must happen (that is, a terminal outcome) before you can safely say the goal will be achieved? Or does it actually produce some intermediate outcome, which would likely be the *real* CSF?

- Are there only three to five CSFs? If there are fewer than three, it may be okay for the particular circumstances in question. If there are more than five—say, six or seven— that may be okay, too. But once you get beyond five, the chances increase dramatically that one or more of them may be a NC that supports one of the "real" three to four CSFs. If this is the case, drop that entity down to the NC level of your tree.

The "10,000-Foot Test"

Once you think you've identified the right number of CSFs and NCs, and you think you've got them all "wired" (that is, connected) properly, cross-check the entire tree with your intuition. How do you do this? Take the "10,000-foot view." If you've ever stood on a mountain top and looked at a valley below, you know that you don't see much detail.

What you *do* see is overall patterns and relationships among physical land features: streams, forests, hills, and so on. Cultivated fields become part of a larger farm. Individual houses blend into crossing streets in a town. Roads intersect in complex patterns you don't see (except in your mind's eye) when you're driving on them.

Try looking at the IO Map in the same way. Do the NCs that support a particular CSF all seem to be part of an integrated pattern, and does that pattern reflect your intuition about how life is, or must be? Are those integrated patterns all topically related (for example, marketing and sales, production, inventory and distribution, engineering, and so on)? And does your intuition tell you that those overall topics are truly indispensable to achieving the goal? If so, your IO Map passes the "10,000-foot test." If not, adjust it until it does.*

8. Enlist Outside Scrutiny of the Entire IO Map

The "10,000-foot test" is only *your individual* effort to verify the completeness and validity of your IO Map. A critical part of verification is outside scrutiny. This is particularly important if you're working on an organizational issue, rather than a personal problem.

Remember that you're "setting the survey stakes" for the layout of a solution to a complex problem. Different people of varying influence will have different perspectives on what the organization should be doing to reach its goal (or even different ideas about what the goal actually is, if senior leadership has not clearly articulated it).

Remember, too, our earlier discussion about span of control and sphere of influence. It's probable that you'll need to work in your sphere of influence, or convince somebody in yours to work in theirs on behalf of the problem solution. It really helps later on, during the heavy lifting of problem analysis and solution generation, if everyone whose help you need is "singing from the same sheet of music"—that is, working from the same understanding of goal, CSFs, and NCs. So, don't be in too much of a rush to charge off into a Current Reality Tree (Chapter 4) until and unless you're certain that your IO Map accurately reflects a destination and a general route that everyone is likely to subscribe to.

---

* Some refer to the "10,000-foot test" as the TLAR (pronounced TEE-lar) method, meaning "That Looks About Right."

NOTE: We're getting a little ahead of ourselves here. In Chapter 8 we'll examine the dynamics of persuasion and consensus building in more detail. For now, suffice it to say that your bigger job of system improvement becomes substantially easier if you know you're working toward the same goal and CSFs that everyone else is.

Figure 3.14 provides an illustrated, abbreviated checklist for constructing an IO Map.

1. Define the System
- Decide on the system boundary: international, national, state, corporate, division, family, personal, and so on.

2. Determine the System Goal
- What is the single outcome for which the system exists?
- What would the system's owners say it is?
- Obtain consensus on the goal if others are responsible for setting it.

3. Determine the Critical Success Factors (CSFs)
- What are the 3-5 high-level terminal conditions that must be satisfied for the goal to be achieved?
- Ensure that they are the last milestones to be achieved before the goal can be declared satisfied.

4. Determine the Key Necessary Conditions (NC)
- What key activities or tasks are required to realize the CSFs? (No more than 3-5 per CSFs.)
- Limit your NCs to no more than two layers in the final IO Map. (If you have more, trim some off.)

5. Arrange the IO Map Components
- Goal at the top
- CSFs below the goal
- NC below the CSFs

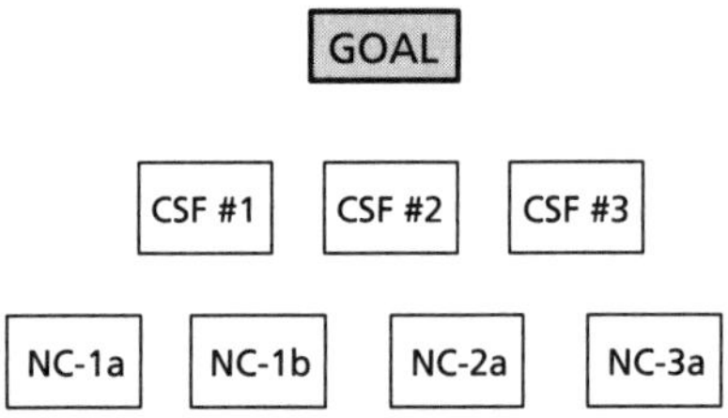

6. Connect the Goal, CSFs, and NCs
- Use single arrows (no ellipses or magnitudinal "AND" symbols).
- Connect vertically.
- Connect horizontally, as dictated by the situation.

7. Verify the Connections
- Necessity logic, not sufficiency
- Cross-check finished connections with your intuition ("10,000-foot view")

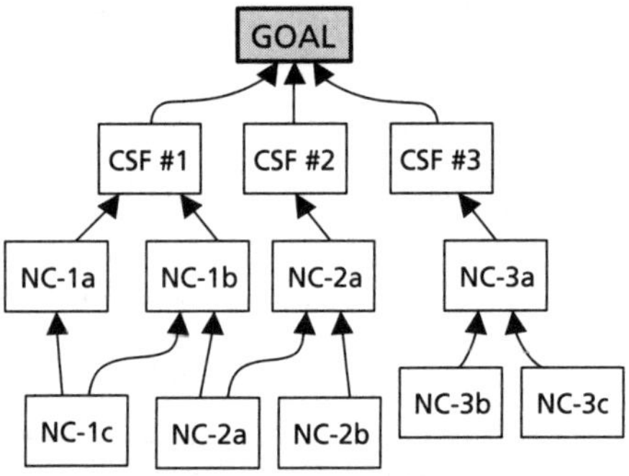

8. Enlist Outside Scrutiny of the Entire IO Map
- Identify and insert any missing CSFs.
- Identify and insert any missing NC.
- Identify and attach any missing connections.
- Rearrange entities to minimize "cross-overs."
- "Trim off" any low-level NCs that would be better addressed in execution planning (not "destination determination").
- Obtain outside scrutiny when you think its complete and as good as you can make it.

Figure 3.14 Procedures for constructing an Intermediate Objectives (IO) Map - abbreviated checklist.

SUMMARY AND CONCLUSION

In the Lerner and Lowe Broadway musical play *Paint Your Wagon,* part of a verse from the title song says:

> *Where am I going? I don't know.*
> *When will I be there? I ain't certain.*
> *All that I know is I am on my way.*

The IO Map is intended to help us avoid that particular situation in real life. It forces us to ask, and agree on the answer to, the question "What is our ultimate goal?" It further demands that we identify the major milestones or accomplishments—the Critical Success Factors—on the road to that goal. And it starts to hint at some of the key necessary conditions, or specific activities, that must be completed for those CSFs to be realized.

Any time and effort spent up front constructing an IO Map is well worth the investment. I facilitated the effort of 35 vice presidents and senior managers in the supply chain of a large U.S. supermarket network (1,800 retail stores and 125 distribution centers) to create their strategic IO Map. While getting 35 executives to agree on anything is no small feat, we completed one in about four hours even though they had no prior understanding of what the IO Map was all about. Not only was there consensus on the accuracy of the map, but one vice president later told me, "In the previous company I worked for, it took us four months to do what we did here in four hours." There's no better testimony than that to the value of taking the time to define the goal, CSFs, and NCs.

Take a look at Figure 3.15 on the next page. This is the kind of outcome you should be striving for: not too detailed, not too high-level, two or three layers of necessary conditions at most. Clearly the critical success factors are high-level terminal outcomes without which the company goal can't be reached. This example is for a commercial manufacturing company. However, the IO Map of a not-for-profit organization would be similar. (Refer to Appendix A to see the IO Map of an educational foundation.)

Now that we have a clear visual image of the destination we should be striving for, we're ready to take a comprehensive look at where we currently are, determine how big the gap is between the two, and identify the action we should take to eliminate that deviation. Our tool for this will be the Current Reality Tree.

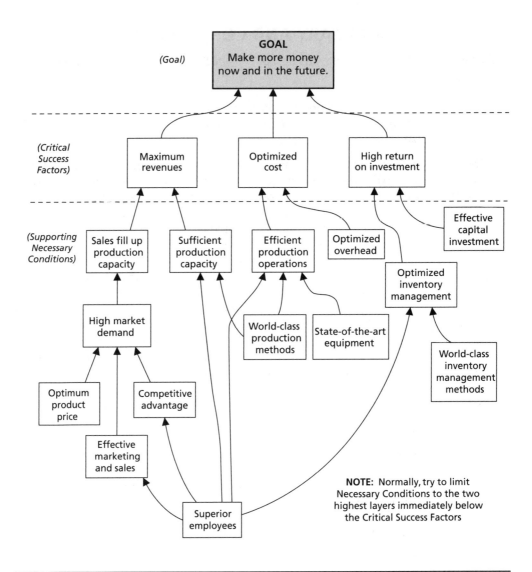

Figure 3.15   Example: a real-world IO Map.

ENDNOTES

1. Bennis, Warren, and Burt Nanus. *Leaders: Strategies for Taking Charge.* NY: Harper-Row Publishing Group, 1985.
2. Covey, Stephen R. *The Seven Habits of Highly Effective People: Powerful Lessons in Personal Change.* NY: Simon and Schuster, 1989.
3. Deming, W. Edwards. *Out of the Crisis.* Cambridge, MA: Massachusetts Institute of Technology Center for Advanced Engineering Study, 1986.
4. Dettmer, H. William. *Strategic Navigation: A Systems Approach to Business Strategy.* Milwaukee, WI: ASQ Quality Press, 2003.
5. http://www.worldofquotes.com/author/Proverb/50/index.html
6. http://dictionary.reference.com/browse/goal

Part II
Gap Analysis and Correction

4

Current Reality Tree

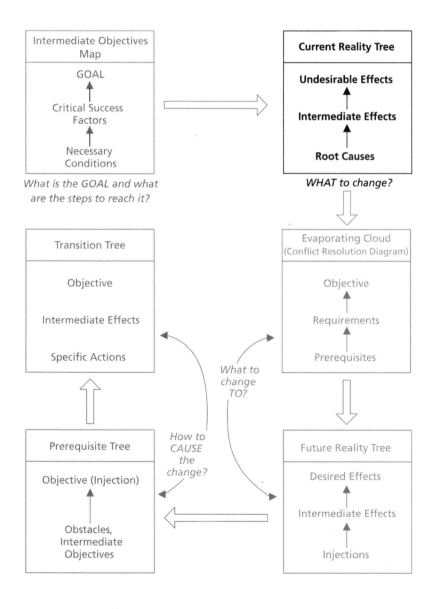

If you can keep your head when all about you are losing theirs,
then you obviously don't understand the problem.

—Evans' Law

"I t's not that simple." How many times have we heard someone say that, usually after a simple solution to a complex problem has been suggested? Does this mean that complex problems can only be solved using complex solutions? No, but it does imply that the complexities of the situation were not fully visible or taken into consideration before a solution was proposed.

Corporate downsizing is a typical example. The indications that a problem exists are usually obvious: Profits are down, sales are sluggish, cash flow may be down to a trickle, and finished (unsold) inventory is high. What's senior management's most common response? Cut costs—lay people off! It's a solution, isn't it? Certainly, but it's not that simple. The causes of the obvious symptoms of this problem are not as clear cut as the downsizing solution would have us believe.

What happens if the problem we've identified—excessive costs—is the wrong one? Inevitably, we would expend time, energy, and resources solving the wrong problem, which means that the original problem would still be with us. And that means the overall situation will probably not improve. Or if it does, the improvement is likely to be minimal and only temporary.

How can we avoid this pitfall—solving the wrong problem—which not only wastes resources but may actually create new problems where none previously existed? Clearly, the first and most important step is to be certain we've identified the real problem correctly. But there's a funny thing about "real" problems in complex situations. They're not usually visible to the naked eye. So, what can we do about that?

One option is to construct a Current Reality Tree—a logic tree Goldratt designed specifically to find hidden system-level problems in complex situations. In this chapter, we'll see what a Current Reality Tree is, what it tells us, and why we can be confident that it has pointed us at the right problem, even though that problem may be hidden beneath many layers of cause and effect.

DEFINITION

A Current Reality Tree (CRT) is a logical structure designed to depict the state of reality as it currently exists in a given system. It reflects the most probable chain of cause and effect, given a specific, fixed set of circumstances. The CRT seeks cause-and-effect connections between visible indications of a system's condition and the originating causes that produce them (see Figure 4.1). It's *functional* rather than *organizational*, blind to arbitrary internal and external system boundaries. Consequently, it can produce a faithful representation of cause and effect.

Please note, however, that a Current Reality Tree is *not* a complete picture of reality. It reflects only the part perceived to be unfavorable. Though it may accurately depict the causal interconnections of the actual situation, it will only show those elements that directly and unavoidably produce undesirable outcomes. So, in circumstances where a system is functioning properly 80 percent of the time, the Current Reality Tree will show only the 20 percent of the situation when it doesn't. In this respect, it could be considered a kind of system-level failure mode effects analysis (FMEA).

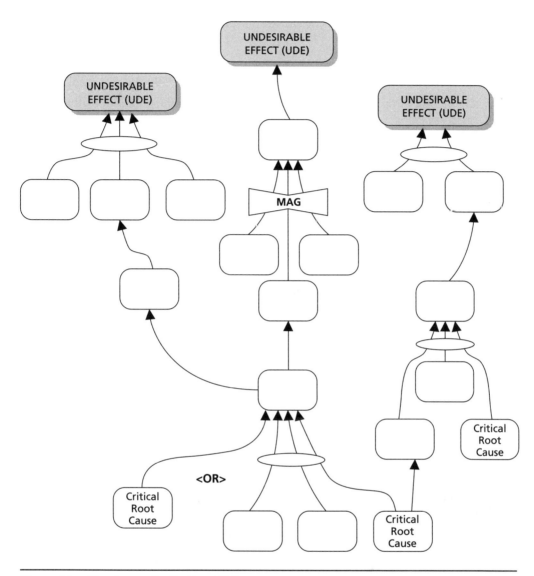

Figure 4.1 The Current Reality Tree (CRT).

PURPOSE

The Current Reality Tree is designed to achieve the following objectives:

- Provide the basis for understanding complex systems.

- Articulate undesirable effects (UDEs) exhibited by a system. Such effects are undesirable when compared with the system's goal, critical success factors, or necessary conditions (see Chapter 3).

- Relate UDEs through a logical chain of cause and effect to root causes (RC).

- Identify the critical root causes that produce a majority of the system's UDEs, including the worst ones.

- Determine which of the root causes lie beyond one's *span of control* or *sphere of influence.*

- Isolate those few causal factors—system constraints—that must be addressed in order to realize the maximum improvement of the system.

- Identify the simplest potential changes that will have the greatest positive impact on the system.

ASSUMPTIONS

The effectiveness of the Current Reality Tree is based on the following assumptions:

- *Cause and effect* is not the same as *correlation.*

- Interdependencies affect system components. A change in one component will produce collateral changes in one or more other components.

- All processes within a system, and the overall system itself, are subject to variation.

- The operation of a system produces both *intended* (desirable) and *unintended* (desirable or undesirable) effects.

- Undesirable effects are undesirable only with respect to the previously defined goal, critical success factors, or necessary conditions of the system.

- Undesirable effects in a system do not exist in isolation from one another.

- All effects within a system (desirable or undesirable) are the products of root causes that may be several steps removed from these effects.

- Cause and effect is governed by the Categories of Legitimate Reservation (CLR) and is verifiable through the CLR.

- Unstated assumptions about reality underlie all cause-and-effect relationships.

- Events related by verifiable cause and effect will be replicable. Another iteration of the chain should give the same effects if no changes to circumstances or to the system are made.

HOW TO USE THIS CHAPTER

- Read "Description of the Current Reality Tree," the next section. This describes what a Current Reality Tree is and how it works.

- Read "How to Construct a Current Reality Tree" and the associated examples. This section explains in detail each of the steps in building a Current Reality Tree and why they're necessary.

- Read "Scrutinizing the Current Reality Tree." This section tells how to ensure that your Current Reality Tree is logically sound and accurately depicts "the way things are."

- Review Figure 4.46, "Current Reality Tree: Fordyce Corporation." This is a complete Current Reality Tree that illustrates the challenges faced by a start-up medical technology company. It is a typical real-world example of just how complex reality can be and how effective the Current Reality Tree is at analyzing complex cause and effect.

- Review Figure 4.45, "Procedures for Building a CRT." This is an abbreviated checklist that you can use to guide you in constructing your own Current Reality Tree. The checklist contains instructions and illustrations for each step. Detailed explanations for each step in the checklists are provided in the chapter itself, under "How to Construct a Current Reality Tree."

- Practice with a "Current Reality Tree Exercise," provided in Appendix C.

DESCRIPTION OF THE CURRENT REALITY TREE

The objective of the Current Reality Tree is to help you isolate what needs changing in any situation. It does this by helping you identify the things that are clearly indicators of system deficiencies and by tracing them back to one or more basic causes. As previously discussed, these visible indicators are called undesirable effects; the factors that originate them are known as root causes.

Why do you need a CRT to identify the undesirable effects and root causes? In some cases you may not *need* one. Some situations are so simple and obvious that the root cause stands out like a sore thumb. But the world is complex, and many (if not most) situations encompass several factors or forces that interact to produce the effects we see around us. In such cases, a complete visual depiction of the situation makes it considerably easier to visualize the interdependencies in the system.

Plant growth, for instance, is normally thought to be the result of three *necessary conditions:* water, nutrition, and light (see Figure 4.2). If a plant fails to grow properly, you must immediately consider deficiencies in one of those three areas. But the failure of a plant to grow may also be the result of factors beyond those three conditions, because while they may be necessary, they may not be sufficient—a favorable temperature range

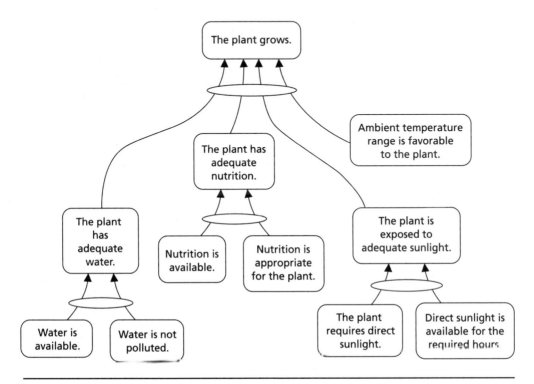

Figure 4.2   CRT: plant growth (example).

is needed, too. Diagnosing the problem may not be as simple as it looks, as most gardeners can tell you.

Because most situations are complex, often with inconspicuous causes driving the results, it can be difficult to decide what to change in order to make the situation right. Combined with effective application of the Categories of Legitimate Reservation, a CRT can help reveal complex relationships.

For example, if your house is consistently too hot or cold, a knee-jerk reaction might be to adjust the thermostat in the central heating/air conditioning unit. Seems simple enough. But if the outside temperature fluctuates significantly during the course of a day, you could find yourself making a lot of adjustments. This might make the inside temperature acceptable, but it might also result in higher utility bills. The simple CRT in Figure 4.3 shows how much more complex the situation could be than it actually seems. It also shows some root causes that, if you only adjust the thermostat, remain unaddressed and will allow the problem to continue or surface again at another time.

A Single Tool or Part of a Set

The CRT can be used by itself to identify root causes of straightforward problems in your daily life. Or it can be used as the first step in the entire Logical Thinking Process, to effect major changes in complex systems. In either case, the process is the same. The final section in this chapter discusses the use of the CRT with other Logical Thinking Process tools.

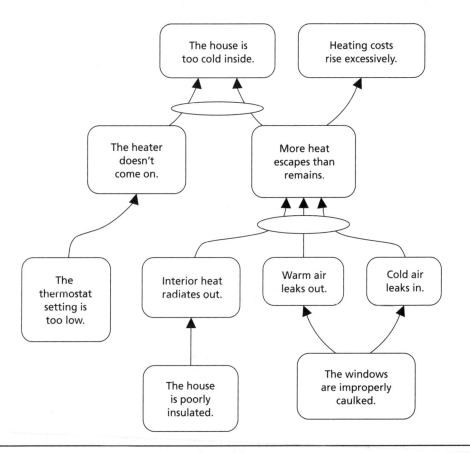

Figure 4.3   CRT: temperature in a house (example).

Span of Control and Sphere of Influence

Before we can effectively explain the CRT, it's necessary to establish the context in which the CRT will be used. In Chapter 3 we discussed the importance of identifying your *span of control* and *sphere of influence*. Now we'll see how this concept applies directly to the use of CRT for deciding which root causes we can reasonably expect to change.

As we saw in the last chapter, we all function in complex systems and have varying degrees of control over our environment. In some areas we have a high degree of control. These areas are said to lie within our *span of control*. We enjoy virtually complete authority to change anything within our span of control. Just outside our span of control lies our sphere of influence, a region of the environment where we can influence things to varying degrees but where we don't enjoy direct control. Beyond our sphere of influence we have neither control nor influence (review Figure 3.1).

Once we understand this concept of reality, a few things about CRT become apparent. In a complex situation, a CRT that accurately depicts reality might conceivably overlap all three regions: our span of control, our sphere of influence, and the outside, or uncontrolled, environment (see Figure 4.4).

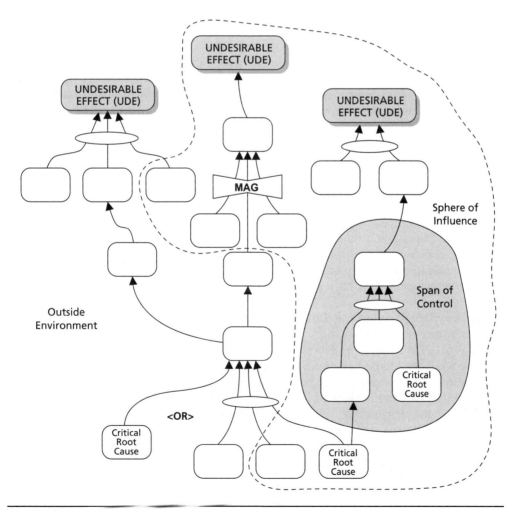

Figure 4.4   Span of control, sphere of influence, and the CRT.

The most significant ramification of this situation is the effect it has on our decisions about what we can change in a system. If the most significant root causes lie outside our span of control, we must depend on others for help. This means persuading others to do things they might not be obligated to do. If the root causes lie outside our sphere of influence, we may not be able to do anything about them at all. If this is the case, we must become truly creative in finding ways to work around root causes over which we have no control.

Keep the concepts of span of control and sphere of influence in mind while you're building your Current Reality Tree, but don't let them limit you in its construction. Follow the cause-and-effect chain wherever it may lead. But after the tree is done, and before you select which root causes to attack, revisit the issue of sphere of influence. Use it to help you decide for which problems you can reasonably expect effective results and for which attack might be futile. Solving problems, especially big ones, is a game to see how far toward the outer limits you can stretch your sphere of influence. "Root Causes" and "Core Problems," later in this section, address this subject in greater detail.

Enthusiasm without knowledge is like running in the dark.

—Unknown

Correlation vs. Cause and Effect

The power of the CRT comes from its basis in cause and effect. Sometimes people confuse cause and effect with correlation. It's important to understand the difference between the two, because CRTs with correlations embedded in them are likely to be invalid: They may isolate the wrong root causes, which could cost you time, energy, and resources in trying to solve the wrong problem. An unidentified embedded correlation will eventually collapse the grandest CRT.*

The difference between correlation and cause and effect is essentially the difference between *how* and *why*. You have a correlation when you can observe patterns and trends and conclude how one phenomenon behaves in relation to another. But the key element that correlation lacks is the answer to the question "Why?" Without knowing why, you'll never know what makes the correlation exist. This means you'll never be sure whether the correlation depends on other variables you haven't identified. In a problem analysis situation, this could cause you to focus on the wrong problem. It also means that you won't be able to effectively predict future instances of the correlation, because you'll never know whether a key variable is present or not.

Predicting Rain in Siberia: A Simple Example of Correlation

In the summer of 2000, a team of American university researchers was studying social and cultural customs in southern Siberia, near the border with Mongolia.[3:36] The researchers camped along the Menza River between the villages of Menza and Ukyr, inhabited by rival populations. In the early part of the 20th century, the rivalry expressed itself in armed conflict but these days it's limited to a few territorial disputes over hunting grounds.

During the dry heat of June, the people of Menza noticed that every time the Americans went swimming in the Ukyr end of the river, rain would follow. After this phenomenon happened three or four days in a row, the jealous residents asked the Americans to swim in the river near Menza, too (see Figure 4.5).

---

* For a humorous but pointed example of the kinds of erroneous conclusions correlation can produce, see Appendix D.

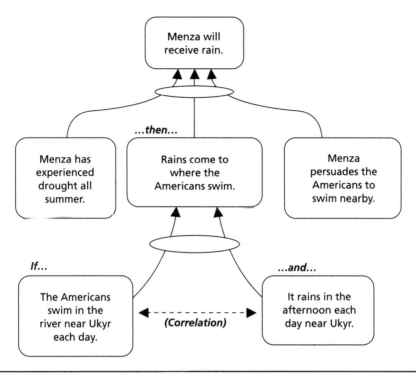

Figure 4.5   Rainfall in Siberia.

A basic assumption in cause and effect is that, under the same circumstances, an expected effect must be replicable from the same cause (see "Assumptions"). It's not known whether the rain followed the Americans to the Menza end of the river, but most people's experience will tell them that it's unlikely to have happened.

Fibromyalgia and Myofascial Pain: A Complex Real-World Example

Take neuromuscular pain, for example. In the last ten years or so, the medical community has identified a condition known as fibromyalgia syndrome (FMS).[2] This is a state of central nervous system sensitization. People with fibromyalgia may be unusually sensitive to pain. They may even find that their bodies translate certain sounds, vibrations, light, and other sensations—even smells—into discomfort or pain. Certain types of sound, such as staccato music or talk, or certain pitches, may be unendurable and may promote increased sensitivity to other stimuli. Diffuse body-wide pain is a part of FMS, but not all of it by any means.

Chronic myofascial pain (CMP) is another malady involving body pain. In fact, it's probably the most common cause of musculoskeletal pain. It is not the same as FMS, though in a substantial percentage of cases (maybe a third or more) they occur at the same time. In fact, a majority of physicians lump them together. But FMS and CMP can occur completely independently, too. The symptoms are difficult to sort out and the treatments are quite different.

Consider how easy it might be for a doctor to correlate the observed pain symptoms with either FMS or CMP, or to observe the widespread body pain and misdiagnose it as influenza, which has similar symptoms.

Decisions based on correlations are inherently less sound than those based on cause and effect. But how do we ensure that we don't fall victim to correlation in our Current Reality Trees? The answer is the Categories of Legitimate Reservation (CLR). Effective application of the CLR ensures that correlation is not confused with cause and effect. As you proceed through this chapter, it will be helpful to refer periodically to Chapter 2, "Categories of Legitimate Reservation." With an understanding of the importance of cause and effect, now let's look at the elements that make up a Current Reality Tree.

Undesirable Effects

One of the first elements you will encounter in a Current Reality Tree is the undesirable effect, or UDE (pronounced "OOH-dee"). What is an undesirable effect? Essentially, it's the most prominent indication you have that something might be amiss in a system. An UDE is something that really exists; something that is negative compared with the system's goal, critical success factors, or necessary conditions (see Figure 4.6). You might be aware of several UDEs. Or you might notice just one. In a complex system, there will probably be several. But you can start a CRT with as few as one.

> **NOTE:** Notice in Figure 4.6 the column labeled "Neutral or Marginally Negative." In your system, a substantial number of negative things might be apparent to you. Very few of these will actually qualify as system UDEs. The IO Map is crucial in separating the real UDEs from people's petty aggravations.

Undesirable by What Standard?

Undesirable effects are not subjective. The IO Map we discussed earlier in Chapter 3, if properly validated by consensus of decision makers, represents an objective benchmark against which to determine undesirability. So the question of "Undesirable to whom?" is really not relevant. Rather, the question should be, "Undesirable by what standard?" As in any human endeavor, subjectivity is difficult to eliminate completely, but a good

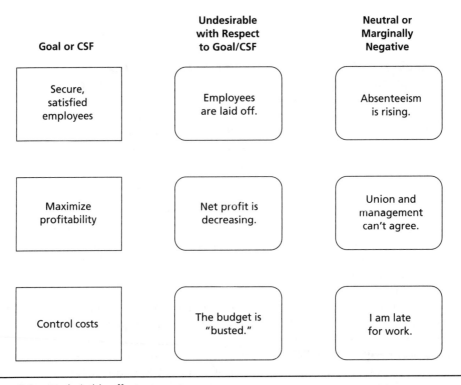

Figure 4.6   Undesirable effects.

IO Map should eliminate as much subjectivity about UDEs as is possible under the circumstances.

> **NOTE:** A good IO Map notwithstanding, disagreement on UDEs is possible. In most cases, this will be an Entity Existence issue, resolvable by producing supporting evidence. However, in a small percentage of situations, disagreement about undesirability can be a "warning flag" that an underlying hidden conflict must be resolved. It could also be a deliberate attempt to suboptimize the system, something that happens when persons or groups seek to maximize their own performance or reputation at the expense of the larger system (organization).

> Don't interrupt building your CRT to handle conflict at this early stage. You may miss some critical element of the conflict by not completing the CRT. Instead, make note of the conflict and consider using the Evaporating Cloud to resolve it. Refer to Chapter 5, "Evaporating Cloud," for more on how to use this powerful tool to resolve conflict.

If you're constructing the CRT solely for yourself (that is, you're operating within your span of control), you can be the final arbiter of what's negative. But if you're doing it to convince others to take action (you're operating in your sphere of influence), you'd be well advised to base your declaration of what is or isn't an UDE on the aforementioned consensus goal, CSF, and NCs of the system under consideration.

How to Identify and Check for Undesirability

To determine whether you've really got an UDE or just a "fact of life," phrase the effect in a complete sentence. Then look for these indications of negativity:

- Are others in my organization or situation likely to agree that these effects are negative with respect to the goal, CSF, and NCs (for example, "decreased profits," "excessive time/cost," and the like)?

  NOTE: Plurality does not establish validity, but consensus could be an indication that a CSF or NC isn't being met.

- Would society at large agree that the effects are negative with respect to its presumed goal, CSF, or NCs (for example, "increased crime rate," "health deterioration," and so forth)?

- Does it constitute an unacceptable deviation from expectations?

- Does it adversely affect the Throughput in your system (however "Throughput" may be defined)?

If you can answer "yes" to any of these questions, you probably have an UDE. But as a last check, give it the "So what?" test. Read the statement as if someone else were saying it to you, and respond, "So what?" Your first reaction will probably be to come up with a "Because…". If you have a valid "because…", that may actually be your UDE. If the statement doesn't cry out for justification, it can probably stand alone as an undesirable effect.

Existence in Reality

The second test of a valid UDE is *existence*. Does it really exist, or is it someone's negative fantasy? Consider the example in Figure 4.7:

If I speak my mind … then my boss fires me.

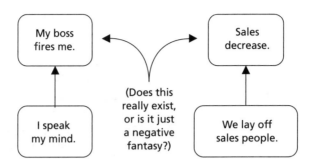

Figure 4.7   Undesirable effects: do they really exist.

The effect is unarguably undesirable to the tree builder. But does it really exist? Is the boss really unable to deal objectively and non-punitively with something he or she may not like to hear? Or is this a worst-case scenario with very little probability of happening? Here's a slightly different example: "Sales decrease." Is that a fact, or is it just somebody's perception? Are there verifiable data to confirm that this effect really exists?

Why the Emphasis on UDEs?
Why is effective UDE identification so important to building an effective Current Reality Tree? We focus on UDEs for the same reason the media focuses on negative stories—they're higher in visibility—and we want to get rid of them. They're what make us feel bad about our situation. We start with UDEs because doing so speeds our analysis of what's wrong with our system and generally leads to faster improvement. UDEs are only the most visible results of much more complex interactions and processes, but like a gopher hole in a perfectly manicured lawn, they're the "gateway" to finding the real underlying problem. If you choose the wrong gateway, you won't find the right problem. So some degree of care is warranted in selecting your UDEs.

> *Complex problems have simple, easy-to-understand wrong answers.*
> —Grossman's Misquote of H. L. Mencken

Root Causes
In building a Current Reality Tree, we work our way from UDEs back through the chain of cause and effect to root causes. The root cause is the beginning of the cause-effect relationship. There may be several intermediate effects and causes between the root cause and the UDE. These may be neutral, or even positive (from a limited, subjective point of view). But when you've worked your way down to a cause and you just can't go any farther, you're at a root cause.

Why might you not be able to go any farther? Theoretically, you could trace cause and effect all the way back to the creation of the world. But from a practical standpoint, you quickly exceed your span of control and soon thereafter your sphere of influence. There's no point in working on something over which you don't have at least some influence. So a prime indication that you may have reached a root cause in your tree is finding yourself at the boundary of your sphere of influence. Historical events in time can't be changed. Policies, practices, or behaviors that persist today because of them can. Consequently, the root cause can be:

- The lowest cause in the chain before passing outside your sphere of influence—the most basic thing you can do something about

- The first cause *beyond* your sphere of influence—something you personally can't do anything about

For example, in Figure 4.8 there are two root causes:

1. "The formal reward system doesn't satisfy important individual needs."

2. "People's behavior is motivated by unsatisfied needs."

The first is a condition of the system itself, which you may have some latitude to change; that is, it lies within your sphere of influence. The second is a condition of human nature, which you are unlikely to have any influence over whatsoever—it clearly lies outside your sphere of influence. *Both* can be considered root causes. One you may have to live with, the other you don't. And being able to identify which is which provides your problem-solving flexibility.

Every Current Reality Tree will have several root causes—maybe even a lot of them. One root cause in any Current Reality Tree is likely to be the origin of a substantial number of UDEs. The primary objective of the CRT is to work backward from UDEs through a chain of cause and effect to identify the few root causes that account for as many of the system's UDEs as possible. Your purpose in building a Current Reality Tree is to try to find the very few root causes that, if corrected, will have the greatest positive impact on system improvement—the most "bang for your buck."

Every cause statement that has arrows coming out of it but no arrows going in is technically considered a root cause (see Figure 4.9). It's worth remembering that a root cause is a point of origin in a CRT—no more, no less. The term does not necessarily connote anything negative.

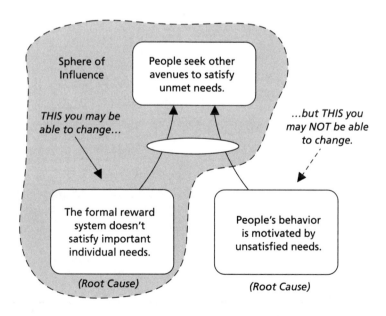

Figure 4.8   Root causes.

For example, "The sun shines every day" might be a root cause of skin cancer, but it's not necessarily negative in and of itself—it's just a fact of life. A root cause may be positive, negative, or neutral, depending on your perception, but most will have no particular significance. A few, however, will.

> *At some time in the life cycle of virtually every organization, its ability to succeed in spite of itself runs out.*
>
> —Brien's First Law

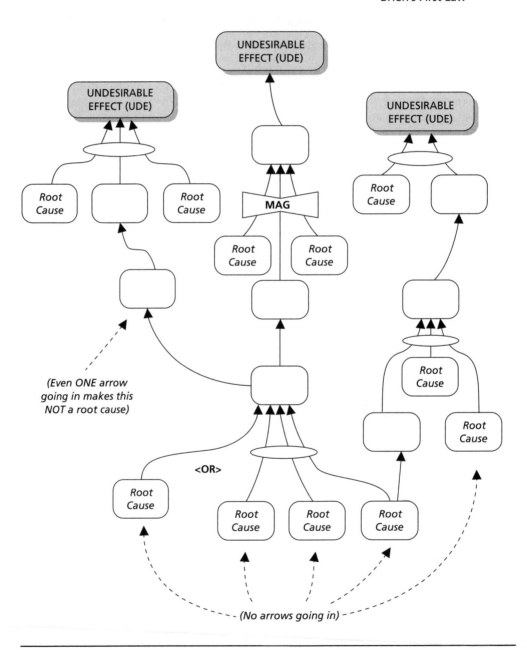

Figure 4.9 Identifying root causes.

Core Problems and Root Causes

From its inception in the early 1990s, the Thinking Process was intended to find what Goldratt referred to as a *core problem*—the one policy or practice that accounted for most of the undesirable effects experienced by a system. Goldratt even went so far as to offer a criterion: a true core problem would account for 70 percent of the UDEs in a system. However, there are two fundamental weaknesses with the idea of a core problem, as Goldratt originally defined it.

The "70 Percent" Criterion

The first weakness is conceptual and had to do with the "70 percent" criterion. Such a rule implicitly assumes that "all UDEs are created equal." If, in fact, every UDE is equally undesirable, then it makes sense to search for a single root cause that accounts for 70 percent of them—or even a simple majority.

But Goldratt originally defined "undesirable" as *negative on its own merits*. In reality, however, *nothing* can be negative on its own merits. Negativity is always relative to some standard of acceptability. Without any kind of objective benchmark, Thinking Process users are left to decide on their own what's negative enough to be called an UDE and what isn't. Naturally, since values differ from one person to another, so too did determination of UDEs.

For example, in a single Current Reality Tree I've seen one UDE that reads "The company loses money" and another that reads "I'm overloaded with work." Think about this question: *Are these two UDEs equally "bad"?* While the second is undeniably negative from the individual's perspective, why should the larger system care about it?

You might make the argument, "Well, the system *should* care, because overloaded people can't complete their work on time, or well. And eventually this degrades the company's welfare. It might even result in financial losses." This is all true. But the company's UDE lies in *these* ultimate system-level results, *not* in a contributing cause (such as an individual's overload) farther down in the CRT.

Moreover, if different people see UDEs differing in value, then all UDEs are *not* created equal. If they're not all equal, what happens if the most important UDEs are in the excluded 30 percent? The obvious answer is that you risk "fiddling while Rome burns" (that is, working on a non-constraint).

Such distinctions were rarely made in defining UDEs for early CRTs. As a result, those CRTs often had dozens of UDEs, and the logical structure needed to connect them all became ponderous, staggeringly complex, and—most of all—daunting in the extreme to people who had to present this level of complexity to decision makers. And what about the decision maker, who was unlikely to have the time or patience to wade through such a CRT? Most of them "tuned out" the presentation, with subsequent adverse consequences on their perception of the common sense (and credibility) of the presenter.

There were other adverse effects of complex CRTs. It didn't take long for people to start thinking, "The CRT is too difficult to create, and the results aren't worth the effort—it's too confusing!"

Inability to Act on a Core Problem

Goldratt's original procedure for building a CRT actually called for a concerted effort to connect disparate branches of a CRT to a single core problem by searching out V-shaped connections (see Figure 4.10). This kind of effort leads to the second weakness in the idea of a core problem, which is purely practical. The wider the variety of UDEs, the broader the statement of a core problem is required to connect them. Or the deeper you must go in cause and effect to reach a unifying core problem. The former leads to problem statements so vague as to be not actionable (for example, "Management is ineffective"). The second leads to root causes well beyond the span of control, or even the sphere of influence, of most decision makers (for example, "Microsoft is a *de facto* monopoly.").

What can any decision maker do about either of these? Nothing! The first is not discrete enough to act upon. You would have to break it down into components of managerial deficiency that somebody could actually *do* something about. The second one may well be outside the influence of even governors, senators, or captains of industry.

A Solution to the Core Problem Conundrum

To help users of the Thinking Process avoid the morass just described, we need a new way of looking at the whole question. One of the aims of this edition is to provide that new look. The solution is two-fold.

First, we must have clear consensus on what is or isn't an UDE. The Intermediate Objectives (IO) Map (Chapter 2) provides the means to achieve this consensus. And starting a Thinking Process analysis with an IO Map not only achieves consensus on what's good for the system (that is, what *should* be happening), by definition it limits what

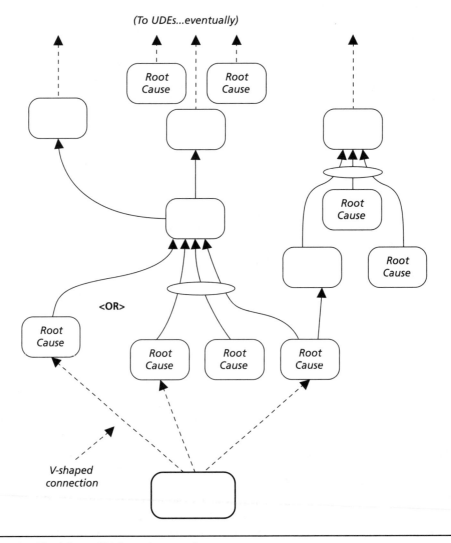

Figure 4.10   The fallacy of V-shaped connections.

can be considered an UDE to a very few entities in a CRT—those that are obviously and demonstrably negative with respect to a limited, focused benchmark and not a wide range of subjective opinions.

Second, in constructing a CRT, we'll cease to strive for a single unifying (but vague and over-broad) core problem. Instead, we'll dig down to a few *critical root causes* that are both actionable and within the sphere of influence of an accessible decision maker. (We'll define "critical root cause" in a moment.) This approach will usually produce no more than four or five things to work on, rather than a single core problem (see Figure 4.11).

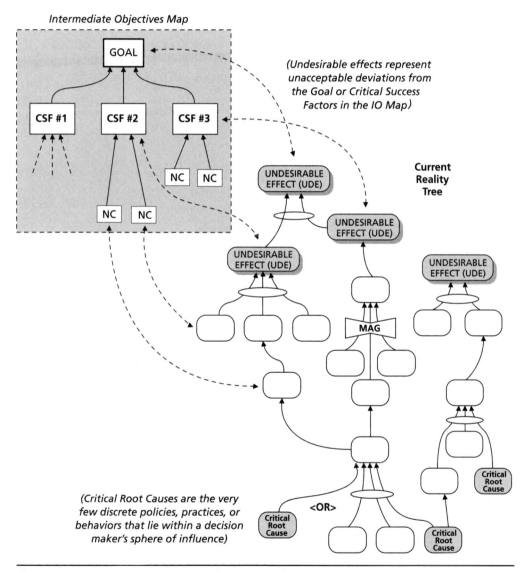

Figure 4.11 A new way to conceive of system problems.

But as Dr. Ray Hansen once observed, "Silver bullets went out of fashion when the Lone Ranger died." The chances for most people to find one simplistic solution to cure all the ills of system are but two: *slim* and *none*. I myself have seen only two such situations in more than ten years of applying the Thinking Process to complex situations. In both cases, the systems were start-up commercial companies, and in both cases the core problem was the same: insufficient start-up capital—an archetypical core problem if ever there were one!

So, avoid "heartburn": Don't begin a Current Reality Tree to begin solving system problems without first completing an IO Map for the same system.

Critical Root Cause: A Definition

In the preceding discussion, we introduced the concept of a critical root cause. It's important to define this term, especially since it represents one of the two foundations of our new way of looking at current reality and complex system problem solving.

> *A critical root cause is a policy, practice, or prevalent behavior that constitutes the lowest level of causality in existing reality lying within someone's sphere of influence to change.*

Notice the two key criteria: *lowest level* and *sphere of influence*. Not all root causes qualify. The lowest level might be a historical event, and that could conceivably be a root cause—but not a *critical* root cause. For a root cause to be critical, it must also reside within someone's sphere of influence to change.

For example, a historical event that can't be changed would be the creation and adoption of the Constitution of the United States. It happened in 1789, and nothing can change that. And almost everything that America has influenced, good or bad, over the past 200-plus years is an effect of that cause. But the Constitution itself is an elastic document that can be interpreted in a variety of ways (and often is). It represents extremely high-level policy that still exists and operates to this day, even though the historical event of its creation has long past. Which means it can be changed—and has been, 26 times since the original articles were drafted in 1789. Thus, a root cause that says, "The Constitution forbids (or requires)…" could be critical root cause.*

Main Body of the CRT

Lying between the UDEs at the top of the CRT and the critical root causes at the bottom is the main body of the tree—all the detailed intermediate causes and effects that connect the two. It's this articulated causality that explains how the root causes actually lead to the undesirable effects.

The details of all this cause and effect will be different for each system we might analyze. The number of differences and their degree will depend on how similar two discrete systems might be to one another. For example, the causality structure for a government organization won't be close at all to one for a commercial company. Besides the obvious differences in size and mission, the nature of their internal structures and functional interactions would be completely different. Neither are their operating environments quite the same. So in the same way reality differs between systems, we should expect the same of the logical structures of cause and effect that characterize them.

---

* Nothing in the definition of a critical root cause can be construed to mean that changing one will be easy. Like changing the U.S. Constitution, it may be within someone's sphere of influence, but it may be extremely challenging and time consuming to achieve.

Archetypical CRTs

Having just said that CRT causality will be unique to each type of system, we must also be aware that *within* types of systems cause-and-effect structure is likely to be similar, maybe even nearly identical. For example, two companies that manufacture the same kinds of products using similar processes, or perhaps produce similar services, would likely have similar IO Maps (that is, requirements for success).

To the extent that the internal challenges they experience are similar, they might have equivalent UDEs. Because their operating functions would be similar, we might expect to see the same topical branches, maybe even the same kinds of critical root causes in the CRTs of each. This similarity would exist even if the specific wording of entities in their trees differed. Seen in their entirety, the same branches and issues are likely to be discernible. This could be true even of organizations that differed substantially, if they compete against one another in the same environment.

Comparable organizations and situations give rise to *archetypical CRTs*—logic trees that might apply to more than one organization. For example, the CRT of one Boy Scout organization or a state transportation department might be valid for another Boy Scout group or a transportation department in another state. The same is true of the *solutions* to the critical root causes identified in the CRT (that is, the FRT).

This carries simultaneously potential benefits and risks. The chief benefit is that for organizations that don't compete with one another, such as different Boy Scout groups, there isn't a need to "re-invent the wheel." The same solution, logically developed and verified, can be adopted by a similar group. The primary risk is that for companies or groups that compete with one another, access to one's CRT (or worse, the FRT) can provide a tactical, perhaps even a strategic advantage. Thus, commercial companies have learned to hold CRTs and FRTs as proprietary information and secure them in order to avoid harm to themselves. No point in giving away the secrets of your success without making the enemy work for them! For this reason, it's usually difficult to find for-profit companies willing to have their Thinking Process analyses trees published or otherwise made available to people outside the company. (For many years, lack of such commercial real-world examples has been an obstacle to spreading the use of the Thinking Process.)

Depicting a Current Reality Tree

The symbology used to depict current reality is straightforward (see Figure 4.12). The symbols used here conform to the standard conventions described in Chapter 2.

A round-cornered rectangle indicates a cause or effect. Effects that are undesirable are highlighted in some way, either by means of stars, asterisks, shading, or perhaps drop shadows. Arrows connect causes with effects. Ellipses are used to indicate that two or more causes must combine to produce the effect.

Entities

As you will notice from reading other chapters of this book, all of the Thinking Process logic trees contain statements bordered by some kind of geometric figure. In the Current Reality Tree you should see only round-cornered rectangles. Evaporating Clouds, Future Reality Trees, and Transition Trees have both round-cornered and sharp-cornered rectangles. Prerequisite Trees have octagons and square-cornered rectangles. These figures and the statements they enclose fall into the general category of "entities." The name itself implies that the idea can stand alone. In accordance with the standard conventions described in Chapter 2, statements in Current Reality, Future Reality, and Transition Trees must be expressed in complete sentences that convey an idea that can stand alone. Entities in IO Maps, Evaporating Clouds, and Prerequisite Trees need not be expressed in complete sentences, provided their meanings are clear.

Entities in a Current Reality Tree
With a Current Reality Tree, the issue is simple: An entity is either a cause or an effect. Or it can be both—that is, the effect of one cause and the cause of another effect. This is what enables us to create chains of cause and effect.

Arrows
Arrows appear in every Logical Thinking Process tool, but they signify different relationships. In the Current Reality, Future Reality, and Transition Trees, they signify sufficiency in a cause-and-effect relationship. Remember, sufficiency implies that the presence of all the contributing causes will *deliver* the stated effect.

In an Evaporating Cloud and a Prerequisite Tree they represent a necessary—but not necessarily sufficient—condition relationship. Remember, necessity implies a minimum (enabling) requirement. A necessary condition (at the tail of an arrow) enables us to accomplish the next entity (at the head of the arrow). But the entity at the head of a necessary condition arrow is *not* an effect.

Refer to the section in Chapter 2, "Sufficiency-Based vs. Necessity-Based Logic Trees," p. 59, for more details on this distinction.

So, in the Current Reality Tree, the arrow implies a sufficiency relationship. In other words, the cause (entity at the tail of the arrow) is sufficient to produce the effect (entity at the head of the arrow). To read a cause-effect relationship (two entities connected by an arrow), attach "If…" to the beginning of the cause statement and "…then…" to the beginning of the effect statement.

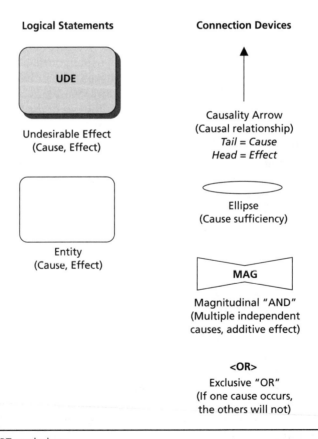

Figure 4.12 CRT symbology.

*If I turn off the light, **then** the room is dark.*

However, you must be careful in using and reading arrows in a Current Reality Tree. The previous example has a catch to it (see Figure 4.13, upper half). It assumes that (a) it's dark (that is, night) outside the room, or (b) there are no windows or other openings that could admit other light. These assumptions aren't stated in the cause-effect relationship, but they're there just the same and they have a direct bearing on the validity of the cause-effect relationship.

Underlying Assumptions

Every arrow in any Logical Thinking Process tree is based on unstated but underlying assumptions about the situation, environment, or laws of nature. For example, consider this cause-and-effect relationship, depicted with entities and an arrow (see Figure 4.13, lower half):

*If I push the glass off the table, **then** it falls to the floor.*

There's an unstated underlying assumption here that the law of gravity applies in this situation. "Well, of course," you're probably thinking, "that's obvious. Gravity always applies." Perhaps. But maybe not. Astronauts in orbit around the earth don't need to

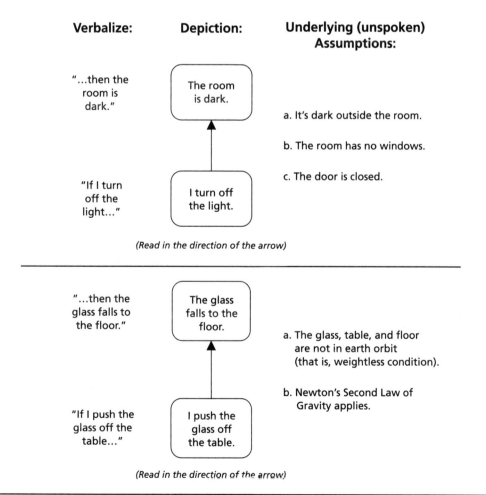

Figure 4.13 Cause-effect relationships and underlying assumptions.

worry about the glass falling to the floor; they have to worry about it floating away, because the underlying assumption about gravity does not apply in their situation. As a result, when the underlying assumptions change, *the same cause can result in a different effect.* Keep this in mind, both when you build your own trees and when you scrutinize someone else's. What assumptions underlie the arrows? And the follow-up question is: "In light of these assumptions, does the cause-effect relationship make sense?" Chapter 2, "Categories of Legitimate Reservation," provides more guidance on analyzing cause-effect relationships.

Ellipses, Magnitudinal ANDs, and Exclusive ORs

Ellipses. The ellipse is unique to sufficiency-based logic trees (Current Reality, Future Reality, and Transition Trees). Its function is to encompass multiple causes that depend upon one another to produce the effect in question (see Figure 4.14). The absence of any one cause whose arrow passes through the ellipse is enough to destroy the cause-effect relationship. However, the most common situation you're likely to encounter is a cause insufficiency—a contributing cause requiring an ellipse to combine it with the one you've already stated.

Let's recall the example, *"If* I turn off the light, *then* the room is dark." It's conceivable that turning off the light alone is not sufficient to make the room dark (see Figure 4.15). You might add another cause: "…and *if* the room has no windows…." Is this now sufficient? No? How about adding: "…and *if* the only door into the room is closed… ." Now it's a pretty tight, or "dry," cause-effect relationship.

REMEMBER: We live in a complex world. Most effects result from multiple causes, some independent, some contributing. An independent cause is a single entity, sufficient by itself to produce the effect. Sometimes, when several independent causes apply, they are referred to as additional causes (see "Additional Cause," Chapter 2, for a more detailed explanation). A contributing cause is one of two or more factors that alone can't produce the effect, but together will. Contributing-cause arrows are always enclosed by an ellipse. You should look at every causality arrow critically and ask yourself the question, "Is an ellipse required?"

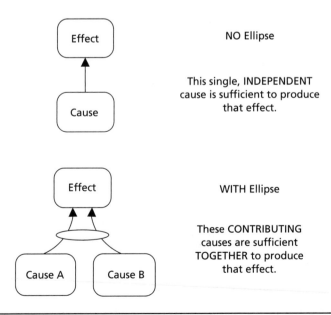

Figure 4.14 Ellipses.

NOTE: It isn't necessary to include every underlying assumption or potential contributing cause in your Current Reality Tree. It would quickly get out of hand if you did. Your decision rule should be: "For whom am I building this tree?" If it's for yourself alone and it's about an environment in which you have good intuitive knowledge, you can leave much more unstated but assumed. If you're going to present your tree to someone else, you have to consider how much they might know about the situation. Trees presented to others must usually be more detailed (that is, with fewer unstated assumptions and more contributing causes) in order to preclude confusion and embarrassment.

Magnitudinal AND. As we saw in Chapter 2, it's possible to have conditions in which two or more causes can produce an effect independently of one another (that is, no ellipse required to enclose them). In some cases, it's possible that these two independent causes exist at the same time. What's more, it's conceivable that when this occurs, two or more causes, though independent of one another, can act additively to increase the magnitude of the effect. This can only happen when the effect is a condition that admits the possibility of a graduated degree. The preferred symbol for a magnitudinal-AND situation is a "bowtie" with the letters "MAG" inside it. Take a look at Figure 4.16, for example.

Notice that the effect—*My gasoline mileage improves*—is not a "zero-or-one" condition.

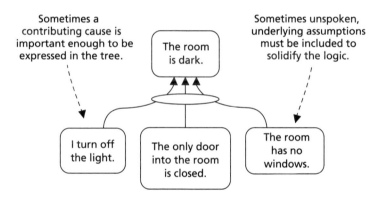

Figure 4.15   Indicating cause sufficiency with an ellipse.

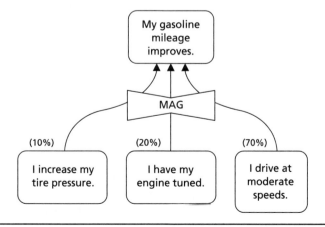

Figure 4.16   Indicating magnitudinal effects.

Rather, potentially it's a graduated effect. This will always be the case with magnitudinal causality. Each added independent cause can be expected to increase the magnitude of the effect to some degree, even if not equally. When the effect is a zero-or-one condition (that is, it is present in some fixed amount or completely absent), it's possible for multiple independent causes to exist simultaneously. But in this case, the removal of just one leaves the entire effect still in place. In order to remove the effect, *all* independent causes must be neutralized or eliminated.

It's important to recognize the distinction between a zero-or-one effect and a graduated effect. In the former case, you have no choice but to eliminate the entire effect, and all independent causes that produce it must be addressed. In the latter case, removal of a cause may reduce the "pain" of the effect to a tolerable level. That may be all that's required in a particular situation, especially if resolving the remaining cause poses extreme difficulties. Knowing the difference between these two situations can make a difference in the options we have for eliminating certain undesirable effects.

Exclusive ORs. There's another situation that merits discussion: the exclusive OR. This situation usually occurs when the effect is a zero-or-one condition, but not always. In exclusive-OR causality, there may be multiple independent causes of an effect, but if one cause is operative, the other will not be. Figure 4.17 illustrates an exclusive-OR situation.

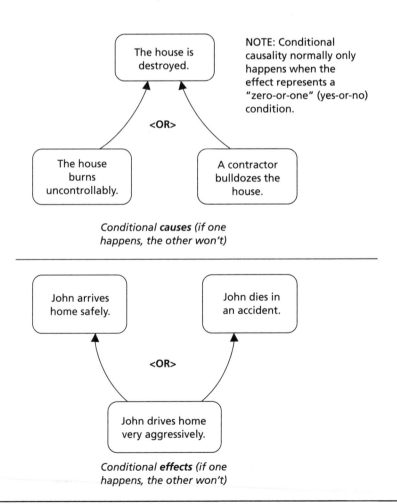

Figure 4.17   Indicating exclusive causality.

Notice that the exclusive OR can apply to multiple causes producing a single effect, or a single cause producing multiple effects. In either situation, however, the **<OR>** symbol is used to indicate that if one of the causal connections occurs, it excludes the other.

Variations on a Theme

The sufficient causality (ellipse), additional causality (independent arrows), magnitudinal cause (bowtie), and exclusive OR can all have variations. Which one applies depends on the reality of the situation being represented. Figure 4.18 shows some of the combinations you might see (or find yourself needing) in a CRT or FRT. There may be others.

Sometimes logic trees (Current Reality, Future Reality, Prerequisite, and Transition) can become quite complex. Figure 4.46 shows just how complicated they can be. An extremely complex tree can be both intimidating and frustrating to a reader, especially someone who isn't familiar with the graphical way of presenting cause-and-effect logic. As tree builders, we have an obligation to make the reader's job as easy as possible. One way to do this is to use an orderly means of numbering entities in a tree. The sidebar, "Numbering Entities in a Tree," describes one such approach. You may elect to use a different one of your own, but the objective should still remain clear in your mind: Keep it simple and easy to follow.

SIDEBAR   *Numbering Entities in a Tree*

A tree can have as few as 10 to 20 entities, or it might have a hundred. The U.S. Transportation Command (U.S. Department of Defense), for example, constructed a Current Reality Tree with 170 entities. Without some kind of coherent numbering system, tracing the chain of cause and effect from root causes to UDEs could be a nearly impossible task. Having a finished product that anyone else could follow would be even less likely.

So how should the entities in a logic tree by numbered? Whatever method you choose should have three basic characteristics (see Figure 4.19):

1. Numbers should increase in the direction of the arrows.

2. If there is more than one page, it should be easy to follow connections to other pages.

3. A given page should be easy to locate quickly, without undue searching.

No single numbering method is necessarily the best. The one suggested here meets the characteristics just mentioned, and offers some other benefits as well. A single numbering sequence will probably suffice if your tree can be confined to one 8½-inch by 11-inch page, or if you're using paper large enough to keep the tree on one page. Once you find that you need two pages or more, start a new sequence for the second page (see Figure 4.19).

- Don't number your entities until you're sure the tree is as logically sound as you can make it (that is, you think all the entities you'll need are present).

- Use a three-digit method, starting with 100. Every time you start a new page, begin a new sequence (for example, 200 on page two, 300 on page three, and so forth) (see Figure 4.19).

- Later, if you decide you need to add entities, don't re-number the entire tree. Instead, use decimal numbers for the new additions (for example, 217.1, 224.5, 234.7, and so forth). Figure 4.20 shows an example.

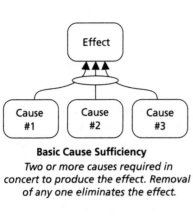

Basic Cause Sufficiency
Two or more causes required in concert to produce the effect. Removal of any one eliminates the effect.

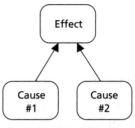

Basic Additional Cause
Two or more causes independently can produce the effect. Both must be removed to eliminate the effect.

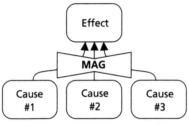

Basic Magnitudinal Cause
Two or more causes independently produce some degree of the effect. Together they increase the total effect. Removal of any one eliminates some (not all) of the effect.

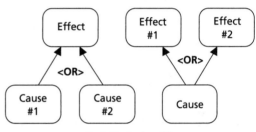

Basic Exclusive OR
Two or more causes independently produce the effect. If one exists, the other will not. Or, one cause produces two possible effects. If one occurs, the other will not.

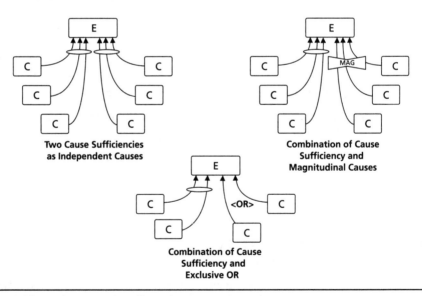

Two Cause Sufficiencies as Independent Causes

Combination of Cause Sufficiency and Magnitudinal Causes

Combination of Cause Sufficiency and Exclusive OR

Figure 4.18   Various causal configurations.

- When a cause on one page leads to an effect on another page, show the "destination entity number" on the cause page, and the "originating entity number" on the effect page (see Figure 4.19). Replicate the cause on the effect page, with a heavy border for emphasis, to draw attention to the fact that it originated on another page. Beside each off-page connection, indicate the page the connection is going to (or the page the entity came from).

One gauge of success is not whether you have a tough problem to handle, but whether it is the same problem you had last year.

—Unknown

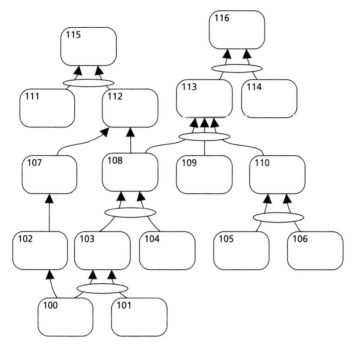

A Cause-Effect Tree on One Page

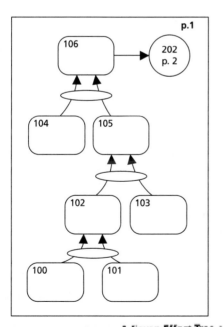

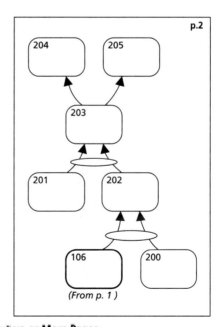

A Cause-Effect Tree on Two or More Pages

Figure 4.19 Cause-effect tree numbering.

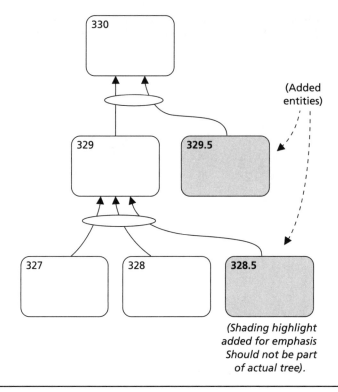

(Added entities)

(Shading highlight added for emphasis Should not be part of actual tree).

Figure 4.20 Adding entities after numbers have been assigned.

THE MOST COMMON LOGICAL ERRORS IN A SUFFICIENCY TREE

As we know, there are eight Categories of Legitimate Reservation. Only seven of these categories can actually be depicted in a Thinking Process logic tree. Of those seven, there are three that you're likely to find most often in either a CRT or an FRT, whether your own or someone else's.

Clarity in the Arrow

The most common error of all is missing intermediate steps. Most people seem inclined to jump several layers at a time. This is a particular failing of beginners, but even experienced users of the Thinking Process fall victim to it. The very first example I saw of this error occurred not in a logic tree but in a television news analysis show. Two analysts debated opposite sides of an issue concerning the passage of a law governing employment benefits. One of the analysts said, "If this law passes in the Congress, half a million jobs will go south of the border." (Meaning out of the United States and into Mexico.) Had this expansive statement been included in a logic tree, it might have looked something like the left side of Figure 4.21. We refer to this as a "long arrow," meaning that it's a long leap of logic between the cause and the effect. (The arrow itself might be physically drawn quite short.)

But now look at the right side of Figure 4.21, which shows how many intervening layers of cause and effect might have been omitted.

Don't Induce Confusion

There are two major risks associated with long arrows. The most obvious is in communicating your logic to a decision maker, or to someone whose support must be enlisted in order for the problem to be solved. If you don't make a clear step-by-step connection between causes (especially root causes) and effects (especially undesirable effects), you risk the credibility of your argument. At best you might elicit only half-hearted support for what you recommend. At worst, you risk outright rejection if the logical connections don't make sense because they skip too many intermediate steps.

Don't Miss Opportunities to Break the Chain of Cause and Effect

The second risk with long arrows is overlooking possible options to solve the problem. Or, if you're building a Future Reality Tree, you might neglect to consider additional actions that need to be taken in those missing intermediate layers. In right side of Figure 4.21, notice that there are at least four unstated root causes in the chain of causality. Because of the sufficiency nature of the tree, removal of any one would serve to prevent the effect at the top. In other words, it might not be necessary to eliminate the Congressional passage of the law—just eliminate one of the unstated contributing factors, which might turn out to be a lot easier to do anyway.

The moral of the story here is to avoid long arrows whenever possible during the problem analysis (CRT) and solution development (FRT) phases of the Thinking Process.

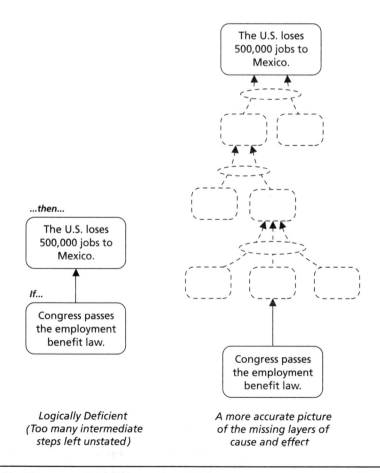

Logically Deficient (Too many intermediate steps left unstated)

A more accurate picture of the missing layers of cause and effect

Figure 4.21 The "long arrow" (clarity).

Try to make your logic as lock-step as possible—no "missing links." If the tree must be streamlined for executive presentation, that can be done later (see Chapter 8 for details). Just remember: It's always easier to leave out logic that you've developed and retrieve it later, if needed, than it is to create missing intermediate steps in the logic "on the fly" in front of an audience of decision makers.

Cause Insufficiency

A typical beginner mistake is failure to acknowledge, and include in a CRT or FRT, all the contributing causes to an effect. The most common indicator of this mistake is a tree that has a lot of single arrows connecting different levels of causality and few, if any, contributing causes with ellipses (see Figure 4.22).

Almost every new user of the Thinking Process falls victim to this trap. Next to "long arrows" (Clarity on the Arrow), this is the most common logical failing in Thinking Process trees. It poses a different kind of risk.

We live in a complex, interdependent world. Very little happens as a result of completely unitary, independent causes. At a minimum, a proposed single cause implies

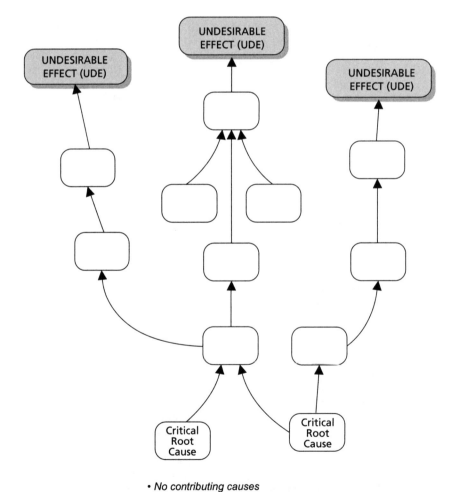

- *No contributing causes*
- *No ellipses*
- *More like a flow chart than a logic tree*

Figure 4.22   The Insufficient Tree.

discrete assumptions about reality that are not stated. And because these assumptions are not stated, they may be completely overlooked.

But if they're critical to the causality, they *shouldn't* remain unstated. People tend to forget, overlook, or disregard what is not acknowledged. What if addressing such an unacknowledged assumption is crucial to solving a problem? What if the unstated assumption is *really* the critical root cause? Ignoring the contributing causes risks failing to identify the right root cause—or at least the one that would most easily and effectively resolve the undesirable effects. The result can be wasted time or resources.*

The lesson here is that there should be *very few* single arrows in either a CRT or an FRT. If you look objectively at your tree and find more than about 25 percent of the connections are single arrows, you had better start examining your logical connections for cause insufficiency.

The Concept of "Oxygen" Revisited

In Chapter 2, "Categories of Legitimate Reservation," we explored the concept of "oxygen" in logic trees. It's time to reinforce that discussion with a brief review. Figure 4.23 illustrates the oxygen issue.

The concept of "oxygen" in logic trees is often used as a rationale for *leaving out* entities—contributing causes—in a CRT or FRT. The argument usually goes something like this: "Well, of course it's a factor, but everybody knows it's there, so there's no need to include it."

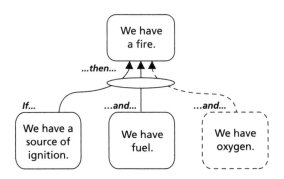

- *Oxygen is critical to the causality, but...*
- *Oxygen is assumed to be present by everyone who knows anything about the situation, and...*
- *Stating it can be omitted*

Figure 4.23   The concept of "oxygen" (revisited).

---

* Not to mention possible loss of life. In 2006, a concrete ceiling panel in the infamous "Big Dig," an underground traffic tunnel in Boston, Massachusetts, fell onto a car, killing the occupant. The "Big Dig" was a $14 billion disaster of a project, costing five times as much as originally forecast and taking 20 years to complete. A CRT would have shown several different critical root causes of the many different UDEs, each dependent on one another. After all this expenditure of time and money and the cost of one life, the tunnel is indefinitely closed pending expensive repairs.[3]

Unfortunately, not everybody knows it's there if you don't state it, and even if they do, it's easy to forget what isn't explicitly expressed. Moreover, the "oxygen" argument is often used as an excuse by people defending their failure to even consider contributing causes in the first place.

The moral of the story is this: When you construct the actual analysis, include as much detail (that is, step-by-step logic and sufficiency) as may be required to persuade a viewer of the tree who knows little or nothing about the situation. When you present the results of the analysis, you can use judgment about how much to streamline the tree. Your judgment should be based on knowing your audience, meaning that you have a good understanding of the listener's personal knowledge of the situation.

This is a little like holding someone's hand as you jump over a chasm together: you never want to attempt a leap longer than the person holding your hand can make with you. It's natural to be concerned about forcing too much detail on people who were not part of the process of building the tree, especially decision makers whose time and patience may be limited. Appendix B provides a way to safeguard your own credibility without "losing your audience."

Entity Existence

The third most common logical deficiency in CRTs is also the most insidious: Entity Existence. We're not speaking here of complete sentences or compound ideas, but rather valid existence in reality. Too frequently, I've seen speculation passed off as fact in cause-and-effect trees. Figure 4.24 is a humorous example intended to drive home this point.* The logical connections are sound, but the outcome is obviously ridiculous because of two failures in Entity Existence. Can you identify which entities they are?

The safest way to ensure that our trees meet the Entity Existence requirement is to ensure that we can provide evidence to substantiate every cause or effect we include in our trees. This can be a tall order, and in some cases you might not need to do it. Whether or not you need to do so is a personal judgment, based on what I call the "regret factor" of the situation—the degree of your distaste for an outcome if you fail to verify the entity existence, multiplied by the probability that the unfavorable outcome will happen (see figure 4.25). In some cases, the probability of disaster is very low, but the impact if it happens might be more than you can stand. In such a case, you might conclude that your regret factor is high enough to warrant checking the entity existence.

> *Facts do not cease to exist because they are ignored.*
>
> —Aldous Huxley

READING A CURRENT REALITY TREE

As with any sufficiency tree, the Current Reality Tree is read from the bottom up. It's relatively easy to read. Since every entity must be worded as a complete sentence, each cause or effect can become a comprehensible clause in a complex sentence. Locate the entity at the tail of the arrow and read it aloud, preceded by the word "If." After that, read the entity at the head of the arrow, preceded by the word "then." If you have several

---

* This example was developed from an exchange between Cliff and Norm, two characters in the American television comedy series *Cheers!*, about the regular patrons of a sports bar in Boston.

"...and THAT, my friend, is why you always feel smarter after a few beers!"

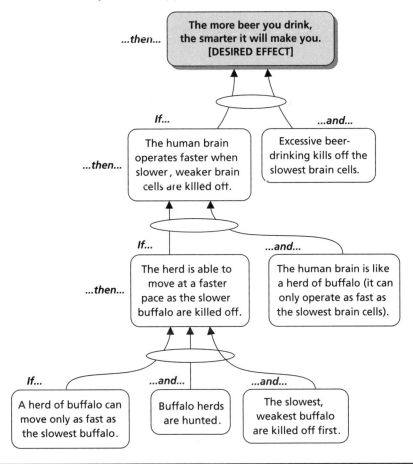

Figure 4.24 "The buffalo effect."

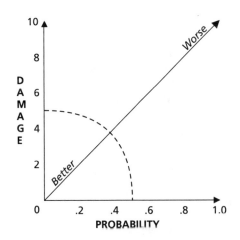

Figure 4.25 Regret factor.

causes joined by an ellipse, read the "If" only once, with the other contributing cause statements joined by "and." For example:

> *If drivers don't stop for red lights,* **then** *odds of accidents increase (see Figure 4.26).*

or

> *If people have little motivation to apply total quality principles,* **and** *successful total quality implementation requires major organizational change,* **then** *people are not likely to be motivated to change as required to successfully implement total quality (see Figure 4.26).*

Get used to reading trees this way. It's a very easy way to verbalize cause-and-effect trees, especially complicated ones, without forgetting where you are in the process. It's particularly important to verbalize cause and effect smoothly when you're presenting your logical construction to others for critique—or to an executive for a decision.

NEGATIVE REINFORCING LOOPS

As you begin building your Current Reality Tree, connecting the UDEs and working your way down to root causes, you might occasionally notice a special relationship between an UDE and a cause lower in the tree. Sometimes it's obvious that an undesirable effect

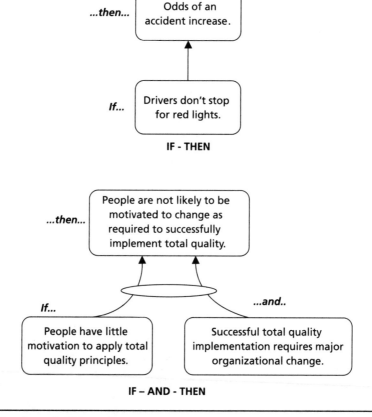

Figure 4.26   Reading a Sufficiency Tree.

actually *reinforces* the cause that produced it. This is known as a negative reinforcing loop. It represents both bad and good news.

It's bad news because you have a self-perpetuating bad situation. It may even magnify the undesirable effect with each iteration of the loop. This is a kind of "death spiral" in which the system causes continual deterioration to itself.

However, the fact that you can identify a negative reinforcing loop is good news, because once you know it's there you can take steps to break it. In fact, you *must* take steps to break this chain of causality. Eliminating the critical root cause that produces a negative reinforcing loop is one of the most powerful changes for good that you can make.

Because of the self-perpetuating characteristic of those entities that are part of the loop, you need to examine the loop carefully:

- Will it disappear if a critical root cause is eliminated?

- Will you need to take additional specific actions to break the loop?

- Is it possible that the right corrective action could turn it into a positive reinforcing loop? (Refer to Chapter 6, "Future Reality Tree," for more on positive reinforcing loops.)

Figure 4.27 is an excerpt from a larger CRT. It describes a devastating condition that drove International Harvester Corporation (later reorganized as Navistar) into bankruptcy.

Reading a Negative Reinforcing Loop

Reinforcing loops are read a little differently than normal cause and effect. As you work your way up to the point where the loop departs the adverse outcome entity and feeds back to the appropriate cause below it, you still read it as "If…then…". The difference is that when you re-read the entity where the negative loop re-enters the tree, you add the word "more" (or perhaps "more and more") at an appropriate place in the sentence. Here's an example, using Figure 4.27:

> "If (111) each individual product/component costs more than it did before, then (105) the total cost of many **more** of IH's components is higher than the industry average."

Each successive effect entity above the re-entry point in the chain of causality should have "more" or "more and more" inserted in it, until the departure entity for the reinforcing loop is reached. This convention highlights the complete loop for anyone who sees it.

If you're verbally presenting a tree with a reinforcing loop (either positive or negative), read the chain of causality the *first time* through the loop departure entity *without* verbalizing "more" (or "more and more"). At the departure entity, mention the negative reinforcing loop first: "At this point, we experience a particularly serious phenomenon…a negative reinforcing loop." Then re-read the departure entity once more, and read the re-entry point entity. Once you re-enter the tree, read each reinforced entity the second time with "more/more and more" inserted.

A negative reinforcing loop is such a detrimental condition that correcting it will often significantly reduce the magnitude of undesirable effects even if nothing else is done to alleviate any other critical root cause.

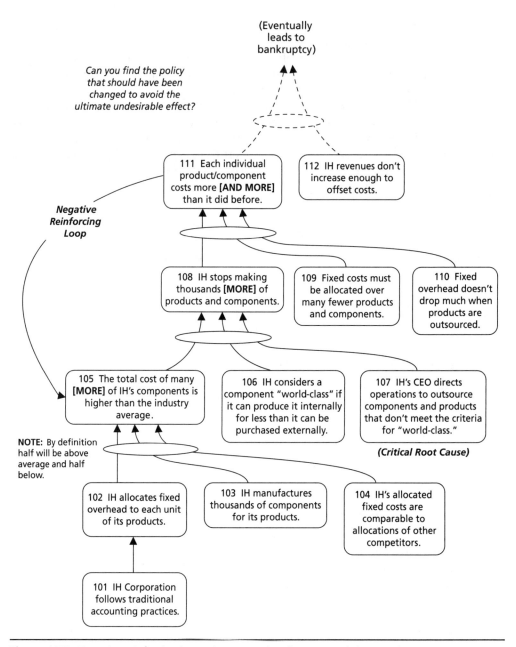

Figure 4.27 Negative reinforcing loop: the International Harvester (IH) example.

It's a simple thing to make things complex, but a complex task to make them simple.

—Meyer's Law

HOW TO CONSTRUCT A CURRENT REALITY TREE

Now you're ready to begin constructing your own Current Reality Tree. Before you start, does your situation qualify for a CRT?

- Do you have adequate intuitive knowledge about the situation, or do you need to do some research first? Are you able to recognize and understand patterns and interactions in your system?

- Do you care about finding a solution to the problem? Have you assumed ownership of the problem? Do you have enough desire to fix it to justify the work that lies ahead?

If you can answer "yes" to these questions, you're ready to proceed. Let's assume that you've already recognized that a Current Reality Tree would be appropriate for your situation. There's something you really need to change about your circumstances. You are able to say, confidently, "My system really needs to improve in these areas…" and put your finger on a few generators of your discontent. What's the first thing you must do?

Gather Materials

CRTs are normally constructed in two forms, either on paper or on a computer using a graphical charting program. My decade-plus of experience in using the Thinking Process has taught me this: unless you already have the entities of the CRT fully formed in your mind with all the causal connections visualized, start your CRT on paper using Post-it Notes. At some point, even before you complete the paper version, you can transition to the computer version. In fact, I do this on almost all my Thinking Process trees (start on paper, finish digitally). If your logic tree is intended for presentation to others at some point, you'll almost certainly have to render it into a printable digital form.

You'll need a large piece of paper (see Figure 4.28) and open wall space adequate for hanging it. Standard 8½-inch by 11-inch paper won't do. You can use flip-chart paper (30 inches by 40 inches, or equivalent), butcher paper, or the back of a sheet of wrapping paper—as long as it's at least 20 inches by 30 inches, preferably larger. If all you have is standard bond paper, tape sheets together until you've approximated those dimensions.

- Use flip-chart or other large paper
- Tape multiple pages together on a wall, if required

Figure 4.28   Large paper required.

Make allowances for the fact that you may even have to tape two pieces of flip-chart paper together, as shown in Figure 4.32.

You'll also need a lot of Post-it Notes—the optimum size is 3 inches by 3 inches—and a bold felt-tip pen for writing on the Post-it Notes. Felt-tip pens are preferable to ballpoint, because the mark they make is legible from somewhat farther away.* Your tree will be built from groupings of these notes (entities). Depending on the complexity of your problem, your tree might exceed a hundred entities, so you'll need an ample supply. I recommend using three different colors: one for UDEs, one for critical root causes, and the third for all the other entities in the tree.

Last but not least, you'll need a few pencils and big erasers. The pencils are for drawing the causality lines on the flip-chart paper. The eraser is for making changes to the routing of these lines, or eliminating some if necessary. As your tree develops, you'll find yourself moving whole connected clusters of entities from one place to another on the flip-chart paper; the old connecting lines will have to be erased, or they'll confuse you later.

1. Define the System to be Modeled

Your first step should be to identify the boundary of the system you're concerned about (see Figure 4.29). You need to know what lies *within* your system and what factors reside *outside* it, in the external environment. For biological, human, or organizational systems this is usually easy to do. The system is defined as a plant, animal, person, family, or organization (members and assets). For societal systems it may be more difficult. How do you define your "community," for example? Economic or ecological systems can be extremely challenging. For these, the transition from internal system to external environment is often not clear.

This is an essential first step, even if you find that you must go back and refine the definition after your analysis is under way. It might be helpful to ask a few leading questions:

- Is this tree about me personally?

- Is it about an organization—business, government, or not-for-profit (whether or not I'm affiliated with it)?

- Is it about a technical or operational process?

- It the tree describing a historical event (for example, for learning purposes, not necessarily for problem solution)?

Once you've answered these questions, you will usually find that you've pretty well defined your system's boundaries. Now that you have a clear mental image of what's inside your system and what's outside, you're ready for the next step.

2. Determine the Undesirable Effects

Remember, this is not a subjective determination. (See Figure 4.30.) It can only be done with reference to verified system benchmarks of performance: the goal, critical success factors, and key necessary conditions of the system you defined in Step 1. An Intermediate Objectives Map (see Chapter 3) is required to do this, so if you don't already have a validated IO Map in hand for your target system, stop now and complete one.

---

* With few exceptions, scrutinizers will view most trees in draft form before they're rendered into digital form. Two or more people trying to read a handwritten tree on Post-it Notes need the 3"x3" size and bold writing to be able to see the content from distances of three feet or more.

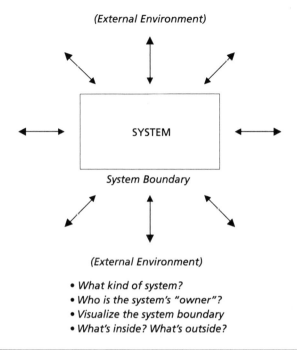

(External Environment)

SYSTEM

System Boundary

(External Environment)

- *What kind of system?*
- *Who is the system's "owner"?*
- *Visualize the system boundary*
- *What's inside? What's outside?*

Figure 4.29   Step 1: Define the system to be modeled.

Compare Reality with Benchmarks of System Success

With the assurance that you know what the system's goal, critical success factors, and necessary conditions are, start comparing these elements one by one with what you know *and can document* (by measurement, testimony, or some other verifiable evidence) is currently happening in your system.

It may be that there are absolutely no deviations at all between current reality and some of these system benchmarks. In that case, the particular critical success factor or necessary condition should not prompt an undesirable effect. If you follow the guidance in Chapter 3 for constructing an IO Map, you're likely to have no more than three to five critical success factors in your system. (Okay, maybe six or seven, but if you have more than five you should be questioning whether one of them is really a necessary condition supporting another CSF.) You may have deviations you can articulate as UDEs with all CSFs. Or maybe just one. Only the actual situation can dictate how many UDEs you'll identify. But you can be sure that you're never likely to see more than about five to seven UDEs form the top of your CRT, if you've done your preliminary work properly.

Create a Starting Matrix

The next part of Step 2 and the first part of Step 3 are more easily and quickly done on a sheet of paper from a tablet. The results can then be transferred to Post-it Notes afterward. Create a three-cell column for each UDE.

Now articulate the UDE—the deviation between reality and the benchmark from the IO Map—in a complete sentence. Write the UDEs in the top cell of each column and number them. When you've done this for all the system benchmarks (goal, CSFs, NCs), you're ready to move on to the next step: filling in the next two cells for each UDE.

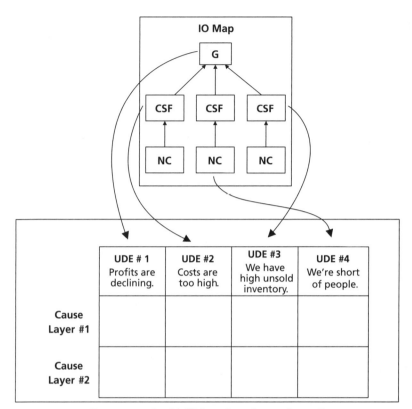

Create a matrix with UDEs and two layers of causality.
* Compare reality with the IO Map
* Create entities for all UDEs

Figure 4.30   Step 2: Determine the undesirable effects.

3. Determine the First Two Levels of Causality

The CRT will be constructed as a number of entity clusters culminating in an UDE. Once the clusters are complete, we'll connect them to form a unified tree. The beginnings of these clusters are the two layers of causality immediately leading to the UDE. (See Figure 4.31.)

Working from one side to the other, one matrix column at a time, articulate the immediately preceding cause of the UDE. Don't "dive down" too deeply (that is, multiple levels of causation). Instead, "peel the onion" one layer at a time. In the first causal layer, write the cause that leads directly and unavoidably to the UDE—no intermediate steps left out. Write this cause in a complete sentence in the matrix cell just below its respective UDE.

Go to the second layer of causality and do the same thing. Write the second-level cause that leads directly and unavoidably to the first-level cause. Write it in a complete sentence in the next matrix cell down. Repeat these actions for all UDEs.

Transfer UDEs and Causes to Post-it Notes

When the matrix is completely filled in, transcribe the UDEs and causes from each layer onto Post-it Notes. Distinguish the UDEs by using different-colored Post-it Notes or by drawing a prominent star (★ or ✱). Number the UDEs, starting with "1."

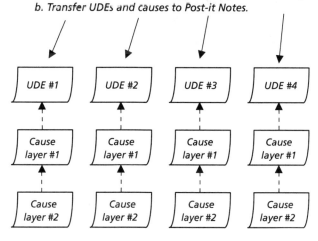

	UDE # 1 Profits are declining.	UDE #2 Costs are too high.	UDE #3 We have high unsold inventory.	UDE #4 We're short of people.
Cause Layer #1	Revenues are too low.	Costs have increased.	Demand and supply are mismatched.	We lose good people.
Cause Layer #2	Sales have dropped.	Fuel prices are up.	Forecasts are wrong.	Job security is threatened.

a. Create a matrix with UDEs and two layers of causality.
b. Transfer UDEs and causes to Post-it Notes.

UDE #1	UDE #2	UDE #3	UDE #4
Cause layer #1	Cause layer #1	Cause layer #1	Cause layer #1
Cause layer #2	Cause layer #2	Cause layer #2	Cause layer #2

Figure 4.31 Step 3: Determine the first two levels of causality.

4. Begin the Current Reality Tree

Affix the Post-it Notes you created in Step 3 onto the flip-chart paper. Lay out the UDE Post-it Notes in a horizontal line near the top of your flip-chart paper, allowing a generous amount of space between each one. Place the two causal layers directly below them, in the same relative position as they were in the matrix (see Figure 4.32). Connect the three levels of entity for each UDE with dotted-line arrows (to signify the conditional nature of the connection).

5. Improve the Logic of the Initial Clusters

Working on each cluster individually, examine the logical relationship between each layer of causality leading to the UDE. Use the Categories of Legitimate Reservation (CLR) to verify and improve each vertical connection (see figure 4.33).

- Clarity: Is the meaning of each statement clear and unambiguous?

- Entity existence: Is each statement a complete sentence, without embedded "if-then" relationships or compound ideas? Is each statement verifiable by some tangible evidence or testimony?

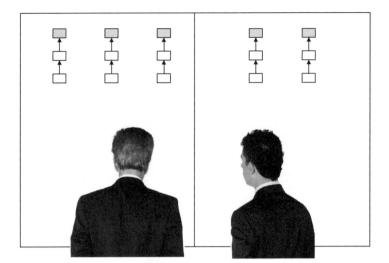

- *Transfer UDEs and first two layers of causes to Post-it Notes*
- *Arrange in vertical columns on flip-chart paper near the top*
- *Allow generous lateral space between columns*

Figure 4.32 Step 4: Begin the Current Reality Tree.

- Causality existence: Does the lowest level cause directly and unavoidably (that is, no intervening steps missing) produce the next level of effect? Does that next level of cause directly and unavoidably produce the UDE? If the answer is no, develop the missing intervening effect/cause entities, write them on Post-it Notes, and insert them where they belong.

- Cause sufficiency: Are the causes, as stated, enough by themselves to produce the stated effect? Are they dependent on some other unstated contributing cause? If so, develop that contributing cause on a Post-it Note, place it beside the other contributing cause, and connect it to the effect. Enclose the causal arrows with an ellipse.

NOTE: Bear in mind that there may be more than one contributing cause.
Unstated key assumptions might also be included as stated entities.

When the logic of all the original clusters is properly solidified, look across the entire arrangement thus far. See if you can identify two clusters that seem to be closely related to one another. For example, clusters on manufacturing production and inventory control would constitute such a pair. When you find such related clusters, move their Post-it Notes, if necessary, to place them beside one another.

The reason for doing this is simple: Since all these clusters are part of the same interdependent system, at some point they'll all end up being connected in a single tree. (These logical structures are called "trees" for a reason.)

As with the shape of a real tree, various branches will converge into a root system at some point (see Figure 4.34). As with real trees, these convergence points are likely to be several more layers of causality downward toward the root. Positioning related clusters together will make it easier to connect converging branches without having visually confusing "cross-over" lines.

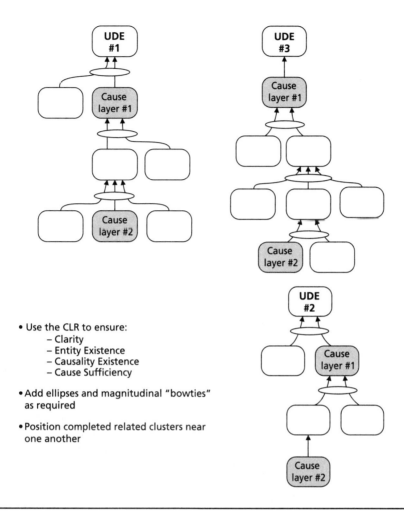

Figure 4.33   Step 5: Improve the logic of the initial clusters.

6. Identify Possible Additional Causes

Our intuitive knowledge of our systems naturally causes us to presume that certain causes, with which we may already be familiar, drive the effects we see around us. In many cases—maybe even most of the time—our intuition is correct, but not always. Sometimes the visible effects we see around us result from different causes that we might overlook, or might have unconsciously discounted without even considering them. It's important for us to avoid this pitfall, and that's why the Additional Cause reservation is so important.

So at this point, before developing any of the clusters any further, we should ask ourselves: "Beside this particular cause, what else could independently produce this same effect?"

For example, let's say we're trying to determine why an ornamental plant in our front yard seems to be turning brown (dying). Based on our experience with other plants, we tend to presume that it isn't getting enough water. But when we investigate closely, we find that there's no shortage of water, fertilizer, or sunlight. Instead, we see the telltale holes that indicate a mole or gopher has been feasting on the roots of the plant, causing it to die. The gopher represents an additional cause.

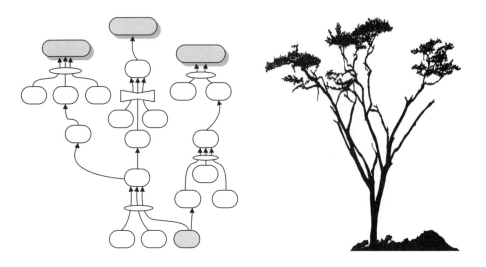

Branches of cause-and-effect logic trees converge toward the roots, much like *real* trees.

Figure 4.34 Logic trees are like real trees (convergence).

Two Criteria for Additional Causes

In Chapter 2, "Categories of Legitimate Reservation," we learned that there are two criteria a proposed cause must meet to be considered a legitimate additional cause. It must be *realistic* and it must be *probable*. Realistic means that if the cause were to happen, it would have the "horsepower" to actually produce the effect. Probable means that the likelihood of that cause occurring is not insignificant. An independent cause of the same effect that is both realistic and probable should be included in the tree.

If you are able to identify a legitimate additional cause, write it on a Post-It note and connect it to the existing cluster (see Figure 4.35).

Take note of a couple of characteristics of the additional cause situation shown in Figure 4.35. Notice first that there are two key assumptions indicated near the causes.

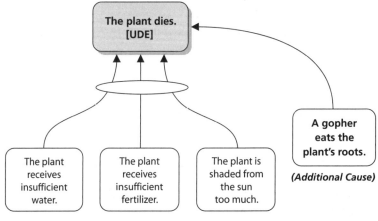

Figure 4.35 Step 6: Identify possible additional causes.

These are clearly "oxygen" to the causality, as discussed in Chapter 2, "The Categories of Legitimate Reservation." They were considered important enough to be included with the tree, but not in the depiction of the logic. With the inclusion of these normally unspoken assumptions, any ambiguity concerning the biology of plant growth is eliminated, yet the tree itself is not made more complicated by the inclusion of additional entities and connections.

Second, notice that there is no magnitudinal relationship here (that is, no "MAG" bowtie symbol used). The effect is not magnitudinal in nature. Life or death of the plant is a "zero-or-one" condition. As stated, it's either living or it's dying. Including the gophers in a magnitudinal relationship with the other causes does not make the plant any more dead.

Work your way though each level of causality in each cluster. Look at the effects, and ask yourself: "Beside these stated causes, what else could independently produce the same effect?" In many cases, you won't be able to think of anything. If not, press on. If you *do* think of an additional cause, however, apply the realistic-and-probable test (see Figure 4.36). Review Chapter 2, "The Categories of Legitimate Reservation," if necessary.

7. Look for Lateral Connections

When your first clusters are thoroughly checked for clarity, entity existence, sufficiency and additional causes, examine the causes and effects among all the clusters for possible lateral connections. A lateral connection is a cause in one cluster that leads to an effect in another cluster.

In some cases, such connections will "jump right out at you." In other words, an existing entity in one cluster connects directly as a cause of an effect in an adjacent cluster. At other times, you will see an entity that will eventually connect to another cluster, but some intermediate effects must be developed first (see Figure 4.37). Draw connecting causality arrows between the entities in the two clusters, from cause to effect. Use the CLR to perfect the logic (refer to Step 5). Reposition or rearrange cluster as required to simplify the visual presentation and eliminate as many "cross-overs" (causal arrows that cross one another) as possible.

Though we put related clusters nearby one another, keep in mind that it's possible for connections to occur between clusters that don't seem related to each other. For this reason, you must check all clusters for lateral connections. If you don't find any, don't be surprised. You will, eventually, because all the clusters in the tree are different aspects of the same integrated system. You'll just need to dig deeper to find them.

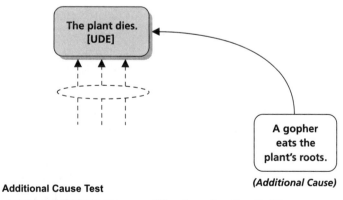

Additional Cause Test
• Is it REALISTIC? (If it happens, will it really produce the effect?)
• Is it PROBABLE? (Is it a remote possibility or a likely occurrence?)

Figure 4.36 Verify possible additional causes.

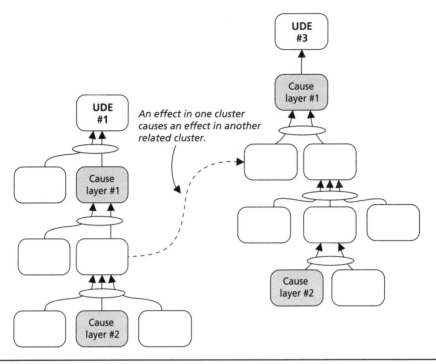

Figure 4.37 Step 7: Look for lateral connections.

8. Build the Cause-and-Effect Chains Downward

Each UDE and its supporting cluster constitute the top of a "branch" in your Current Reality Tree. Your objective is to trace the cause-and-effect chain downward in each branch until all the branches converge at a very few common, critical root causes (see Figure 4.38). Choose one branch and start building downward. Then do the same for the other branches. Use the same prescriptions we discussed in Steps 5 and 6. To construct each successive level, answer the following questions for each cluster:

- Why does your lowermost entity exist? The "because ..." that answers this question will be the next lower cause in each branch.

- What is the direct and unavoidable cause of your lowermost entity? This answer should be the same as the "because..." for the preceding question. If it's not, keep looking for an appropriate "because... ."

- Is that the only cause? Could something else cause or contribute to the same effect (the lowermost entity)? Hint: You're continually looking for additional causes here.

- Are there negative reinforcing loops in your tree? Remember the International Harvester example (Figure 4.27)? Examine each UDE and, using the CLR, determine whether it might possibly reinforce or amplify an entity at a lower level in the tree. If you find such situations, depict the loop in the CRT by drawing an arrow from the UDE back down to the entity it reinforces. It may be necessary for you to insert an intermediate entity or two between the UDE and the reentry point.

As you add each successive lower layer of cause, compare that new cause with the lower levels in adjacent clusters. In other words, as you build each layer downward, look for opportunities to cross-connect.

Repeat this process until you've achieved two objectives:

- You reach the lowest level of causation that you or someone within your sphere of influence has the authority to change, and

- All clusters are cross-connected into a single, logically sound tree.

Your finished tree should look like Figure 4.38.

9. Scrutinize the Entire Current Reality Tree

Now that the tree is complete, at least for the first pass, it must be "scrutinized" in its entirety. For our purposes, scrutiny means more than just to "look carefully" at it. In the domain of logic trees, scrutinizing is a distinct, formal process of evaluating the tree against three terminal criteria:

- Is it complete? Are all the important UDEs and critical root causes of them included?

- Is the logic "tight," meaning is each connection sufficient?

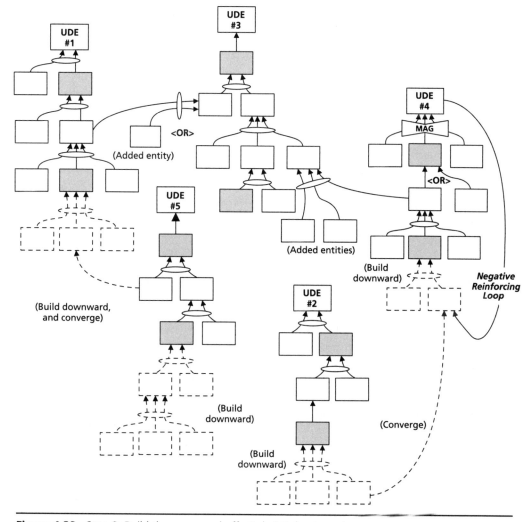

Figure 4.38 Step 8: Build the cause-and-effect chains downward.

- Is the tree, in its entirety, an accurate reflection of reality as people in the system perceive it? If you showed it to others involved in the system, would they agree that it's an accurate picture of what's happening?

It's at this point that you get to actually test the last of the preceding bulleted questions. When you think that your CRT is as good as you can possibly make it, it's time to show it to others and solicit their scrutiny of its details. It isn't necessary for outside scrutinizers to understand the Categories of Legitimate Reservation, though that can be helpful. It *is* necessary, however, that they be intimately familiar with the subject matter of the CRT. You need scrutinizers who can tell you when your tree's Entity Existence and Causality Existence are questionable, and only those familiar with the system can do that.

These outsiders will naturally advise you when your logic seems lacking, though you won't hear such terms from them as "causality existence reservation" or "cause insufficiency." Instead, as they "talk around" what they perceive as deficiencies, you'll recognize the words that characterize one or more of the formal reservation categories.* Especially if you are preparing a CRT for a higher decision maker, or in any other career-critical situation, *external scrutiny of your work is essential.*

10. Decide Which Root Causes to Attack

Now it's time for the fun part: deciding where to focus your improvement efforts to realize the most "bang for your buck." The whole concept of constraint management is intended to help you find those few factors that exercise the most impact on your system. In the case of the CRT, this impact is negative, which means that turning those negatives into positives requires doing something about those critical root causes that account for all the UDEs. As you will notice when you're working on your own systems, some of those root causes will lie within your span of control—you have unilateral change authority over them.

More likely, however, the critical root causes will be within authority of someone else to change, often a senior decision maker. Once you have a finished CRT (see Figure 4.39), you'll need to decide if you can change a particular critical root cause directly or whether you'll need the help of someone with more "horsepower." (Refer to "Span of Control and Sphere of Influence," earlier in this chapter.) One way to make this determination is to scribe a perimeter on your CRT that defines your span of control.** Then examine all the entities in your tree and decide which ones you can influence, either directly or by persuading others to do so for you. Scribe another perimeter line around those entities, too (see Figure 4.39). Maybe make it a dotted line.

Any entities that lie outside your sphere of influence are ones that you will likely have to live with because you can't cause them to be changed. This is why it is *so* crucial to reflect sufficiency (that is, all contributing causes, even if they're static conditions) in your CRT, especially at the root cause level. The mere presence of two or more causal arrows passing through an ellipse provides you with multiple options for modifying actual causation. One of those causes is likely to lie within your sphere of influence. Thus, sufficiency in a CRT helps you focus your efforts on things that you can change, bypassing things that you can't. Your effectiveness multiplies geometrically when you do that.

---

* This is why it's essential for you to understand the Categories of Legitimate Reservation completely.

**It may be that your span of control on a particular CRT is so small that it can't even be depicted. In this case, you'll have to work exclusively within your sphere of influence.

Have you ever heard of "the serenity prayer?" *God, grant me serenity to accept the things I cannot change, the courage to change the things I can, and the wisdom to know the difference.* Well, the CRT may not provide you serenity, but it can certainly help you differentiate the things you can do from those you can't and give you the wisdom to know the difference. Before we move on to another topic, let me leave you with this thought:

> *Your success or failure in accomplishing what you want in life is, in the final analysis, a game. And the name of the game is "How far am I willing to push the limits of my sphere of influence?"*

If you think you can do it, you *may* be right. If you think you *can't* do it, you'll *always* be right.

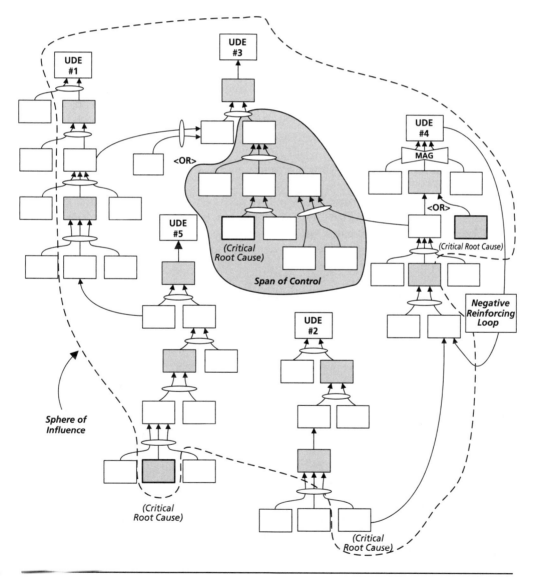

Figure 4.39 The finished Current Reality Tree.

Figure 4.45 at the end of this chapter is an abbreviated illustrated checklist you can use when you construct your own CRT. Figure 4.46, immediately following the abbreviated checklist, is an example of a real-world CRT.

> *Be thankful for your problems. If they were less difficult, someone with less ability might have your job.*
>
> —Unknown

SCRUTINIZING THE CURRENT REALITY TREE

We've discussed scrutiny of logic trees in Chapter 2, "The Categories of Legitimate Reservation," and again earlier in this chapter, "The Most Common Logical Errors in a Sufficiency Tree." This is the penultimate step in the process of building a Current Reality Tree, and it's perhaps the most critical because it's your final "safety net"—the one that will save you from embarrassing fatal credibility errors when it comes time to use your work to persuade decision makers to act the way your analysis indicates that they should. So there are a few other topics we need to cover concerning Current Reality Trees before we move on to the next tool.

Scrutinizing is the process of critically examining a logic tree and strengthening it as much as possible. It involves locating and eliminating weaknesses in logic at any point in the tree. As you've probably noticed, you do a lot of scrutinizing during the building process—so much, in fact, that you may have to force yourself go back over it again after it's completed.

Moreover, we are all blind to our own mistakes. Despite your best efforts, while your tree looks "just right" to you, it will undoubtedly have sufficiency and additional cause errors, at the very least. No matter how many times you go over the tree, you probably will see right through them. That's why it's important to have someone else look at your tree. Clearly, if you plan to present the tree to someone else for the purpose of persuading him or her to do something, it's absolutely critical to have an independent set of eyes review it for you.

The Categories of Legitimate Reservation

As we mentioned earlier, outside scrutinizers need not be well versed in the Categories of Legitimate Reservation (CLR), though it certainly helps if they are. All that's really necessary for effective scrutiny of a Current Reality Tree is that the person have intuitive knowledge of the tree's subject matter. As long as you understand the CLR, you'll be able to translate questions and comments into reservations from one of the eight categories.

You can expect the majority of reservations expressed by external scrutinizers to fall into the categories discussed earlier in "Most Common Logical Errors in a Sufficiency Tree." It's worth reviewing those just before you begin outside scrutiny.

Techniques for "Shortstopping" Logical Challenges

You can take some preventive steps to eliminate characteristics in your logic trees that might invite challenge. These fall under the heading of techniques, rather than procedures, because they're more a matter of personal style and execution than prescriptive steps. The first of these techniques involves wording entities in such a way that they don't invite unwarranted dispute.

When "All" or "None" Are Not Acceptable

Consider this statement: "People are naturally paranoid." Would you agree with it if somebody else said it? It's strongly inclusive. Without any qualifying adjectives, it implies that everybody is paranoid. What about you? Are you paranoid? If not, you might take exception with such an inclusive statement: "I think that's wrong. Not everybody is paranoid."

What if the person who made that statement had, instead, said: "Some people are naturally paranoid." Could you agree with that? Most of us probably could. What's the difference between the one you might accept and the one you'd contest? Clearly, it's the presence of the word "some." It's a "qualifier."

Inclusive and Exclusive

In this world, very little is all "black" or all "white," except maybe for two colors of paint. This means that in building logic trees, we must consider the possibility that our statements may not be valid if they're completely inclusive or exclusive. We may have to qualify our statements, especially if we intend to present our trees to others. Otherwise, we risk compromising our own credibility.

Qualifying Words

Qualifying words can save our credibility. Words like "some," "many," "most," "few," and "a majority" acknowledge the fact that very few situations are "all or none." But how do you know which to use, and when? The scale in Figure 4.40 provides a possible benchmark. Consider it a starting point. You may choose to redesign it, or modify it in any way you like. Its sole function is to permit you to evaluate your situation and put some kind of logical limit on your statement, a limit that will make it more acceptable to the average reader.

For example, if you think that 10 percent of people or fewer (but more than zero) are paranoid, you might say, "a few people are naturally paranoid." If you think the number

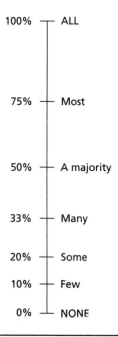

Figure 4.40 All or none: a sliding scale.

is closer to 25 percent, you might say, "Some people are naturally paranoid." If you think that 45 percent of the population likes baseball, you might say, "Many people like baseball." If you think that 60 percent are displeased with a baseball strike, it might translate to "A majority of fans oppose the strike."

Once you get above 75 percent, you might be safe in saying that "Most fans oppose the strike." (Technically, 51 percent or more could constitute "most." You're free to establish your own thresholds for each of these qualifiers, but you should consider using them to add credibility to your logic.)

Once you've decided how to qualify a statement that will be an entity in your tree, you must decide how the combination of two or more "qualified" statements will play out in the effect. Are "some" and "some" sufficient to produce "many"? Will "many" and "some" produce "a majority"? How about "many" and "many"—will they give you "most"? Figure 4.41 shows some possible combinations and their proposed effects. You'll undoubtedly be able to think of others. Experiment with "qualifiers" until you're certain the logic of your cause-and-effect connections is as tight as you can make it.

Too Many Arrows?

A common error in sufficiency trees is too many arrows passing through an ellipse between cause and effect. This normally results when a tree builder fails to question whether some of them might be additional causes rather than contributing sufficient causes.

A simple way to avoid this pitfall is to use the number 3 as a starting benchmark. Although there are situations in which a causal connection may have more than three arrows, these are rare. So if you are tempted to run four or more arrows through an ellipse to an effect, consider that a "warning flag." Evaluate the proposed connections for sufficiency and additional cause.

One way to do this is to cover up each cause and its arrow in turn and ask yourself, "Are the remaining causes sufficient to produce the effect?" If the answer is "yes," then the one you've covered up is likely to be an additional cause. If not, then it belongs with the ellipse. If you have more than four arrows passing through an ellipse, you should

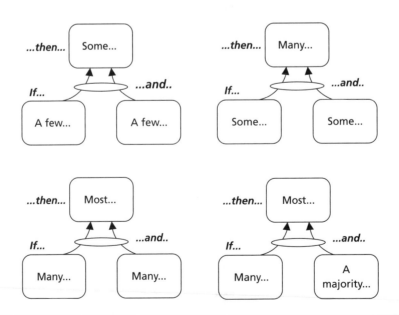

Figure 4.41 Combining "qualifiers" in effects.

assume that you've embedded an additional cause in the ellipse somewhere and start evaluating each cause individually to determine whether one or more might stand alone.

Simple Logical Aid #1: Means, Method, and Motivation

A couple of simple aids can help you avoid the too-many-arrows problem by constructing logically sound causal connections in the first place. The first of these is to consider means, method, and motivation. This concept isn't exactly new—it originated with Aristotle.*

Aristotle suggested that observed effects are the result of three equally important causal factors:

- Means (resources)

- Method (a way to act)

- Motivation (the desire or determination to act)

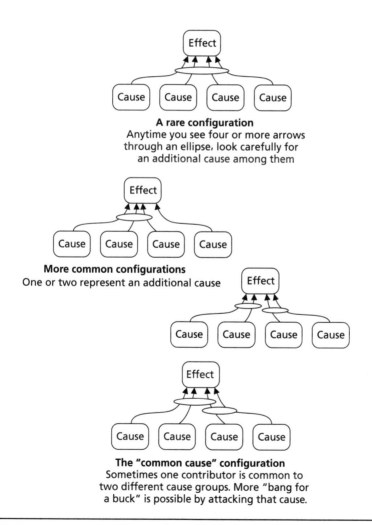

A rare configuration
Anytime you see four or more arrows through an ellipse, look carefully for an additional cause among them

More common configurations
One or two represent an additional cause

The "common cause" configuration
Sometimes one contributor is common to two different cause groups. More "bang for a buck" is possible by attacking that cause.

Figure 4.42   Too many arrows? Other possible configurations.

---

* I'm indebted to Dr. Mel Anderson for introducing me to this useful concept.

It's fairly easy to read each cause entity and determine whether one of these causal factors is represented. Figure 4.43 shows a simple example. Keep in mind that in the real world, things may not be quite as clear cut as this particular example. Means and method can be inherent in the same cause. In that case, there would probably be only two arrows indicated. It may not be possible to apply means-method-motivation in all cases, but when you can, it can provide insurance that you'll have sufficiency without too many arrows.

Simple Logical Aid #2: The Syllogism

The syllogism also originated with Aristotle and it's a useful tool to ensure that you have the right number of arrows without including too many. Syllogisms are the quintessential expression of deductive logic, which is the foundation of the entire Thinking Process.

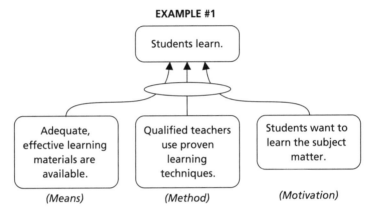

Assumption #1: Students have no disability that would preclude effective learning.
Assumption#2: Materials and techniques are available to accommodate learning-disabled students.

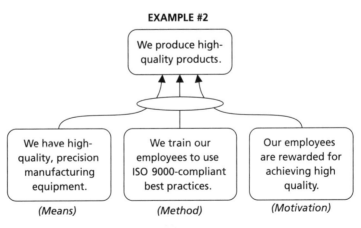

Assumption: Other policies and practices don't degrade equipment or methods.

Figure 4.43 Means, method, and motivation.

A syllogism is composed of three parts: a major premise, a minor premise, and a conclusion. Here's an example:

MAJOR PREMISE: Hare Krishna men shave their heads.

MINOR PREMISE: John is a Hare Krishna.

CONCLUSION: John's head is shaved.

Here's how that looks in a sufficiency relationship (bottom part of Figure 4.44).

From our discussion of entity existence in Chapter 2, we know that each entity must be expressed in a complete sentence. Although a subject and a verb are often enough to comprise a complete, valid sentence, more often we see a subject, verb, and object. For the purposes of this discussion, let's assume that an effect and the two causes that produce it (the upper part of Figure 4.44) each have a subject, verb, and object.

Now if we look at the syllogism (the bottom part of Figure 4.44), we see that the major premise, the minor premise, and the conclusion also have subjects, verbs, and objects. For a causal connection to be valid and sufficient, *we must be able to find evidence of the subject, the verb, or the object from each contributing cause somewhere in the effect* **and** *a common link with at least one other contributing cause.*

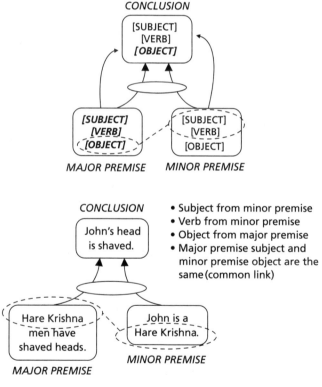

- Look for evidence of the major premise in either the subject, verb, or object of the conclusion

- Look for a common link between the major premise and the minor premise

- Any entity not providing either of the subject-verb-object or the common link is probably superfluous to this connection

Figure 4.44 The syllogism.

If you find a cause (or are contemplating including one within a sufficiency ellipse) that does not provide part of the subject, verb, or object of the effect and doesn't link with one of the other causes, then it must be considered a possible additional cause of the effect, separate from the ellipsed contributors and evaluated using the CLR independently.

USING THE CRT WITH OTHER PARTS OF THE THINKING PROCESS

The Current Reality Tree is a superb tool by itself. It becomes invaluable when used in concert with other parts of the TOC Thinking Process. The times when you'll use it in isolation are likely to be few. After all, what good does it do you to identify critical root causes if you're not going to move ahead and do something about them? While the other logical tools have great utility by themselves as well, the Current Reality Tree is designed to lead into two other parts of the Thinking Process: the Evaporating Cloud and the Future Reality Tree.

The Current Reality Tree and the Evaporating Cloud

Why do critical root causes exist? If they're such a serious drag on a system's performance, you'd expect that someone would have stepped up and solved them before now. There are two possible reasons why this hasn't happened: a) The problem has gone unrecognized, or b) there is hidden conflict underlying the situation. If the problem hasn't been recognized, the very exposure of the root cause may be enough to prompt action to fix it: "We never realized that this was a problem before—now that we understand it, we can do something about it."

Frequently a critical root cause is perpetuated by some hidden conflict. This may not be as obvious as animosity between two people or organizations. It may be merely a conflict of interests. Sometimes those involved are tacitly aware of the conflict, but often they are not. However, the possibility of conflict should always be investigated before moving on to the solution stage. Failure to address hidden conflict will undermine any solution you might develop. The same "infection" will cause the patient (system) to relapse if the underlying conflict is not resolved. This is the function of the Evaporating Cloud, and in the next chapter we'll see how it helps us develop effective solutions to critical root causes.

The Current Reality Tree and the Future Reality Tree

Presuming that there is no underling conflict stalling the resolution of critical root cause or that any such conflicts have been resolved, at some point the time will come to start creating a new configuration of your system, one that will eliminate the UDEs you identified in your CRT. Creating that new configuration—the way you want the system to function in the ideal world—is the role of the Future Reality Tree (FRT).

However, the FRT is rarely a completely new creation. How many cases are you aware of in which the entire system, its structure, relationships, and functions, were thrown away in order to make a new start with a clean sheet of paper? It almost never happens.

What happens instead is some modification, sometimes rather significant, to an existing system that doesn't radically change its functional interactions. Since these unchanged interactions are usually captured to some degree in the CRT, it makes sense that the future configuration of the system is likely to conform to them, though the "polarity" of the outcomes will change from negative (in the CRT) to positive (in the FRT).

What this portends for the FRT is that a substantial portion of the CRT—many of the same or similar entities, causal connections, and sufficiencies—are likely to be transferable to the FRT. In other words, there will be significant parts of the wheel that won't have to be reinvented.

It's been said that a well-defined problem is more than half solved. The CRT represents that good definition of a problem, and failing to take advantage of that benefit by jumping directly to a Future Reality Tree not only risks solving the *wrong* problem, it risks taking longer than necessary to create the solution. The moral of this lesson is that CRTs and FRTs go hand in hand. The situations in which you would jump directly to a Future Reality Tree without first completing a CRT should be few and far between. In Chapter 6 we'll learn how to create FRTs.

Now take a look at the Current Reality Tree in Figure 4.46. It's the CRT of a start-up company. While the context of the company's situation and competitive environment are not provided, it still shows an accurate picture of the company's current reality (in 2002), and its logic is "tight." As such, it's a good example of what a CRT should look like.

SUMMARY

We've seen how a Current Reality Tree can help us find the hidden, underlying root causes that produce our system's problems—what to change in our system. Now it's time to start the second phase of problem solution: what to change to. The first part of that phase is the Evaporating Cloud—the subject of Chapter 5.

> *The greatest obstacle to discovering the shape of the earth, the continents, and the ocean was not ignorance but the illusion of knowledge.*
>
> —Daniel J. Boorstin, *The Discoverers*

1. Define the system to be modeled.
- Is it:
  - A person?
  - An organization?
  - A process?
  - A historical event?
- Create a clear mental image of what lies within the system and what lies in the external environment in which the system operates.

(External Environment)

SYSTEM

System Boundary

(External Environment)

2. Determine the Undesirable Effects (UDE).
- Construct an IO Map (if not already done).
- Identify the system performance benchmarks:
  - Goal
  - Critical Success Factors (CSF)
  - Necessary Conditions (NC)
- Assess current reality against each benchmark:
  - Is there a deviation?
  - If so, define and articulate it in a complete sentence.
- Write and number the deviation as an UDE on a uniquely-colored Post-it Note.
- Arrange the UDEs horizontally on the workspace.

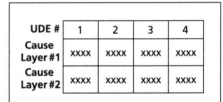

3. Determine the Two Preceding Layers of Causes.
- On a tablet, create a two-layer matrix of causes for each UDE:
  - Determine the two preceding causes of each UDE.
  - Enter these as complete sentences in the appropriate block of the matrix.
- When the matrix is completely filled, transfer the causal statements to Post-it Notes.
- Position the causal Post-it Notes directly beneath their respective UDEs.
- Connect the three entities vertically with dotted-line arrows.

UDE #	1	2	3	4
Cause Layer #1	xxxx	xxxx	xxxx	xxxx
Cause Layer #2	xxxx	xxxx	xxxx	xxxx

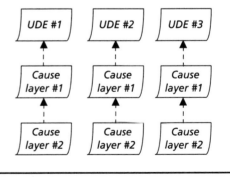

Figure 4.45 Procedures for constructing a Current Reality Tree (CRT) – abbreviated checklist.

(Continued)

(Continued)

4. Begin the Current Reality Tree.
- Transfer the Post-it Notes you created in Step-3 to a large sheet of paper.
- Arrange the Post-it Notes with the UDEs at the top, the FIRST causal layer below them, and the second causal layer below that layer.
- Retain the same relative position as in the matrix.
- Connect causal layers with a single dotted-line arrow.
- Allow adequate lateral space between clusters.

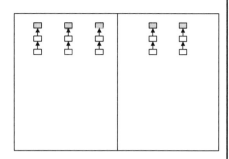

5. Improve the Logic of the Initial Clusters
- Use the CLR to evaluate and perfect each connection in each cluster:
  - Clarity
  - Entity Existence
  - Causality Existence
  - Cause Insufficiency
- Add entities, arrows, and ellipses where required.
- Stop only when you are sure the logic of each cluster individually is "tight."
- Reposition as required to place related clusters beside each other.

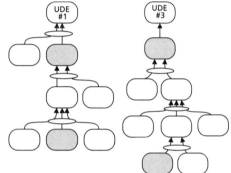

6. Identify Possible Additional Causes.
- Look for other independent causes of the same observed effect.
- Any proposed additional cause must be:
  - REALISTIC
  - PROBABLE
- Write the additional cause on a Post-it Note.
- Place it in the tree and connect it to the appropriate effect.

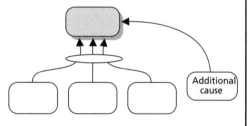

(Continued)

7. Look for lateral connections.
- Identify causes in one cluster that produce effects in another.
- Examine first the related clusters (Step 5) related to one another (but don't ignore other clusters as well).
- Connect the causes to their effects with causality arrows.
- Refine the logic of the new connections (refer to Step-5).
- Re-position the clusters as necessary to eliminate as much as possible arrows that cross over one another.

8. Build the Cause-and-Effect Chain Downward.
- Extend the cause-and-effect of each cluster downward:
  - Continue by asking "why?" for each lowermost cause.
  - With each new layer of cause, look for lateral connections with other clusters.
  - As you add each new layer, look also for new additional causes.
  - Look for negative reinforcing loops, label them where they occur.
- Stop:
  - When you reach the lowest level of cause that is within a decision maker's sphere of influence to change.
  - When all clusters have converged into a single tree.

9. Scrutinize the Entire Current Reality Tree.
- Examine the tree in its entirety:
  - Is it complete? (Are all the important UDEs and critical root causes included?)
  - Is the logic of each connection sufficient?
  - Will it make sense (that is, achieve consensus) for those who did not participate in building the tree?
    - Enlist the aid of others who were not part of the construction process to scrutinize the tree.
    - Their knowledge of the CLR is not required, only subject matter knowledge of the situation.

(Continued)

10. Decide Which Root Causes to Attack.
- Identify critical root causes (those few causes that account for *all* the UDEs):
  - Trace the chain of dependency from each root cause to each UDE.
  - Determine which root causes are within your sphere of influence.
  - Identify the ones that offer the most potential for improvement as *critical root causes.*

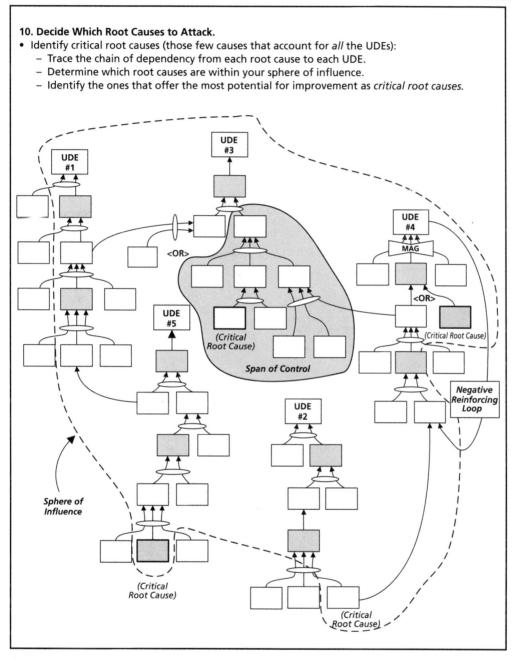

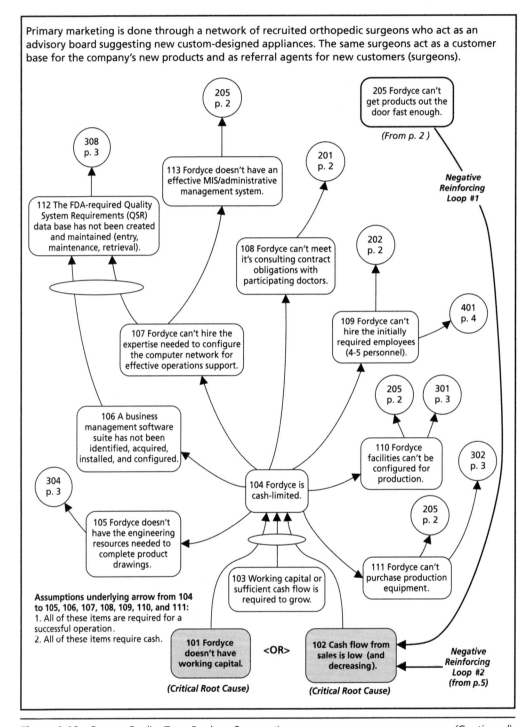

Primary marketing is done through a network of recruited orthopedic surgeons who act as an advisory board suggesting new custom-designed appliances. The same surgeons act as a customer base for the company's new products and as referral agents for new customers (surgeons).

205 p. 2

308 p. 3

205 Fordyce can't get products out the door fast enough.

(From p. 2)

Negative Reinforcing Loop #1

113 Fordyce doesn't have an effective MIS/administrative management system.

201 p. 2

112 The FDA-required Quality System Requirements (QSR) data base has not been created and maintained (entry, maintenance, retrieval).

108 Fordyce can't meet it's consulting contract obligations with participating doctors.

202 p. 2

107 Fordyce can't hire the expertise needed to configure the computer network for effective operations support.

109 Fordyce can't hire the initially required employees (4-5 personnel).

401 p. 4

106 A business management software suite has not been identified, acquired, installed, and configured.

205 p. 2

301 p. 3

110 Fordyce facilities can't be configured for production.

302 p. 3

304 p. 3

104 Fordyce is cash-limited.

205 p. 2

105 Fordyce doesn't have the engineering resources needed to complete product drawings.

111 Fordyce can't purchase production equipment.

Assumptions underlying arrow from 104 to 105, 106, 107, 108, 109, 110, and 111:
1. All of these items are required for a successful operation.
2. All of these items require cash.

103 Working capital or sufficient cash flow is required to grow.

101 Fordyce doesn't have working capital.

<OR>

102 Cash flow from sales is low (and decreasing).

Negative Reinforcing Loop #2 (from p.5)

(Critical Root Cause)

(Critical Root Cause)

Figure 4.46   Current Reality Tree: Fordyce Corporation.   *(Continued)*

(Continued)

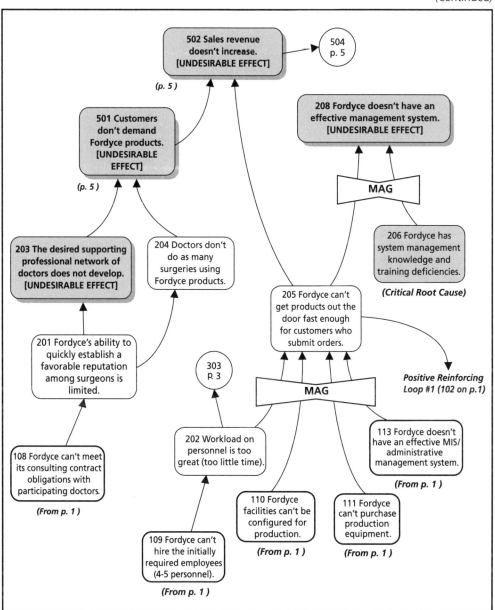

(Continued)

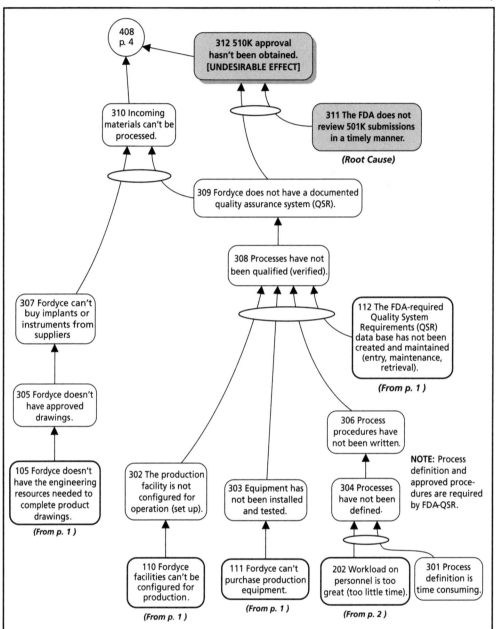

(Continued)

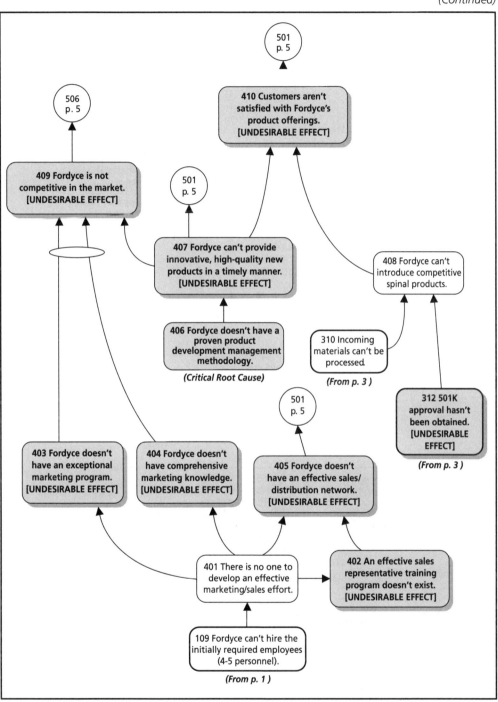

501
p. 5

506
p. 5

410 Customers aren't satisfied with Fordyce's product offerings. [UNDESIRABLE EFFECT]

409 Fordyce is not competitive in the market. [UNDESIRABLE EFFECT]

501
p. 5

407 Fordyce can't provide innovative, high-quality new products in a timely manner. [UNDESIRABLE EFFECT]

408 Fordyce can't introduce competitive spinal products.

406 Fordyce doesn't have a proven product development management methodology.

(Critical Root Cause)

310 Incoming materials can't be processed.

(From p. 3)

501
p. 5

312 501K approval hasn't been obtained. [UNDESIRABLE EFFECT]

(From p. 3)

403 Fordyce doesn't have an exceptional marketing program. [UNDESIRABLE EFFECT]

404 Fordyce doesn't have comprehensive marketing knowledge. [UNDESIRABLE EFFECT]

405 Fordyce doesn't have an effective sales/distribution network. [UNDESIRABLE EFFECT]

401 There is no one to develop an effective marketing/sales effort.

402 An effective sales representative training program doesn't exist. [UNDESIRABLE EFFECT]

109 Fordyce can't hire the initially required employees (4-5 personnel).

(From p. 1)

(Continued)

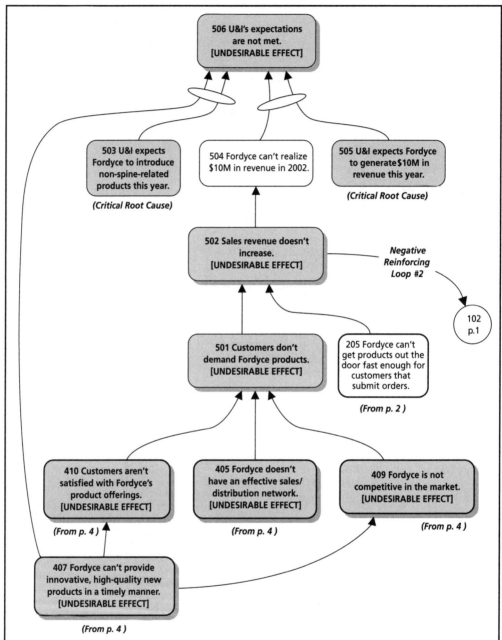

(Continued)

No.	Subject	Type	Possible Disposition
101	Fordyce doesn't have working capital.	CRITICAL ROOT CAUSE	Resolve in Future Reality Tree.
102	Cash flow from sales is low (and decreasing).	CRITICAL ROOT CAUSE	"OR" condition with 101. Evaluate which to work on in Future Reality Tree.
206	Fordyce has system management knowledge and training deficiencies.	CRITICAL ROOT CAUSE	Resolve in Future Reality Tree.
311	The FDA does not review 501K submissions in a timely manner.	CRITICAL ROOT CAUSE	Federal government issue; probably outside sphere of influence.
406	Fordyce doesn't have a proven product development management methodology.	CRITICAL ROOT CAUSE	Resolve in Future Reality Tree.
503	U&I expects Fordyce to introduce non-spine-related products this year.	CRITICAL ROOT CAUSE	"AND" condition, but requires short-term relief; Future Reality Reality Tree can't possibly resolve systemic issues within U&I-mandated time horizon.
505	U&I expects Fordyce to generate $10M in revenue this year.	CRITICAL ROOT CAUSE	"AND" condition, but requires short-term relief; Future Reality Tree can't possibly resolve systemic issues within U&I-mandated time horizon.

ENDNOTES

1. http://en.wikipedia.org/wiki/Big_Dig
2. http://www.sover.net/~devstar/define.htm
3. University of Southern California. *Trojan Family Magazine*, Spring 2001, p.36

5
Evaporating Cloud

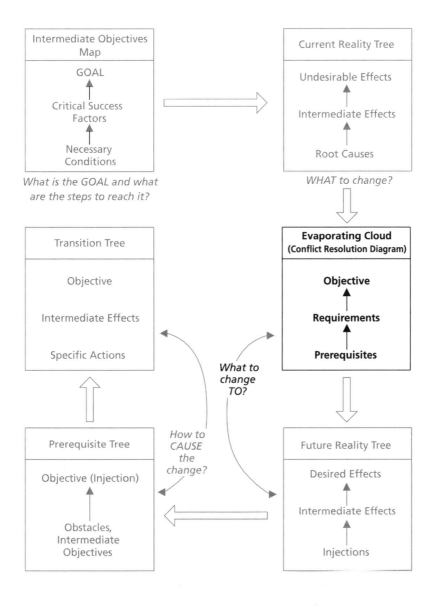

Just as most issues are seldom black or white, so are most good solutions neither black nor white. Beware of the solution that requires one side to be totally the loser and the other side to be totally the winner. The reason there are two sides to begin with usually is because neither side has all the facts.

—Stephen R. Schwambach

Why do root causes of undesirable effects (UDE) exist? Often it's because some hidden conflict stagnates or thwarts efforts to change the status quo. This isn't always the case, but it happens frequently enough to justify a concerted effort to search for an underlying conflict that might be perpetuating a particularly persistent problem.

Like root causes in a Current Reality Tree, conflict is not always obvious. In most complex situations, it's usually insidious. So how can we determine if some hidden conflict is the culprit? How can we "ferret out" the contending elements that keep us from a prompt solution to our problem? The Thinking Process provides an ingenious tool for resolving conflict in a way that leaves both sides "winners"—the Evaporating Cloud, often referred to as a conflict resolution diagram (CRD).

DEFINITION

Goldratt named this tool an Evaporating Cloud (EC) because of its capacity to "evaporate" conflict. It's a *necessary condition* structure designed to identify and display the important elements of a conflict situation and open people's minds to ways to resolve it. The diagram includes the system objective, necessary-but-not-sufficient requirements that lead to it, and the conflicting prerequisites that satisfy them (see Figure 5.1).

Conflict is generally rooted in the hidden, underlying assumptions operating on each side. The EC helps to reveal such assumptions that, though accepted as valid, are actually questionable and subject to invalidation. If this can be done, the conflict can often be rendered moot. The EC opens the playing field to ideas that can be converted into solutions to complex problems.

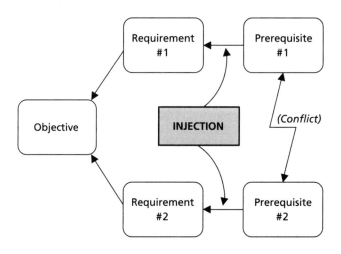

Figure 5.1   The Evaporating Cloud (conflict resolution diagram).

PURPOSE

The Evaporating Cloud is intended to achieve the following purposes:

- Confirm that conflict actually exists
- Identify and articulate the conflict perpetuating a major problem
- Identify all assumptions underlying problems and conflicting relationships
- Resolve conflict
- Avoid compromise
- Create solutions in which both sides win
- Create new, "breakthrough" solutions to problems
- Explain in depth why a problem exists

ASSUMPTIONS

The effectiveness of the Evaporating Cloud is based on the following assumptions:

- Problems exist because influential, competing forces perpetuate them.
- Competition at some point becomes conflict.
- Conflict within a system is an indication of suboptimization.
- Conflict is not always visible, obvious, or overtly confrontational.
- Accomplishing a system goal usually means satisfying more than one underlying requirement, each of which is necessary but not sufficient alone. By definition, these necessary conditions cannot be in conflict with one another.
- Underlying requirements are driven by prerequisites, which is the real level at which conflict usually occurs.
- Conflicting forces can exist at several levels, both functionally and organizationally.
- Conflicts may originate from either policies or from human relationships.
- Conflict results from one or more underlying invalid or no-longer-relevant assumptions.
- Assumptions underlying conflict can be identified and their validity successfully determined.
- Successful conflict resolution depends on effectively breaking, or invalidating, one or more assumptions underlying opposing or competing positions.
- Conflict frequently involves complex interaction among several factors; it is not always bipolar.
- Most conflicts cannot be resolved with "silver bullets" (that is, single actions or changes that make the entire problem go away).
- Ideas—even "breakthrough" ideas—are not solutions.

HOW TO USE THIS CHAPTER

- Read "Description of the Evaporating Cloud."

- Read "Constructing an Evaporating Cloud."

- Read "Scrutinizing an Evaporating Cloud."

- Review Figure 5.34, "Evaporating Cloud – Wurtzburg Corporation." This is a completed EC on developing new capabilities to satisfy markets. It illustrates in a typical real-world example how hidden conflict can be resolved with an Evaporating Cloud.

- Review Figure 5.32, "Procedures for Constructing an Evaporating Cloud." This is an abbreviated checklist that you can use to guide you in constructing your own ECs. The checklist contains brief instructions and illustrations for each step. Detailed explanations for each step in the checklist are provided in the chapter itself, under "Constructing an Evaporating Cloud."

- Practice the "Evaporating Cloud Exercise" provided in Appendix D.

- For your convenience, blank EC worksheets are provided in Figure 5.33. You may reproduce or reconstruct this format for use in building your own ECs.

> *We are all faced with great opportunities...brilliantly disguised as impossible situations.*
>
> —Unknown

DESCRIPTION OF THE EVAPORATING CLOUD

As the name implies, the Evaporating Cloud is designed to expose and resolve conflict. "Resolve" does not mean compromise. A compromise has been described as a solution with which everybody is equally unhappy because nobody really gets what they want. True conflict resolution, however, requires a "win-win" solution—that is, both sides feel as though they've come out winners.

> *The compromise will always be more expensive than either of the suggestions it is compromising.*
>
> —Juhani's Law

Another function of the Evaporating Cloud is to facilitate the generation of new ideas—potential "breakthrough" solutions to difficult problems. Obviously, there is some overlap here with conflict resolution. "Win-win" solutions often require us to come up with new ways of doing things, new solutions to old problems that might also be described as "breakthroughs." But even if a conflict is not obvious in solving a problem, the Evaporating Cloud can serve as a "creative engine," stimulating ideas. In other words, there's more than one way to skin a cat and you don't necessarily have to throw away the skin afterward—or the cat.

The Nature of Conflict

Conflict is often painfully obvious. Some of its indicators may include loud voices, angry words, hard feelings, or clearly opposing positions. A classic example of conflict is rancorous labor negotiations leading to a strike. But conflict is even more often likely to be subtle—more like different opinions on the same subject, the difference between what you need to do and what you're allowed to do, or two different parties competing for exclusive use of the same resources (for example, time, money, labor, and equipment).

Conflict Is Not Always Obvious

When the conflict is obvious, techniques especially designed for the purpose are trotted out to help resolve it: collective bargaining, negotiation, and binding arbitration. But when it's not obvious, the conflict frequently goes unrecognized. Nobody is aware that an underlying conflict, with a life of its own, is even affecting the situation. As a result, the problem may be difficult or even impossible to effectively resolve.

> *The obvious is that which is never seen until someone expresses it simply.*
>
> —Kahlil Gibran

Two Types of Conflict

Because "conflict" has such a pejorative connotation, most people tend to think only of the overt indications of conflict mentioned earlier. But for the purpose of identifying and solving problems, it's sometimes better to think in terms of "competing forces." These competing forces are usually of two types: opposite conditions or different alternatives.

Opposite Conditions

In this situation, one force pushes us to *"do* this." The other force pushes us to *"not do* this" (or to do something that is the diametric opposite). For example, one side of the conflict might tell us to "save money," while the other side might say "spend money." This particular conflict is inherent in the problem of reducing the federal budget, where one school of thought says "Spend money to stimulate the economy," while the other says "Reduce federal spending to cut the deficit."

Different Alternatives

This kind of conflict forces us to choose between two alternatives that are not opposite conditions but are, for some reason, mutually exclusive. This kind of conflict is inherent in any resource shortage. In other words, "We only have so much money; we can do either 'A' or 'B,' but we can't do both." This is a classic conflict condition: the choice between equally desirable alternatives that we can't do at the same time. Any "either-or" situation implies a hidden conflict of this type.

Compromise, "Win-Lose" or "Win-Win"?

When it comes to resolving conflict, there are three basic paths: *compromise, win-lose,* and *win-win.* Though two of these may be necessary at times, only one is truly desirable. In a compromise, neither side gets everything it expected. In win-lose, one side gets what it expected—maybe more—while the other side doesn't get what it expected—and maybe gets nothing. In a win-win, however, both sides get more than they expected.

Compromise

The first idea that almost everybody thinks of when a conflict or contention arises is, "Let's split the difference—you take half, and I'll take half." If both sides are willing to live with a compromise, it's probably the easiest and fastest way to resolve differences. But what if the conflict doesn't have an acceptable compromise? That leaves two other alternatives.

"Win-Lose"

This type of resolution assumes that the situation is a zero-sum game: One side must win and the other side must lose. If I win, you can't win, and vice-versa. This is okay—maybe even desirable—for athletic contests. But in big business, careers, interpersonal relationships—the "games of life"—it's neither necessary nor desirable. All it does is create hard feelings and lasting resentment.

"Win-Win"

This is an ideal situation. When both sides win, nobody feels exploited. Both sides probably get more than they'd hoped for. And most important of all, good will is generated on both sides, which bodes well for the future of the relationship.

An Indication of Hidden Conflict

If the conflict isn't obvious, how do we know we really have one? A principal indication of an underlying, hidden conflict is a sense of stagnation: "We have a problem, and, despite our best efforts, we haven't been able to make any headway on it." This situation forces us to ask the question, "What's keeping us from solving this problem?"

One way to confirm that a conflict may be causing undesirable effects is to look closely at how management spends its time. Typically, a hidden conflict can eat up as much as 50 percent of senior management's time and energy. If you see this happening, you can be reasonably sure a hidden conflict is perpetuating the problem.

How can we be sure a conflict is involved? In fact, it may not always be. Maybe the only reason we can't resolve our problem is that we just don't have enough intuitive knowledge about the situation to work it out—and if we did, we would. But if it's a serious, nagging problem that knowledgeable people have tried unsuccessfully to solve, chances are that a conflict is perpetuating the problem's existence. If inadequate knowledge was really the roadblock, good minds and better intentions should have overcome this obstacle and solved the problem already. The only way to know for sure whether the problem is perpetuated by a conflict or inadequate knowledge is to try to build an Evaporating Cloud. If a conflict is really present, it will show up in the EC.

"Breakthrough" Solutions

Evaporating Clouds help explain why problems exist and what perpetuates them. They serve as a kind of template or environment in which to develop "breakthrough" solutions. The key word here is "breakthrough," because it implies the challenging of traditional assumptions—those associated with the phrase "but that's the way we've always done it."

> *Creative thinking may simply mean that there's no particular virtue in doing things the way they have always been done.*
>
> —Rudolph Flesch

When the problem has you at a standstill, "the way we've always done it" probably won't be good enough anymore. Or, as Goldratt once said, "yesterday's solution is tomorrow's historical curiosity." ("Isn't that the funniest thing you ever saw? Why on earth do you suppose they did it *that* way?")

Elements of the Evaporating Cloud

The typical Evaporating Cloud has seven elements, six of them connected by arrows:

- One objective

- Two necessary, but not sufficient, requirements

- Two conflicting prerequisites

- Underlying assumptions

- One or more injections

Symbology

The symbols used to depict an Evaporating Cloud are relatively straightforward (see Figure 5.2):

- Since objectives, requirements, and prerequisites are essentially conditions of existing or desired reality, a round-cornered rectangle encloses their respective statements. These entities are arranged in a five-sided figure that resembles baseball's "home plate" lying on its side (refer back to Figure 5.1 on page 160).

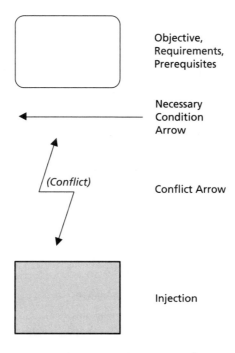

Figure 5.2   Evaporating Cloud symbology.

- The objective, requirements, and prerequisites are connected by necessary-condition arrows. Necessary-condition arrows may look like the sufficiency arrows used in the Current Reality, Future Reality, and Transition Trees, but they signify very different things. NC arrows imply the presence of hidden underlying assumptions about the relationship between the entities they connect. (See "Assumptions.")

- Between the two prerequisites the arrow has a "zig-zag" and barbs on either end to indicate the presence of a conflict or competing conditions.

- In the center of the Evaporating Cloud are one or more sharp-cornered rectangles indicating *injections*, the ideas developed to break the conflict.

Objective

The objective of an Evaporating Cloud is essentially a common purpose. In a negotiation, for example, even though both sides may be at odds over some things, there is an elemental reason they are in the same room, at the same table, attempting to negotiate. Labor and management basically want the same thing—a profitable company—because it's essential to the well-being of both sides. It's their common purpose, or objective (see Figure 5.3). If an Intermediate Objectives Map has been constructed for the system in question—a *strategic* IO Map—the goal articulated in that IO Map is usually a safe choice for the objective in an Evaporating Cloud.

Requirements

A requirement is a *necessary condition*—something that *must* be satisfied in order to achieve the objective. Each requirement is necessary but not sufficient alone to achieve the objective. There may be many of these requirements, like spokes in a wheel, and in most cases these requirements don't conflict with each other. They may even seem so benign that they're often not noticed (see Figure 5.4).

For example, in order to have a profitable company, we might need to maximize sales revenue, control costs, or minimize inventory. We might have to create a popular product or service, lower operating costs, stabilize production, effectively market and sell, or establish other conditions important to profitability. There is no direct conflict here, and each of these requirements can be considered necessary, though not sufficient alone. In the accompanying example, the objective "A profitable company" depends on several requirements, two of which are "increase sales revenue" and "control costs" (see Figure 5.5). Requirements are often the critical success factors from an IO Map.

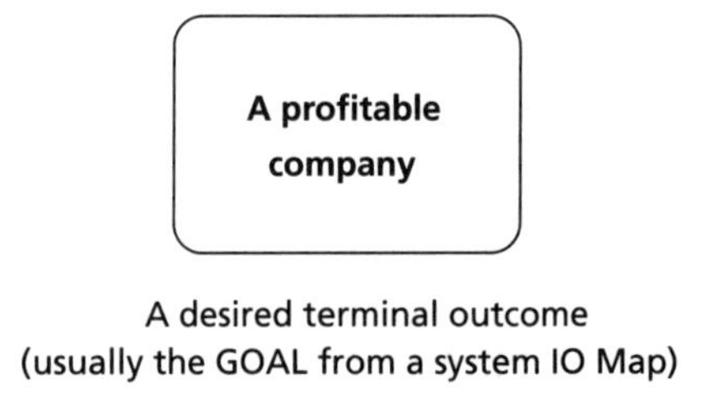

A profitable company

A desired terminal outcome
(usually the GOAL from a system IO Map)

Figure 5.3 An example of an objective.

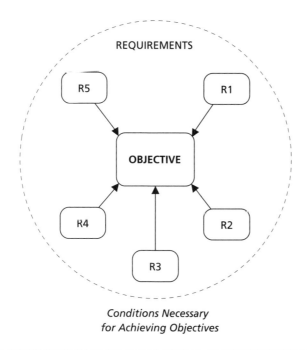

Figure 5.4   Requirements.

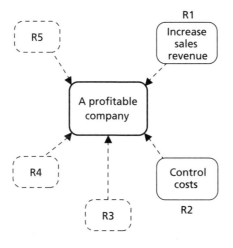

Figure 5.5   Objectives depend on requirements.

Prerequisites

Satisfying the necessary conditions, or requirements, usually demands some actions on our part—things that we must *do*—that are better defined and more specific. The action is *prerequisite* to satisfying the requirement, so that's what we call it—a prerequisite. (See Figure 5.6.)

In the preceding example, the requirement "increase sales revenue" might require the specific action "spend more money on advertising." This specific action seems to be a prerequisite for satisfying the requirement "increase sales revenue." But another requirement, controlling costs, would seem to demand a different prerequisite—*not* spending more money (see Figure 5.7).

Immediately the conflict becomes apparent. On the one hand, we have to spend more money to satisfy one necessary condition. But on the other hand, we have to *not* spend more money to satisfy another equally necessary condition. Both requirements are necessary conditions—by definition they can't be in conflict with one another—however, the prerequisites we generate to satisfy them are.

So it's at the prerequisite level that conflict usually occurs, where forces compete. Remember, not all prerequisites conflict; perhaps only two or three do. But these are usually enough to stall progress toward satisfying the requirements—the necessary conditions—that they support. And since *all* the requirements are necessary to achieve the objective, failure to satisfy any one can prevent achievement of the objective. As few as two prerequisites in conflict with one another can "shortstop" the objective.

Even though there may be many requirements and an equal number of prerequisites, it's the ones in conflict that we're most interested in. That's why the "pie" configuration pictured in Figure 5.8, though it effectively illustrates the whole objective/requirement/ prerequisite situation, is not as useful to us in resolving the conflict as is the "slice," which

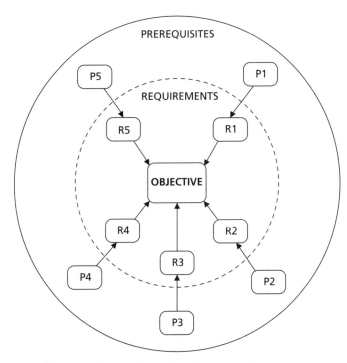

Prerequisites satisfy Requirements
Requirements are Necessary to Achieve Objectives

Figure 5.6   Prerequisites satisfy requirements.

we configure to resemble "home plate" lying on its side (see Figure 5.8). So when you see the Evaporating Cloud, keep in mind that it's really a piece of a larger structure, most of which we're not immediately concerned about because it doesn't pose a problem.

We should note at this point that conflict is not always bipolar. There may be three or more prerequisites in conflict with one another (a complicated, vexing situation in the rare instances when it occurs). It may also be that a solution—an injection—to one conflict creates a new conflict that didn't previously exist with some other prerequisite.* When this happens, the preferred strategy is to deal with one conflict at a time, using the EC. Figure 5.9 shows an example of a particularly difficult tripartite conflict.[4]

How the Evaporating Cloud Relates to the Current Reality Tree

We began our examination of the Thinking Process with the Intermediate Objectives Map, which defined the destination we're trying to reach and the major milestones we must meet to get there. Then we discussed the Current Reality Tree and saw that it defines the magnitude and direction of the gap, or mismatch, between where we currently are and where we're striving to be. A little earlier in this chapter we learned that the critical root causes in a CRT might result from conflict, and we're about to delve into the EC in detail to try to resolve the conflicts surrounding those root causes. But before we do that, it's important to visualize the relationship between the EC and the CRT. In my experience with the Thinking Process over the past decade, I've seen a lot of really bad Evaporating Clouds (by bad I mean poorly constructed—the conflicts themselves are usually always inherently bad expressions of the situation). In this edition, I hope to help Thinking Process practitioners eliminate poorly-constructed ECs by offering a more detailed examination of the relationship between the EC and the CRT.

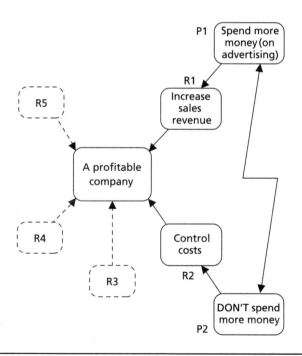

Figure 5.7 An example of conflicting prerequisites.

---

* As Eric Sevareid once observed, "The chief cause of problems is solutions."

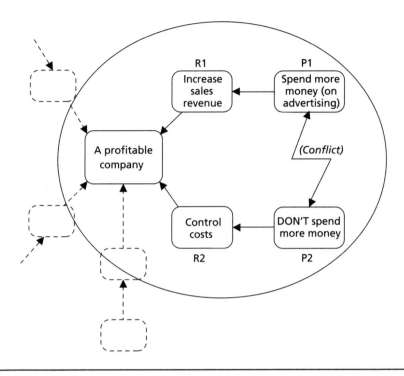

Figure 5.8 The EC: a "slice of the whole pie."

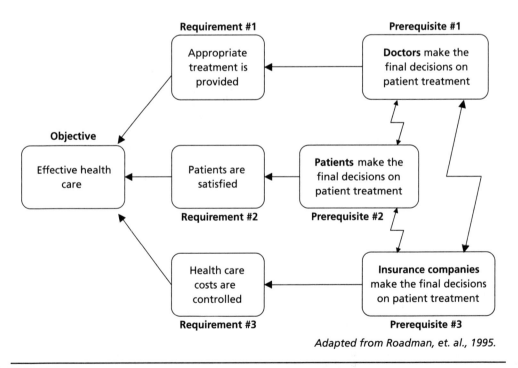

Adapted from Roadman, et. al., 1995.

Figure 5.9 Tripartite conflict: who has final authority for medical treatment?

Why Do Root Causes of Undesirable Effects Exist?

If the UDE is the result of a phenomenon of nature—drought or flooding, for example—the cause is physical and natural. Neither floods nor droughts are undesirable in and of themselves—rather their impact on our lives is where the undesirability lies. For most of us, however, the systems we're primarily concerned with have a significant human component. They may, in fact, be almost exclusively human-oriented or human-based systems. The very presence of humans in a system implies some degree of free will.

Free will means that, at some level, components of the system have some latitude to *decide* what to do or how to do it—maybe both. The more substantial the role of humans in a system, the more opportunities exist (and the greater the likelihood) for free will to be exercised and decisions to be made. Thus, we can safely say that in most of the situations we might be concerned about, the root causes of our undesirable effects stem from the decisions we choose to make.*

Even in the case of flooding—say, the disastrous Mississippi River floods of 1993—the victims bore as much responsibility as Mother Nature for the damage they suffered, because they chose to build or buy property in the flood plain of a huge river with a known history of flooding at irregular intervals.

Policies and Constraints

To the extent that a particular decision leads to a repetitive practice—in other words, future behavior is modified as a result of the decision—a *policy* is created. Thus, *a policy results from a decision intended to standardize behavior from the decision point onward into the future.*

We tend to think of policies as formal—written prescriptions or prohibitions captured on paper. And most policies are. Laws, government regulations, corporate rules, and "best practices" are all formal attempts to standardize current and future behavior through policies.

But "policies" can have a broader interpretation than just written rules alone. Often they're no more than verbal. Cultural custom at some point takes on the aura of policy. Have you ever heard someone say, "*That's* the way we do things around here"? Or even more ominously, "That's *not* the way we do things around here"? If you have, you're hearing the verbal expression of a policy that may not actually be written anywhere. It may be no more than social custom.

The policies we follow in our companies, society, and personal lives normally serve a good and useful purpose: they bring structure and order to our lives. But sometimes the "law of unintended consequences" rears its ugly head. In some cases a policy created to produce one outcome is actually detrimental in some other respect. In organizations, a policy that does this can actually degrade or limit overall system performance. When this happens, the policy itself becomes a constraint to improved performance—*a system constraint.*

Policy Constraints: A Source of Conflict

In complex organizational systems, because of the law of unintended consequences, policy constraints are often a source of conflict. In other words, policies intended to satisfy some valid requirement in one part of the system, or the system as a whole, can cause headaches—perhaps culminating in undesirable effects—in other parts of the system.

---

* There's no way around it—no matter what our undesirable effects might be, *we're* responsible for them. Or, in the immortal words of Pogo, from the comic strip of the same name by Walt Kelly, "We have met the enemy and he is us!"

For example, consider a policy that says, "Raw materials will always be purchased in economic-order-quantity lots." Many companies operate with this policy. It's intended to make purchasing as efficient as possible, meaning the maximum quantity is acquired for the least cost-per-unit. And this policy certainly makes the purchasing departments "numbers" look good. But it also leads to buying a large amount of material that may not be needed immediately, creating the need for warehouse space to store it. Moreover, in normal up-and-down business cycles, it might sit on the shelf for a long time—and may eventually be disposed of as scrap or manufactured into products that for whatever reason can't be sold. The inventory manager's "numbers" then tend to look bad. What's desirable for the purchasing department becomes undesirable for the warehouse manager.

This idea of the law of unintended consequences has some relevance to what we've seen so far. Whether or not people have deliberately identified an unequivocal system goal and critical success factors (through an Intermediate Objectives Map), these elements actually *do* exist. And the policies in place were likely put there to satisfy them.

From Chapter 4 we know that the Current Reality Tree is intended to depict the causality of *only* the unfavorable system outcomes—the deviation from critical success factors. But in most cases, major parts of the system are "doing just fine, thank you," and for that reason they're not included in the Current Reality Tree. In fact, it could be said that the CRT is only *a negative branch of current reality,* not all of it (see Figure 5.10). Yet the parts of the system that are hurting are inextricably connected to parts that aren't.

Knowing this, it should be easy to understand why a concerted effort to "fix" a critical root cause—a policy that results in an UDE in the CRT—is likely to create problems for people in parts of the system that are working just fine. To those people, we may be upsetting *their* applecart as we try to fix the root cause of *our* problems. And what is their natural tendency when this happens? They *push back,* of course: "You can't change *that* because…" And such push-back or opposition is a subdued form of conflict* (see Figure 5.11).

Conflict is Usually Embedded in the CRT
As you can see in Figure 5.11, most conflict concerning complex systems involves things that are part of the CRT and other things that are not. Resolving this kind of conflict demands an approach that transcends the system—the parts that are depicted in the CRT and those that are not alike. The Thinking Process provides such a capability in the Evaporating Cloud.

Assumptions
As with any of the Logical Thinking Process trees, the presence of an arrow indicates the existence of hidden underlying assumptions about the relationship between entities of the Evaporating Cloud. These assumptions are the key to unlocking the conflict. An assumption is a statement about reality that is accepted as true or valid without question or demand for proof. It's likely that there are several assumptions underlying each arrow in an EC. Some of these assumptions are invariably valid.

Invalid Assumptions
But what makes assumptions so important to the conflict resolution process are not the valid assumptions, but the *invalid* ones. They may never have been valid. Or, if they were, changes in the environment may have rendered them invalid. Resolving conflict or solving problems with an Evaporating Cloud calls upon us to expose *all* the underlying

---

* Whereas such differences of opinion were once settled by physical conflict, these days the vehicle of choice is either verbal argument or passive resistance (which by any other name is essentially conflict).

assumptions we possibly can about the entire prerequisite-requirement-objective relationship and separate the ones that are invalid. You can expose assumptions by brainstorming, using the Crawford Slip Method[1], or using some other means of idea generation.

Some Assumptions Can Be Invalidated

In some situations it may seem to you that all the assumptions you identify are valid. If you haven't been able to come up with any invalid assumptions, try evaluating the valid ones you already have. Maybe you can think of a way to make *one* invalid. Doing so will usually involve finding a substitute for the entity at the tail of the connecting arrow. We

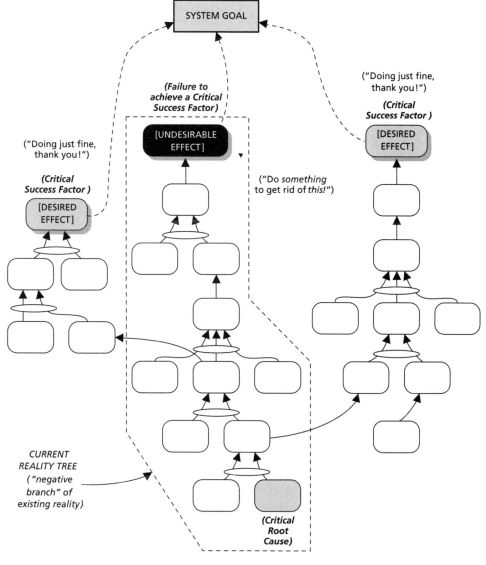

- The CRT is NOT a complete picture of reality
- It only depicts the causality that produces Undesirable Effects
- Yet some of that causality may also cause Desired Effects
- Those Desired Effects are critical in achieving the system's goal

Figure 5.10   The CRT: a "negative branch" of reality.

refer to this substitute as an "injection." More on injections a little later in this chapter. For the moment, let's return to the intriguing idea of rendering moot an apparently valid assumption. Take a look at the accompanying sidebar.

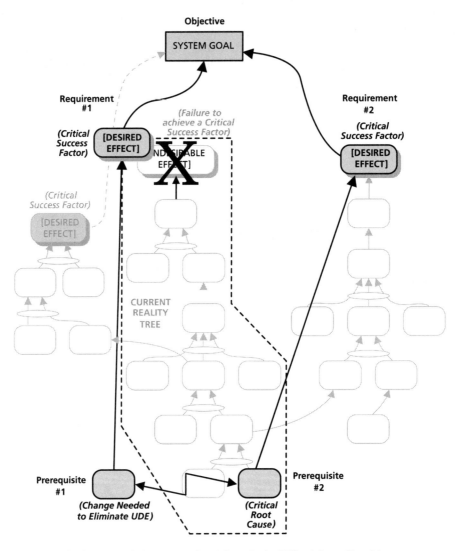

The change needed to convert the UDE to a Desired Effect is in conflict with the original root cause of the UDE, which is needed to satisfy some other Critical Success Factor not depicted in the CRT

Figure 5.11 The EC is partially embedded in the CRT.

Why Assumptions Are So Critical

Assumptions provide the hidden rationale for why the relationship between the entities exists. Consider the following example:

"In order to have high-quality federal construction [REQUIREMENT], Congress must change the existing contracting law [PREREQUISITE], because:

ASSUMPTIONS

1. Existing law always favors the lowest bidder above all other considerations

2. Existing law always drives contractors to cut costs to the bone

3. Heavy cost cutting always encourages cutting corners on quality

4. Use of inexpensive, low-quality materials is the only way to cut costs

5. Low-*quality* materials never last as long as customers expect

6. Low-*cost* materials never last as long as customers expect

7. Contractors are never required to guarantee their work

In this example there are seven assumptions underlying the arrow. There may be more. Can you think of any others? Are these all valid assumptions? At first cut they all look reasonable, and some undoubtedly are, but there are probably one or two whose validity might be challenged.

Are the assumptions really valid? For the sake of argument, let's assume that all the assumptions are valid except numbers 5 and 6. If low-cost, high-quality, durable materials were possible, the product would last much longer, even if all of the other assumptions remained valid and unchallenged. If such a "miracle material" could be found, assumptions 5 and 6 would no longer apply, but it might not be necessary to eliminate the prerequisite (change the existing law) because the requirement (high-quality federal construction) might have been satisfied without having to do so. Finding high-quality, low-cost building materials becomes the injection we use to break the conflict between prerequisites.

"Win-Win" vs. "Win-Lose"

Consider the implications of this kind of problem resolution. Obviously, the other side of the conflicting relationship in the sidebar is the opposite of our stated prerequisite: "Don't change existing contracting law." Somebody is certainly going to be entrenched in that position. But by invalidating the key assumptions that we did (numbers 5 and 6), we have eliminated the need to choose one prerequisite over the other—a "win-lose" situation. Instead, we found a way to satisfy the requirement (high-quality federal construction) without making anyone a loser—the essence of a "win-win" solution.

Five Potential "Break Points"

If you look at a typical Evaporating Cloud (Figure 5.12), you'll notice that there are five arrows that have assumptions underlying them. Theoretically, the conflict can be broken at any of these arrows, or "break points." But in practicality, the odds of finding invalid assumptions are likely to be lower with some arrows than with others.

For example, if the EC is properly constructed to begin with, the arrows between the two requirements (R1 and R2) and the objective (O) are less likely to have invalid assumptions associated with them than the arrows between the prerequisites and the requirements (P1 to R1, P2 to R2), or between the two prerequisites (P1 and P2). Why do you suppose this is?

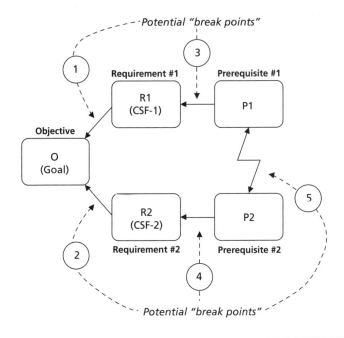

Figure 5.12 "Break points:" arrows indicate hidden underlying assumptions.

If you've properly determined the requirements in the first place, it's likely that they really *are* truly necessary for the attainment of the objective. Take another look at Figure 5.11. Notice that it indicates the Desired Effects are really the satisfaction of critical success factors from the IO Map. And the objective of the EC is really a statement of the goal from that same IO Map. If you've identified real, verifiable critical success factors in your IO Map, then by definition they are valid requirements (that is, no invalid underlying assumptions). This means that for you to break the conflict at one of those two arrows, *you* would have to initiate some *major* change to reality that would render one requirement or the other no longer relevant to achieving the system goal. This is not likely to happen.

In the case of the conflict arrow connecting P1 and P2, there's a slightly greater likelihood of being able to find an invalid assumption there. But the assumptions underlying this arrow have little to do with the content of P1 and P2. Rather, they're more related to the conflict itself. In other words, the assumptions under this arrow relate to why you can't have both prerequisites.

In almost all ECs, however, the two places where the majority of invalid assumptions lie are between the prerequisites (P1 and P2) and their paired requirements (R1 and R2). This is why it's usually easiest to begin with the presumption that the conflict will more likely be broken at these two arrows than at any of the others. Only if breaking the conflict between prerequisites and requirements proves difficult or impossible will we contemplate breaking it between the requirements (R) and the objective (O), or between the conflicting prerequisites.

Invalid Assumptions: An Example
Let's look at our continuing example from earlier in this chapter (Figure 5.13). Presuming for now that the connections between prerequisites and requirements offer the greatest potential for harboring invalid assumptions, let's look at what the various assumptions might be. Once we've identified as many as possible, we can evaluate each one for validity.

ASSUMPTIONS:
1. Our markets traditionally respond well to advertising campaigns
2. Our superior value proposition allows us to avoid competing via price reductions
3. Spending more money on advertising is the ONLY way to increase sales revenue
4. Bigger advertising expenditures ALWAYS produce more sales
5. Bigger advertising expenditures are ALWAYS cost-effective

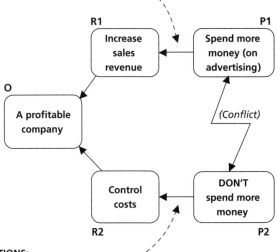

ASSUMPTIONS:
6. Limiting spending is the ONLY way to control costs
7. Not spending more money ALWAYS provides cost control
8. Not spending more money NEVER has a negative effect on revenue generation
9. No other part of the operation is EVER adversely impacted by holding the line on spending
10. Bigger advertising expenditures are NEVER cost-effective

Figure 5.13   Invalid assumptions: an example.

Five assumptions have been articulated for each side of the conflict. It won't always be this nicely balanced. Of the five underlying the P1-to-R1 arrow, assumptions 1 and 2 are likely to be valid. But 3, 4 and 5 are questionable. Moving to the other side of the conflict, assumptions 6 and 7 are likely to be valid as well, while numbers 8, 9, and 10 virtually invite challenge to their validity.

Injections: The Role of Invalid Assumptions

Now the question arises: what shall we do with these invalid assumptions after we identify them? The answer is that they point the way to the direction of new ideas—potential solutions to break the conflict.

Take assumption 3, for example: "Spending more money is the ONLY way to increase sales revenue." Doesn't that statement virtually invite a challenge? Can't you just hear a marketing expert say, "Wait a minute! We don't have to spend more money on advertising. Instead we could…" And with the unstated end of that last sentence, an idea for breaking the conflict is born— an idea that increases revenue (R1) without the need to spend more money (P1).

Likewise, take a look at assumptions 8 or 9. While they may never be explicitly verbalized by anyone in a commercial organization, people clearly behave as though they subscribe to them, which implies that they *do* drive behavior. But their validity is clearly questionable. No rational leader or manager in an organization could argue that failure to spend more money in some circumstances doesn't have an adverse effect on the company as a whole.

In deciding what to do about this conflict, we see that because the argument on both sides is somewhat shaky, an "injection"—an idea for a solution—could be advanced for either side. And in truth, this may be the best way to address the conflict. Money might be spent judiciously on some things that, if carefully selected, could produce more payback than they cost. Costs could still be controlled (R2). At the same time, a second injection might be to evaluate all alternatives for spending targets to identify the ones with the best potential benefit-to-cost ratio, which is another way of saying revenues would increase (R1).

Thus the conflict is resolved by replacing both P1 and P2 with two ideas that a) satisfy the two non-negotiable requirements, and b) are themselves not in conflict with one another (see Figure 5.14).

How Are Injections Related to Assumptions?

Remember that the conflict exists because of the assumptions each side makes about reality. The odds are high that some of these assumptions are erroneous—or invalid—in the first place. Yet one or both sides operate as if they *were* valid. The conflict is rooted in the idea that each side is convinced that *"our* assumptions are valid and *theirs* are not." In reality, there may be invalid assumptions on both sides. To resolve a conflict using the

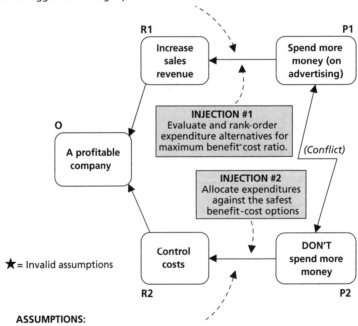

ASSUMPTIONS:
1. Our markets traditionally respond well to advertising campaigns
2. Our superior value proposition allows us to avoid competing via price reductions
★ 3. Spending more money on advertising is the ONLY way to increase sales revenue
★ 4. Bigger advertising expenditures ALWAYS produce more sales
★ 5. Bigger advertising expenditures are ALWAYS cost-effective

ASSUMPTIONS:
6. Limiting spending is the ONLY way to control costs
7. Not spending more money ALWAYS provides cost control
★ 8. Not spending more money NEVER has a negative effect on revenue generation
★ 9. No other part of the operation is EVER adversely impacted by holding the line on spending
★ 10. Bigger advertising expenditures are NEVER cost-effective

Figure 5.14 Conflict resolved: an example.

Evaporating Cloud, injections—"breakthrough" ideas—must be created that play specifically to the invalid assumptions.

An injection is an alternative way—an action or a condition—to achieve the entity at the head of an EC arrow without needing to have, or perform, the entity at the tail. The injection basically bypasses the invalid assumption—that is, makes it not even necessary to consider.

For example, take the relationship in the top half of Figure 5.15. When invalid assumptions are clearly identifiable, they virtually point to ways to satisfy the requirement without needing the prerequisite. But when all the assumptions on both sides seem valid, we must find a way to replace a prerequisite *in spite of* the valid assumptions. Both approaches preserve the requirement while still allowing the replacement of one

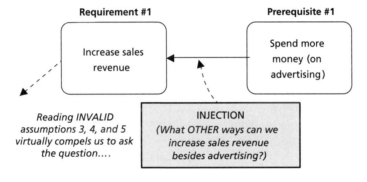

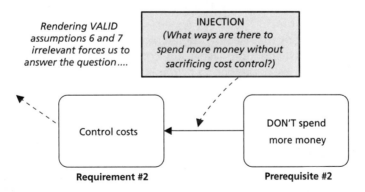

Figure 5.15 Injections and invalid assumptions.

assumption or both. Coming up with a way to replace a prerequisite in spite of valid assumptions is a highly creative challenge—but one that must be addressed in some of the most intractable conflicts.

Injections: Actions or Conditions?

Let's revisit the issue of injections for a moment. It should be obvious from the example in Figure 5.14 that these two injections are directive in nature—they articulate specific *actions* to be taken. When possible, it's usually better to have injections that represent discrete actions. They're considerably easier to execute. But it's not always possible—and maybe not advisable—to use actions for your injections in all cases.

An Evaporating Cloud can have its prerequisites in the specific or the general. If the prerequisites are as specific as they are in Figure 5.14, it makes sense to apply injections that are direct actions, such as the ones in that figure. But if the prerequisites are at a higher or more conceptual level of the system, it makes more sense to create an injection that is a condition or outcome that must be put into place.

For example, take a look at Figure 5.16. The upper conflict is relatively discrete. It addresses objective requirements that are clearly at a personal or family level, which makes them relatively simple. The lower conflict, however, involves a more complex system with many more variables than the one above. Expanding existing business is not a matter of taking a single specific action. Rather, business expansion would be the *outcome* of a number of discrete but interdependent activities, each of which may comprise several steps. Likewise, the development of new product lines is equally complicated.

The lesson here is that the more limited in scope the conflict is, the more likely it is that you'll be able to find specific, discrete, conflicting actions to put into the prerequisite blocks of the EC. The broader or higher-level the conflict, the more likely the prerequisites will have to be statements of complex conditions. And the level at which the conflict exists (that is, personal, group, system, and so on) will also have implications for the kind of injection—action or condition—most appropriate to break the conflict, too.

"Silver Bullets"

When we find invalid assumptions, we create injections (actions or conditions) to break them. Different invalid assumptions may need separate injections to break them. If the situation is simple, perhaps one injection might be enough. It's also possible that one injection may break several assumptions, or, conversely, that several injections may be necessary to break one assumption. The lesson here is to avoid locking your thinking into a one-to-one relationship.

But single injections that cleanly kill the conflict— "silver bullets," if you will—are extremely rare. In most situations, especially complex ones, it's unlikely that one single "mother of all injections," whether an action or a condition, will suffice to completely eliminate the conflict. (That happens only in the movies.*) What's much more likely is that it may take several injections to do the job. But the EC is equal to the task of identifying them all.

Creating "Breakthrough" Ideas to Resolve Conflict

The most challenging, intractable problems usually require some kind of breakthrough in thinking. This kind of thinking is a creative exercise, often of the highest degree. It requires "thinking outside the box."

---

* As Dr. Ray Hansen once observed, "Silver bullets went out of style when the Lone Ranger died."

All Arrows Are Fair Game

In the federal construction example earlier in this chapter, we examined the assumptions underlying just one arrow in the Evaporating Cloud: the one between a prerequisite and a requirement. But remember, there are *five* arrows in each EC and assumptions underlie them all. You need not confine yourself to trying to break the assumptions between only prerequisites and requirements.

The world is constantly changing. It's possible that an assumed requirement is no longer a valid necessary condition to attaining the objective, but if you never examine the assumptions underlying that arrow, you'll never know. If the relationship between requirements and the objective turns out to be easier to eliminate than any other, failing to examine it may cost you unnecessary aggravation as you work on a more difficult assumption perpetuating the conflict. And who needs that?

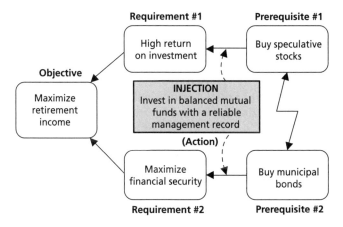

This conflict is resolvable by **discrete action**,
because the prerequisites are specific actions

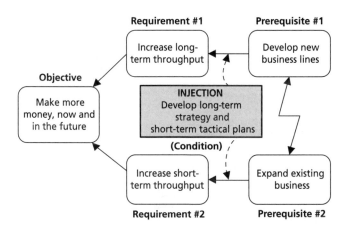

This conflict requires a condition or outcome as an injection,
because the prerequisites are themselves complex conditions

Figure 5.16   Injections: actions or conditions?

Is the Idea Feasible?

Notice that nowhere in this chapter have we considered the *feasibility* of our idea (injection). That's not the purpose of the EC—the purpose is creating new ideas. Other tools, namely the Future Reality Tree and the Prerequisite Tree, test feasibility and identify paths around the obstacles that might obstruct implementing the idea. In other words, the EC creates a "working area" for *idea generation.* As with brainstorming, Crawford Slip, and other idea-generating methods, if we let feasibility enter into the equation during the creative stage of problem solving, we dramatically decrease the chance of inventing breakthrough solutions.

Reading an Evaporating Cloud

At some point, it's inevitable that we'll have to verbalize the conflict we've depicted in an Evaporating Cloud. Even if it's your own "Hamlet"-style conflict, eventually you'll find that you're talking to yourself.* If you're working on a conflict between different people, groups, or systems, it's even more important to be able to verbalize the conflict. At some stage of the game you'll have to negotiate a resolution among parties, and that means being able to state the conflicting issue succinctly enough that the other side will say, "Yes, that accurately describes the problem."

With this in mind, Goldratt conceived a way to verbalize the EC that remains effective today. We read the EC from left to right, starting with the objective and working toward the conflicting prerequisites. Because the EC uses necessity-type logic rather than sufficiency, we don't use the "if–then" format of the Current Reality Tree. Necessary

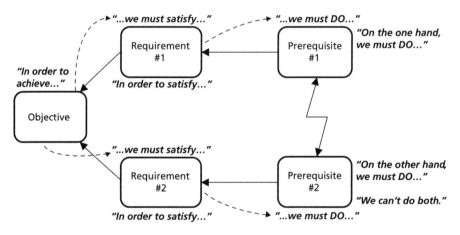

"In order to achieve [the Objective], we must satisfy [Requirement #1].
In order to satisfy [Requirement #1], we must do [Prerequisite #1]."

"In order to achieve [the Objective], we must satisfy [Requirement #2].
In order to satisfy [Requirement #2], we must do [Prerequisite #2]."

"On one hand, we must do [Prerequisite #1].
On the other hand, we must do [Prerequisite #2].
We can't do both."

Figure 5.17   How to read an Evaporating Cloud.

---

* "To be or not to be, that is the question…" Shakespeare: Hamlet, Act III, scene 1.

conditions are expressed as "In order to…we must…" And instead of reading in the direction the arrow is pointing (from tail to barb), we read the EC the opposite way because we're trying to get to the antecedent. Figure 5.17 illustrates this way of reading the EC.

Feel free to vary the wording to fit the text in the various boxes. You might have to substitute "have" in place of "satisfy", or just use the verb included in the prerequisite statement, if there is one. You should try to make the statements flow smoothly and logically to the conflict statement (P1 versus P2).

Verbalizing Assumptions

Eventually, you'll have to get all the assumptions out on the table or on the wall for everyone to see. This means that you'll have to verbalize those at some point, too. The best way to do this is to read the last "in-order-to-we-must" statement, then add "because…" before articulating each assumption (see Figure 5.18).

> *If the assumptions are wrong, the conclusions aren't likely to be very good.*
>
> —Burns's Balance

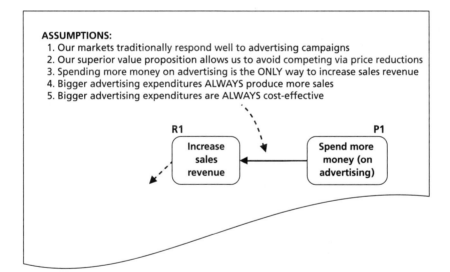

ASSUMPTIONS:
1. Our markets traditionally respond well to advertising campaigns
2. Our superior value proposition allows us to avoid competing via price reductions
3. Spending more money on advertising is the ONLY way to increase sales revenue
4. Bigger advertising expenditures ALWAYS produce more sales
5. Bigger advertising expenditures are ALWAYS cost-effective

R1 — Increase sales revenue

P1 — Spend more money (on advertising)

"In order to increase sales revenue, we must spend more money (on advertising), BECAUSE…"

…our markets traditionally respond well to advertising campaigns, and BECAUSE…

…our superior value proposition allows us to avoid competing via price reductions, and BECAUSE…

…spending money is the *only* way to increase sales revenue, and…

Figure 5.18   How to verbalize assumptions.

WHAT TO REMEMBER ABOUT EVAPORATING CLOUDS

Here are the key points to remember about Evaporating Clouds:

- In any conflict situation, there are usually five arrows indicating underlying assumptions.

- Each arrow implies the existence of at least one, but probably more, assumptions.

- Expose as many assumptions underlying each arrow as you can to:

  – Improve your chances of finding an easy one to invalidate, and

  – Open the range of potential solutions as wide as possible.

- The injections you develop to invalidate assumptions are ideas, not solutions. They should not be constrained by premature considerations of feasibility.

- In complex conflict situations, injections are likely to be conditions you want to create, rather than actions you expect to perform. Many separate actions may be necessary to achieve these conditions.

> *Changing things is central to leadership. Changing them before anyone else does is creativeness.*
>
> —Jay's First Law of Leadership

HOW TO CONSTRUCT AN EVAPORATING CLOUD

Now that we've examined the Evaporating Cloud in detail, it's time to start learning how to build one of your own.

A Nine-Step Path to Conflict Resolution

There are three stages in resolving a conflict using an Evaporating Cloud:

- Construct the cloud

- Expose the underlying assumptions

- Create "breakthrough" ideas to resolve the conflict

These three stages are completed in nine steps. Presuming that all relevant background information about the conflict is known or readily available, the first seven steps can often be completed in about 30 to 45 minutes. Depending on how problematic the conflict is, the last two steps (creating and selecting possible solutions) might take somewhat longer and require outside participation.

> **NOTE:** I must point out that a completely different approach to constructing Evaporating Clouds has been advanced over the years. This method, referred to as the "3-UDE Cloud," has been offered as a way of getting to a so-called generic or core conflict. I don't recommend the 3-UDE Cloud method, for reasons that I've provided in Appendix E. Because it avoids the fallacies of the 3-UDE Cloud, I recommend the procedure that follows for constructing Evaporating Clouds in almost all circumstances. However, if you're contemplating the 3-UDE Cloud approach, I suggest you read the detailed analysis in Appendix E.

1. Construct a Blank Evaporating Cloud

This is probably the easiest step in constructing any of the trees in the Logical Thinking Process. It's as easy as drawing and connecting five empty round-cornered boxes, as shown in Figure 5.19.

Label the five boxes Objective, Requirement #1, Requirement #2, Prerequisite #1, and Prerequisite #2.*

2. Articulate the Conflicting "Wants" of Each Side

In most situations, the conflict is relatively easy to state. It's the issue that you're contesting with someone else, or, if it's internal to you alone, the dilemma—the choice—you're faced with. The two positions in the conflict are recorded in the blanks labeled prerequisites 1 and 2.

Sometimes the conflict is between individuals. Other times it's between courses of action, or between what needs to be done and what a rule, policy, or law mandates. Sometimes it's a confrontation between what the organization requires and a personal agenda. Whatever the conflicting positions may be, *in five words or fewer* write each one in a prerequisite box (Figure 5.20).

The conflicting prerequisites can be either opposite conditions or different alternatives (see "Two Types of Conflict"). To help articulate the prerequisites, verbalize them using "On one hand... on the other hand... ." Adjust the wording of the prerequisites until they make sense when read this way. Use *action* verbs *(do)*, not conditions *(be* or *have)*. Remember from our earlier discussion that conflict normally resides at the level of *action* perceived necessary to satisfy a higher-level condition (the requirements).

If you find that you can define one side of the conflict but have trouble articulating the other, you may need to "come in through a back door." Starting with the side of the conflict you prefer, ask yourself the question, "What stops me from doing my side?" The answer to this question can form the basis of the other side of the conflict.

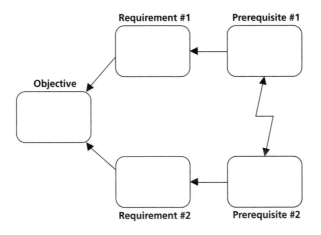

Figure 5.19 Step 1: Construct a blank Evaporating Cloud.

---

3. Determine the "Needs" of Each Side

The needs of each side are non-negotiable necessary conditions, outcomes that must be satisfied to achieve the common objective. What are the necessary conditions that each prerequisite is trying to satisfy? Why does each side think the prerequisites are required? One way to come up with effective wording of the needs is to read the "in-order-to-we-must" statement backwards, and try to fill in the blank (see Figure 5.21). For example:

We must do [PREREQUISITE] in order to have/satisfy [REQUIREMENT].

State both requirements succinctly—again, five words or fewer. Assess the validity of each requirement statement: Is this really the reason each side is demanding the prerequisite? Adjust the wording of the requirements until they make sense when read left-to-right in the normal "In order to have..." form. For example:

In order to have/satisfy [REQUIREMENT], we must do [PREREQUISITE].

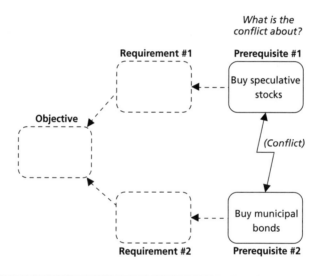

Figure 5.20   Step 2: Articulate the conflicting "wants" of each side.

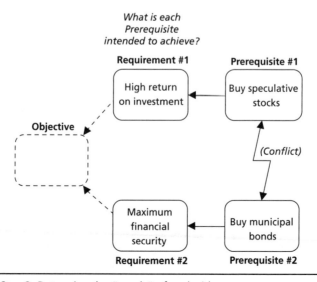

Figure 5.21   Step 3: Determine the "needs" of each side.

Write the final requirement statements in the appropriate box (R1 or R2), properly paired with its prerequisite.

The "Easy Way" to Articulate Requirements

Personally, I don't like to work harder than I have to. And from my experience with the Thinking Process (and teaching it), I've discovered that zeroing in on the right requirement is often difficult. Strange as it may seem, people usually know what they're trying to do, but they frequently find it challenging to explain precisely why their actions are necessary—in other words, what they hope to achieve with them.

So here's a kind of short-cut to the requirements. You'll recall that in our discussion of the Current Reality Tree, we saw that undesirable effects were much easier to articulate when we had a frame of reference with which to compare our situation. And that frame of reference was the Intermediate Objectives (IO) Map, which contains the system goal, critical success factors, and necessary conditions. The IO Map holds the clues to the requirements of the EC (and, eventually, in Step 4, the objective as well).

Go back and look at Figure 5.11 on page 174. We're trying to change undesirable effects that constitute violations of critical success factors or high-level systemic necessary conditions. These CSF and NC are usually found in the IO Map. So it's reasonable to conclude that one of our prerequisites is a change we're trying to make to eliminate the undesirable effect—to satisfy that CSF or NC. Thus, a CSF or NC from the IO Map is a natural candidate for a requirement paired with one of the Prerequisites. The same is true of the other requirement and prerequisite.

For example, let's consider an organizational conflict (Figure 5.22).

The conflicting prerequisites are intended to satisfy two requirements that would most likely be critical success factors—or at least high-level necessary conditions—taken from the organization's IO Map. In Chapter 3 we discussed the usefulness of having an IO Map to establish standards, or benchmarks, of system performance. It doesn't matter whether the system is an organization, a social group, or an individual; the utility of articulated standards is the same. Having these standards pre-determined in an IO Map

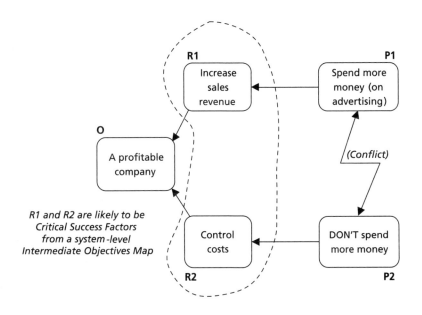

Figure 5.22   Where do requirements come from?

makes construction of a robust EC on the first attempt much easier and more reliable. If you're having difficulty coming up with the Requirements for your EC, go back to your IO Map and see which CSF or NC jumps out at you as the ultimate reason the Prerequisite seems to be required. (If you haven't already prepared an IO Map, it might be a good time to go back to construct one.)

It's worth noting at this point that the requirements are never in conflict with one another. By definition, necessary conditions *can't* be in conflict, or one of them isn't really necessary. If you think that your requirements are in conflict with each other, then you've probably misidentified as requirements statements that should really be prerequisites.

4. Formulate the Objective

Construction of the Evaporating Cloud is complete when a common objective of both requirements is formulated (Figure 5.23).

There was a time, early in the life of the Thinking Process, when this was often the most difficult part of constructing an Evaporating Cloud.* But no more. The same aid available to determine requirements—the IO Map—can also provide the common objective of an EC. Normally, this would be the ultimate goal of the system. It might be a critical success factor, if both requirements are necessary conditions that support that CSF. (Refer to Figure 5.24.)

But whether you're using an IO Map to determine your EC Objective or not, the two characteristics of the Objective are that: a) it's at least one level of dependency up from the highest requirement, and b) *both* requirements can be justified as being essential for attainment of the objective.

Why Use an Intermediate Objectives Map?

There are two compelling reasons to use a previously constructed system IO Map to help you determine the objective and requirements of an Evaporating Cloud: *speed and quality*. In the past 14 years of using the Thinking Process, I've seen innumerable "lousy" Evaporating Clouds. Almost all of them had well-thought-out conflict statements (prerequisites) but

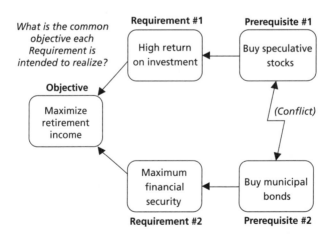

Figure 5.23   Step 4: Formulate the objective.

---

* Frequently, people would insert some meaningless, fluffy statement (for example, "Manage well") just to come up with something that could be remotely related to each Requirement.

poorly formulated objectives and requirements. The most common failing is that the logical connection between at least one requirement and the common objective is weak or non-existent—in other words, one or both of the requirements aren't really necessary for achieving the objective.

I've concluded that the reason for this is that without some prior considerations for the goal and critical success factors of the system in question, determining the elements of the left side of the EC becomes a hit-or-miss proposition. Remember that there may be multiple layers of cause and effect implied by the connections between Ps, Rs, and O (see Figure 5.25); in other words, R1 or R2 may not be the next level of outcome. A robust IO Map can make it infinitely easier to identify an objective that aligns with the system goal and requirements that are truly necessary to reaching that goal.

The lesson here is worth emphasizing one last time:

> *Use your Intermediate Objectives Map to point you toward the right requirements and common objective. If you haven't constructed an IO Map, it's worth taking a few minutes to do so.*

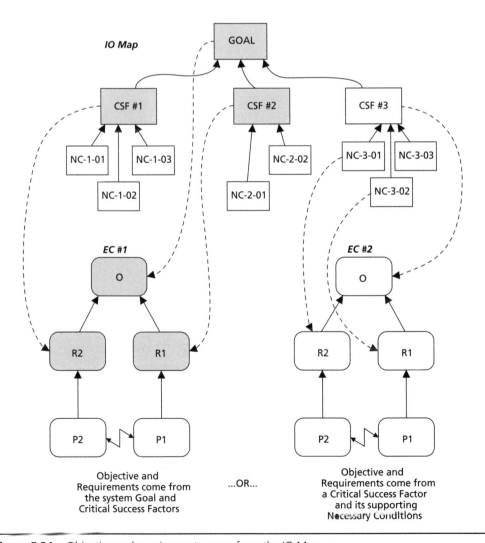

Figure 5.24   Objective and requirements come from the IO Map.

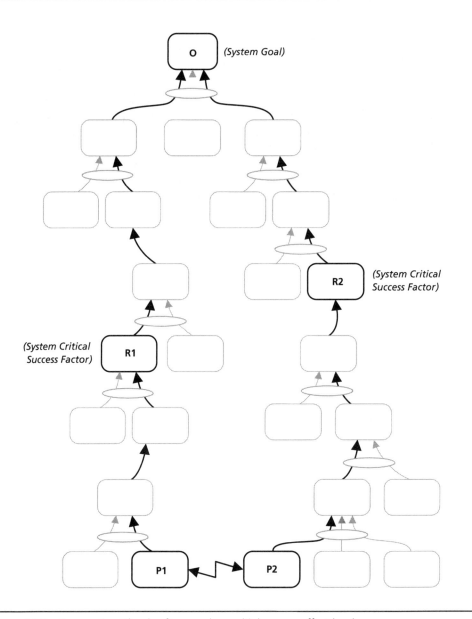

Figure 5.25 Evaporating Clouds often overlay multiple cause-effect levels.

5. Evaluate the Whole Relationship

No Evaporating Cloud is more than a first draft when you reach the point of having all five blocks completed. Before you can move on, you should check this draft to see if it makes sense.

- Are the requirements really necessary to realizing the objective?

- Do the prerequisites really reflect accurate (or consensus) statements of the perceptions of the conflict?

- Do all the elements "sound right" when verbalizing the connections?

The easiest way to validate the whole relationship is to read it from left to right, using the "in-order-to-we-must" form. And read it out loud, not just silently. (You'll be amazed at how quickly a weak or invalid statement pops out at you.) As a whole, does your construction accurately reflect your intuition on the issue? If not, go back to the parts that seem weak and refine them. Enlist help from others knowledgeable in the issue, if necessary. When you're satisfied that the EC represents an accurate statement of the situation, move on to the next step.

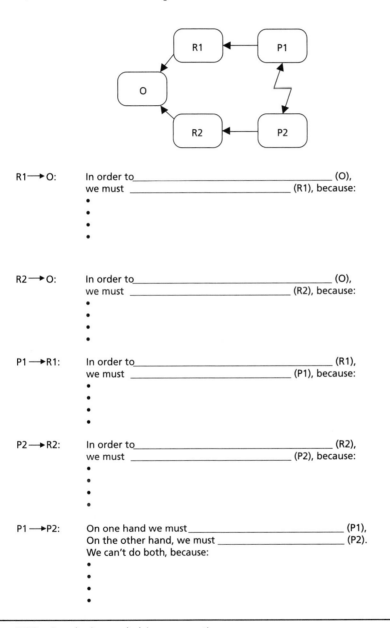

R1⟶O: In order to_____ (O),
         we must _____ (R1), because:
         •
         •
         •
         •

R2⟶O: In order to_____ (O),
         we must _____ (R2), because:
         •
         •
         •
         •

P1⟶R1: In order to_____ (R1),
         we must _____ (P1), because:
         •
         •
         •
         •

P2⟶R2: In order to_____ (R2),
         we must _____ (P2), because:
         •
         •
         •
         •

P1⟶P2: On one hand we must_____ (P1),
         On the other hand, we must _____ (P2).
         We can't do both, because:
         •
         •
         •
         •

Figure 5.26   Developing underlying assumptions.

6. Develop Underlying Assumptions

Conflict is inherent in the assumptions that underlie it, and conflict resolution hides in the invalid assumptions of each side. In the 15th century, Michelangelo started with a whole block of marble and progressively chipped away everything that didn't seem to be part of David. Getting at the invalid assumptions is a little like that. You start with all the assumptions you can muster for each side of the conflict. Eventually, you'll cull out the valid assumptions and be left with only the invalid ones. But first you have to have a complete list.

There's no hard-and-fast rule about how many assumptions there might be underlying each arrow in an EC. Generally, the arrows between the requirements and the objective have the fewest, and those between the prerequisites and the requirements have the most. All arrows rest on *at least one assumption*. The most assumptions I've ever seen in a single EC is 37, with 16 under one arrow alone. But that's the exception, rather than the rule. Use your best judgment about when to stop looking, but keep pressing until you run out of ideas. Try using the format in Figure 5.26 to array your assumptions for effective review.

Beneath each statement, list all the "becauses" you can think of for each statement. These are the assumptions. When your creative well is dry on one statement, go on to the next.

Extreme Wording

There's a technique in writing assumption statements that will later help you zero in on the invalid ones—the ones you'll want to challenge. Instead of writing a fairly bland statement, word the assumption in the most extreme, outrageous way you can think of. For example:

> *Instead of:*   *"We can't eat without having money."*
>
> *Try:*   *"Of course, there's absolutely no way we can eat without having money."*

The latter wording virtually invites challenge: "Oh, yeah? Well, I don't need money to eat. Instead, I can…" We'll address the rest of this line of thought in the discussion of injections, in Step 8. For now, suffice it to say that extreme wording makes invalid assumptions fairly jump off the page at you when you get to step 7.

Here are some typical phrases you might use to convert neutral expression to extreme:

- "Of course we *must*…"
- "Of course we *can't*…"
- "We can *never*…"
- "We must *always*…"
- "There's *absolutely* no way…"
- "It's *absolutely impossible* to…"

NOTE: Here's another way to surface assumptions under the arrows connecting the prerequisites with the requirements. Try turning the Evaporating Cloud on its side, so the objective is at the top and the prerequisites are at the bottom. Below each prerequisite make two columns, one labeled "PRO" and the other labeled "CON." Then in each PRO column begin listing as many advantages to having each prerequisite as you can.

Do the same with the drawbacks for each side. The PROs might become assumptions why each prerequisite is needed to satisfy each requirement. The CONs might become assumptions for the opposite side of the conflict (see Figure 5.27).

Assumptions underlying the conflict arrow reflect competing, rather than supporting, positions. As such, these particular assumptions are generally limited to factors directly related to the nature of the conflict itself: "We can't do both, because... [why?]." The most common assumptions underlying conflict arrows are:

- "They absolutely have to be done at the same time."

- "They are always mutually exclusive."

- "There are never enough resources to do both."

Remember that in organizational settings the most common conflicts are resource shortages (for example, time, material, money, people, and so on), which manifest themselves as *different alternatives*.

After your first pass through all the assumptions, go back through each one again, looking for any you might have missed and possible duplicate entries (that is, the same assumption that might apply to more than one statement). After you think you've accounted for all the assumptions, ask another knowledgeable person to review your work and suggest assumptions you might have missed.

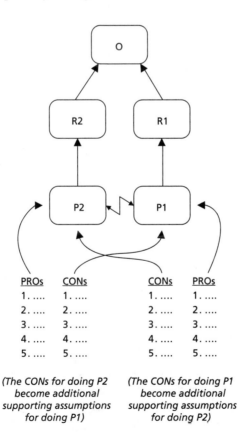

Figure 5.27 Another way to surface underlying assumptions.

NOTE: Don't fall into the trap of building a "bulletproof" Evaporating Cloud—one that has only valid assumptions listed. If the only assumptions you list are valid, then you've proposed an unbreakable conflict, and that's not why we build Evaporating Clouds. We want to resolve conflict, not set it in stone. Consequently, to the best of your ability be sure that your assumptions reflect commonly held perceptions of current reality. Doing so should help ensure that the invalid assumptions, as well as the valid ones, are exposed.

When you're relatively certain you have all the assumptions listed, begin at the top and number them consecutively for ease in differentiating them.

7. Evaluate Assumptions

Now it's time to find the invalid assumptions. If you used the extreme wording technique described in Step 6, this should be relatively easy. Reread each assumption and mark the invalid ones with a question mark ("?") or other distinguishing symbol beside the number of the assumption. Figure 5.28 shows a complete list of assumptions with potentially invalid ones highlighted.

NOTE: Notice in Figure 5.28 that assumptions 1 and 3 are not highlighted as invalid. While a case might be made that they could be invalid, even with the extreme wording there is some validity to these assumptions. After all, increased efficiency is usually the reason most organizations undertake improvement efforts in the first place, so a successful improvement effort could reasonably be expected to mean that the organization really is more efficient. Likewise, a more efficient operation *may not* need as many people to do the same work afterward. By comparison, the other assumptions are so invalid that they virtually draw attention to themselves.

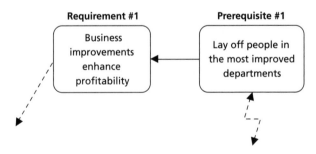

ASSUMPTIONS (P1 ⟶ R1):
"In order for business improvements to enhance profitability, we must lay off people in the most improved departments, because:

   1. Improvements ALWAYS mean better efficiency.
★ 2. Lean organizations are ALWAYS more profitable.
   3. The most improved departments NEVER need as many people afterward.
★ 4. Layoffs are the ONLY WAY to enhance profitability.
★ 5. Layoffs are the BEST WAY to enhance profitability.
★ 6. There is NEVER any residual psychological effect on those remaining after layoffs.
★ 7. "Survivors" will ALWAYS work just as diligently (or more so) than before after seeing their compatriots laid off.
★ 8. We ALWAYS know EXACTLY how many people to lay off without compromising organizational performance.

Figure 5.28   Finding invalid assumptions ("separating the wheat from the chaff").

It may be that you have some arrows for which all the assumptions seem completely valid. When it's time to start formulating injections, you'll be better off focusing your attention on the other arrows—the ones that *do* have invalid assumptions underlying them.

But before you discard the apparently valid assumptions entirely, it's worth challenging your creativity to determine whether there might be changes you could institute that would *invalidate* an apparently valid assumption. More on this concept in the next step.

8. Create Injections

The key word here is "create," and this step is the most creative part of the Evaporating Cloud process. You now have to come up with the best not-yet-existing condition or action that will neutralize the conflict. In other words, the injection will constitute a change that will render one or both competing positions irrelevant. Coming up with a "best" injection implies that you have a number of options to choose from.

How do we do this? It isn't possible, or even desirable, to reduce the creative process to a set of restrictive, rote steps. But two general approaches can help make the job of creating injections a little easier.

First, validate the requirements (R1 and R2). Let's resolve not to waste our efforts unnecessarily. Remembering that the whole purpose of the Evaporating Cloud is to eliminate conflict, we can save ourselves a lot of trouble by first checking to see if both R1 and R2 are still really valid. Maybe one of them was established under conditions that no longer pertain to the current environment—in other words, it may have outlived its usefulness. If so, the conflict may really be a mirage.

If either R1 or R2 isn't really necessary, it can be eliminated, thus voiding the conflict outright. In this case, an injection might not be necessary—or it would be "Delete the requirement and the practices that fulfill it." Or a requirement might be modified in such a way that it still leads to the objective but eliminates the need for the contentious prerequisite that supports it. Either way, validating R1 and R2 requires that you look first at the assumptions associated with arrows connecting them to the objective (O).

Since requirements are often system-critical success factors or necessary conditions for valid reasons, it may be more difficult to attack the conflict on the left side of the Evaporating Cloud (O, R1, R2, and their connecting arrows). In most cases, changes to the way the requirement is satisfied—that is, the prerequisites on the right side of the diagram—are more likely within your span of control or sphere of influence.

The Alternative Environment

You may use any method you like as an "idea generator" to create injections. Some of the most common techniques are brainstorming, the Crawford Slip method, and nominal group technique. Another tool that's especially useful for technical conflicts is TRIZ,* a problem-solving method invented in Russia by Genrich Altshuller. The best sources on TRIZ I've found are Domb[3] and Terninko[5]. Appendix F describes a notional case study detailing how the combination of an Evaporating Cloud and TRIZ, had they been known at the time, might have prevented the Challenger space shuttle disaster.

For those without experience in these idea-generation methods (or the time or stamina to research them), there's another quick-hit technique that works very well, called the alternative environment. It's based on the old adage that "there's more than one way to skin a cat."

To use the alternative environment, ask yourself, "How can I have the requirement without needing its prerequisite?" Then you "shotgun" as many different ways as you can to satisfy the requirement without needing the prerequisite. Refer to Figure 5.29 for an example of the alternative environment technique.

---

* TRIZ is a Russian acronym that stands for *theory of inventive problem solving*.

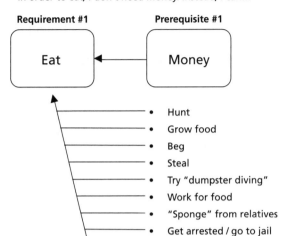

"In order to eat, I don't need money. Instead, I can..."

Figure 5.29 The alternative environment technique.

Once you've compiled all the ways you can think of to satisfy the requirement (R1 or R2) without needing the prerequisite (P1 or P2), you essentially have a list of injections.

Conditions or Actions?

Remember that injections can be either conditions or actions. If you know exactly what action you must take to replace a prerequisite, make it easy on yourself: Choose the *action* (a "do" verb, rather than "have"). But if you don't know exactly what action to take, or if there might be a complex set of actions necessary, try wording your injection as a condition (a "have" verb, rather than "do").

For example, in Figure 5.30, "Have a $1,000,000 retirement fund" is a condition-type injection you might create to satisfy the requirement of "Financial security in declining years." You may later have to develop specific steps needed to realize that injection, but for the moment it's enough to state it as a condition of desired future reality. An injection formulated as an action in this example might look like "con Mom and Dad out of $1,000,000." But if your parents aren't rich (or gullible), the condition wording might be more appropriate until you can figure out what specific steps you need to take.

9. Select the Best Injection(s)

Now you have a list of injections to choose from. If you repeated the alternative environment technique for every assumption you marked as invalid, you may be like the cat that happens on a nest of mice in the basement: You may not know which injection to chase first. In a situation like this, it helps to have a few "decision rules." Some helpful ones might be to choose the injection that:

- Is easiest to do

- Is the least expensive that shows promise of doing the job

- Achieves the minimum acceptable performance the fastest

- Provides the maximum possible improvement in system performance

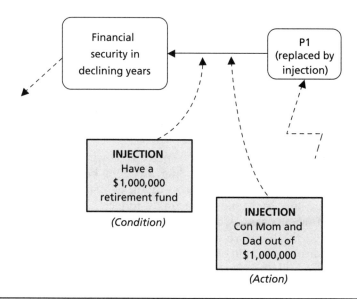

Figure 5.30 The injection: condition or action?

Obviously, some value judgments must be applied here. And you might choose several injections if you can't make up your mind, if you need redundancy to ensure success, or if it seems clear that more than one will be required to break the conflict.

Don't discard any injections that you decide not to use immediately, for two reasons. First, you might find later that you'll have to go back to resurrect one or two of them if the original ones you chose don't do the job you expected. Second, you might find that several injections are required and you might not have originally chosen them all (remember the "silver bullet" warning!) If you've retained the injections you didn't immediately use, you can save a lot of time you might otherwise waste if you had to go back and develop the additional injections from scratch.

Your Evaporating Cloud is now complete. You've articulated the conflict for all to see by identifying the objective, the requirements, and the opposing prerequisites. You've exposed the assumptions and identified the invalid ones. You've created injections to break the invalid assumptions. You're almost ready to think about implementing change, but first there's one last thing you really should do.

SCRUTINIZING AN EVAPORATING CLOUD

Scrutiny of an Evaporating Cloud is substantially different from scrutiny of a sufficiency-type tree such as a Current Reality or Future Reality. There are really only two tests of an Evaporating Cloud's validity.

Reflection of Current Reality

The Evaporating Cloud is basically a depiction of what is happening now—not what we *think should be* happening. Consequently, the EC must reflect current reality with reasonable accuracy. This is purely a subjective judgment on your part, based on your intuitive knowledge of the situation.

Perception

Unlike the Current Reality Tree, however, your worst enemy is a "dry," solid, logical EC. Why? Remember that the purpose of the EC is to reveal faulty logic in an existing situation so as to expose an opportunity to break a conflict, not entrench it. This means that there had better be some faulty logic there to find—if your cloud is "bullet-proof," you're likely to find it much more difficult to break. The key to breaking conflict is to recognize that in addition to a heavy dose of verifiable reality, each EC also usually contains perceptions that might be challenged.

The entity at the tail of each arrow should be perceived by most people to be necessary to achieve the entity at the barb. The word "perceived" is key. It may not actually be necessary—but if it's generally accepted as necessary, the EC can be considered acceptable. So as a final check, be sure that your EC actually reflects the consensus of people's perception of the existing situation. After the EC is complete, you should be able to look at it and ask yourself "Is this what we see?" rather than "Is this what *is?*"

Figure 5.31 provides an example of reward-system conflict. Figure 5.32 provides an abbreviated checklist for building your own ECs. Figure 5.33 contains a sample of a blank form you can reproduce for use in building your ECs. And finally, Figure 5.34 provides an example of a real-world conflict resolved.

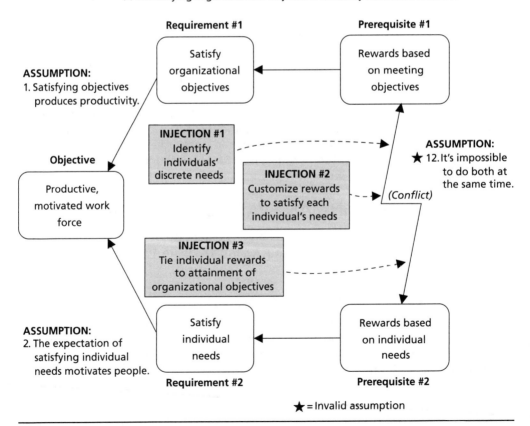

ASSUMPTIONS:
3. The organization needs to have its objectives realized.
4. Behavior is motivated.
5. Success requires behavior motivated toward organizational objectives.
★ 6. Satisfying organizational objectives naturally motivates behavior.

Requirement #1

Satisfy organizational objectives

Prerequisite #1

Rewards based on meeting objectives

ASSUMPTION:
1. Satisfying objectives produces productivity.

Objective

Productive, motivated work force

INJECTION #1
Identify individuals' discrete needs

INJECTION #2
Customize rewards to satisfy each individual's needs

ASSUMPTION:
★ 12. It's impossible to do both at the same time.

(Conflict)

INJECTION #3
Tie individual rewards to attainment of organizational objectives

ASSUMPTION:
2. The expectation of satisfying individual needs motivates people.

Satisfy individual needs

Requirement #2

Rewards based on individual needs

Prerequisite #2

★ = Invalid assumption

Figure 5.31   Evaporating Cloud: reward systems.

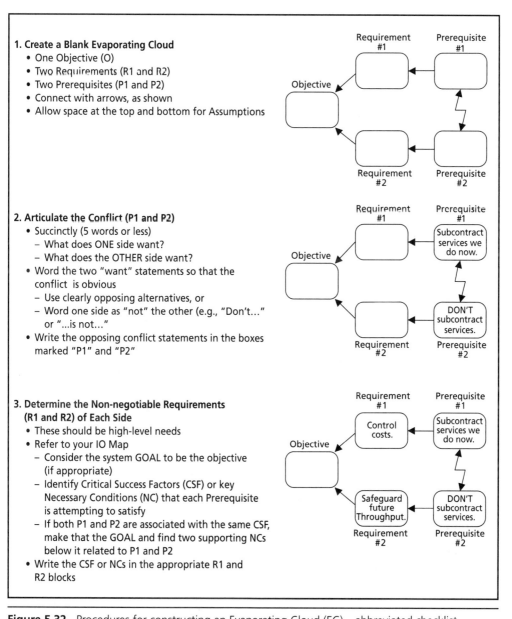

1. Create a Blank Evaporating Cloud
- One Objective (O)
- Two Requirements (R1 and R2)
- Two Prerequisites (P1 and P2)
- Connect with arrows, as shown
- Allow space at the top and bottom for Assumptions

2. Articulate the Conflict (P1 and P2)
- Succinctly (5 words or less)
  - What does ONE side want?
  - What does the OTHER side want?
- Word the two "want" statements so that the conflict is obvious
  - Use clearly opposing alternatives, or
  - Word one side as "not" the other (e.g., "Don't…" or "…is not…"
- Write the opposing conflict statements in the boxes marked "P1" and "P2"

3. Determine the Non-negotiable Requirements (R1 and R2) of Each Side
- These should be high-level needs
- Refer to your IO Map
  - Consider the system GOAL to be the objective (if appropriate)
  - Identify Critical Success Factors (CSF) or key Necessary Conditions (NC) that each Prerequisite is attempting to satisfy
  - If both P1 and P2 are associated with the same CSF, make that the GOAL and find two supporting NCs below it related to P1 and P2
- Write the CSF or NCs in the appropriate R1 and R2 blocks

Figure 5.32   Procedures for constructing an Evaporating Cloud (EC) – abbreviated checklist.

(Continued)

(Continued)

4. **Formulate the Objective (O)**
   - Determine the common objective of both Requirements (R1 and R2)
   - Refer to your IO Map
     - If you used CSF in Step 3, use the GOAL in this step
     - If you used NC in Step 3, use a CSF in this step
   - Write the GOAL or CSF, as appropriate, in the Objective block

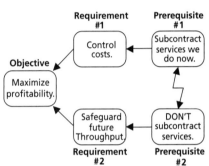

5. **Evaluate the Entire Relationship**
   - Read the Evaporating Cloud from left to right
     - Verbalize "In order to...we must..."
     - Read the top leg first, then the bottom leg
     - Then read the conflict (P1 and P2) as "On one hand... on the other hand..."
   - Determine whether the verbalization "sounds right"
     - Adjust the wording as needed
   - Does the entire conflict accurately reflect the perceptions of both sides?
     - If not, adjust the wording as needed

6. **Develop Underlying Assumptions**
   - Start with the relationship between R1 and P1
     - Re-read it as "In order to...we must..."
     - Add "...because..." and list as many reasons why as you can think of (first-order assumptions)
     - For each "why" statement, if practical add "...because..." and add to the list as many reasons why (second-order assumptions) as you can think of
     - Use *extreme* wording where appropriate
   - List all the assumptions on the EC diagram in the space above the R1-P1 leg
   - Repeat this process for the R2-to-P2 leg
   - Repeat the process again for the O-to-R1 and O-to-R2 legs

ASSUMPTIONS (R1-to-P1):
1. Services done internally *always* impose high overhead on the company.
2. Overhead *always* includes salary and fringe benefits for full-time employees.
3. Subcontracting services *always* allows headcount reductions.
4. Headcount reductions *always* save money.
5. Savings from headcount reductions always offset the cost of subcontracted services.
6. Subcontractors *always* provide equivalent service with never a compromise to reliability, quality, or timeliness.

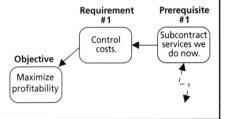

(Continued)

7. Evaluate the Assumptions
- Start with the R1-to-P1 leg
- Differentiate the VALID assumptions from the INVALID ones
  - Examine each assumption individually
  - Pay close attention to the ones that use extreme wording
- Highlight the INVALID assumptions with a distinctive mark

ASSUMPTIONS (R1-to-P1):
1. Services done internally *always* impose high overhead on the company.
2. Overhead *always* includes salary and fringe benefits for full-time employees.
★ 3. Subcontracting services *always* allows significant headcount reductions.
4. Headcount reductions always save money.
★ 5. Savings from headcount reductions *always* offset the cost of subcontracted services.
★ 6. Subcontractors *always* provide equivalent service with never a compromise to reliability, quality, or timeliness.

8. Create "Injections"
- For each leg of the conflict, think of alternatives that can satisfy R1 or R2 without having to be committed to P1 or P2
  - Let the INVALID assumptions suggest alternatives
  - Use an "idea generation" technique such as alternative environment, brainstorming, etc.
  - List as many alternative ideas as you can think of
  - Don't pre-judge or rank-order alternatives until all are identified
- Determine which Prerequisite each potential injection replaces
  - Annotate the injection with a "P1" or "P2"
- Word the injection as an action or condition, as appropriate
  - Action, if the injection is a simple activity or task you know how to do
  - Condition, if the injection is a complex condition of future reality, or the outcome of a series of component activities

> **INJECTION**
> Hire a subcontractor that guarantees its work.
>
> *(Action)*

> **INJECTION**
> Identify Throughput generating work that can be done with the surplus headcount.
>
> *(Condition)*

9. Select the Best Injection(s)
- Decide on a decision rule. E.g., "Select the injection that..."
  - Is easiest to do
  - Is completed the fastest
  - Is least expensive
  - Breaks the most critical assumption
  - Produces the maximum positive benefit for the system
- Recognize that there are no "silver bullets"
  - More than one injection will likely be required in most cases

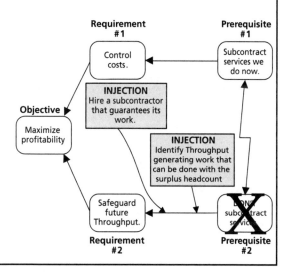

In order to have **O**, we must have **R1**, because:

ASSUMPTIONS:
1.
2.
3.
4.
5.

In order to have **R1**, we must do **O**, because:

ASSUMPTIONS:
1.
2.
3.
4.
5.

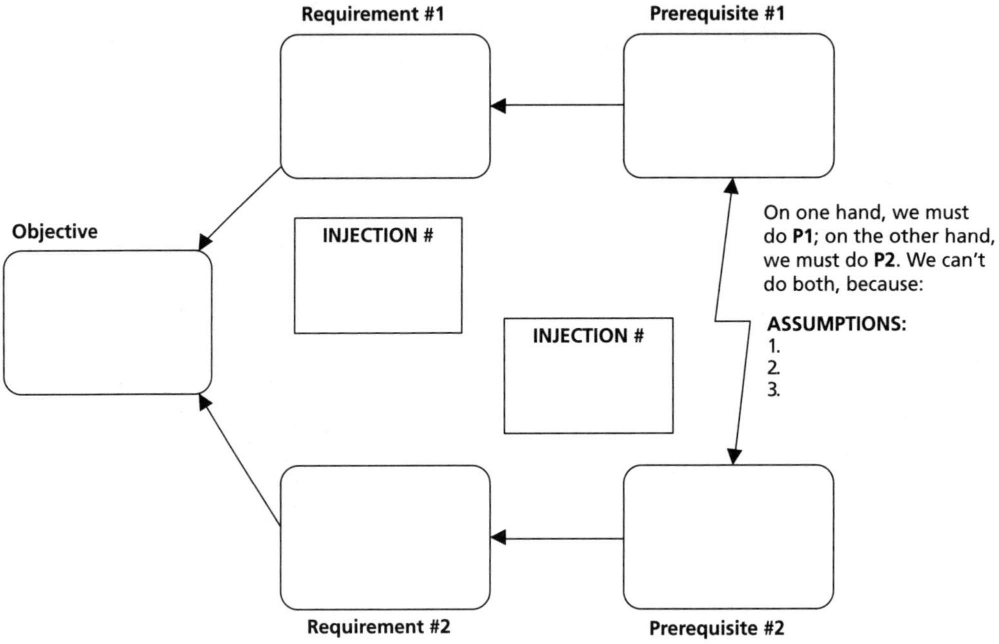

Requirement #1

Prerequisite #1

Objective

INJECTION #

INJECTION #

On one hand, we must do **P1**; on the other hand, we must do **P2**. We can't do both, because:

ASSUMPTIONS:
1.
2.
3.

Requirement #2

Prerequisite #2

In order to have **O**, we must have **R2**, because:

ASSUMPTIONS:
1.
2.
3.
4.
5.

In order to have **R2**, we must do **P2**, because:

ASSUMPTIONS:
1.
2.
3.
4.
5.

Figure 5.33   Evaporating Cloud (EC): master blank form.

★ = *Invalid assumption*

★★ = *Valid assumptions that can be invalidated*

Assumptions:

2. We know metal stamping well.

★ 3. We don't have the capability to learn new skills/technologies.

4. We know nothing about laser-cutting, machining, tube-bending, etc.

5. We know the metal-stamping market intimately.

6. We don't know the market for other metal-forming technologies at all.

★★ 7. There is high risk of failure in technologies and markets we don't know well.

★★ 8. Developing capabilities in new technologies/markets requires money we don't have.

9. We are risk averse.

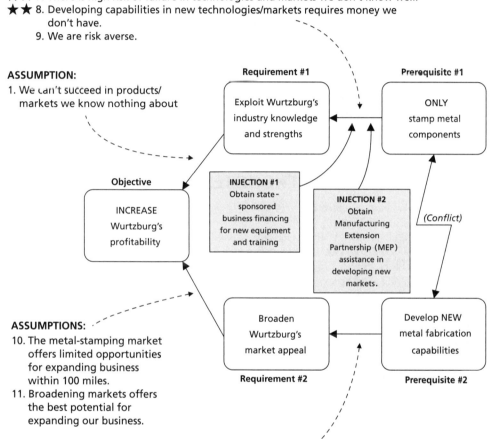

ASSUMPTION:

1. We can't succeed in products/markets we know nothing about

ASSUMPTIONS:

10. The metal-stamping market offers limited opportunities for expanding business within 100 miles.

11. Broadening markets offers the best potential for expanding our business.

ASSUMPTIONS:

12. Our market for stamped components within 100 miles is limited.

13. We can't respond to short-notice new opportunities with stamping.

14. Stamping alone ties us to excessive lead times.

15. Long lead times and no flexibility require long-term contracts (long production runs) for profitability.

16. Modern technologies (computer-controlled) provide speed, flexibility, and shorter lead times.

17. Customers like shorter lead times, faster response, and later decision points.

18. We are more likely to be "the solution" to the customer's challenges.

19. Risk of adopting a new technology can be mitigated.

Figure 5.34 Evaporating Cloud: Wurtzburg Corporation.

SUMMARY

As we've seen, success in using the Evaporating Cloud is based on bringing to the surface the underlying assumptions we make about current reality—assumptions whose validity is questionable. Once we've determined that our conflict is based on invalid assumptions, the door is opened to new ways of satisfying our requirements is opened—ways that completely bypass the original conflict. And the EC helps us to creatively assemble new alternatives.

But new ideas are not solutions. Until they're tested and implemented, they're just ideas. Now that we have an idea for a solution, it's time to verify it. Will it really do what we want it to do? And will it do so without creating more problems than it solves? Verifying the effectiveness of our idea is the job of the second part of determining what to change to: the Future Reality Tree. This is the subject of Chapter 6.

> *It is not because things are difficult that we do not dare. It is because we do not dare that they are difficult.*

> —Seneca

ENDNOTES

1. Dettmer, H. William. *Brainpower Networking Using the Crawford Slip Method.* Victoria, BC (Canada): Trafford Publishing, 2003.
2. Domb, Ellen, Ph.D., and H. William Dettmer. "Breakthrough Innovation in Conflict Resolution: Marrying TRIZ and the TOC Thinking Process." *Proceedings, Constraints Management SIG Symposium,* APICS, 1999.
3. Domb, Ellen, Ph.D., and Kalevi Rantanen. *Simplified TRIZ: New Problem-Solving Applications for Engineers and Manufacturing Professionals.* Boca Raton. FL: St. Lucie Press (2002).
4. Roadman, Charles M., et.al. *Proceedings, Constraints Management SIG Symposium,* APICS, 1995.
5. Terninko, John, Alla Zusman, and Boris Zlotin. *Systematic Innovation: An Introduction to TRIZ.* Boca Raton. FL: St. Lucie Press (1998).

6
Future Reality Tree

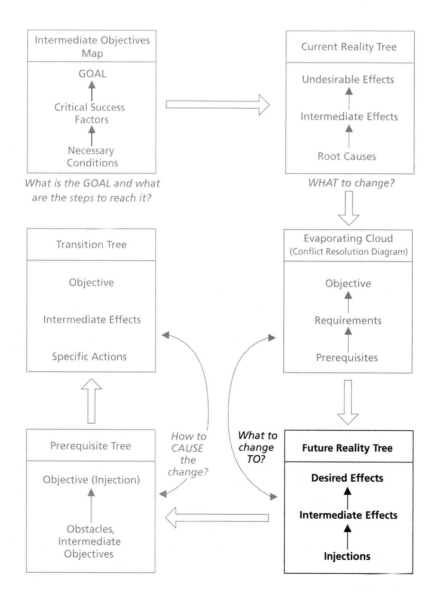

To introduce something altogether new would mean to begin all over, to become ignorant again, and to run the old, old risk of failing to learn.

—Isaac Asimov

Picture yourself responsible for the performance of a complex system—for example, a state education system. For the sake of argument, let's say it's failing the students it's charged with educating. You know you have to make significant changes or watch it collapse completely. And you have no shortage of people telling you what you should do to "fix" the system—and naturally, all of them have different opinions about what should be done. Yet this is not a decision to be entered into lightly. You know it's likely to cost millions of dollars to put the system back on track again, and you really have only one chance to get it right. What will you do?

Would you simply choose a course of action that feels good and say, "That looks about right!"? Or would you rather have some confidence that the decision you're about to make will actually deliver the results you expect—and in the process not dig the hole you're in any deeper?

Naturally, most of us would choose the latter, not the former. Nonetheless, many of us make big decisions in our professional and personal lives with no better assurance that we're doing the right thing than "that feels right!" What if we had a way to "bench test" an idea before we commit a lot of time, energy, and resources to executing it? Wouldn't that be preferable to a "by-guess-and-by-gosh" approach?

The Future Reality Tree can give us confidence born of logic that our chosen path is the right one. In fact, it was specifically intended to do just that.

DEFINITION

The Future Reality Tree (FRT) is a sufficiency-type logic structure designed to predict how changes to the status quo would affect reality—specifically to produce desired effects (DE) (see Figure 6.1). It's an expression of a reality that doesn't yet exist. The FRT visually unfolds the cause-and-effect relationship between changes we make to existing systems and their resulting outcomes.

Though it can be used by itself, without input from preceding stages of the Thinking Process, it wasn't conceived that way. Rather, it was originally intended to follow the Current Reality Tree and Evaporating Cloud in sequence. With the introduction of the Intermediate Objectives Map, another stage in the systems analysis process now precedes the FRT.

The entire logical analysis of a system starts with the determination of expected performance standards, using an Intermediate Objectives Map (Chapter 3). The next stage is the use of a Current Reality Tree to assess the deviation between what *is* happening and what *should be* happening (Chapter 4). Any conflicts attending the critical root causes of the deviations are resolved using Evaporating Clouds (Chapter 5). The Future Reality Tree begins with the outputs of the IO Map, the CRT, and the EC, and provides a roadmap for eliminating the deviations identified earlier in CRT.

Consider the FRT a simulation model of the future. Since the FRT is a projection of the future from the starting point of the present, it's constructed from the bottom upward, rather than from the top downward, the way a Current Reality Tree is.

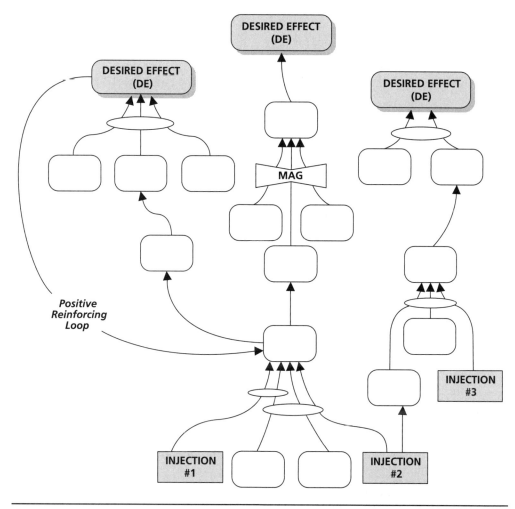

Figure 6.1   The Future Reality Tree (FRT).

PURPOSE

The Future Reality Tree serves eight basic purposes:

- It ensures that any contemplated changes will actually advance the goal and critical success factors of the system.

- It enables effectiveness testing of new ideas before committing resources (time, money, people, and so on) to implementation.

- It logically determines whether proposed system changes will, in fact, produce the desired effects without creating devastating new side effects.

- It reveals, through negative branches, whether (and where) proposed changes will create new or collateral problems as they're solving old problems.

- It helps make beneficial effects self-sustaining through the deliberate incorporation of positive reinforcing loops.

- It provides a way to assess the impacts of localized decisions on the entire system.

- It provides an effective tool for persuading decision makers to support a desired course of action.

- It serves as an initial planning tool for changing the course of the future.

ASSUMPTIONS

The effectiveness of the Future Reality Tree is based on the these assumptions:

- System components are interdependent. A change in one affects others.

- A definite progression of cause and effect governs the functioning of all systems.

- Change has both intended and unintended effects.

- Unintended effects of change can be anticipated.

- Unintended effects can be beneficial, neutral, or detrimental.

- Some changes can cause more problems than they solve.

- It is possible to determine, with reasonable confidence, what effects, both intended and unintended, a change will have on a system.

- Negative effects can be anticipated, located, and prevented.

- Cause-and-effect logic applies equally effectively to the future as it does to the present or past.

- Ideas can't be considered solutions until they have been validated as effective and then implemented.

- All processes within a system, as well as the overall system itself, are subject to variation.

- The concept of cause and effect is regulated by the Categories of Legitimate Reservation (CLR) and is verifiable through the CLR.

- Unstated assumptions about reality underlie all cause-and-effect relationships.

HOW TO USE THIS CHAPTER

- Read "Description of the Future Reality Tree." This section describes what a Future Reality Tree is and how it works.

- Read "How to Construct a Future Reality Tree" and the associated examples. This section explains in detail each of the steps in building a Future Reality Tree and why they're necessary.

- Read "Scrutinizing a Future Reality Tree." This section tells how to ensure that your Future Reality Tree is logically sound and that it accurately depicts "the way things will be" after you make a change.

- Review Figure 6.29, "Future Reality Tree Example: Fordyce Corporation." This is a complete Future Reality Tree on a real-world start-up company. It illustrates how effective the Future Reality Tree is at mapping the route from proposed changes to the desired effects.

- Review Figure 6.27, "Procedures for Constructing a Future Reality Tree." This is an abbreviated checklist that you can use to guide you in constructing your own Future Reality Tree. The checklist contains brief instructions and illustrations for each step. Detailed explanations for each step in the checklist are provided in the chapter itself, under "How to Construct a Future Reality Tree."

Repetition does not establish validity.

—Souder's Law

DESCRIPTION OF THE FUTURE REALITY TREE

How many times have you heard the term "computer simulation model"? Simulation modeling is used extensively in complex, high-technology design processes. New airplane designs are exhaustively tested for stability, airworthiness, and flight-handling characteristics long before the first real airplane rolls down the runway. Why are simulation models so valuable? Aside from the cost of losing an expensive prototype in a crash (not to mention danger to the pilot), consider the risk of committing billions of dollars to an aircraft production program without knowing until too late whether it will do what it was intended to do.

Is it conceivable that this same approach—the simulation model—can apply to other complex situations? That, in essence, is what the Future Reality Tree does. While it isn't an interactive computer model, the FRT's greatest potential value lies in its ability to simulate the future: to identify "bright ideas" that are, in reality, not very bright—that is, they won't get the job done or, worse yet, they'll create more problems than they solve.

A Real-World Example

Consider the Immigration Reform Act of 1986. The U.S. Congress committed no small amount of time, energy, money, and agony trying to get this legislation passed—in spite of political gridlock and over the objections of special interests. The intent of the law was simple: to end illegal entry of aliens into the United States (see Figure 6.2).

Did it succeed? Twenty years after its passage, the influx of illegal aliens is higher than ever. Clearly, the legislation failed at the job it was designed to do. Worse yet, it created at least one collateral problem that didn't previously exist. The law's requirement for employers to verify residency status before hiring spawned a cottage industry in forged documents of all kinds: drivers' licenses, ID cards, Social Security cards, and—worst of all—birth certificates that are virtually indistinguishable from legitimate ones except by close professional examination. The net result of this forgery is a drain on Social Security, Medicaid, and other entitlement resources by people not legally authorized to have them. Surely the U.S. Congress did not anticipate or intend for this to happen.

The chief cause of problems is solutions.

—Sevareid's Law

How much of this outcome might have been foreseen and precluded before the fact? By making good use of an FRT, virtually all of it. Before you invest time, energy, and money trying to make something happen, an effective FRT can give you a measure of assurance that your idea will work. If it reveals that your plan is flawed in some way, this knowledge affords you the opportunity to eliminate the flaws before you begin something that might be destined to fail.

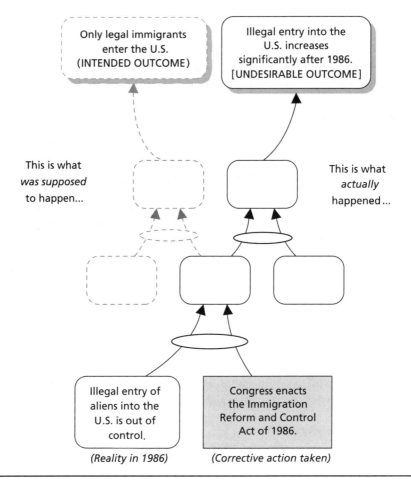

Figure 6.2 A real-world example: the Immigration Reform and Control Act of 1986.

A Framework for Change

The Future Reality Tree provides you with a framework, or drawing board, with which you can design and refine change. It combines elements of existing reality with injections (new ideas) that you create to produce new outcomes, or expected outcomes. In other words, you can plot your proposed changes as a chain of cause and effect leading to your desired future condition.

For example, one element of existing reality is Bernoulli's Principle, which describes the relationship between air flow over a surface and pressure on that surface. What if we combine that bit of reality with a new idea that we create? That idea is to make a device that enables us to sustain and control air flow over a specially designed surface. The immediate outcome is an airfoil, or wing; the ultimate effect is powered flight (see Figure 6.3). This is essentially how the Wright brothers changed the world as we know it. They combined existing reality with an injection of their own creation to produce an expected effect that did not exist at the time. The rest, as they say, is history.

The Wright brothers didn't have the benefit of an FRT to help them, but you do.

> *Nothing is ever so bad that it can't get worse.*
>
> —Gattuso's Extension of Murphy's Law

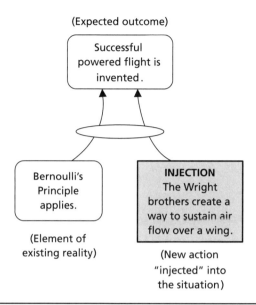

(Expected outcome)

Figure 6.3 A framework for change.

Negative Branches

Anytime you change the status quo, one of three possibilities will occur: things will get better, things will stay the same, or things will get worse. The first is eminently desirable. The second may be acceptable. The third is to be avoided at all costs—unless, of course, it was your intent to make things worse in the first place.

But if your intent is not to make things worse, the *negative branch* aspect of the Future Reality Tree can prove invaluable to you. In fact, the negative branch is so powerful you can use it by itself, in daily applications, without needing a complete FRT. The negative branch enables you to expose the hidden undesirable outcomes that might proceed from any action you're contemplating (see Figure 6.4). Moreover, by using the procedures to identify negative branches, you can locate the exact point in your FRT where the chain of cause and effect begins to turn sour. If you decide to proceed in the face of possible negative consequences, the negative branch will help you decide on ways to minimize or eliminate the negative consequences. The section on negative branches later in this chapter will show you how to take advantage of this powerful tool.

The Positive Reinforcing Loop

Another powerful aspect of the Future Reality Tree in designing the future is the positive reinforcing loop (see Figure 6.5). Nothing is more frustrating than to initiate a change for the better, only to have it fall apart because it wasn't continually monitored and reinforced. Wouldn't it be ideal to implement a solution that was self-sustaining—a solution that reinforced its own existence? The purpose of the positive reinforcing loop is to do precisely that. In an FRT, a desirable effect is deliberately routed back down toward one of its causes, perhaps combined with another element of reality or a subsequent injection, and the original desirable effect is ultimately magnified. This loop relationship reinforces the stability of the new reality and helps make it self-sustaining. Moreover, you need not depend on chance to have a positive reinforcing loop. You can design one into your FRT. The instructions for constructing an FRT later in this chapter will show you how to do just that.

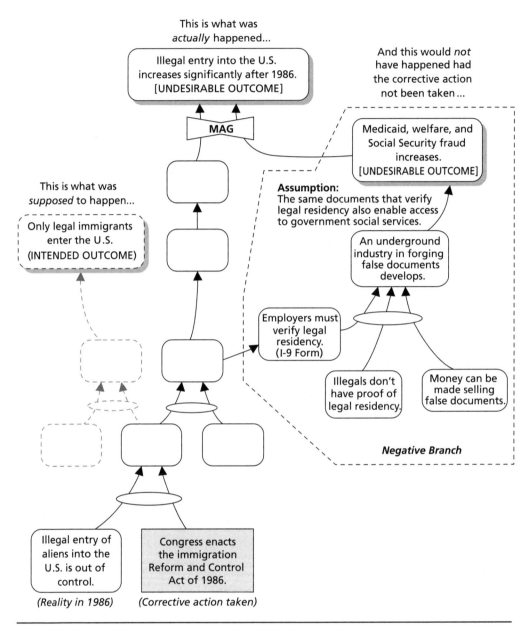

This is what was
actually happened...

Illegal entry into the U.S.
increases significantly after 1986.
[UNDESIRABLE OUTCOME]

And this would *not*
have happened had
the corrective action
not been taken ...

MAG

Medicaid, welfare, and
Social Security fraud
increases.
[UNDESIRABLE OUTCOME]

This is what was
supposed to happen...

Only legal immigrants
enter the U.S.
(INTENDED OUTCOME)

Assumption:
The same documents that verify
legal residency also enable access
to government social services.

An underground
industry in forging
false documents
develops.

Employers must
verify legal
residency.
(I-9 Form)

Illegals don't
have proof of
legal residency.

Money can be
made selling
false documents.

Negative Branch

Illegal entry of
aliens into the
U.S. is out of
control.

Congress enacts
the immigration
Reform and Control
Act of 1986.

(Reality in 1986)

(Corrective action taken)

Figure 6.4   Example of a negative branch.

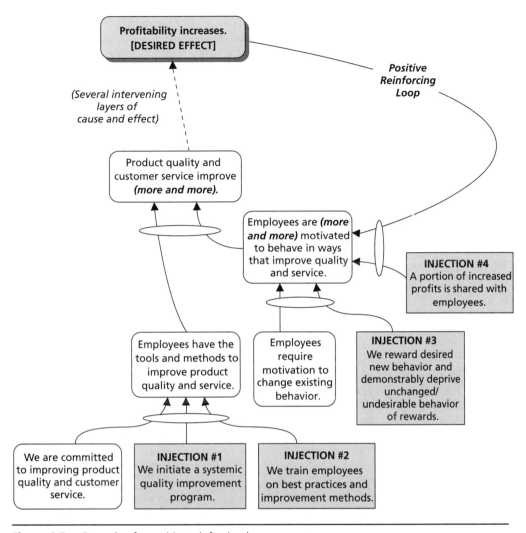

Figure 6.5 Example of a positive reinforcing loop.

Future Reality Tree Symbology

The symbols used in a Future Reality Tree are similar to those used in a Current Reality Tree (see Figure 6.6). A round-cornered box indicates a condition of existing reality or an expected effect. Expected effects may be desirable or undesirable. Desired effects (DE) and undesirable effects (UDE) are reflected by adding shading or a drop-shadow to a basic entity box. A cause-effect arrow indicates a causal relationship, with the cause lying at the tail and the effect at the barb. An ellipse encloses several dependent cause-effect arrows that contribute to an effect. A "bowtie" indicates multiple independent causes that combine to produce an increase in the magnitude of the effect. And a conditional "OR" indicates mutually exclusive effects that might be produced by the same cause.

The significant new symbol in the FRT is a sharp-cornered box, which represents an injection.

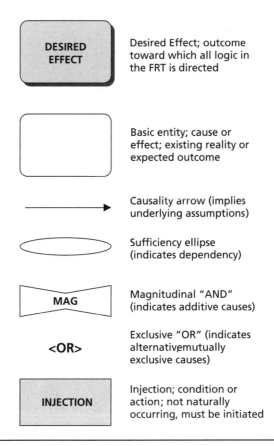

Figure 6.6 Future Reality Tree symbology.

Injections

The entity that gives the Future Reality Tree its flexibility and unlimited potential is the injection. In essence, an injection is a new condition or action that does not exist in current reality. It's something you must *make happen* in order for future reality to unfold the way you want it to. The FRT's flexibility comes from the fact that injections are not fixed or predetermined. You have many choices. By changing injections, you can redesign or revise the way the future develops.

Consider, for example, how differently your personal future might turn out if you substitute one of these injections for another:

- "I go directly from high school to college."

- "I enlist in the Marine Corps directly from high school."

Remembering that an FRT is like a computer simulation of the future, injections become the variables you can change to see how differently the subsequent simulations turn out. Don't lose sight of the fact that *injections are not solutions*—they're *ideas* for solutions. The difference between the two is that solutions have been tested, the kinks have been worked out, obstacles have been overcome, and implementation has been thoroughly planned.

If you've previously constructed an Evaporating Cloud (refer to Chapter 5), injections might come from there. But the FRT can also be used alone, without the other trees. So injections may originate from anywhere—from your imagination or someone else's.

Injections: Actions or Conditions?

Visualize yourself starting the steps necessary to change current reality into desired future reality. Ideally, you'll know exactly what you should do and how to do it. If this is the case, consider yourself fortunate and structure your injection as a specific action.

For example, let's say your desired effect is to realize long-term financial independence. But right now you don't have much money. If you know exactly how to get it, you can make an injection out of the action you'll need to take (see Figure 6.7). The action injection shown here is to embezzle a large sum of money from a company. (That action might lead to financial independence, but it also has a significant negative branch associated with it!)

But as we discussed in Chapter 5, in many cases the changes we need to make represent complex future outcomes—perhaps the result of many component actions, any number of which we might not yet have identified. We also might not know exactly *what* to do at all—in other words, some creative idea generation might be needed.

You might decide to reach financial independence through the more complex process of developing a long-term investment strategy. The establishment of a well-diversified stock portfolio could certainly help you achieve your ultimate goal. But that particular injection would be condition, not an action, because it would represent the culmination of a series of component activities, such as researching investments, identifying a broker, and managing changes in the portfolio over time.

In either case, it isn't necessary (or even desirable) to include such excruciating detail in the FRT. It's usually sufficient for the purpose of outcome testing to indicate some intermediate result—a condition of some kind—as the injection. Let's continue our financial independence example. For the purpose of your FRT, you wouldn't include each individual action in setting up a particular investment (for example, searching out and contacting a financial adviser, researching potential investments, transacting each individual stock purchase, and so on). Rather, you'd consider your injection to be something like, "I have a well-diversified stock portfolio." (See Figure 6.7.)

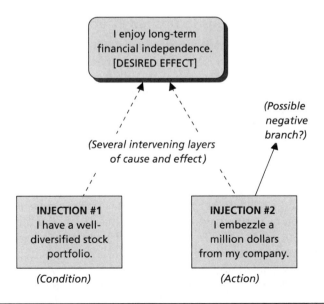

Figure 6.7 Injections: actions or conditions?

At this point you may be thinking, "But how do I determine what all those individual steps might be, and in what sequence I should complete them?" The answer is that such details are the stuff of implementation (execution) planning. You certainly can't ignore them, but it's not productive to spend time on those details in the FRT, when your purpose in completing this tree is to determine whether that well-diversified stock portfolio will actually advance you toward your ultimately desired effect: financial independence. For that purpose, a condition injection—an intermediate outcome of several discrete steps—is sufficient. We'll determine what those steps should be, and their appropriate sequence, in the Prerequisite Tree (Chapter 7).

If your injections are actions, you can expect to have a substantial number of them. If you limit your injections to conditions (outcomes of component actions), you can expect to see considerably fewer of them. Each new condition or action you introduce into reality constitutes an injection.

The Risk of Actions as Injections

There are two potential pitfalls associated with making your injections actions:

- By settling too quickly on a specific action, you may foreclose other possibilities that might turn out to be less expensive, easier to do, or more effective. For example, "Build a central warehouse" forecloses some less expensive options such as renting space. "Have a central warehouse" is a condition, rather than an action, which opens options other than construction. Remember that designing future reality is a creative exercise. Don't constrain your creativity unnecessarily with preconceived solutions by zeroing in on any specific action too soon.

- By focusing too soon on a specific action, there's a tendency to start worrying about implementation before the overall solution is completely and effectively tested for its ability to do the job without creating unacceptable adverse effects.

Don't forget the purpose of the Future Reality Tree: *validation of a proposed course of action*. If you jump too quickly to specific actions, you risk missing the FRT's benefits.

Build Upward, from Injections to Desired Effects

You begin your FRT with a basic injection that comes either from a preceding Evaporating Cloud or from your imagination. This injection, combined with a fact of existing reality, leads to an immediate expected result that didn't exist before. It may automatically produce several successive layers of effects. But invariably, causal momentum "dissipates" at some point. You're likely to find that you're further along than you were when you started, but not yet at your desired effect—and you're at a standstill. You may not be able to advance further without some new injection, one that you hadn't previously foreseen. This is okay—it's one of the things an FRT is designed to tell you: *what additional things must I do to make my original idea effective?*

The answer to this question will represent another injection which, combined with the last outcome, produces still another new result. This process continues until the desired effect is reached. You continue to add effects, new injections, and other statements about reality into your Future Reality Tree as required to maintain logical sufficiency and progress toward the desired effect. Each additional injection is like a course correction keeping you on track toward your ultimate outcome.

How will you know when to add a new injection? The Categories of Legitimate Reservation will tell you. When you encounter a cause insufficiency in a Future Reality

Tree between one level and the next, you must add the not-yet-existing injection needed to complete the logical causality.

Example: Building a House

Let's use the building of a house as an example to see how this works. Your earlier injections included purchasing a lot to build on and selecting an architect to create the plan. The condition of reality that you included near the bottom of the tree was the winning of a million dollars in the lottery. This reality and the two injections have brought you to the point of standing in the middle of an empty lot with a set of plans in your hand. You're further along than when you started, but you're not yet living in the home of your dreams.

And you never will be, either, until and unless you execute some more injections, beginning with the hiring of a general contractor to do the construction. You then keep adding injections as needed until the ultimate effect produced is "I am living in the home of my dreams."

Remember that the Future Reality Tree is a broad simulation model of the future. As such, it's not likely to contain a lot of detail. Though injections may be worded as desired future conditions, if you expect to implement your model of the future these "condition" injections must eventually be translated into outcomes of specific activities that will be developed in Prerequisite Trees (see Chapter 7).

Multiple Injections: The "Silver Bullet" Fallacy

In building a Future Reality Tree, your aim should be to make the simplest change to existing reality that will produce the future conditions you desire. Unfortunately, as we discussed in Chapter 5, because most situations in which you'd need an FRT are complex, it's not likely that you'll find a single "mother of all injections" that will do the job for you. Neat, one-shot solutions are rare in the real world.

Let's say, for example, that a major injection in your FRT is to change a broad policy. You may find that several discrete faulty parts of that policy must be addressed separately in order to ensure the elimination of different undesirable effects. Each of these policy changes might constitute a discrete injection.

In summary, you're likely to need several injections in order to realize most conditions of desired future reality. You may start with only one injection, but you'll undoubtedly add others as you go along.

Where Injections Come From

The obvious question now presents itself: How do I determine what these various injections are? Where do they come from? They can come from a number of sources:

- *The Current Reality Tree.* If you've begun your analysis with a CRT, it can suggest possible injections. Look for critical root causes in the CRT. They may point to the injection(s) necessary to eliminate them. In any case, they're likely to be entering arguments in the FRT because they're conditions of existing reality. If they lead to an undesirable effect in the CRT, they are a starting point that can be combined with an injection in the FRT to favorably modify the future. Though the injection is intended to replace the root cause, in the FRT it's more likely to be combined with it, as shown in Figure 6.8. Moreover, if the root cause also generates positive effects, you probably won't want to replace it. Remember our discussion in Chapter 5 and Figure 5.10 about CRTs being negative branches of current reality? Now would be a good time to revisit that illustration.

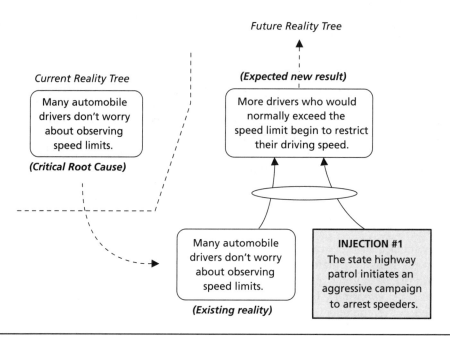

Figure 6.8   Critical root causes: a "stimulant" for injections.

- *The Evaporating Cloud.* If you used an EC to help solve your problem, the injections you developed with it will form the foundation layers of your FRT (see Figure 6.9). Refer to Chapter 5, "Evaporating Cloud," for more on how to use an EC to develop injections.

- *Spontaneous Creativity.* If you haven't used an Evaporating Cloud, you might use some other structured idea-generation method (brainstorming, Crawford Slip Method, Delphi, TRIZ, or other technique) to create your initial injections.

- *Logical Additions.* In the final analysis, you may depend on logical sufficiency to help you identify needed injections. We just alluded to this approach, under "Build Upward from Injections to Desired Effects." Essentially, you start with existing reality and your expected result or desired effect, then ask the question, "What must I add to existing reality to produce the desired effect?" (See Figure 6.9.) After you create an action or condition to add to the relationship, check the connection using the Categories of Legitimate Reservation. They should immediately tell you if your cause is insufficient.

NOTE: As your Future Reality Tree begins to take shape, most of the causality arrows should be passing through ellipses—substantially more than you might expect to find in a CRT. Because injections constitute changes, they must always be combined with existing reality entities to produce a new expected effect. By definition, then, single arrows from injections to effects should be extremely rare. Moreover, the same is generally true of new effects created by combining injections with existing reality. The expected effects will also need to merge with realities or other effects to produce the ultimate desired effect. So if you see a single arrow in an FRT, examine it carefully. An additional injection or unstated reality might be needed. Use the cause insufficiency test: "Can all parts of the effect be accounted for in the cause?" If not, determine what's missing and include it.

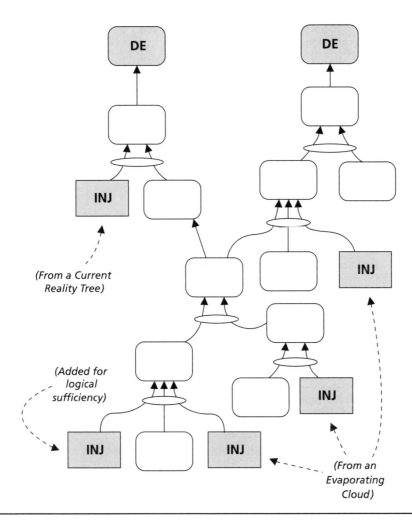

Figure 6.9   Sources of injections.

The Future Reality Tree and Other Thinking Process Trees

You can build an FRT from scratch, without the help of the other Logical Thinking Process trees, but that can require some "brute force." After all, why would you be trying to change the future unless you're dissatisfied with the present? And if you're dissatisfied with the present, how will you know what to change about the present—or what to change it to for the future—without some prior problem analysis?

The Future Reality Tree and the Current Reality Tree

Even if you're strategically planning the future rather than solving a specific problem, you'll be starting from a reference point in the present that will need to be clearly expressed. This is the essential function of the Current Reality Tree. Whatever you define as a critical root cause in a CRT, it's conceivable that your future objective could be the diametric opposite of that situation. If you have undesirable effects in existing circumstances, you probably want them converted into their opposites—desired effects—in your future (see Figure 6.10).

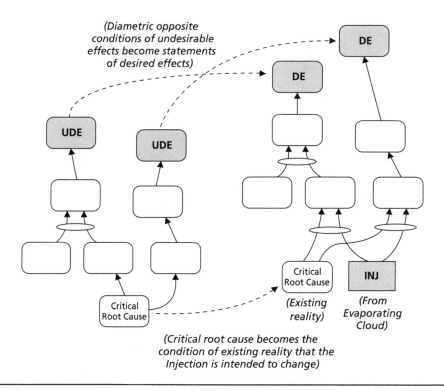

(Diametric opposite conditions of undesirable effects become statements of desired effects)

(Critical root cause becomes the condition of existing reality that the Injection is intended to change)

Figure 6.10   Undesirable effects determine desired effects.

Moreover, it's often very difficult to plan the future unless you're intimately familiar with the causes and effects of the present. The Current Reality Tree can be, in effect, the beginning of the road map to future reality.

The Logical Structure of Reality, Current and Future

If you've already constructed a CRT, you'll find that much of that structure may be usable in building your FRT. Basic relationships in reality are not likely to change very much, so the same logical causality you developed in your CRT will probably apply to the FRT. Parts of the CRT—statements of reality and assumptions for example—may be transferable directly to your FRT. Even undesirable effects can be useful, because "reversing the polarity" of their wording provides an excellent starting point for the desired effects in the FRT.

The most important contribution a well-constructed CRT can offer, however, is its structure. Since the existing general cause-effect relationship will remain the same in the future, you should find similar, comparable branches in your FRT. Figure 6.11 illustrates these similarities.

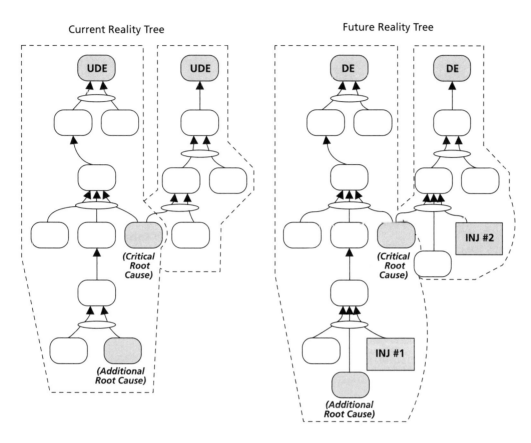

Current Reality Tree

Future Reality Tree

The CRT displays two distinct branches...   *...which also manifest themselves in the FRT*

Figure 6.11   The FRT retains the same basic structure as the CRT.

The Future Reality Tree and the Evaporating Cloud

Effectively changing future reality requires that you know what to change it to. An Evaporating Cloud can provide part of the answer to that question by suggesting injections as alternatives to the causes in existing reality. The Future Reality Tree then answers the rest of the question, logically testing the effectiveness of those injections (see Figure 6.12).

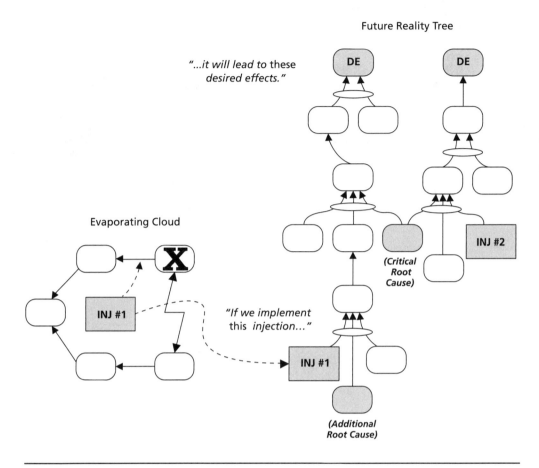

Figure 6.12 The FRT logically verifies injections from an Evaporating Cloud.

If you use both a CRT and an EC to help structure your Future Reality Tree, you'll have some very important elements already in place as you begin to make logical connections. Figure 6.13 shows how essential elements of the EC and CRT can provide a "connect-the-dots" type of framework for your Future Reality Tree.

The Future Reality Tree and the Prerequisite Tree

The FRT occupies a unique position in the Logical Thinking Process. It serves as a bridge between the analysis of the present, as embodied in the CRT, and the implementation of change in the future. Once the ideas for problem solution are developed and properly validated, all that remains is to execute them. The Prerequisite Tree (PRT) is the Logical Thinking Process tool that facilitates implementation and it uses the FRT injections as its starting points. Execution and PRTs will be covered in more detail in the next chapter, but for now Figure 6.14 shows the relationship of the FRT to the PRT.

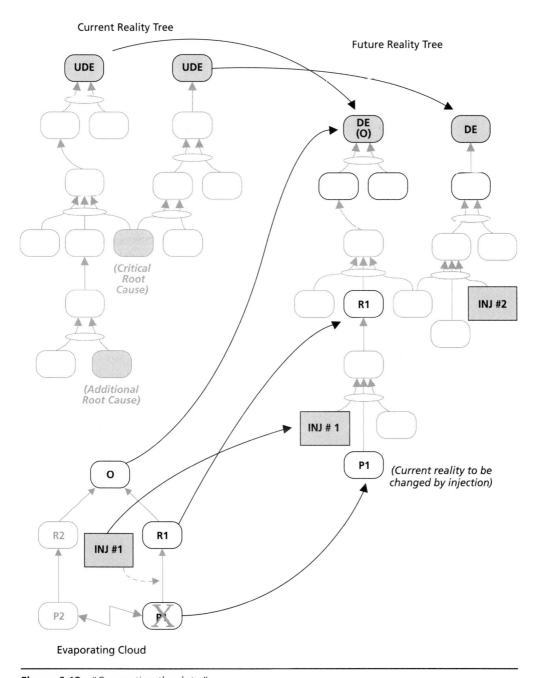

Figure 6.13 "Connecting the dots."

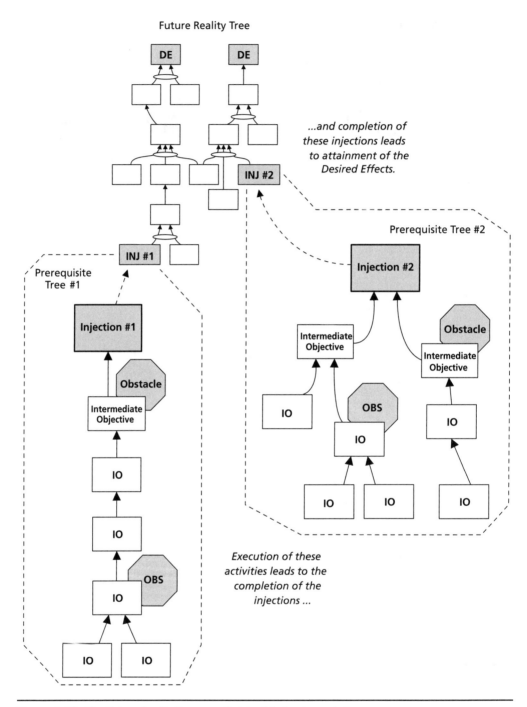

Figure 6.14 The Future Reality Tree as a "bridge" to implementation.

The Future Reality Tree as a "Safety Net"

One of the strengths of the Future Reality Tree is its ability to act as a safety net for the Current Reality Tree and the Evaporating Cloud. What this means is that you don't have to have a perfect CRT or EC to have an effective FRT. If you don't precisely identify the critical root cause in the Current Reality Tree, it's not critical—you only need the CRT to get you into the area of the critical root cause. If you don't identify all the assumptions that need to be broken in the EC, don't worry. As long as you have a major invalid assumption to attack, you have enough to get started. The sufficiency characteristic of the FRT will catch any omissions from the EC or the CRT through negative branches. Goldratt once observed, "It's better to be approximately correct than precisely incorrect." That observation is still valid today. So don't agonize over unnecessary precision in the CRT or EC. The FRT is where you must be precise. If you're thorough and conscientious with your logic in the FRT, you'll catch any deficiencies overlooked with the other two tools.

> *In our haste to deal with the things that are wrong, let us not upset the things that are right.*
>
> —Unknown

Negative Branches

The negative branch is one of the most powerful features of the Future Reality Tree. It can save planners and problem solvers much heartache and aggravation during implementation.

The negative branch is a kind of predicted effect existence reservation. (Refer to Chapter 2, "Categories of Legitimate Reservation," for more on the predicted effect existence reservation.) But instead of using them to prove the existence of an intangible cause, we use predicted effects to expose any possible undesirable outcomes associated with an injection we're thinking of using. For example, let's say that your injection is "I lend you my car." The outcome I desire is "You drive my children to school." (See Figure 6.15.)

My desired outcome is probably entirely reasonable, but some other conditions of reality might be considered (for example, "You've had four accidents in the last six months"). In a situation like this, the following negative branch then becomes a real possibility: "You wreck my car."

Using the Negative Branch as a "Stand-Alone"

The preceding example also illustrates a feature of negative branches that makes them extremely useful in daily application: You don't need any of the other Thinking Process trees to make good use of negative branches, not even a Future Reality Tree.

If you're called upon to render a decision that seems questionable, ask for some time to consider the issue: "Let me think about that for a few minutes." Then see if you can construct a quick negative branch. If you decide there are no realistic negative consequences, you'll be more confident about your decision. If there are undesirable outcomes, the negative branch may help you do one of two things:

- Decline the request tactfully, without incurring animosity

- Find an alternative means (injection) of satisfying the original intent without incurring the risk of an undesirable outcome

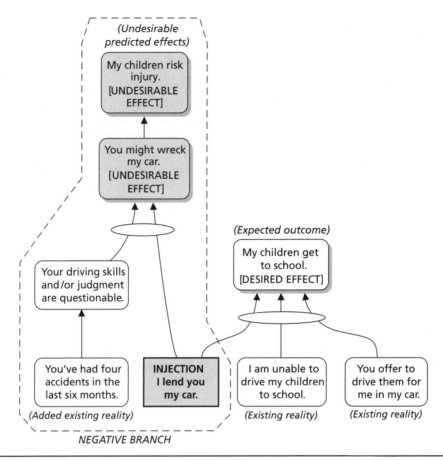

Figure 6.15   Negative branch: an example.

For example, if you had approached me to borrow my car, I could have begun with the injection "I lend you my car" and developed a negative branch all by itself, without resorting to an FRT. If I really perceive a risk of your wrecking my car, the negative branch might steer me to this response: "If you can wait until lunchtime, I'll drop you by your appointment on my way out and pick you up on my way back." The negative branch helps make your response "palatable" for others to accept without incurring ill feelings.

Day-to-day decisions can be effectively and analyzed and "unpleasantries" avoided this way. Figure 6.16 shows how a different negative branch might be "trimmed." Figure 6.28, "Using the Negative Branch as a Stand-Alone Tool," provides abbreviated steps for using a negative branch without a complete Future Reality Tree.

Added Realities
If your negative branch is a growth on a Future Reality Tree, it's likely to result from the combination of your injections with other conditions of reality that you haven't previously identified in the basic FRT. In Figure 6.16, for example, when introducing the injection "We buy a new laser-cutting machine," we have to consider more than just the anticipated beneficial outcomes (that is, the new business that might be captured).

We also have to anticipate the debt we'll incur for the machine's purchase. If we don't pay cash for the machine (an underlying, possibly unstated assumption), we'll have a sizable debt to pay off. In most cases, we'd plan to finance that debt with the increase in new business from the added capability the laser cutter gives us.

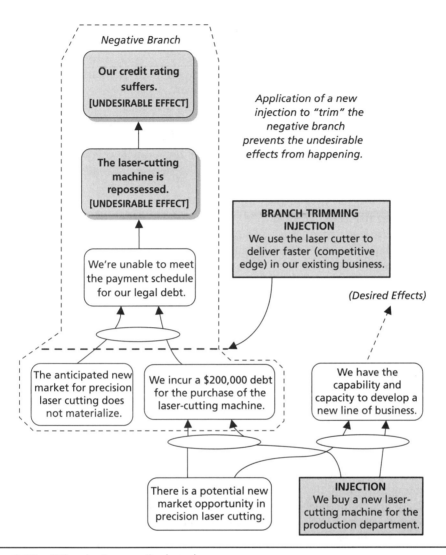

Figure 6.16 "Trimming" a negative branch.

But what if that new market doesn't develop for some reason? Now we're left with a capital debt and no way to pay it off. At some point, our bank will repossess the machine, which would adversely affect our credit rating. Both the repossession and the degraded credit rating are undesirable effects that grow out of the injection—the action we plan to take. That action itself is not negative, nor is it negative when considered with the other conditions (expected new market demand) we include in our FRT. It's only when we add unfavorable conditions of reality that might occur that the causal path turns negative.

Is this speculation? Of course! But so is our intended (desirable) future reality. What the negative branch helps us consider, before damage is inflicted on us, is the potential negative outcome of the same decision that's supposed to deliver good outcomes. Obviously, there are probabilities associated with both the good and bad causal paths. We'll have to consider these on a case-by-case basis. The negative branch only shows what *could* happen if an unfavorable probability actually does happen.

Assumptions

Remember that, as with Current Reality Trees and Evaporating Clouds, the arrows in a negative branch also imply the presence of underlying assumptions. In fact, we just mentioned one in the Figure 6.16 example. The ones that are particularly important in a negative branch are those associated with the arrows connecting neutral entities or injections to the negative entity. It is at this point that the Negative Branch begins to turn "sour" and trimming must be done.

You should identify as many assumptions as possible underlying these crucial arrows, and develop new injections to negate or neutralize them, much as you would do with an Evaporating Cloud. In fact, you can use an EC to help you create injections to trim negative branches.

"Trimming" Negative Branches

Once you have the added realities and the additional injections needed to break the assumptions that turn the branch negative, you're on the verge of trimming the negative branch.

You incorporate the added reality and the new injection— or injections, if more than one is required— into your Future Reality Tree at the point where the branch had begun to turn from positive or neutral to negative. Then recheck the logic of the entire tree downstream from (that is, above) the trim point. Make any subsequent adjustments to meet CLR requirements, not just at the trim point (see Figure 6.17).

When to Raise Negative Branch Reservations

In many situations as you're building a Future Reality Tree, you'll notice places where it's highly probable that a negative branch might develop. These places may be obvious. As the builder of the tree, if you see such indications, mark them in some prominent way and continue building your FRT. Don't become side-tracked trying to deal with them before the FRT is completed. Always make your basic FRT as logically tight as you can during construction, then go back afterward to address any potential negative branches you might have identified.

As you work, remember that the tree builder's inherent "blindness" to logical deficiencies may cause you to overlook negative branches. It might require someone else's independent scrutiny of your tree to point them out.

If you present your tree to others for scrutiny, ask them to make note of any negative branch they might see but to wait to tell you about it until after the entire tree has been presented. Figure 6.28, "How to Trim a Negative Branch," provides detailed directions for constructing and trimming negative branches.

> *The time it takes to rectify a situation is inversely proportional to the time it took to do the damage. EXAMPLE: It takes longer to glue a vase together than to break one.*
>
> —Drazen's Law of Restitution

Positive Reinforcing Loops

In building a Future Reality Tree, you'll occasionally notice situations where a desired effect might feed back and amplify another entity lower in the tree. That lower entity may originally be neutral or positive, but the outcome of the desired effect higher up is to reinforce or increase the magnitude of the entity below (see Figure 6.5).

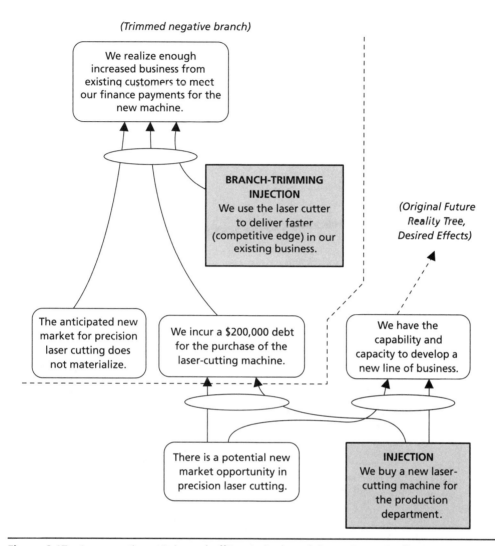

Figure 6.17 Incorporating a "trimmed-off" negative branch into a Future Reality Tree.

As we've previously discussed, this effect is called a positive reinforcing loop, and it's highly desirable in any Future Reality Tree. In fact, it's so desirable that if you don't notice one occurring naturally, you should actively search for ways to make the ultimate desired effects reinforce their causes lower in the tree. By doing so you can frequently make your desirable condition self-sustaining and synergetic. The more positive loops you have, the greater the probability of a self-sustaining solution.

Figure 6.18 presents a more detailed example. Figure 6.27 (on page 244), "Procedures for Building a Future Reality Tree," includes a specific step prompting you to create positive reinforcing loops.

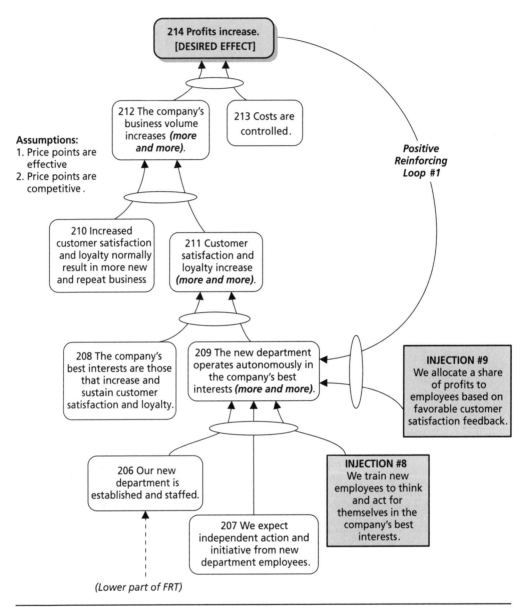

Figure 6.18 Positive reinforcing loop: an example.

Strategic Planning with a Future Reality Tree

So far we've examined the Future Reality Tree in a problem-solving role as a "solution tester"—a way of validating the effectiveness of ideas for solutions and exposing any undesirable collateral effects of these ideas. This is probably the mode in which you'll most frequently use it. But the FRT's capability as a strategic planning model is potentially its most valuable application. The FRT can substitute for a traditional strategic plan by visually representing what needs to be done.

The subject of strategic planning using the Logical Thinking Process is beyond the scope of this book. However, it is explained in detail in *Strategic Navigation: A Systems Approach to Business Strategy.*[1]

HOW TO CONSTRUCT A FUTURE REALITY TREE

Now you're ready to begin building a Future Reality Tree. The following procedures will lead you through the process. An abbreviated checklist of these same procedures may be found in Figure 6.27, "Procedures for Constructing a Future Reality Tree."

Now it's time to start applying what we've covered so far on Future Reality Trees.

1. Gather Necessary Information and Materials

While it is possible to start building a Future Reality Tree from scratch with no inputs from previous logic trees, it's not the easiest way to do it. At the very least, you should have an Intermediate Objectives Map to articulate the system-level goal and critical success factors your tree should be trying to achieve. It only takes about 15 minutes to complete an effective IO Map, so if you haven't already done one, go back and do it now. (Refer to Chapter 3, "Intermediate Objective Map").

If you already have some previous related logic trees, now would be a good time to bring them out. In addition to an IO Map, you might already have a Current Reality Tree and one or more Evaporating Clouds. From the CRT, make a list of undesirable effects and the critical root causes. From the EC, add to your list the objective, the two requirements, and any injections you have developed. Keep the assumptions from your EC close at hand, too. (Figure 6.19)

Information:

Goal, CSF, NC (IO Map)	Undesirable Effects (CRT)	Evaporating Cloud(s)
Goal CSF #1 CSF #2 CSF #3 CSF #4 NC NC NC NC	1. ..... 2. ..... 3. ..... 4. ..... 5.	Objective Requirement #1 Requirement #2 Injection Injection Prerequisite #1 and/or #2 Assumptions: 1. ..... 2. ..... 3. ..... 4. ..... Etc. Etc.

Materials:

1. Flip-chart paper
2. Post-it Notes
3. Indelible bold pens
4. Pencils
5. Large erasers
6. Scotch tape

Figure 6.19   Step 1: Gather all necessary information and materials.

You'll need an oversized sheet of paper, an indelible bold pen, pencils, erasers, and Post-it Notes, just as you had for the CRT. Some clear tape would be useful, too, for securing the Post-it Notes in their final positions before taking the large paper off the wall or easel.

2. Formulate Desired Effects

Begin your tree by writing, on Post-it Notes, statements of the desired effects you're trying to achieve (see Figure 6.20). If you have a CRT to start from, extract all of the undesirable effects (UDE) from it. Then rephrase each one in an opposite, or desirable, way. For example, if the UDE reads "The company loses money," the opposite (desirable) phrasing might be "The company makes money." These desired effects will be the ultimate targets of the FRT.

Positive, Not Neutral
Be sure the wording you use to express the desired effect, the opposite of the UDE, is truly positive and not merely neutral (that is, be sure it expresses "good," rather than just "not bad").

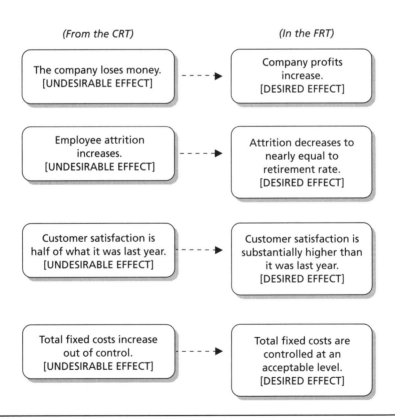

Figure 6.20 Step 2: Formulate the desired effects.

Use Present Tense

Avoid future tense in wording all entities in your FRT. Consider it a real-time computer simulation, as if it's happening right now. Use present-tense wording (for example, "is," "are," and "can," not "will be").

Lay Out Desired Effects

Start by arranging the desired-effect Post-it Notes horizontally across the top of your paper. Remember that future reality will have the same basic branch configuration as current reality, but with opposite "polarity." Adjust the placement of the desired effects as appropriate to approximate the same structure as the CRT. (See Figure 6.21.)

In other words, if your desired effects come from UDEs in a CRT, they will occupy the same relative positions in the FRT. The basic relationships of reality will usually remain the same.

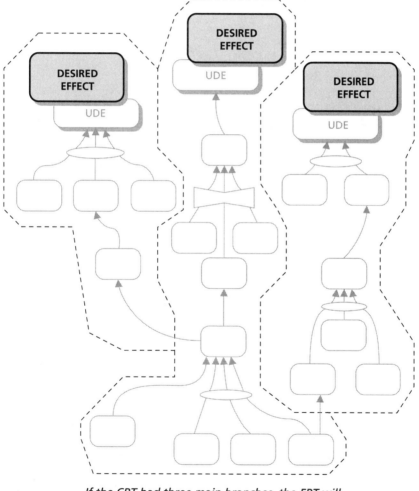

If the CRT had three main branches, the FRT will likely have three comparable main branches

Figure 6.21   FRT branch structure is similar to the CRT.

3. Add Injection(s) and Evaporating Cloud Requirements

Place your injection Post-it Notes at the bottom of the page (see Figure 6.22). In order for the future to unfold differently from the present, some change in what's currently happening must be initiated. You must do something different, or create conditions favorable to the development of the future along your intended path. The changes you make will constitute injections.

Where Do We Find Injections?

If you're starting your Future Reality Tree without having completed a CRT or Evaporating Cloud, you'll have to be creative in deciding what to change and what form the changes should take. Idea-generation methods such as brainstorming, nominal group technique, TRIZ, and the Crawford Slip Method can be useful in developing injections. But if you have a CRT or EC, much of the creative work may be already done. The EC, besides helping resolve conflict, is a natural "idea generator." Chances are, if you've constructed an EC, you'll already have one primary injection and maybe some secondary

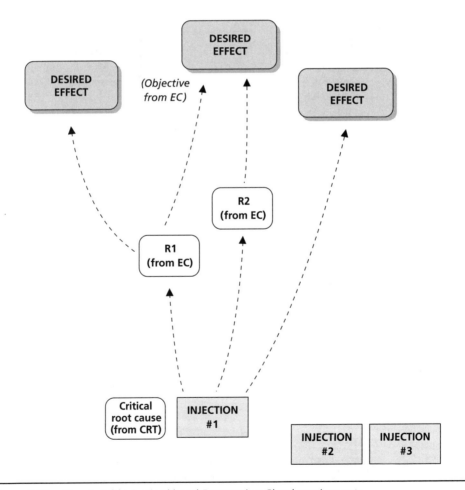

Figure 6.22   Step 3: Add injection(s) and Evaporating Cloud requirements.

ones. Write your injections on Post-it Notes. Distinguish them from other entities by using different colored notes or by outlining the edges.

Injections at the Bottom

Put your primary injection at the bottom of the paper, in the center. If you have additional injections you expect to use, arrange them temporarily in a horizontal "holding pattern" to one side along the bottom edge of the paper (see Figure 6.22).

> **NOTE:** If you already have a CRT or EC relating to your problem, you can add a few more elements. Some might be the statements of critical root causes. Two others might be the requirements from the EC (that is, R1 and R2). The latter would show up as effects of the primary injection (probably several layers of cause and effect above the injection itself). The objective of the EC is likely to show up in the FRT as a desired effect.

4. Fill in the Gaps

You now have a framework in which to build your Future Reality Tree.

Build Upward

Starting with your primary injection at the bottom, build upward toward the desired effects. Combine your injection with an entity of current reality—a critical root cause from your CRT, for example. Use an ellipse to combine multiple causes into an expected effect (one that does not yet exist).

For example, let's assume that your current reality is "Our order-to-delivery times are longer than our competitors' times." That might prompt the question, "So what?" An additional statement about existing reality that provides motivation might be added: "New and existing customers are attracted to short delivery times." Your injection might be "We optimize production for fast delivery." The expected effect of these three entities might be "New and existing customers are attracted to our faster delivery times." With each layer of cause and effect we must adhere to the requirements of the Categories of Legitimate Reservation, with special attention to cause insufficiency (see Figure 6.23).

The direct and unavoidable effect of the conditions of reality, combined with the injection, should produce an effect that is a step closer to one of the intermediate "milestones"—a requirement from the Evaporating Cloud, for example.

Continue Building from the Expected Effect

Each successive layer of effects should move you progressively closer to your desired effects. Check to be sure this is happening. The expected effect may be enough to propel the causality through more than one subsequent layer. But if it's not, "causal inertia" may die unless you help the process along with another injection (see Figure 6.24).

In the previous example, optimizing production for faster delivery resulted in order-to-delivery times that would probably be attractive to customers. But that attractiveness alone doesn't translate directly to the desired effect: increased profitability. No further progress is possible without taking some additional action—that is, adding another injection. In this case, the additional injection, ensuring that prospective customers know about the improved capability, moves the cause-and-effect process another level closer to securing more business and ultimately to improved profitability.

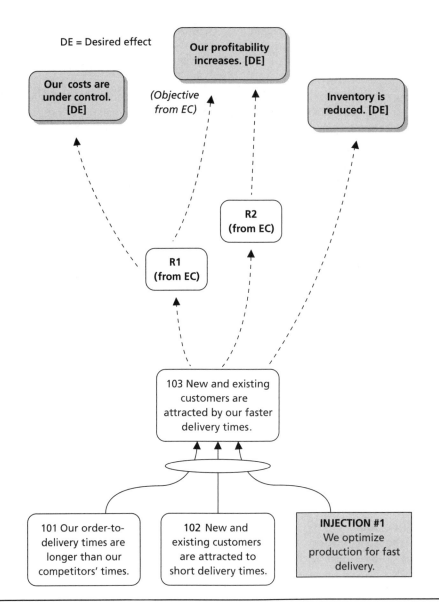

Figure 6.23 Step 4: Fill in the gaps.

Having a CRT available makes the job of filling in gaps much easier. If you don't have a CRT to work from, you may have to "hack your way through the jungle" a bit to reach your desired effects. In any event, continue building upward until you connect with the EC requirements, and on up to the desired effects.

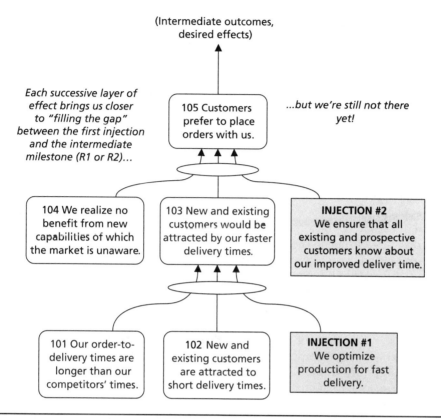

(Intermediate outcomes, desired effects)

Each successive layer of effect brings us closer to "filling the gap" between the first injection and the intermediate milestone (R1 or R2)...

105 Customers prefer to place orders with us.

...but we're still not there yet!

104 We realize no benefit from new capabilities of which the market is unaware.

103 New and existing customers would be attracted by our faster delivery times.

INJECTION #2 We ensure that all existing and prospective customers know about our improved deliver time.

101 Our order-to-delivery times are longer than our competitors' times.

102 New and existing customers are attracted to short delivery times.

INJECTION #1 We optimize production for fast delivery.

Figure 6.24   Add injections to maintain forward progress.

5. Build In Positive Reinforcing Loops

Once all the connections are completed from required injections to desired effects, examine each desired effect (DE) as a possible candidate for a positive reinforcing loop. Then, starting at the bottom of the tree, try to find an effect entity below the desired effect that the DE will amplify or reinforce.

If none present themselves naturally, try to add entities and injections as necessary to create a positive loop. It may be necessary to combine the arrow from the DE with any added entities using an ellipse. (See Figure 6.18.)

Be sure that the entity at the reentry point of the loop will withstand an additional cause reservation. In other words, be sure that the entity the loop leads to can't be produced by any other independent cause. If it can be produced by another cause, you'll never know whether your loop is really the cause of the reinforcement. You may think it is, but if that additional cause suddenly goes away, you could lose your reinforcing effect and not understand why.

> *What we anticipate seldom occurs. What we least expected usually happens.*
>
> —Benjamin Disraeli

6. Look for Negative Branches

Remember from our discussion of the Current Reality Tree (Chapter 4) that the CRT is really only a negative branch of existing reality—it doesn't include the beneficial parts of the system, because its purpose is to analyze gaps or mismatches between expected performance standards (as articulated in the IO Map) and actual system performance. Consequently, aspects of the system that are performing acceptably are omitted from the CRT. The FRT will only reflect desired effects that represent "cures" to the deficiencies identified in the CRT.

> **NOTE:** As we discussed with the law of unintended consequences, sometimes changes we make (or injections we apply) can also produce unpleasant consequences—new undesirable effects that didn't exist before the injection was applied. In many (perhaps all) cases, such new UDEs represent deviations from critical success factors or necessary conditions in the IO Map that were not considered problems before. As a rule of thumb, evaluate the new developments in your FRT against these elements from the IO Map that weren't reflected in the original CRT. Ask yourself, "Will this new course of action adversely affect any CSF or NC that were problem free under the CRT?" This can help you locate potential negative branches more quickly.

Starting at the bottom of the Future Reality Tree, systematically examine each expected effect of every injection for possible negative outcomes (see Figure 6.25). Ask yourself, "Besides this desired outcome, what else could result from this injection that would be detrimental to the system?"

Since negative branches can develop at any subsequent point, don't become complacent if you don't find one immediately above the injection. Work upward from the injection along each branch to the top of the Future Reality Tree. Don't overlook negative outcomes associated directly with the desired effects, either. It's so easy to focus on the desirable outcomes of the FRT that the adverse impacts may be overlooked. There's a tendency to breathe a sigh of relief when you reach the desired effects and ignore their downsides. What are the possible undesirable effects of your reaching that pot of gold at the end of the rainbow? (Ever hear the saying, "He was a victim of his own success"?)

Why Negative Branches Require Attention

Why should we be concerned about negative branches? Other than the obvious reason (that is, we may not like the outcome), we might have to consider other people as well. Frequently it's necessary to work outside our span of complete control in order to change things. What if you need the assistance of other people to achieve the desired effects? And what if those people can see downsides to your proposed course of action, maybe disadvantages that affect them directly? How can we expect their support, unless we can demonstrate that we've already identified those disadvantages and taken steps to neutralize them? Part of the persuasion process in such cases involves addressing negative branches in the presentation of the Future Reality Tree to others. (Refer to Chapter 8 for more discussion on persuading others with your logic.)

> **NOTE 1:** Don't start looking for negative branches before your FRT is complete. It's too easy to become sidetracked and the tree may never develop its basic shape. In pursuit of negative branches, you may be diverted from your original purpose, which is to build up to the desired effects. So save work on negative branches until after the FRT is done, even if you're certain you know where some might pop up.

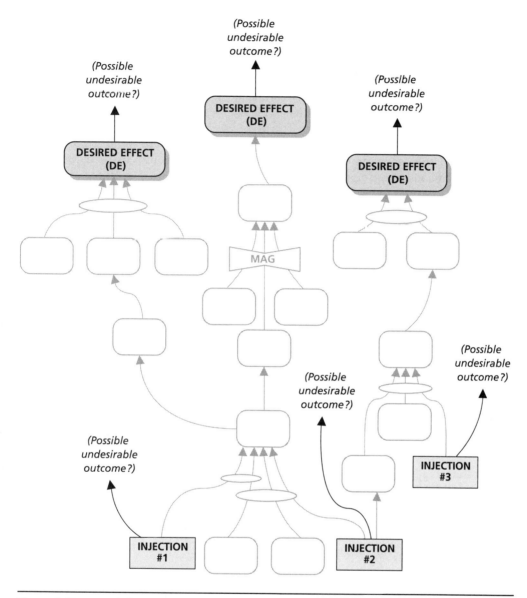

Figure 6.25   Search for negative branches.

NOTE 2: Remember that, as with any personal creation, you have "pride of authorship" in your tree. To some extent, this can blind you to its deficiencies. Moreover, it's likely that you'll be unable to see all the negative possibilities associated with it. Even if you find a few negative branches, you might need the help of "outside eyes" to locate them all. Before acting on your tree, you'd be well advised to have someone else scrutinize your tree—someone with intuitive knowledge of your situation. Even if he or she doesn't point out any more negative branches, the additional review is likely to help you clarify and strengthen the logic of your FRT.

7. Develop Negative Branches

If you find possible negative branches, write the entities on Post-it Notes and place them in their proper positions. To preclude confusion, you may want to develop your negative branch on a separate piece of paper. Include additional reality entities and ellipses as required. Continue building the negative branch upward, just as you did with the main FRT, until you reach effects that are undesirable with respect to the goal or critical success factors (see Figure 6.26).

Don't expect your injection to produce an undesirable effect directly. Instead, it's more likely to lead through some intermediate effects that are neutral, or perhaps slightly negative, before reaching something that is definitely undesirable. The same is true of the relationship between injections and desired effects. So be prepared for your negative branch to be more than just one or two entities—possibly even very complex.

8. Trim Negative Branches

When the negative branch is fully developed, decide how to "trim" it off the FRT. This requires the addition of a "branch-trimming" injection. The first step in trimming a negative branch is similar to the initial step in resolving an Evaporating Cloud: *identify the underlying assumptions.* And it's the same for a similar reason. Injections to trim a negative branch are inherent in the underlying assumptions of an associated arrow, just as they are in an Evaporating Cloud.

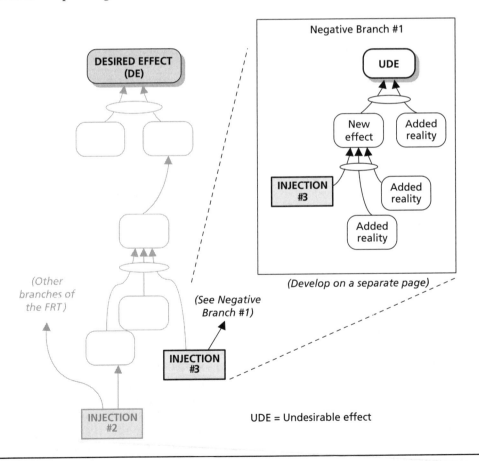

Figure 6.26   Develop the negative branch.

We're not concerned with all the assumptions in a Negative Branch, only the ones associated with the *transitional arrow*. The transitional arrow is the one that leads into the first clearly negative entity—the place where we can definitely say, "Things are starting to go badly here," even if we're not yet to the point of an UDE.

We read the connection in this case a little differently. Remember that in the Evaporating Cloud we read the relationship, "In order to...we must...". To get to the underlying assumptions in a negative branch, we read, "If [cause]...then [effect], *because* [assumption]."

Normally, you won't find more than a few assumptions associated with a transitional arrow in a negative branch—and sometimes only one. But one is probably enough to suggest an injection, especially if you use the extreme wording technique in your assumptions (see Chapter 5).

Once you've articulated the underlying assumptions at the transitional arrows, create an injection to trim the branch at that point. This means that such an injection, combined with the causes at the tails of the transitional arrows, will produce a benign or even positive effect, rather than the negative one you started with. Develop this causality on a separate piece of paper (see Figure 6.29 p. 6, for an example). This "trimmed" causality is no more than the projection of the branch-trimming injection to its logical conclusion—and that had better be favorable (or at least neutral), otherwise you've chosen the wrong injection.

Verify the "trimmed" causality using the Categories of Legitimate Reservation, and be sure that your branch-trimming injection doesn't create any negative branches of its own. Figure 6.27 includes an abbreviated list of steps for how to trim a negative branch, along with an illustration.

9. Incorporate the "Branch-Trimming" Injection into the FRT

Once the branch-trimming effort is verified with the CLR, you must go back and incorporate this "trimmed" logical construction into the original FRT. Why? Basically, for two reasons.

First, when it comes to planning implementation of the FRT, if the branch-trimming injection doesn't appear in the main FRT with all the others, there's a chance you might forget to execute it. (Remember, you constructed the negative branch and the trimmed part on separate pages.)

Second, if this negative branch occurred to you, it might well occur to others. Eventually, you'll probably present your FRT to decision makers for approval—or at least to contemporaries to enlist support. In either case, it's faster and "cleaner" to show that you've anticipated a problem with the proposed solution yourself, rather than to have someone point out a "show-stopping" negative branch at the last minute. By putting the branch-trimming logic into the main FRT, you kill both of these birds with one stone.

10. Scrutinize the Entire FRT

Once all negative branches have been identified and trimmed, reread and scrutinize the entire tree using the Categories of Legitimate Reservation. This is a good time to bring in someone else to help. Helpers don't really need to understand the CLR; they just need intuitive knowledge about the situation. Even though they may not articulate logical reservations the way we've become accustomed to doing, you'll recognize a comment such as, "I don't think decreasing inventory makes profits to go up" as a causality reservation. As part of the scrutiny process, determine whether any parts of the FRT are unnecessary to attaining the desired effects. If so, trim those parts from the tree; the fewer superfluous entities, the more readable your tree will be.

NOTE: Don't forget that the FRT may have more desired effects than the CRT had undesirable effects. In planning future reality, we want to be sure that even the parts of current reality we didn't try to change remain intact and without adverse effect.

In building the Future Reality Tree, we added injections for two reasons: (1) to correct our progress back "on course" toward our desired effects, and (2) to trim negative branches. Often one injection can do double duty (that is, fulfill both these functions), but because we inserted injections individually for different purposes, we never noticed this duplication. In scrutinizing the entire FRT, including negative branches at this step affords us the opportunity to find ways to consolidate injections, thus simplifying the tree.

This step also lets us question whether we have elements in the Future Reality Tree that really don't contribute to achieving our desired effects. If so, these parts of the tree can be eliminated without adverse consequence.

Figure 6.27, "Procedures for Constructing a Future Reality Tree," contains abbreviated steps for constructing an FRT.

SCRUTINIZING A FUTURE REALITY TREE

Checking the logic of a Future Reality Tree is similar to checking that of a Current Reality Tree. The Categories of Legitimate Reservation (refer to Chapter 2) are used to test the logical connections between entities of the Future Reality Tree. However, there are a few differences to consider when using the CLR in an FRT.

Existence Reservations

In Chapter 2, we discussed the second level of the Categories of Legitimate Reservation—existence, both entity and causality. While this level of reservation is important in the Future Reality Tree, there are some definite limitations to its use. Take entity existence, for example. One of the tests for entity existence is whether it is a valid statement of existing reality. Clearly, this test won't be of as much use in an FRT, because outcomes of actions we haven't yet taken don't currently exist. They can only exist in the future. So the only parts of the entity existence reservation that might apply in an FRT would be completeness (a complete sentence) and structure (no embedded "if–then" statements). Instead of validity, a better criterion by which to evaluate expected effects would be *probability*.

Causality existence—whether the stated cause does, in fact, lead to the stated effect—likewise must be used with caution. Obviously, in a Future Reality Tree the effect does not exist now. The question is whether it will exist as an expected outcome of an injection; that is, will the injection effectively do the job it's designed to do? Again, probability would be more useful in this situation. The predicted effect reservation is also likely to be much more useful in verifying outcomes of injections that don't yet exist.

Additional Cause

There is one reservation that we can ignore in scrutinizing a Future Reality Tree: additional cause. Why? Because we aren't really concerned about whether something else might produce our intermediate or desired effects—we're only concerned that the actions we take will do so. Think about the example of demolishing an old building to make space for a new one. Do we really care whether an earthquake will do the job? It's too uncertain to depend on that kind of outside force. What we really care about is whether the demolition team we've selected to do the job at the time of our choosing is equal to the task.

So for all intents and purposes, you can dispense with additional cause checking in FRTs.

Scrutinizing Injections

The most important scrutiny you can apply concerns whether the injection can actually be done and whether it will eventually produce the desired effects. Be careful about rejecting an injection as "undoable" at face value. The electric light was undoable, until Thomas Edison did it. Instead, consider the subjective probability of being able to complete the injection. If your intuition tells you that the injection is likely to happen only "when pigs fly," you might be well advised to look for another one—or multiple injections to accomplish the same purpose. Whether the injection will produce the desired effect is really a future causality issue.

"Oxygen"

A single arrow always implies unspoken "oxygen"—maybe a lot of it. This is especially true in Future Reality Trees. And the assumptions people are willing to make about current reality might be less acceptable in projections of the future. In the FRT, you're usually better off displaying "oxygen" visually as an existing reality entity, which you combine with an injection or an expected effect of an injection. There should be very few single arrows in an FRT.

SUMMARY

Take a look at Figure 6.29 (p. 1 through p. 6). It's the Future Reality Tree, with trimmed negative branch, of the same start-up company depicted in the CRT at the end of Chapter 4 (Figure 4.46). It's a good example of what a Future Reality Tree should look like.

By the time you've completed a Future Reality Tree, you'll have fairly high confidence that your idea for a solution to your system problem will actually work—that it will give you the results you want. You'll also be reasonably certain that your idea won't cause any new problems. Or, if it does, the negative branches will be clear for everyone to see, and you'll know how to trim them before they even develop.

Only now are we ready to consider the phase of the problem that kills the most promising ideas: how to cause the change. Good ideas go sour in implementation for three reasons:

- First, we never verified whether or not they'd really succeed before jumping right into execution. (We've taken care of that with the Future Reality Tree.)

- Second, we aren't aware of what obstacles stand in our way, or how to overcome them.

- Third, and probably most crucial, we ignore the behavioral changes required in the system for the injections to succeed in delivering the desired effects. (More on this is Chapter 8.)

Uncovering and overcoming obstacles to implementation is the first part of the final phase, determining how to cause the change, which is the subject of Chapter 7.

> *An act, a habit, an institution, a law produces not only one effect, but a series of effects. Of these effects, the first alone is immediate; it appears simultaneously with its cause; it is seen. The other effects emerge only subsequently; they are not seen; we are fortunate if we foresee them.*
>
> —Frédéric Bastiat (1801-1850)
> French economist

1. **Gather all Necessary Information and Materials**
   - Large paper (flip-chart size)
   - Indelible pens, pencils
   - Post-it Notes (3" x 3")
   - Key elements from IO Map, CRT and EC

2. **Formulate the Desired Effects**
   - Write on Post-it notes
   - Formulate DEs from UDEs (diametrically opposite wording)
   - Use positive, not neutral wording
   - Use present tense
   - Lay DEs out near the top of the page, in the same approximate spatial arrangement as the UDEs in the CRT

3. **Add the Injection(s) and EC Requirements**
   - Collect injections from the EC (or use other "idea generator")
   - Position injections at the bottom of the page
   - Choose one to start the tree; set the others aside
   - Position the EC requirements between the injections and the Desired Effects

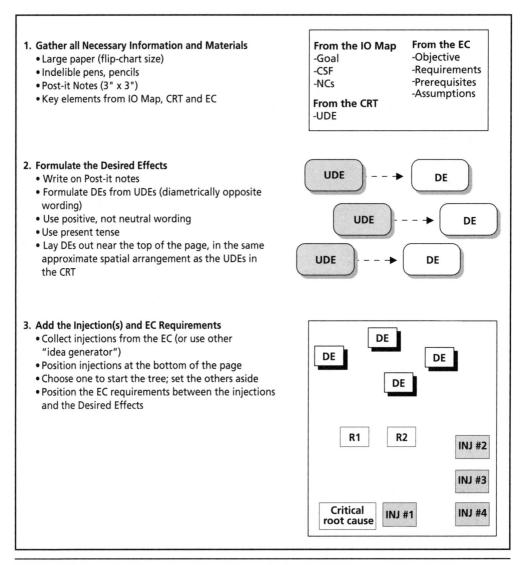

From the IO Map
-Goal
-CSF
-NCs

From the CRT
-UDE

From the EC
-Objective
-Requirements
-Prerequisites
-Assumptions

Figure 6.27 Procedures for constructing a Future Reality Tree (FRT) – abbreviated checklist.

(Continued)

(Continued)

4. Fill in the Gaps
- Build UPWARD from injections to expected effects
- Add existing statements of reality as required
- Include entities from CRT that are still relevant in the future
- Build upward from one level to the next
- Work consistently toward:
  - Requirements from EC
  - Desired Effects
- Add injections as required to maintain progress toward the Desired Effects

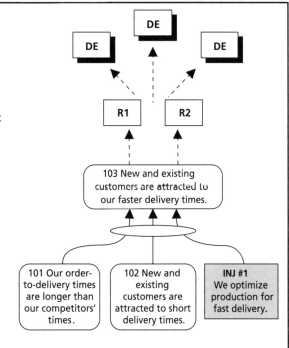

5. Build in Positive Reinforcing Loops
- Find Desired Effects that might amplify other effects lower in the tree
- Identify the effects they amplify
- Connect the DE to the amplified effect with an arrow
- Add injections, reality entities, and ellipses as required
- Check to be sure the re-entry (amplified) entity can withstand an additional cause reservation
  - That is, could some completely different cause (not previously identified) cause the amplification?

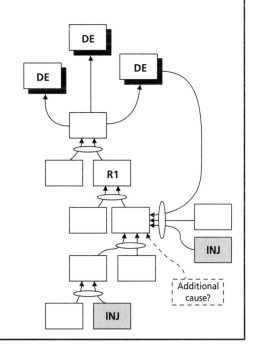

(Continued)

6. Look for Negative Branches
- AFTER the FRT is completed to the Desired Effects
- Solicit outside help if necessary
- Evaluate each expected effect
- Besides *this* effect, what *else* could result that might be unfavorable?
- Don't overlook Negative Branches that might grow out of Desired Effects

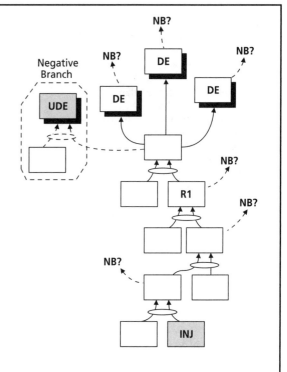

7. Develop Negative Branches
- Use a separate sheet of paper
- Build upward from the originating injection to the Undesirable Effect(s)
- Add previously unstated entities, if required
- Identify the "turning point"
- Identify all assumptions underlying the transitional arrow; list them to one side of the NB

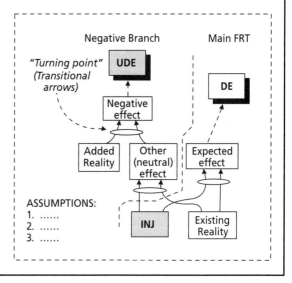

(Continued)

8. Trim Negative Branches
- Develop branch-trimming injection(s) to break key assumptions
- Validate injection(s) on a separate sheet of paper
- Logically project the direct and unavoidable consequences of the injection(s)
- Combine injection(s) and effects with additional, previously unstated reality entities as required
- Build upward until you reach the opposite condition of the Negative Branch's Undesirable Effect
- Make sure the branch-trimming injection doesn't create any new UDEs of its own

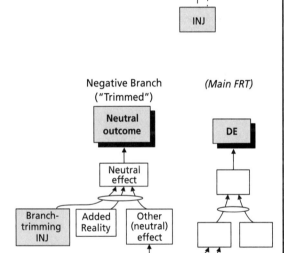

Negative Branch ("Trimmed")

Neutral outcome

Neutral effect

Branch-trimming INJ   Added Reality   Other (neutral) effect

(Main FRT)

INJ

9. Incorporate the Branch-Trimming Injection into the FRT
- On the original FRT, combine the branch-trimming Injection with the effect entity from the Injection that caused the Negative Branch
- Write a reference to the NB beside the branch-trimming Injection
- Save the supporting NB pages

Negative Branch ("Trimmed")   *(Main FRT)*

Neutral outcome   DE

Neutral effect

Branch-trimming INJ   Added Reality   Other (neutral) effect

INJ

10. Scrutinize the Entire FRT
- Re-read and scrutinize the entire tree
- Use the Categories of Legitimate Reservation
- Enlist someone else to assist you
  - Understanding of CLR *not* required
  - Intuitive knowledge of the content *is* required
- Identify any parts of the FRT not needed to reach the Desired Effects or trim Negative Branches
- Trim superfluous entities from the FRT

DECISION: "Should we invest in a web site (e-business)?"

1. List all the POSITIVES and NEGATIVES
On a sheet of paper, in two columns
- List all potential positive outcomes of the decision
- List all potential negative outcomes of the decision
  - These become the UDEs

POSITIVES	NEGATIVES
1. There is potential to reach a much larger customer base	1. Web sites are passive, requiring customers to know you're there
2. Market can be international	2. "Drive by" business (from web surfing) is uncertain
3. Sales can be transacted faster through the web site	3. Sales may not offset investment
4. Costs can be minimized	4. There is a high probability of losing money

2. Draft the Negative Branch Injection
On a second sheet of paper
- Write the proposed decision as an injection on a Post-it Note
- Position the injection at the bottom of the page
- Write the UDEs on Post-it notes
- Position the UDEs at the top of the page

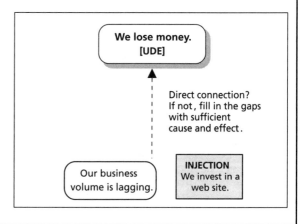

3. Analyze the Decision (Injection)
Does an UDE result directly from the Injection?
- If so, connect the Injection directly to the UDE
  - Include additional entities and ellipses for sufficiency, if required
- If not, begin building the chain of causality upward from the Injection to the UDEs
  - Include additional entities and ellipses for sufficiency, if required
- Stop when you can connect the last effect to the UDE as a direct and unavoidable cause

Figure 6.28   Using the negative branch (NB) as a stand-alone tool – abbreviated checklist.

(Continued)

(Continued)

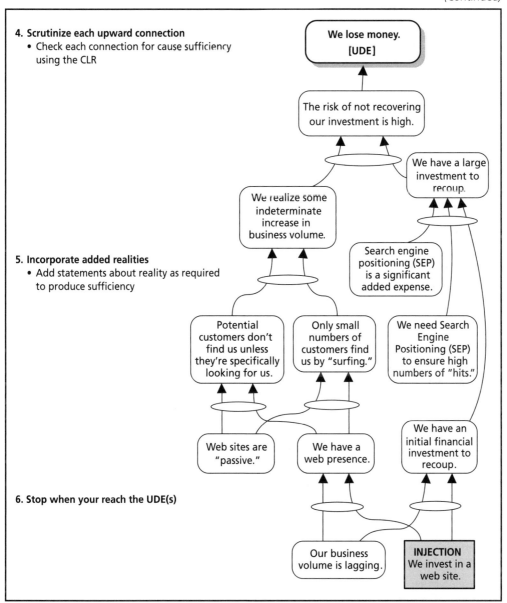

4. Scrutinize each upward connection
- Check each connection for cause sufficiency using the CLR

5. Incorporate added realities
- Add statements about reality as required to produce sufficiency

6. Stop when your reach the UDE(s)

(Continued)

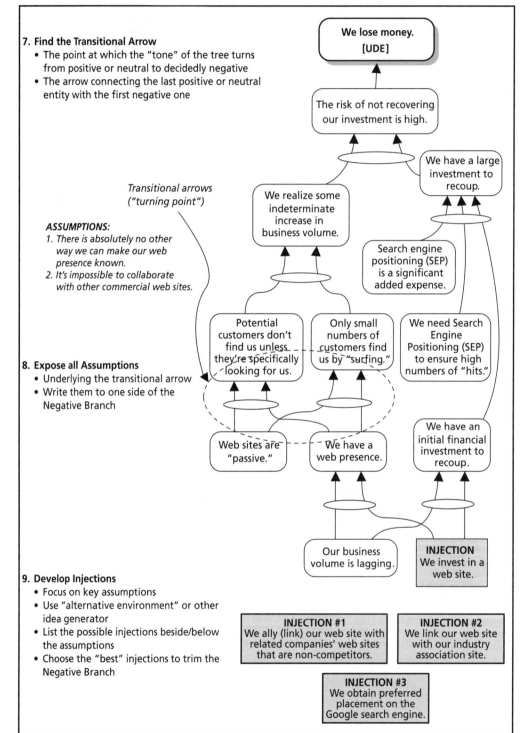

7. Find the Transitional Arrow
- The point at which the "tone" of the tree turns from positive or neutral to decidedly negative
- The arrow connecting the last positive or neutral entity with the first negative one

Transitional arrows ("turning point")

ASSUMPTIONS:
1. *There is absolutely no other way we can make our web presence known.*
2. *It's impossible to collaborate with other commercial web sites.*

8. Expose all Assumptions
- Underlying the transitional arrow
- Write them to one side of the Negative Branch

9. Develop Injections
- Focus on key assumptions
- Use "alternative environment" or other idea generator
- List the possible injections beside/below the assumptions
- Choose the "best" injections to trim the Negative Branch

We lose money.
[UDE]

The risk of not recovering our investment is high.

We have a large investment to recoup.

We realize some indeterminate increase in business volume.

Search engine positioning (SEP) is a significant added expense.

Potential customers don't find us unless they're specifically looking for us.

Only small numbers of customers find us by "surfing."

We need Search Engine Positioning (SEP) to ensure high numbers of "hits."

Web sites are "passive."

We have a web presence.

We have an initial financial investment to recoup.

Our business volume is lagging.

INJECTION
We invest in a web site.

INJECTION #1
We ally (link) our web site with related companies' web sites that are non-competitors.

INJECTION #2
We link our web site with our industry association site.

INJECTION #3
We obtain preferred placement on the Google search engine.

(Continued)

10. Validate the Chosen Injection(s)
- Rewrite the last entity before the "transitional" arrow
- Write your chosen Injection beside it
- Develop the logical chain of cause-effect of combining the two
  - Add other reality entities as necessary
  - Continue building upward until you're certain the UDE has been neutralized or turned into a Desirable Effect
- Check to be sure the new Injection doesn't create any new NBs of its own

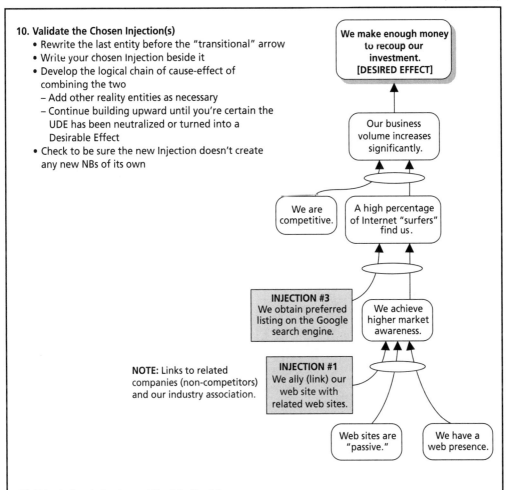

11. Take Action to Implement the Injection(s)
- If you constructed the Negative Branch in response to someone else's request, meet with that person
- Review the POSITIVE outcomes of the decision or action, from your original list (Step 1)
- Present the Negative Branch completely and without interruption, all the way to the Undesirable Effect
- DON'T offer YOUR Injection as a remedy. Hold it in reserve and wait for a response from the requestor
- Allow the requestor to offer a workable alternative (Injection)
  - If the requestor's solution is as good as or better than yours, accept it (as long as you can live with it)
  - If NOT, steer the discussion toward your alternative, but give the requestor EVERY opportunity to become part of the solution FIRST

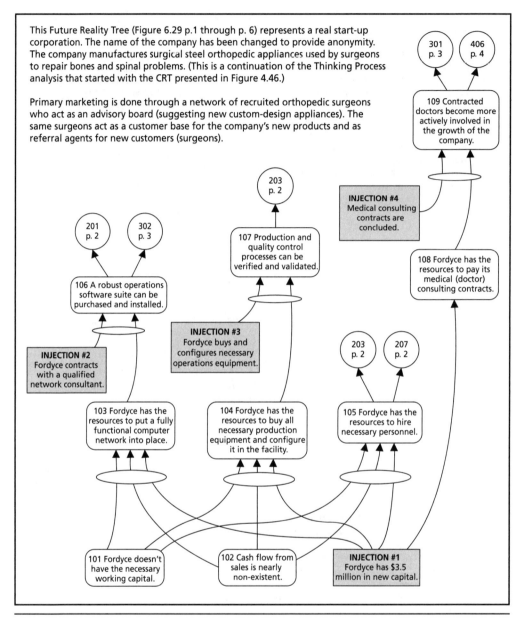

This Future Reality Tree (Figure 6.29 p.1 through p. 6) represents a real start-up corporation. The name of the company has been changed to provide anonymity. The company manufactures surgical steel orthopedic appliances used by surgeons to repair bones and spinal problems. (This is a continuation of the Thinking Process analysis that started with the CRT presented in Figure 4.46.)

Primary marketing is done through a network of recruited orthopedic surgeons who act as an advisory board (suggesting new custom-design appliances). The same surgeons act as a customer base for the company's new products and as referral agents for new customers (surgeons).

301 p. 3

406 p. 4

109 Contracted doctors become more actively involved in the growth of the company.

203 p. 2

INJECTION #4
Medical consulting contracts are concluded.

201 p. 2

302 p. 3

107 Production and quality control processes can be verified and validated.

108 Fordyce has the resources to pay its medical (doctor) consulting contracts.

106 A robust operations software suite can be purchased and installed.

INJECTION #3
Fordyce buys and configures necessary operations equipment.

203 p. 2

207 p. 2

INJECTION #2
Fordyce contracts with a qualified network consultant.

103 Fordyce has the resources to put a fully functional computer network into place.

104 Fordyce has the resources to buy all necessary production equipment and configure it in the facility.

105 Fordyce has the resources to hire necessary personnel.

101 Fordyce doesn't have the necessary working capital.

102 Cash flow from sales is nearly non-existent.

INJECTION #1
Fordyce has $3.5 million in new capital.

Figure 6.29 Future Reality Tree: Fordyce Corporation (p. 1). *(Continued)*

(Continued)

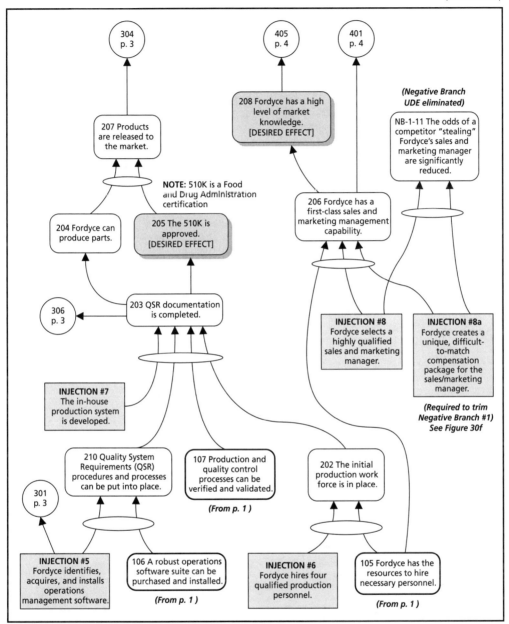

Figure 6.29 Future Reality Tree: Fordyce Corporation (p. 2).

(Continued)

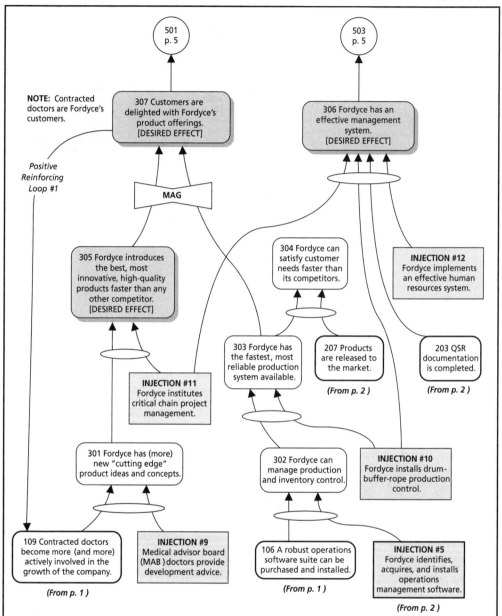

Figure 6.29 Future Reality Tree: Fordyce Corporation (p. 3).

(Continued)

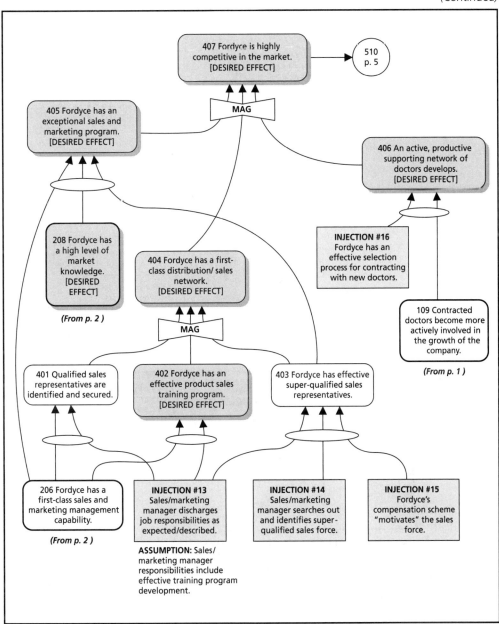

Figure 6.29 Future Reality Tree: Fordyce Corporation (p. 4).

(Continued)

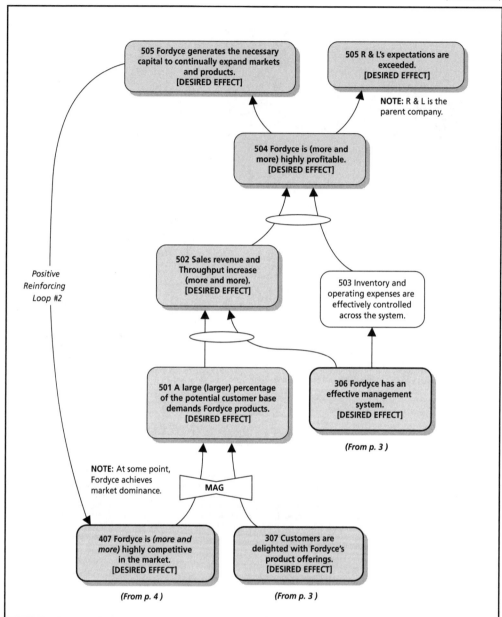

Figure 6.29 Future Reality Tree: Fordyce Corporation (p. 5).

(Continued)

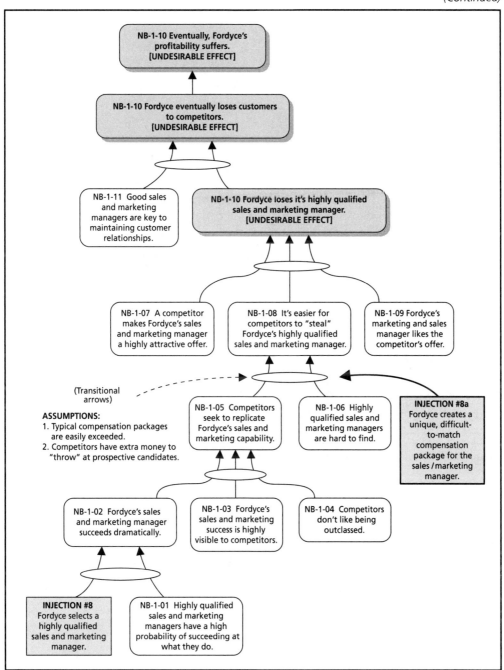

Figure 6.29 Future Reality Tree: Fordyce Corporation (p. 6, negative branch).

(Continued)

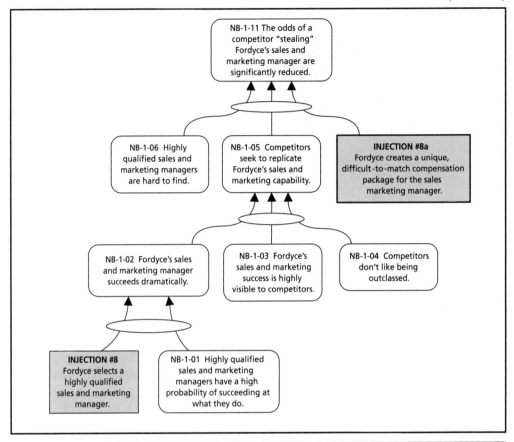

Figure 6.29   Future Reality Tree: Fordyce Corporation (p. 6, negative branch "trimmed").

ENDNOTES

1. Dettmer, H. William. *Strategic Navigation: A Systems Approach to Business Strategy.* Milwaukee, WI: ASQ Quality Press, 2003.

Part III
Executing Change

7
Prerequisite and Transition Trees

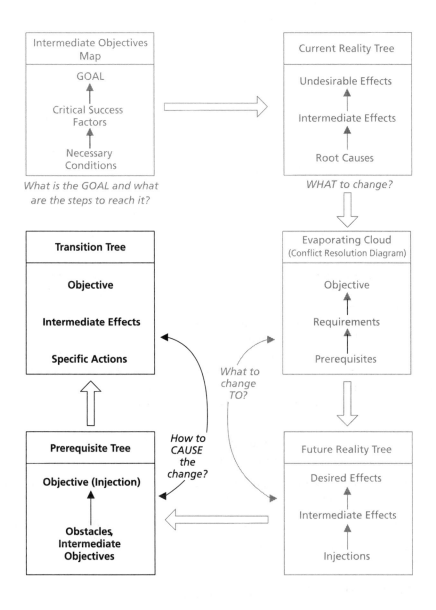

Intermediate Objectives Map		Current Reality Tree
GOAL ↑ Critical Success Factors ↑ Necessary Conditions		Undesirable Effects ↑ Intermediate Effects ↑ Root Causes

What is the GOAL and what are the steps to reach it?

WHAT to change?

Transition Tree

Objective

Intermediate Effects

Specific Actions

Evaporating Cloud
(Conflict Resolution Diagram)

Objective ↑ Requirements ↑ Prerequisites

What to change TO?

How to CAUSE the change?

Prerequisite Tree

Objective (Injection) ↑

Obstacles, Intermediate Objectives

Future Reality Tree

Desired Effects ↑ Intermediate Effects ↑ Injections

The devil is in the details.

—Unknown

A CONSOLIDATION OF TWO TREES

The first edition of this book separated the discussion of Prerequisite Trees and Transition Trees, treating each as distinctly individual tools. This edition merges the discussion of the two logic trees into a single chapter and de-emphasizes the Transition Tree substantially. In fact, the Transition Tree will be only briefly addressed, and more as a matter of historical interest than as an ongoing application.

There is a compelling reason to do this: The usefulness of the Transition Tree has proved to be limited. Over the course of the past ten years of teaching and applying the Logical Thinking Process, I've discovered that it has turned out to be the least valuable of the Thinking Process tools for nearly all practitioners. I'll discuss the reasons for this later in the chapter, under the section entitled "The Transition Tree."

I don't intend my de-emphasis of the Transition Tree to imply that the execution phase of a systemic solution is less important than the problem definition, idea generation, or validation phases (Current Reality Tree, Evaporating Cloud, and Future Reality Tree). The quotation above this section should dispel any doubts about that. Rather, I believe that there is a better way to execute a new solution than to map it out with a Transition Tree.

That better way is three-fold:

- Develop a more detailed Prerequisite Tree

- Convert the Prerequisite Tree to a project activity network and manage implementation as a project using Critical Chain Project Management

- Devote proper attention to the human element in systemic change (Chapter 8 is completely devoted to this topic)

Good ideas often founder in implementation. It's one thing to come up with an idea for a solution to a problem. It's another thing entirely to make it happen. Just wanting to do something doesn't get it done. That's why one of the principles we discussed earlier says, "Ideas are not solutions." It's not a solution until it's implemented and doing what it's supposed to do. Maybe we generated an excellent idea with an Evaporating Cloud and we might have proven its worth in a Future Reality Tree. But without effective execution, it's a good idea "on paper" only. How can we ensure that our idea will be effectively implemented? A Prerequisite Tree (PRT) can be the first step.

What do we need to know when we consider execution of change? Basically, four things:

- We need to be sure that what we contemplate doing will work the first time—that there will be no false starts or failures.

- We also need to know what component tasks must be completed and what intermediate outcomes accomplished.

- We need to know what obstacles stand in our way and what to do about them.

- Finally, we need to know in what sequence the second and third items must happen.

The Prerequisite Tree is capable of answering all of these questions.

DEFINITION

The Prerequisite Tree is a logical structure designed to identify all obstacles and the responses needed to overcome them in realizing an objective, usually an injection from a Future Reality Tree. It identifies minimum necessary conditions without which the objective cannot be achieved (see Figure 7.1).

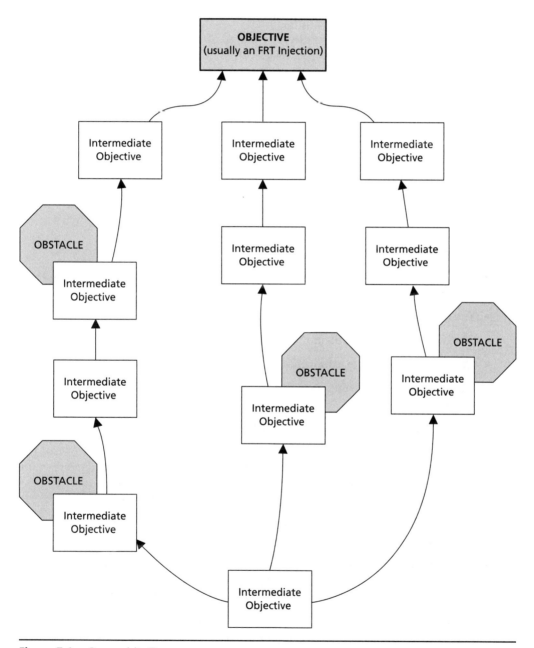

Figure 7.1   Prerequisite Tree.

PURPOSE

The Prerequisite Tree is intended to do several things:

- Identify all the tasks or activities required to achieve a limited objective.

- Determine the sequence of these tasks or activities.

- Identify all obstacles preventing achievement of a desired objective (most often, an injection from a Future Reality Tree).

- Identify the remedies (conditions or states of nature) needed to overcome or neutralize obstacles to a desired objective.

- Identify and depict previously undefined steps to an objective end when one does not know precisely how to achieve it.

- Structure the execution of a Future Reality Tree, which identifies major accomplishments or milestones in complex problem solutions, into a time-sequenced "projectized" implementation plan.

- Array discrete implementation tasks and activities for assignment of accountability for completion.

ASSUMPTIONS

The effectiveness of the Prerequisite Tree is based on the following assumptions:

- Any complex outcome depends on the completion of some determinate number of component tasks or activities.

- The minimum required component tasks or activities can be identified.

- Obstacles to a desired outcome actually exist in reality.

- Obstacles can frustrate achievement of desired outcomes.

- Obstacles must be overcome with specific, deliberately focused efforts (intermediate objectives).

- It is not necessary to eliminate obstacles—bypassing them with work-arounds is acceptable.

- There is at least one alternative, or intermediate objective, capable of overcoming each obstacle. In all probability, there will be several alternatives. Some obstacles may require more than one intermediate objective to overcome them.

- Successful outcomes depend on a specific, possibly unique, sequence in which component tasks or activities must be completed.

- Obstacles and their associated intermediate objectives usually have a sequence-dependent relationship (that is, some obstacles must be overcome with intermediate objectives before another task or activity can be completed).

- A Prerequisite Tree is not static; it is likely to need changing as it is implemented. New or unforeseen obstacles requiring new intermediate objectives present themselves.

HOW TO USE THIS CHAPTER

- Read "Description of the Prerequisite Tree" below. This section describes what a Prerequisite Tree is and how it works.

- Review Figure 7.31, "Procedures for Constructing a Prerequisite Tree," and the associated examples. This section explains in detail each of the steps in building a Prerequisite Tree and why they're necessary. Then practice with a complex injection of your choice.

- Read "Scrutinizing a Prerequisite Tree." This section tells how to ensure that your Prerequisite Tree is logically sound, contains all required tasks/activities, accurately depicts real obstacles, and accurately reflects what must be done to overcome them.

- Review Figure 7.33, "Prerequisite Tree: Conference Planning and Management."

DESCRIPTION OF THE PREREQUISITE TREE

The Prerequisite Tree (PRT) is intended to lay out the components of complex execution for the realization of some desired outcome. It can answer the question, "What must I do to achieve 'the impossible'?" Your objective—what you want to achieve—might be as limited as tuning up your car. Or it may be only one step in the solution of a much larger problem. For example, you might want to know how to gain admission to a certain college as one step in embarking on a professional career, or how to introduce a new product line. Whether your objective is great or small, individual or organizational or societal, the Prerequisite Tree can help you determine what you need to do to realize it, what would keep you from successfully achieving it, and how to work around the obstacles. A PRT can help you objectively identify obstacles and determine what to do about them, without regard for who is responsible for taking action. (That comes later.)

Necessity vs. Sufficiency

The Prerequisite Tree is not like the Current Reality Tree (CRT) or the Future Reality Tree (FRT). It's more like the IO Map and the Evaporating Cloud. The big difference is that the PRT is a *necessity* structure, while the CRT and FRT are *sufficiency* structures.

What's the difference? Simply, the CRT and FRT convey a different message from the PRT. A CRT/FRT says that all entities at the tail of arrows are *enough* to actually *produce* the entities at the heads. (See Figure 7.2.) A PRT shows the minimum that you must do before you can go on to the next step.

For example, to build a house you need significant quantities of cement, lumber, steel, and a place to build. Without them, you can't *begin* the actual work of construction. These four factors are "show-stoppers." You can't proceed without them. Obtaining them must take place first. That's the concept of necessity—completing tasks or activities that must be done before some other task is done, or before some outcome is achieved. (See Figure 7.3.)

In fact, the analogy of building a house is a good one to use for conceptualizing the PRT. It is clearly an implementation of an idea for a solution (in the house example, it's a safe, secure, gratifying, pleasant way to escape the elements). So let's consider that our objective in an example we'll examine a little later to see how a PRT is developed.

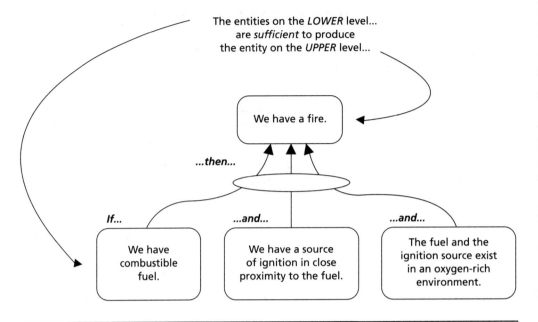

The entities on the *LOWER* level...
are *sufficient* to produce
the entity on the *UPPER* level...

We have a fire.

...then...

If...

We have combustible fuel.

...and...

We have a source of ignition in close proximity to the fuel.

...and...

The fuel and the ignition source exist in an oxygen-rich environment.

Figure 7.2   Sufficiency.

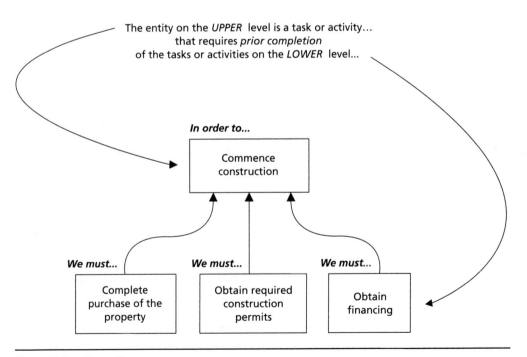

The entity on the *UPPER* level is a task or activity...
that requires *prior completion*
of the tasks or activities on the *LOWER* level...

In order to...

Commence construction

We must...

Complete purchase of the property

We must...

Obtain required construction permits

We must...

Obtain financing

Figure 7.3   Necessity.

The PRT reflects necessity—the minimum requirements for going ahead to the next step—not sufficiency. To reach the outcome, or result, of having a house built and ready for occupancy, we need much more than just the minimum (a lot, cement, steel, and lumber). We also must provide money, nails, roofing material, drywall, electrical wiring and fixtures, plumbing, flooring, and paint. You must also provide other factors as well (plans, tools, skill, time, and so forth) to be able to say, "This is sufficient to *have* a house."

REMEMBER: The necessity concept of a Prerequisite Tree answers the question, "What keeps me from achieving (not *having*) my objective or IO?" Continuing the analogy from above, "To *complete* this house, what must I do or have that I haven't done, or don't have now?" That's the difference between sufficiency and necessity.

Depicting a Prerequisite Tree

With the exception of the Intermediate Objectives Map (which is really a simplified form of Prerequisite Tree), the PRT requires fewer symbols than any of the other trees:

- *The Objective.* A rectangle at the very top of the tree signifying the outcome of all activities indicated by intermediate objectives. (Distinguish the objective from IOs in some way, by a different color/shade, or a heavier border, or both.)

- *Intermediate Objectives.* Rectangles arranged in a vertical hierarchy, indicating the activities or tasks that are components of the effort to achieve the objective.

- *Obstacles.* Octagons ("STOP" signs, because they can stop progress if not overcome*) reflect obstacles that can frustrate progress toward the objective. Notice that where obstacles exist, one or more IOs are collocated to overcome them. The IOs are positioned to partially overlay the obstacle, conveying the idea that the IO overcomes the obstacle.

- *Necessary Condition Arrows.* Arrows connecting the IOs (not the obstacles) from bottom to top. The direction of flow indicated by the arrows reflects the sequence in which the IOs must be performed.

The Objective

Construction of a PRT is a little like peeling the layers of an onion: we start with the end in mind, as Stephen Covey would say,[1:95] and work our way backward to the beginning. The end, in our case, is the *objective* of the PRT. Usually, this is the completed implementation of an injection from a Future Reality Tree (see Figure 7.4). Notice that the PRT is appended to the FRT at the point of the injection. Many, if not most, of the injections in your FRT will have PRTs appended to them. You won't show them in the FRT itself, but the connections will be there just the same. The execution of a Future Reality Tree is accomplished by the completion of injections, which are themselves the outcome of the component detailed activities reflected in the PRT.**

It doesn't always work this way, however. You will undoubtedly find situations where the PRT is an appropriate stand-alone tool, the one you would go to first. There might not be a Future Reality Tree involved at all. Whether you call it an injection or not, the objective of the PRT is the common beginning for constructing a PRT.

---

* I'm indebted to Dr. Paul Selden for suggesting the idea of octagons to represent Obstacles and having Intermediate Objectives overlay part of the Obstacle to suggest "overcoming" them.

** Conceptually, the tasks and activities in a PRT require "hands-on" action to complete, but once the objective of the PRT—the injection—is achieved, the cause-and-effect reflected in the FRT should unfold automatically, like dominoes falling, all the way to the Desired Effects.

Intermediate Objectives

As you can see in Figure 7.1, the PRT's objective is realized by accomplishing component tasks and activities. We refer to these as intermediate objectives (IO). Visually, they exist in a hierarchical relationship in the PRT, with arrows from the ones that must precede leading to the ones that follow. In the real world, these arrows reflect sequence, or precedence, not really hierarchy. Why do we refer to them to as "intermediate"? It's because they constitute transitional steps (actions) that must be completed before we can attain our ultimate objective.

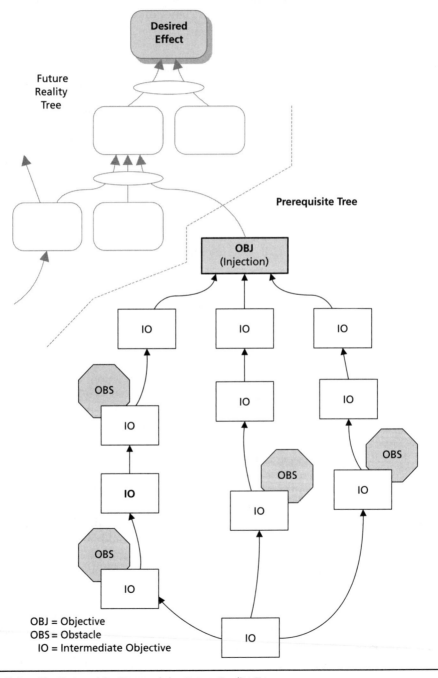

Figure 7.4   The Prerequisite Tree and the Future Reality Tree.

Most IOs are required tasks that we probably know how to perform. They're included in the PRT because they're "enablers" of the next step in the process. There may not be any particular challenge associated with completing them, even though they may be tedious. They're just known things that must be done and we include them in the PRT because we don't want to overlook or forget them.

But some IOs serve a unique purpose: they're needed to overcome specific, discrete obstacles that stand in the way of realizing the PRT's objective. We might consider them problem solutions on a small scale.

For example, let's say that to complete the building of our house, we need to have electrical wiring installed that satisfies local government code requirements. But we face a major obstacle—we don't have the knowledge or skill to do that kind of work ourselves. The code may actually require someone with an official certification to do the work, and perhaps we don't have such a certification. What can we do about this obstacle? You've probably already figured out a way around it: we hire a certified electrical contractor to wire the house. (See Figure 7.5.)

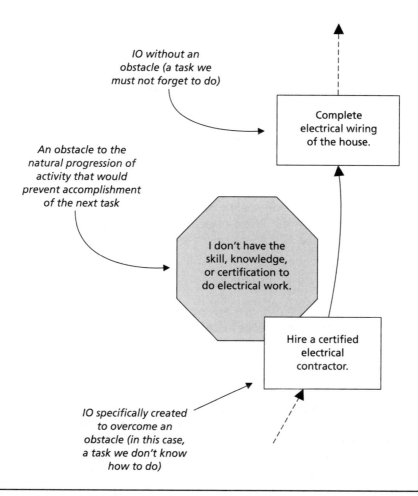

Figure 7.5   Obstacles and intermediate objectives.

Different Alternatives

As you develop intermediate objectives to overcome obstacles, you'll undoubtedly find that there's more than one way to skin the cat. In other words, two completely different and independent IOs might each effectively overcome the obstacle in question. For example, if your next intermediate objective is do something on the opposite side of a river (the obstacle), you might consider swimming, rowing a boat, or building a bridge as possible IOs to overcome the obstacle. Each alone could do the job satisfactorily. Which of several possible IOs you select should be determined by evaluating each against six criteria:

- Which is the fastest to complete?

- Which does the job most effectively?

- What is the first one that comes to mind that does the job with minimum required effectiveness?

- Which IO is the easiest to do?

- Which IO incurs the least expense?

- Which IO produces the fewest negative or collateral side effects?

Not Always a One-to-One Relationship

In most cases, a single IO can effectively overcome a given obstacle, but not always. Two or more may be required. If more than two are necessary, check carefully to see if there is really a sequence between one of them and the other two. If three IOs really are required to overcome one obstacle—a rare occurrence—overlap one of the IOs on another to minimize the number of connecting arrows, for visual clarity. (See Figure 7.6.)

Obstacles

As we just mentioned, most IOs are merely discrete tasks we must perform in a specified sequence in order to realize the PRT's objective. But sometimes there are real, even tangible obstacles that stand in the way of completing a particular task. Some of these obstacles might include:

- Insufficient or non-existent knowledge

- Lack of adequate resources

- Laws or regulations that limit or forbid certain kinds of activity

- Human resistance

There may well be others. To simplify things, we define an *obstacle* as something that keeps you from doing what you need to do to reach the objective, what you would otherwise be able to accomplish were the obstacle not preventing it.

Clearly, in executing an injection not every component task is performed to overcome an obstacle. But failure to identify a "show-stopping" obstacle can bring execution to a complete halt. Once you've determined all the things you must do to reach the PRT's objective, you should search for obstacles to completing those tasks and create work-arounds.

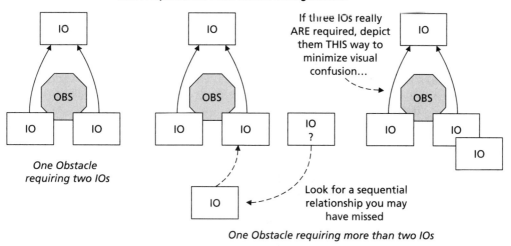

Figure 7.6   Multiple intermediate objectives.

Overcome, Not Obliterate

The term "work-around" is important. Notice in Figure 7.5 the IO that neutralizes the obstacle is depicted as slightly overlaying the obstacle symbol. The implication here is that the IO "overcomes" the obstacle. Notice, too, that the arrow goes *around* the obstacle symbol to reach the next IO. This conveys the idea of bypassing the obstacle.

Let's assume that you're on one side of a river and achieving the objective of your PRT requires you to be on the other side. It's not necessary to wipe out the river (dam it or re-route its course) so that you can just walk across. You can leave the river intact, but work around it—row across in a boat, build a bridge, or even just swim. Though you may actually anticipate some perverse pleasure in destroying the obstacle in front of you, try not to let it distract you from your ultimate intent.*

---

* On the other hand, if you don't sacrifice time, resources, ethics, or morals in obliterating your obstacle (and if doing so gives you some short-term gratification), indulge yourself—and wallow in it! ☺

Enlist Assistance to Identify Obstacles

If what you're trying to do is complex or happens in a complex environment, you alone may not recognize all the obstacles you might be facing. It might be necessary to enlist the help of others more knowledgeable than you to identify all the obstacles. Fortunately, the PRT lends itself well to group as well as individual effort. Furthermore, don't be too concerned if you haven't identified all the obstacles. The beauty of the PRT is that as you and others scrutinize it, any obstacles you might have overlooked will probably jump right out at you.

> *Obstacles are those frightful things you see when you take your eye off the goal.*
>
> —Hannah More

A Single Tool or Part of a Set

As suggested earlier, the Prerequisite Tree need not depend on the prior completion of a Future Reality Tree. Consider the PRT as you would a hammer in a toolbox. You can use the hammer just to drive a nail to hang a picture. Or you can use it in concert with all the other tools in the box to build an entire house. Similarly, the PRT can be used either by itself to overcome routine obstacles in your daily life, or to formulate the activity network of a larger project. Or it can be used as an integral part of the entire Logical Thinking Process to resolve some complex problem and implement the solution.

As we saw in Chapter 6, not all FRT injections require a PRT. Whether or not you need a PRT depends on your answer to two questions:

- Is my objective a complex condition?

- Do I already know exactly how to achieve it?

If your injection is a simple, straightforward action, don't even bother considering a PRT. But if it's an outcome of a complex series of interdependent actions, a PRT can help you sequence all these intermediate steps. Moreover, if you don't already know exactly how to achieve your objective—that is, there are obstacles in your way that you're not sure how to get around—you might *need* a PRT to help you figure that out.

Intermediate Objectives: Actions or Conditions?

In the CRT and FRT, we tend to see causes and effects primarily as conditions—that is, outcomes of preceding causes. The objective of a PRT is definitely such an outcome, so it should be worded as a condition. But the intermediate objectives in a PRT are most assuredly tasks or activities, which naturally imply action. The logical flow of the PRT sounds something like this: "If we *do* these two IOs, then nothing stands in the way of our commencing to *do* the next IO." Notice that it doesn't say, "We *have* the next IO."

The only exception to the action wording is the objective. In our house construction example, the final objective would be a condition: The house is completed.

Obstacles: Always Conditions

Obstacles, however, should always be worded as conditions, using such words as "is" or "have." For example, the obstacle might be phrased "We don't have . . ." or "We don't know…" Obstacles should never be worded as needs (for example, "We need . . ."). A *need* is not an obstacle. The *condition* of that need not being satisfied *could* be an obstacle.

For example, "I need to get around traffic jams" is not an obstacle. "Traffic is congested" might be. Notice the difference in the wording: "is" (condition), versus "need." And the intermediate objective that might overcome that condition-obstacle, "Take an alternate route to work," is an *action*.

To summarize the action-condition discussion, take a look at Figure 7.7. All the obstacles are conditions. All the IOs that overcome them are actions (activities or tasks). Only the overall objective is a condition. Notice, too, that the arrows are drawn to connect the IOs, not the obstacles. Since not all IOs are likely to have obstacles, this is really the only way it can be done.

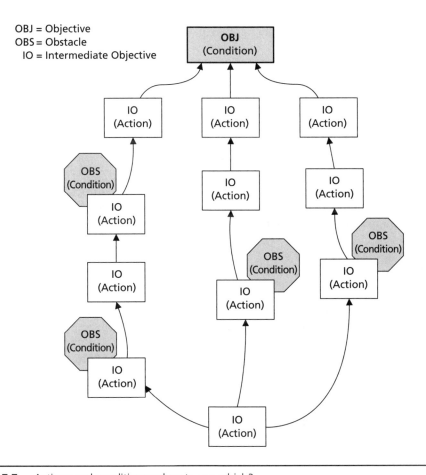

Figure 7.7   Actions and conditions: when to use which?

Sequence Dependency

In solving any complex problem, one of the critical questions is, "What do we do first?" The Prerequisite Tree answers this question. After identifying obstacles and ways to overcome them, the next most important function a PRT serves is sequencing these ways (intermediate objectives) in the right order.

Experience over the last decade has shown that when it comes to deciding in what sequence tasks should be completed, some people have difficulty with the concept of "earlier versus later." For example, as we'll see when we get to the procedures for constructing a PRT, at one step in the process we'll have a collection of individual Obstacles and IOs (that is, not yet connected to one another). We'll have to decide which ones to place near the bottom of the tree ("earlier") and which ones go nearer the top ("later").

Here's an example of sequence dependency. Let's say your objective is to attend college. Before that can happen, you must be accepted for enrollment (see Figure 7.8). But before a college accepts you, you must apply to the college *and* you must qualify for their acceptance. Before you can apply, you must decide which college you want to attend. Before you can decide which college to attend, you must know whether it offers the course of study you desire. Before you can determine that, you have to know what field of study you wish to pursue. Before that can happen, it would be nice to have some kind of career goal in mind.

A sequence dependency exists among intermediate objectives. The more complex the problem you're trying to solve, the more important it will be to identify and properly sequence time-dependent events. This will occur as a matter of course as you construct the PRT.

The easiest way to make that distinction is to visualize the PRT as the depiction of the flow of project activities. Picture yourself a thousand feet above the activities, which are laid out like a production line. Pose the question to yourself: *Which of these IOs must take place closer to the beginning of the process, and which take place nearer to completion?* Viewed in this way, the proper sequence usually presents itself with no difficulty. If you're having difficulty seeing where a particular IO fits into a given sequence, it may well be that it doesn't fit there at all—it may be part of a different sequence in the tree. Which brings us to the topic of…

Parallelism

Much as production processes or projects have different activities going on simultaneously, PRTs can have them as well. In fact, such parallelism is desirable because it can shorten the duration of solution implementation if different components can be executed by different people at the same time.

While it isn't unusual to have a simple PRT with a single "branch" or sequence of IOs, it's more common to see multiple branches in a PRT. Figure 7.9 illustrates parallelism in PRTs. In constructing your PRTs, you should make every effort to identify which sequences of IOs can be completed separately from, and one would hope, simultaneously with others. Normally, such branches are organized by function and converge at some logical integration point.

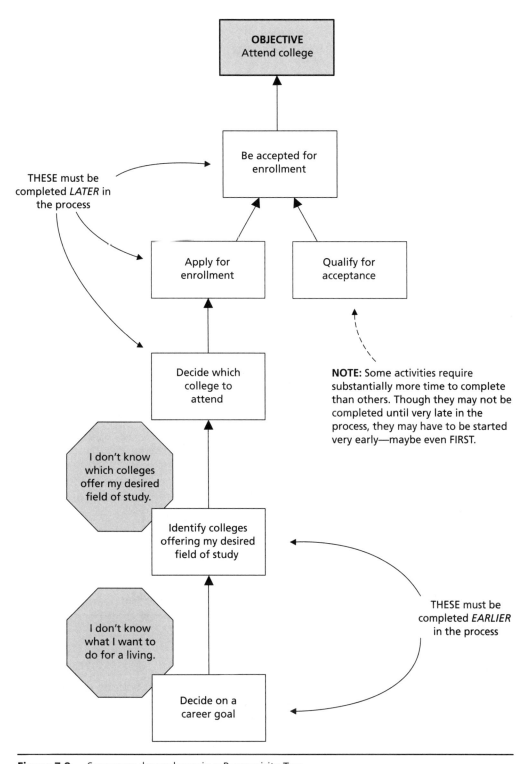

Figure 7.8   Sequence dependency in a Prerequisite Tree.

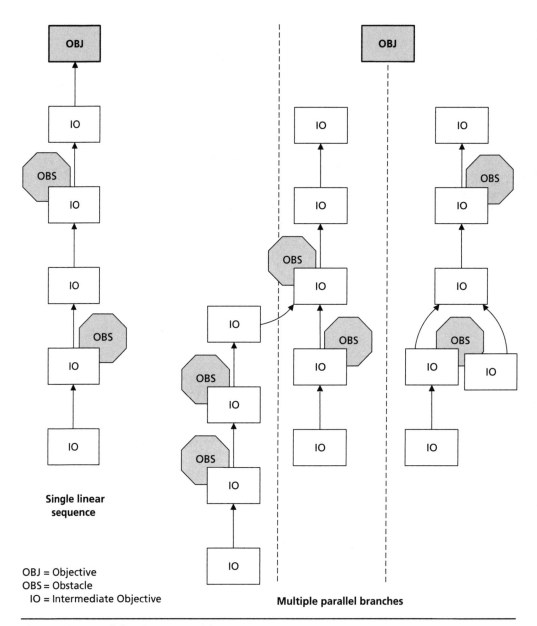

Figure 7.9 Parallelism in a Prerequisite Tree.

Reading a Prerequisite Tree

Prerequisite Trees can be read from bottom to top or from top to bottom, depending on your personal preference. It's not an easy tree to verbalize, especially when obstacles are involved.* However, there are two ways that I've found work reasonably well. Choose the way that is easiest for you.

_____

* Fortunately, it isn't likely that you'll have to verbally present Prerequisite Trees in front of an audience. Most formal presentations to decision makers will focus more on what the problem is (a CRT) and how to solve it (an FRT). If executives are at all interested in how the solution will be executed, it would make more sense to present a visual representation of a project activity network, or perhaps a flow chart.

Top to Bottom

If, like Stephen Covey, you prefer to "start with the end in mind," begin at the top with the objective and work downward to the earliest intermediate objective. Read the tree this way (see Figure 7.10):

> *In order to...[OBJECTIVE or IO], we need to ...[IO].*
>
> *or*
>
> *In order to...[UPPER IO], we must...[LOWER IO] because...[OBSTACLE].*

Another way to read the Prerequisite Tree from top to bottom—one that may "flow" a little more easily for some people—is this:

> *We need to...[UPPER IO], but [OBSTACLE] stands in our way, so we must...[LOWER IO].*

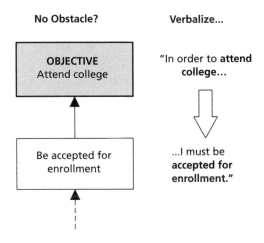

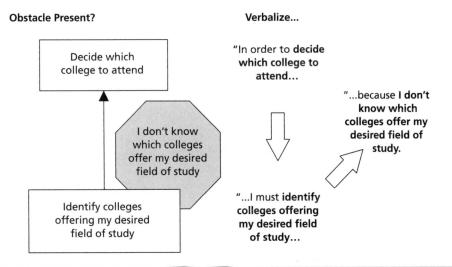

Figure 7.10   Verbalizing Prerequisite Trees: top to bottom.

Bottom to Top

If you're more comfortable working forward chronologically, start from the bottom, reading the tree this way (see Figure 7.10):

> *We must...[LOWER IO] to be able to...[UPPER IO]*
>
> *or*
>
> *We must...[LOWER IO] to overcome [OBSTACLE] in order to...[UPPER IO].*

However, my personal experience leads me to conclude that most people will prefer the top-to-bottom approach.

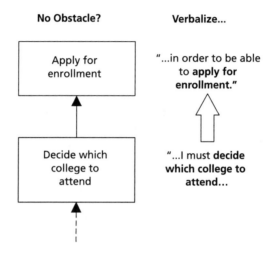

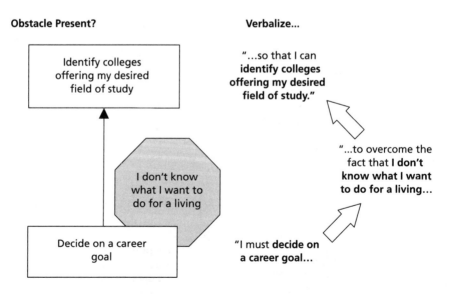

Figure 7.11   Verbalizing Prerequisite Trees: bottom to top.

BUILDING A PREREQUISITE TREE

Whether you intend to use the Prerequisite Tree as a stand-alone tool or as part of a complete Thinking Process analysis (that is, executing an injection from a Future Reality Tree) you can use this procedure. It is somewhat similar to the procedure for building an Intermediate Objectives Map (Chapter 3), but there are differences resulting from the level of focus. The IO Map is directed at the strategic level of the system, whereas the Prerequisite Tree is intended to support tactical execution. Level of detail and scope are the two most significant differences.

1. Determine the Objective

The first step is to establish the desired outcome of the effort that the PRT will reflect. This is comparable to determining the system's goal in the IO Map procedure, but the PRT objective is both finite and limited. It's the completion of a complex activity, such as a development project or organizational change of some kind. Like the IO Map goal, the PRT implies a time horizon for completion, though the tree itself doesn't address time, only sequence.

In most cases, you'll use the PRT to determine the specific tasks and activities required to implement a specific injection from a Future Reality Tree. The logical way to begin is to modify the wording of the targeted injection so that it reads as a condition of achievement or completion. (See Figure 7.12.)

2. Identify All Intermediate Objectives

The second step requires some skill at visualization. You need to be able to picture in your mind all the diverse and various tasks and activities that must be completed in order to realize the objective. This is an exercise in "brainstorming." Don't limit yourself to only what you can think of. If possible, enlist the assistance of others to brainstorm with you.

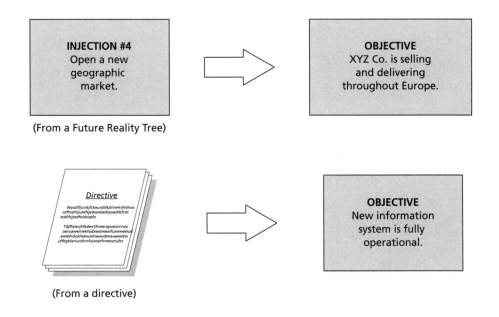

Figure 7.12 Step 1: Determine the objective.

You should strive to identify all the component activities that are required for the attainment of the objective. Some of these may be broader activities that are themselves composed of lesser component tasks. List them all. Use Post-it Notes and stick related notes together. Eventually different discrete functions may become separate branches in the PRT. (See Figure 7.13.)

> **NOTE:** The use of Post-it Notes is more useful in the Prerequisite Tree than in any of the other trees. It's possible to construct any of the other trees sequentially using computer graphics programs, because the Current Reality Tree, Evaporating Cloud, and Future Reality Tree are constructed from top to

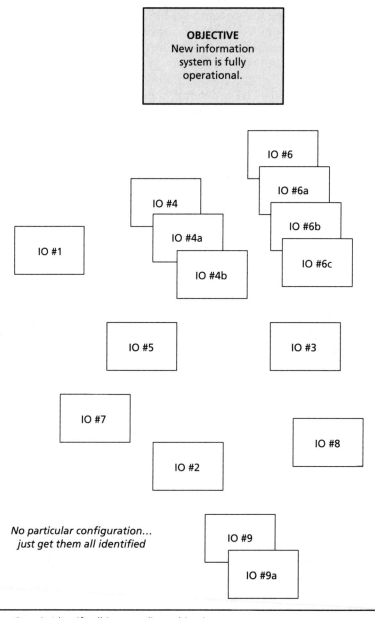

Figure 7.13   Step 2: Identify all intermediate objectives.

bottom an entity at a time, or from bottom to top. The PRT is the only one in which you first create a large number of entities, then piece them together, like a jigsaw puzzle. For this reason, the flexibility of being able to move Post-it Notes around is invaluable. It's possible to build a PRT initially from scratch on a computer, but for most people it's much more cumbersome (and slower) that way. Once the PRT pieces are in place on Post-it Notes, data entry into a flowcharting program goes much more quickly.

When you think you've identified all the IOs you can, go on to the next step.

3. Surface All Possible Obstacles

Examine each Intermediate Objective you identified in Step 2. Are there any that seem obviously difficult? By difficult, I mean:

- You aren't sure how to do the required task
- Some external factor might intervene to delay or stop progress
- Required resources are unavailable to you
- You don't know where the resources will come from
- You don't know all of the critical inputs for the IO

As you think of obstacles, write them on Post-it Notes, preferably of a different color than the IOs. Attach the obstacle Post-it Notes to the IO notes they obstruct. (See Figure 7.14.)

> **NOTE:** Don't try to contrive an obstacle for every intermediate objective. Not every IO will have one, so don't create more work for yourself or complicate the visual impression of the PRT by trying for "artificial symmetry." As Goldratt originally conceived the PRT, it was only intended to identify and overcome implementation obstacles. In this generation of the PRT, we are striving to make it as complete as possible, so we're including among the IOs tasks and activities that are necessary to achieving the objective but which may not have any obstacle to their completion. It may be that your PRT has few obstacles—possibly even none, though that would be unusual. The only determinant for how many real obstacles you have is the reality of your situation.

4. Organize the Intermediate Objectives and Obstacles

Now that most of the pieces are on the board, it's time to organize them. This requires some intuitive and inductive thinking.

Picture yourself viewing the implementation unfolding from a high altitude. Consider all the activities or tasks in the aggregate. Sort the IOs and obstacles into functional categories. For commercial companies, these categories might be marketing/sales, production, supply chain, distribution, or human resources. Or they might be hardware, software, training, compensation, or any number of other types of categories. What you're trying to do is find an "umbrella" under which to classify kindred IOs and obstacles. The actual categories will depend on the situation you're modeling.

If all else fails, try three categories called "means, method, and motivation." Or combinations of any of the above.

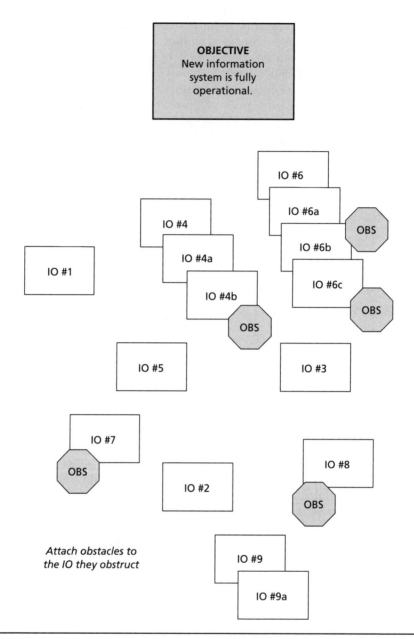

Figure 7.14   Step 3: Surface all possible obstacles.

What we're trying to do here is to establish the major structure of branches within the PRT. All topically related IOs will likely be included in the same branch. If the tree has only one branch (that is, a linear sequence), then they'll all be in a straight line. Figure 7.15 shows what a sorted configuration might look like.

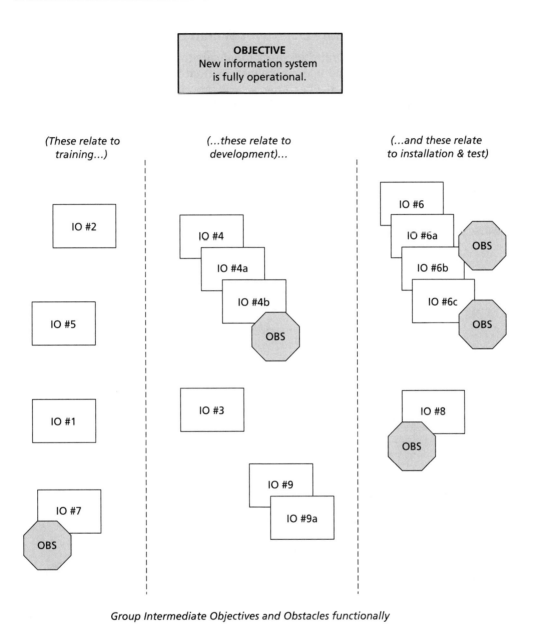

Figure 7.15   Step 4: Organize the intermediate objectives and obstacles.

If you're using the PRT as a stand-alone tool (that is, not for implementing injections from a Future Reality Tree), you won't have an injection to guide you. You'll have to formulate the objective on your own. This shouldn't be too difficult, since you probably already have a sense of the outcome you're trying to achieve. For example, an aerospace manufacturer wouldn't need an FRT to establish the outcome statement for a particular development project. The objective would be something like, "The customer is satisfied with the cost-effective delivery of the first Boeing 787." This concise statement embodies all the characteristics of a successful development project: performance, cost, schedule, and customer satisfaction.

5. Sequence the Intermediate Objectives Within Each Branch

Now examine each of your branches (functional categories) individually. Determine which IOs should be completed later in the process (that is, closer to the objective) and which must occur earlier, near the beginning of the process. If you have a large number of IOs in a branch (say, five or more), your first pass at this might just group them into two categories—"near the beginning" and "near the end."

Once you've sorted all the IOs in a branch this way, look in the "beginning" group and decide what order the IOs must be completed. Then do the same for the "end" group. Figure 7.16 illustrates this sequencing.

NOTE: As you move IOs around, make certain that any Obstacles obstructing an Intermediate Objective remain attached to the IO they obstruct.

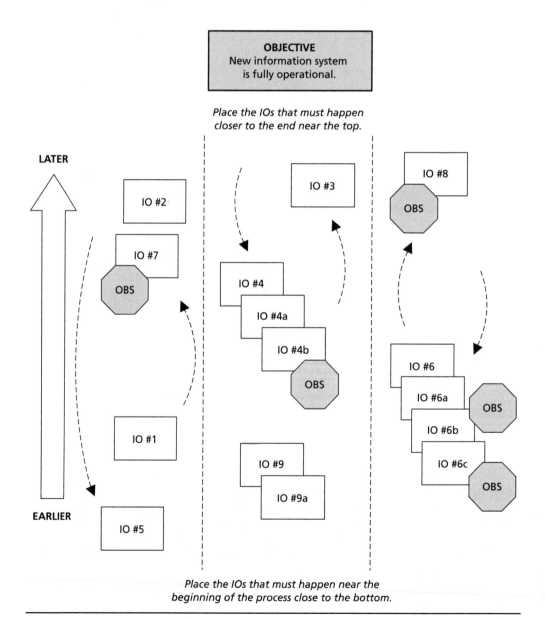

Figure 7.16   Step 5: Sequence the intermediate objectives within each branch.

Notice that up to this point there are not yet any *arrows* in the PRT. For now, we're merely trying to arrange the pieces of the puzzle in the proper configuration.

6. Connect the Intermediate Objectives

Now it's time to finalize coherent branches. Start at the top and work downward. Ignore the objective for the moment—we're concerning ourselves only with the IOs for now.

Connect the top IO with the one below it (the arrow flows from bottom to top). Evaluate that connection using the following criteria:

- Does the lower IO indicate the task that must immediately precede the upper IO?

- Is some other previously unstated intermediate task/activity missing (vertically)?

- Does the completion of that lower IO mean that nothing else (laterally) stands in the way of commencing the upper IO? If needed, create another IO for the missing task or activity.

- Is there any previously unstated obstacle to completing the newly added IO?

Repeat this process for each layer of IOs, from top to bottom in the branch. (See Figure 7.17.)

7. Overcome the Obstacles

Notice that so far we haven't done anything about the obstacles except to move them around with the intermediate objectives they obstruct. That's about to change. Now it's time to overcome the known obstacles.

It should be obvious that an obstacle to completing a particular IO must be overcome by *doing* something prior to the obstructed IO. Your choice of what to do to overcome an obstacle will be informed by the nature of the situation (the IO obstructed) and the technical, economic, and political realities of your environment. It may also be constrained (or liberated) by your creativity.

Once again, as with injections in an Evaporating Cloud or Future Reality Tree, determining IOs to overcome obstacles is an exercise in creativity. Don't hesitate to bring the knowledge and creativity of others into the challenge.* "Brainstorm" as many ideas as you can, then select the best one according to some decision rule. You might choose the "best" by whatever standard you like:

- Easiest to do

- Incurs the least expense

- Fastest to complete

- Does the job most effectively

- First one that comes to mind that does the job with minimum required effectiveness.

- Produces the fewest negative or collateral side effects

---

* Consider the Crawford Slip Method, a proven technique that gathers many ideas quickly, independently, and anonymously, and one that can be conducted simultaneously at different locations. Refer to Dettmer, *Brainpower Networking Using the Crawford Slip Method*.[2]

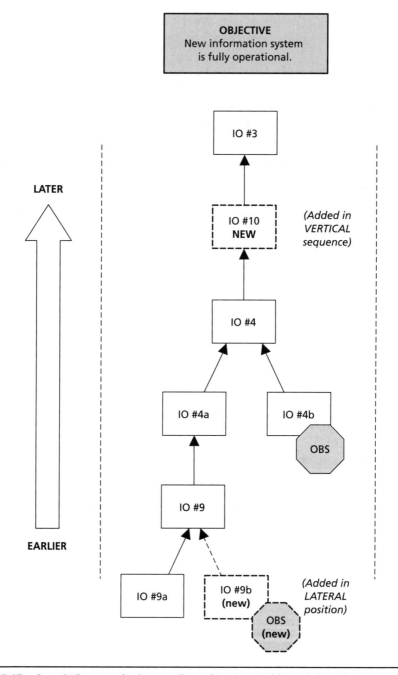

Figure 7.17 Step 6: Connect the intermediate objectives within each branch.

Once you've decided on an IO (or more than one) to overcome an obstacle, position it (or them) below the obstructed IO and *move* the obstacle from the obstructed IO to the IO that overcomes it. (See Figure 7.18.)

At this point, each branch should be more or less complete in final form. All that remains is to integrate the branches and connect the result to the objectives.

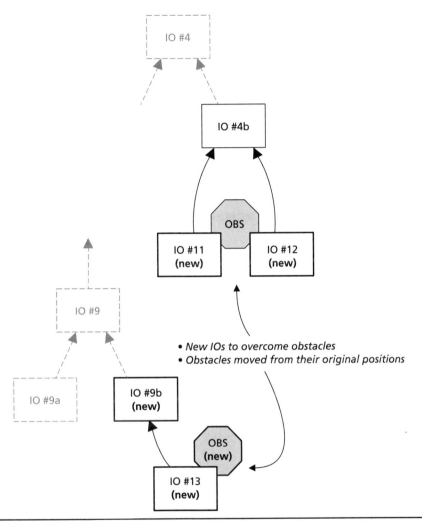

Figure 7.18 Step 7: Overcome the obstacles.

8. Integrate the Branches

Once each individual branch is complete, the branches must be connected into a single tree. Normally, the branches of a PRT converge as you get closer to the top. In few cases are the branches likely to connect independently to the objective. In most cases, different branches will converge with one another before the final connection to the objective is closed.

To integrate the branches, choose one and focus your attention on the top-most intermediate objective. Examine each of the other branches in turn, from top to bottom, and try to find an IO where a connection can logically be made. In other words, find an IO in a second branch that requires the completion of the top-most IO in the first branch as an entering argument (prerequisite). When you find such a condition, rearrange the completed branches in their entirety to facilitate a logical connection, then make that connection. (See Figure 7.19.)

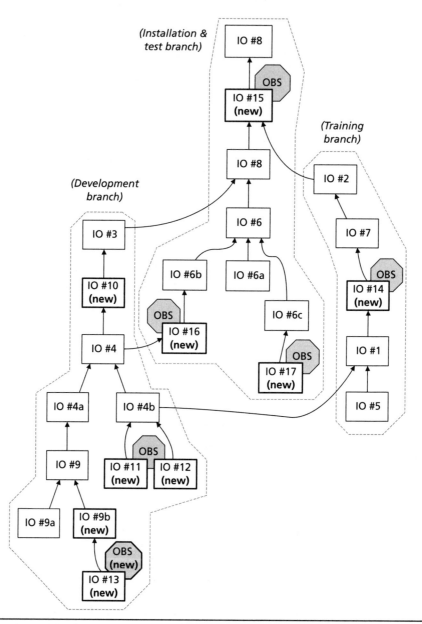

Figure 7.19 Step 8: Integrate the branches.

9. Connect the Main Body of the Tree to the Objective

Now we're ready to make this a complete Prerequisite Tree. It's time to connect the integrated branches to the objective. At this point, it's most likely that this will be just a simple action of drawing an arrow between the top-most intermediate objective and the objective of the PRT. However, if upon examining that connection you discover another sequential activity or task missing, insert the missing element between the two as a new IO. (See Figure 7.20.)

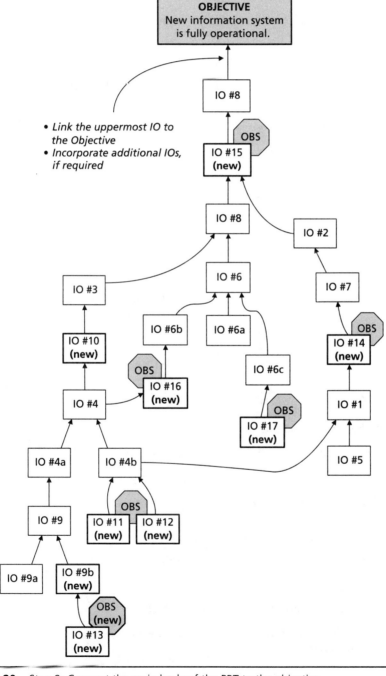

Figure 7.20   Step 9: Connect the main body of the PRT to the objective.

10. Scrutinize the Entire Tree

When you think the Prerequisite Tree is finally done, you should scrutinize it one last time. It's often helpful to enlist the assistance of someone else with knowledge of (and interest in) the topic of the PRT. You're looking for any IOs or obstacles you might have overlooked during construction. This is what the Air Force refers to as a "last chance" check before takeoff.

Here are the format requirements you should be looking for when you scrutinize a PRT:

- Is the objective worded as a condition or outcome?

- Are all intermediate objectives worded as tasks or activities (start with an active verb)?

- Are all obstacles worded as conditions?

- Are all IOs connected by arrows to other IOs (not to obstacles)?

Once you've verified that the PRT conforms to the proper format, you must verify its logic. The next section explains how scrutiny of a Prerequisite Tree differs from that of Current or Future Reality Trees. If your scrutiny turns up some overlooked IOs or obstacles, or if it indicates that an IO or obstacle isn't truly necessary, make corrections to the PRT.

SCRUTINIZING A PREREQUISITE TREE

How do we know whether the IO–obstacle relationship we (or someone else) created is valid? The answer is, "Scrutinize it," much as you would a Current or Future Reality Tree. Does an obstacle really prevent the IO above it? Does a lower IO really overcome the obstacle above it? Have all IOs been accounted for?

Unfortunately, the Categories of Legitimate Reservation (Chapter 2) were designed to verify sufficiency-type trees (that is, CRT and FRT). They ask, "Is the cause *sufficient* to produce the effect?" But the Prerequisite Tree, like the Evaporating Cloud, is a necessity-type tree: It identifies the conditions necessary to enable progressing to the next step as well as factors that might impede that progress. A sufficient logical relationship is expressed:

> *If... [CAUSE], then... [EFFECT].*

But a necessity-based logical relationship is expressed:

> *In order to have ... [OBJECTIVE], we must... [ACTION/ACTIVITY].*

And if an obstacle is associated with the higher-level objective, we add:

> *because of...[REASON/OBSTRUCTION].*

In scrutinizing a PRT, you're questioning whether:

- All intermediate objectives have been identified

- An obstacle really exists

- A proposed IO is likely to neutralize an obstacle

Fortunately, some of the Categories of Legitimate Reservation can be applied in a limited way to validate PRT logic.

Entity Existence

Entity existence applies with respect to either an intermediate objective or an obstacle. In the case of IOs alone, we're trying to determine whether completion of a lower IO really enables commencement of the upper IO.

In the case of the obstacle, we want to verify that it really exists, that it isn't just somebody's negative speculation. Take, for example, the fear of getting fired for expressing your true opinions to your boss (see Figure 7.21). Undoubtedly, some people have been fired for speaking their minds, but is this a realistic probability in the situation at hand? If so, then it is a legitimate obstacle. If not, it isn't.

Cause Sufficiency

Each of two vertically connected IOs, and an intervening obstacle if there is one, can be separated into two relationships that taken together can support or refute the validity of the IO–obstacle relationship. In Figure 7.22, the relationship is valid if you can make a convincing case that:

- If C, then A is blocked, and

- If B, then C is overcome

Another way to check causal validity is to ask two questions:

- Is C sufficient to block A?

- Is B sufficient to overcome C?

If you can't answer "yes" to either of these questions, the IO-Obstacle relationship isn't valid. If you don't really have an obstacle, you'll be wasting your time trying to overcome it. If the lower IO is ineffective, you'll never realize the upper IO.

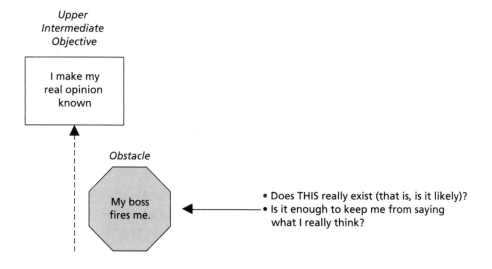

Figure 7.21   Entity existence in a Prerequisite Tree.

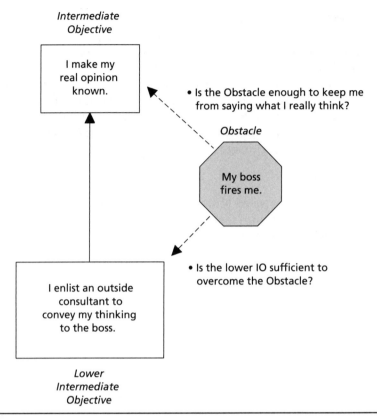

Intermediate Objective

I make my real opinion known.

• Is the Obstacle enough to keep me from saying what I really think?

Obstacle

My boss fires me.

• Is the lower IO sufficient to overcome the Obstacle?

I enlist an outside consultant to convey my thinking to the boss.

Lower Intermediate Objective

Figure 7.22 Cause sufficiency in a Prerequisite Tree.

Additional Cause

We also want to find out at this point whether completion of a stated lower IO *alone* is enough to allow us to start the upper one, or if another IO is required. And we want to determine whether there is an additional unidentified obstacle—one you haven't already thought of—that might prevent starting on the upper IO.

For both IOs and obstacles, you have to ask yourself, "Is there something else?" Less-apparent obstacles may occur to you (or to someone else) only while you're examining the most obvious one. Additional obstacles don't directly affect the validity of your primary one, but they merit examination in their own right for their capacity to prevent you from reaching your objective. Figure 7.23 illustrates additional cause reservations in a PRT.

The IO–Obstacle Validity Test

To summarize, Figure 7.24 is a six-question template for validating your PRTs. You can use this as a PRT scrutiny checklist, omitting the ones pertaining to obstacles if you determine that none actually exist:

- Does the primary obstacle really exist?

- Does the primary obstacle really block the higher IO objective?

- Does the lower IO really overcome its paired obstacle?

- Is the lower IO alone enough to overcome the primary obstacle? Is another lower IO needed?

- Is there anything else (that is, a second obstacle) that might prevent achieving the higher IO?

- Is the original lower IO enough to overcome any new secondary obstacle? Is another lower IO needed?

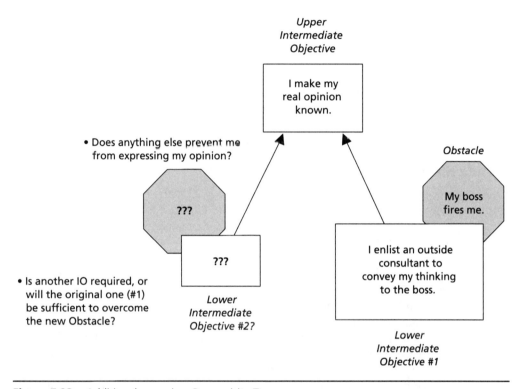

Figure 7.23   Additional cause in a Prerequisite Tree.

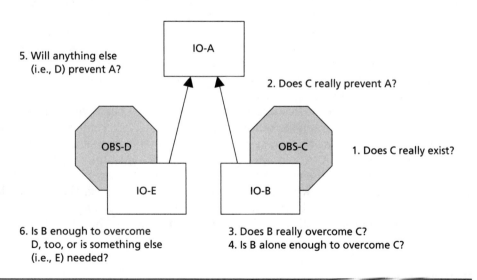

Figure 7.24   The IO-Obstacle validity test.

THE TRANSITION TREE

When Goldratt originally conceived the Logical Thinking Process in the early 1990s, he introduced five different trees intended, collectively, to answer three questions about effecting change in systems:

- What to change?

- What to change to?

- How to make the change happen?

To answer the first question, Goldratt offered the Current Reality Tree. The second was addressed by a combination of the Evaporating Cloud (for idea generation) and the Future Reality Tree (for validating and "bullet-proofing" ideas). The third question was supposed to be answered by the Prerequisite and Transition Trees.

A Little History

Originally, the function of the Prerequisite Tree was only to identify obstacles to implementation and create ways to overcome them. Goldratt intended the step-by-step details of implementation to be developed in another cause-and-effect tree, a Transition Tree, which was meant to achieve what the name implies—transition from the current state to a future state. The first edition of this book adhered to this process.

But in teaching and practicing the Logical Thinking Process between 1996 and 2006, I observed that most students and clients had no patience for creating detailed Transition Trees to "flesh out" the detail that had been omitted from a Prerequisite Tree. In fact, as I observed students constructing their Prerequisite Trees, I noticed that they tended to include considerably more detail than just obstacles and the intermediate objectives needed to overcome them. In fact, some solution implementations, though somewhat complex in activities, had few (or sometimes no) obstacles at all. The primary challenge in these cases seemed to be proper sequencing of tasks and activities that the users already knew how to do.

I noticed another phenomenon, too. People tend to be slaves to format and structure, especially when learning and applying a new skill. My students were contriving obstacles (that weren't really obstacles) just to have something to pair with intermediate objectives they knew had to be completed to achieve FRT injections. They were "garbaging up" their PRT with unnecessary detail that only contributed to sensory overload. In other words, they tended to get away from Goldratt's original intention for the Transition Tree by inadvertently incorporating its details into the Prerequisite Tree, so naturally the Transition Tree seemed redundant to them.

After swimming against this stream for several years, I began to see that for most people, the Transition Tree was superfluous. It seemed to have become a convoluted way of creating work-task instructions and explaining to people why they needed to do each step in sequence. But in nearly all cases, my clients and students were working professionals. They knew their jobs and systems very well. It wasn't necessary to build a tree that explained how and why individual tasks needed to be done. They already knew or recognized that. Moreover, there are far superior tools to a Transition Tree for generating work-task instructions.*[2] I began to look for an alternative to the Transition Tree.

---

* The Crawford Slip Method is probably the best tool ever developed for creating coherent task instructions.

The obvious solution was to augment the Prerequisite Tree. Instead of merely including known obstacles to implementation and the ways to overcome them, why not put in all the key tasks and activities required to achieve a PRT objective? Many of these tasks would not have obstacles associated with them, yet they needed to be properly sequenced with the ones that did. The net result of doing this would be a single logic tree that would guide implementation.

After trying this out with students several times, I discovered that a robust PRT was more than an adequate stand-alone implementation tool—it was also more flexible and effective than any Transition Tree I'd ever seen. Moreover, students and clients alike embraced it much more willingly. They appreciated a "big picture" opportunity to implement an injection on one or two pages, rather than spread across two different trees that used different logic (necessity for one, sufficiency for another). Basically, a single, detailed PRT was easier for them to "get their arms around." Finally, without the baggage of a Transition Tree, it was easier to get students and clients alike to visualize implementation (PRTs) as being "appended" to the FRT at the injections. Any visualization that improves people's ability to see details as an integral part of a larger system is always beneficial.

Finally, accepting the idea of a more detailed PRT facilitates the most important benefit of all. If you have a PRT that includes all the indispensable tasks and activities networked together in parallel and in sequence, whether they have Obstacles associated with them or not, you have the "skeleton" of a project activity network. A robust PRT, with all the Obstacles set aside (leaving only the Intermediate Objectives and the Injection), can be rotated ninety degrees and converted into a Program Evaluation and Review Technique (PERT) chart. This is the first step in "projectizing" implementation (that is, establishing performance, cost, schedule, and accountability for a "deliverable"). Figure 7.25 illustrates how such a conversion might be done.

For this edition of the book, I have eliminated the step-by-step explanation of how to construct a Transition Tree. Instead, as a matter of historical perspective, I've included a brief description of what a Transition Tree looks like and why it was structured that way. Readers who have a burning desire to learn how to construct Transition Trees are welcome to contact me directly.

Prerequisite Tree and Transition Tree: Original Concept

Goldratt's original concept for implementing changes (injections) created in a Future Reality Tree was two-fold. First, determine what obstacles stand in the way of effecting change and neutralize them. Second, identify all the step-by-step actions required to fully implement an injection.

Since there usually aren't many true obstacles to implementation, Prerequisite Trees were sparse. But since there was much more to implementation than merely removing obstacles, Transition Trees could be detailed, especially if a particular injection turned out to be fairly complex. Figure 7.26 shows the relationship between a PRT and a TT.

It's clear from Figure 7.26 that there is significant "developmental" work involved in constructing a Transition Tree. Even with the IOs identified in a PRT as a starting point, a lot of interpolation and "fleshing out" is required.

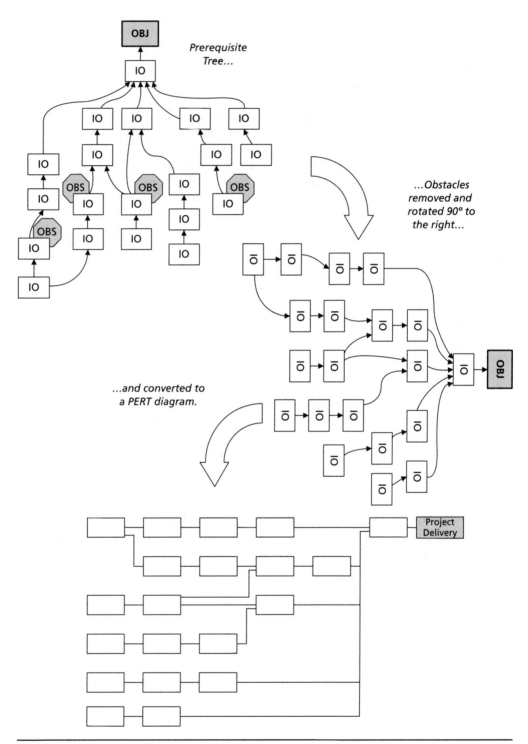

Figure 7.25   Converting a Prerequisite Tree to a PERT chart.

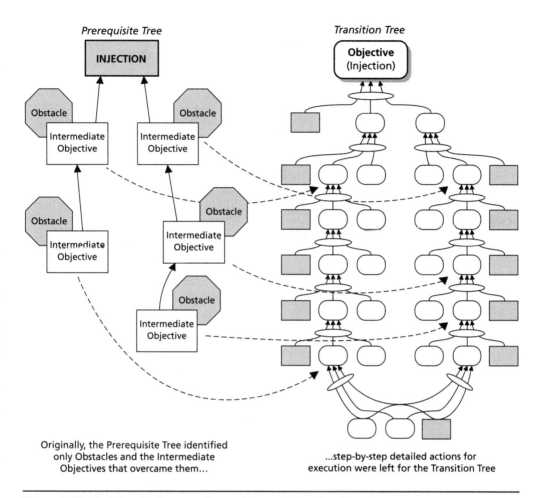

Figure 7.26   Relationship between Prerequisite and Transition Trees.

Transition Tree Structure

A Transition Tree looks at first glance like a sufficiency-type cause-and-effect tree—which it is. But on closer examination, one can see a rigidly repeating structure of existing reality, need, action, and expected effect (see Figure 7.27).

Notice that the placement of each of these elements draws attention to the step-by-step nature of the TT. It's easy to visualize just the actions alone proceeding in sequence from bottom to top, until the injection is attained. Even if the tree divides into multiple branches, it eventually converges again at the top.

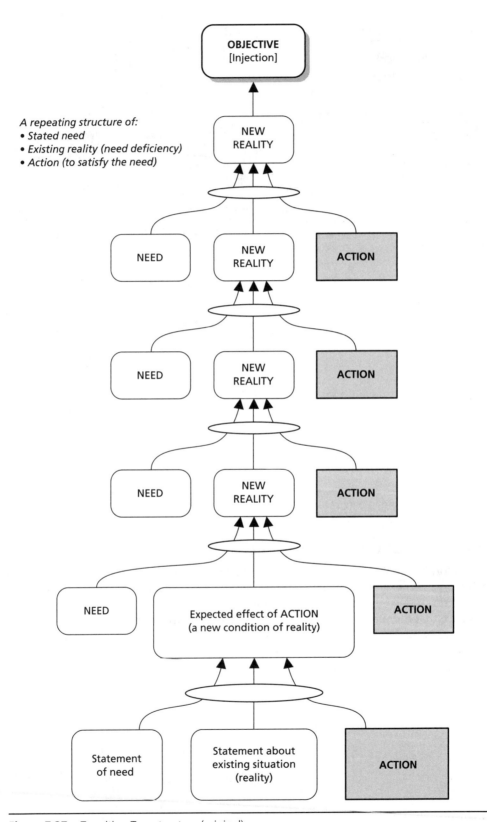

OBJECTIVE
[Injection]

NEW
REALITY

A repeating structure of:
• Stated need
• Existing reality (need deficiency)
• Action (to satisfy the need)

NEED   NEW
REALITY   ACTION

NEED   NEW
REALITY   ACTION

NEED   NEW
REALITY   ACTION

NEED   Expected effect of ACTION
(a new condition of reality)   ACTION

Statement
of need   Statement about
existing situation
(reality)   ACTION

Figure 7.27 Transition Tree structure (original).

The Five-Element Transition Tree

Sometime around the mid-1990s, Goldratt decided that a Transition Tree could serve an additional purpose besides structuring step-by-step implementation actions: it could provide the rationale for why each particular action was required at that specific point in the process. The repeating structure of the original TT had only four elements. With the addition of a fifth, Goldratt thought the "why do this?" question would be answered. Figure 7.28 shows the differences between the four-element and five-element TTs.

By adding this "why" rationale, Goldratt attempted to address the behavioral issue of motivating people to complete the TT actions in sequence. Surely, if people knew why they were being asked to do some specific things in a particular sequence, they would understand and embrace the need to do so and move forward eagerly with it. Unfortunately, the intricacies of human motivation and behavior are a little more complex than that, as we'll see in Chapter 8.

The five-element TT succeeded at one thing, however: it made the Transition Tree even more ponderous and unappetizing to potential users than its predecessor was. For these reasons, I have elected to dispense with a detailed explanation of how to construct a Transition Tree. Instead, I offer a different approach to implementation, one that is a combination of methods.

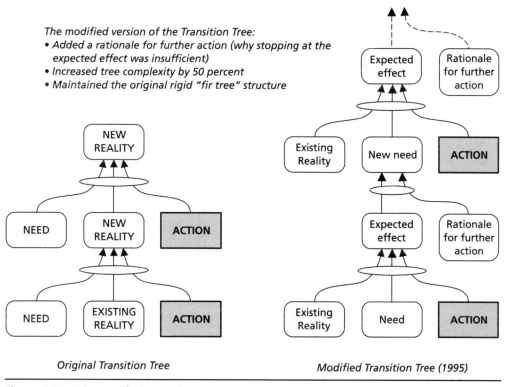

Figure 7.28   The modified Transition Tree.

IN SEARCH OF ROBUST EXECUTION

We've already explored the idea of a comprehensive Prerequisite Tree, one that incorporates much more than just the identification and neutralization of obstacle. With the modified PRT as an effective roadmap, only two things remain to be done: create an execution plan and address the behavior change issues. The first of these we'll visit here. The second is discussed in more detail in Chapter 8.

Managing Change as a Project

Most people are well aware that project management as a discipline is used for technical challenges such as hardware or software development or construction. It's less obvious that the same discipline can be applied to organizational change, which is what the implementation of FRT injections really represents. Nevertheless, it's true.

A comprehensive Prerequisite Tree accomplishes the first big challenge in any change implementation: it lays out a detailed roadmap of tasks and activities that must be accomplished to achieve the desired outcome. For some changes, such as developing and introducing a new product line or spinning off part of an organization into a separate new one, the structure of tasks can be very complicated. A robust PRT is potentially a valuable starting point.

As indicated in the preceding section, such a PRT lends itself very easily to conversion to a project activity network. So rather than spend time trying to plan execution in a Transition Tree, I recommend instead that you consider using accepted (and new) techniques and principles of project management.

Critical Chain Project Management

Successfully managing organizational change as a project first requires a well-grounded understanding of project management. The project management discipline has long been studied and developed, and other sources address the principles and techniques in much more detail than we can do here. Readers interested in applying project management are encouraged to consult these sources to educate themselves in its nuances. Several of these are cited in the endnotes at the end of this chapter.[5,6,8]

However, one particular project management technique is worth mentioning here for no other reason than it has proved to enhance schedule, cost, and performance reliability in projects well beyond the capability of traditional project management practices. Considering the uncertainty of the heavy behavioral component in any significant organizational change, anything that can help manage change more reliably merits consideration. This technique is *Critical Chain Project Management* (CCPM).

As with the traditional principles and techniques of project management, there's much more to CCPM than we can explore in a book about the Logical Thinking Process. Fortunately, there are several excellent sources[3,4,7] available that explain Critical Chain Project Management in detail. For now, I'll just summarize the technique and explain why I believe people should use it to manage change.

What Critical Chain Project Management Does

Since it was originally conceived as a way of scheduling and monitoring progress of complex projects in the late 1950s, project managers have used a combination of the Program Evaluation and Review Technique and Critical Path Method (PERT/CPM) to help assure effective performance, cost, and schedule adherence. But since that time, enough projects have failed in one or more of those parameters to raise the question whether the projects that succeeded did so *because* of PERT/CPM or *in spite* of it. By some estimates as many as 85 percent of projects are either over budget, delivered late, or underperforming. That leaves only about 15 percent that could be considered completely successful.

What Critical Chain Project Management Requires

CCPM was conceived to try to turn that statistic around—to improve the odds of success to something closer to 80 to 85 percent. It does this through a combination of practices that seem counterintuitive to most people. Prominent among these are:

- Scheduling projects to minimize resource contention (that is, the instances where the same resource is required to complete two different tasks in the same time period)

- Eliminating the requirement to complete component project tasks on a firm fixed deadline

- Effective use of time buffers at key points in the project and prior to delivery

- Discouraging people from multitasking (that is, starting-stopping-changing tasks before a task is completed)

- Consistent buffer management during project execution

The net effect of successfully applying CCPM has, in fact, proved to be an almost exact reversal of the historical failure rate of projects. With CCPM, original project schedules are shorter to begin with and have a much higher probability of being met than PERT/CPM schedules.

A Three-Phase Change Management Framework

I'm referring to this as a framework because it doesn't pretend to be prescriptive enough to constitute a procedural process. Once a problem is clearly identified and a potential solution developed and logically tested using the Thinking Process, the solution can be implemented in three phases (see Figure 7.29).

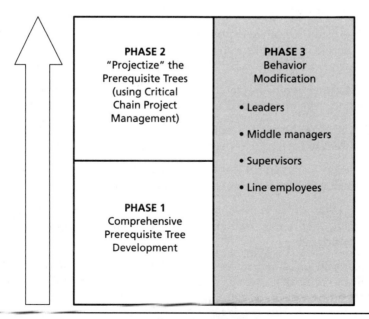

Figure 7.29   A three-phase change management framework.

The first is to develop comprehensive Prerequisite Trees—as many as required to support the injections identified in a Future Reality Tree. This might be as few as one or as many as half-dozen or more. Each of the injections that requires a PRT represents a discrete project in its own right. The different projects will vary in complexity, duration, and resource requirements.

The second phase is "projectizing" the PRTs. This means first converting all PRTs to task/activity networks, as depicted in Figure 7.25, from which individual properly-buffered CCPM schedules can be constructed. Then the individual PRT/projects are staggered around the availability of the most restrictive resource. Completion and coordination of the individual projects are monitored by executives as a single "meta-project," or program. (See Figure 7.30.)

The third phase actually takes place simultaneously with the first and second phases. This is the behavioral aspect of change management. In almost every instance, changes that are worth anything (that is, the ones that promise great rewards or payback for successful implementation) require basic modification of behavior at all levels of the organization:

- In the example that executives set
- In the leadership of both executives and middle management
- In the practices and procedures by which the organization's mission is discharged
- In the measurements of success
- In the behavior reinforcement at all levels

This third phase is addressed in somewhat more detail in Chapter 8, but even so the behavioral issue demands more study and leadership attention. Failure to do so is the most prevalent reason why change fails, even changes that seem apparently "bullet-proof" technically and economically.

SUMMARY

Let's summarize what we've covered in this chapter:

- The Prerequisite Tree can help you identify, organize, and sequence all the tasks or activities necessary to achieve an injection in a Future Reality Tree, even when you don't know ahead of time exactly what they might be or how to do them.

- The PRT can help you completely expose the obstacles to implementing an FRT injection and develop intermediate objectives to overcome them.

- The PRT provides the detail needed to start transforming a projection of the future (a Future Reality Tree) into a specific action plan (a project activity network).

- The Transition Tree as an aid to implementation has proven to be less effective than desired. Better tools are available for work-task development.

- A combination of a more comprehensive PRT and Critical Chain Project Management offers a robust alternative to Transition Trees for managing successful execution of change.

- When all is said and done, successful change depends at least as much (if not more) on the effectiveness of leadership and behavioral modification than on the technical and economic merits of the solution.

Now it's time to explore the implications of this last bullet, above, in Chapter 8.

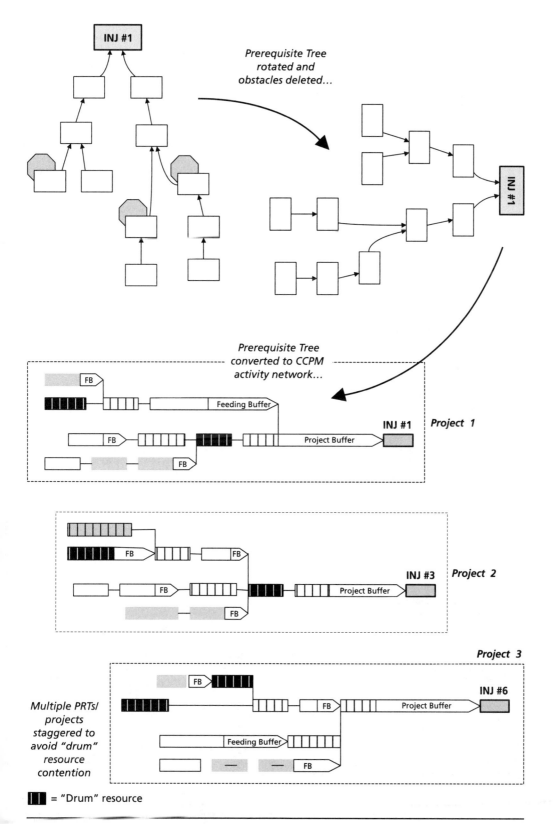

Figure 7.30 Converting a Prerequisite Tree to a Critical Chain Project Network.

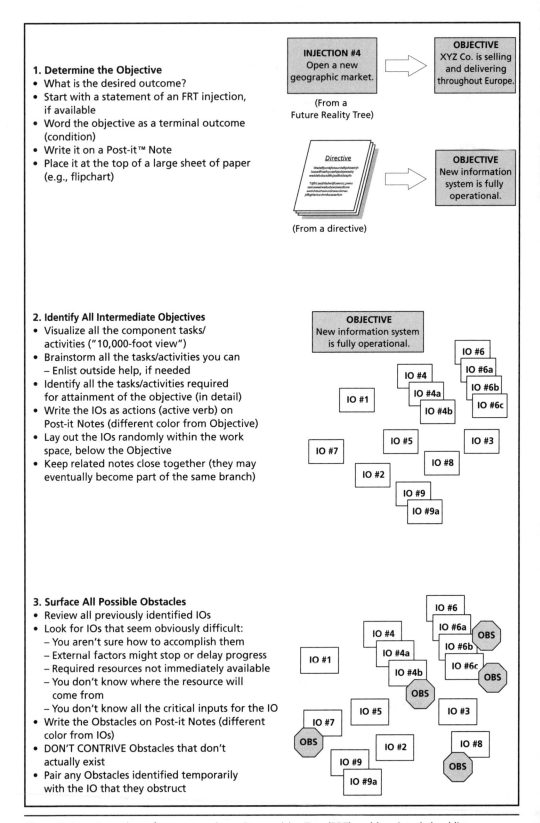

1. Determine the Objective
- What is the desired outcome?
- Start with a statement of an FRT injection, if available
- Word the objective as a terminal outcome (condition)
- Write it on a Post-it™ Note
- Place it at the top of a large sheet of paper (e.g., flipchart)

INJECTION #4
Open a new geographic market.

(From a Future Reality Tree)

OBJECTIVE
XYZ Co. is selling and delivering throughout Europe.

Directive

OBJECTIVE
New information system is fully operational.

(From a directive)

2. Identify All Intermediate Objectives
- Visualize all the component tasks/activities ("10,000-foot view")
- Brainstorm all the tasks/activities you can
  - Enlist outside help, if needed
- Identify all the tasks/activities required for attainment of the objective (in detail)
- Write the IOs as actions (active verb) on Post-it Notes (different color from Objective)
- Lay out the IOs randomly within the work space, below the Objective
- Keep related notes close together (they may eventually become part of the same branch)

OBJECTIVE
New information system is fully operational.

IO #6
IO #6a
IO #6b
IO #6c
IO #4
IO #4a
IO #4b
IO #1
IO #5
IO #3
IO #7
IO #8
IO #2
IO #9
IO #9a

3. Surface All Possible Obstacles
- Review all previously identified IOs
- Look for IOs that seem obviously difficult:
  - You aren't sure how to accomplish them
  - External factors might stop or delay progress
  - Required resources not immediately available
  - You don't know where the resource will come from
  - You don't know all the critical inputs for the IO
- Write the Obstacles on Post-it Notes (different color from IOs)
- DON'T CONTRIVE Obstacles that don't actually exist
- Pair any Obstacles identified temporarily with the IO that they obstruct

IO #6
IO #6a OBS
IO #6b
IO #6c OBS
IO #4
IO #4a
IO #4b OBS
IO #1
IO #5
IO #3
IO #7
OBS
IO #2
IO #8 OBS
IO #9
IO #9a

Figure 7.31 Procedures for constructing a Prerequisite Tree (PRT) – abbreviated checklist.

(Continued)

(Continued)

4. Organize the Intermediate Objectives and Obstacles
- Look at all the IO Post-it Notes collectively
- Sort them into functional categories
- Each category/function will become a discrete branch
  - May be linear sequence
  - May be parallel, or converge

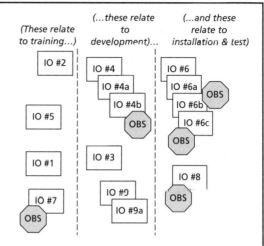

5. Sequence the Intermediate Objectives Within Each Branch
- Look at each branch individually
- Sort the IOs into "earlier," "later," and "in between"
  - Position "earlier" near the bottom
  - Position "in between" in the middle
  - Position "later" near the top
- Examine each sub-group (earlier, in between, later) individually
  - Decide on the sequence for the IOs within each sub-group
  - Rearrange IOs within each sub-group so that the last activity is at the top of the group
- Do the same for each functional branch

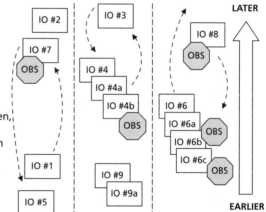

6. Connect the Intermediate Objectives
- Start at the top and work downward
- Connect the top IO with the one below it
- Evaluate each connection:
  - Is the lower IO the immediately preceding task?
  - Are any previously unstated tasks missing?
  - Does nothing else (laterally, on the layer below) preclude starting on the IO?
  - Is there a previously unstated Obstacle to the IO?
- Repeat this process for every layer of IOs in all branches, from top to bottom

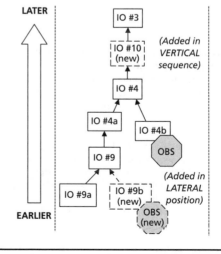

(Continued)

7. Overcome the Obstacles
- Examine the Obstacles you've identified (attached to the IO they obstruct)
- Brainstorm ways around the Obstacle
  - Overcome, don't obliterate
  - Think of as many different ways as you can
- Enlist help if needed to think of IOs to overcome Obstacles
- Choose one or more IOs that are:
  - Easiest to do
  - Fastest to complete
  - "Best" (by whatever standard you choose)
  - First that comes to mind
- Write the new IOs on Post-it Notes
- Attach the IO to the Obstacle and move the two slightly below the obstructed IO
  - Position the OBS-IO pair between previously identified IOs as necessary and connect in the chain

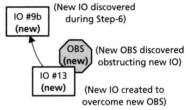

8. Integrate the Branches
- Look for lateral connections and convergences
  - More likely as you approach the top of the tree
- Compare entities among branches
  - Look for cross-connections, i.e., an IO in one branch that is a prerequisite for an IO in another branch
  - Link branches laterally where they obviously connect
  - Move branches up or down as required and rearrange on the page as necessary to facilitate visually simple connections

9. Connect the Main Body of the Tree to the Objective
- Complete the final connects
- Connect the top level of IOs with the Objective
- Add IOs anywhere it becomes obvious that a step/task/activity is missing, and connect to the network

10. Scrutinize the Entire Tree
- Is the Objective worded as an outcome?
- Are all IOs worded as tasks or activities (active verbs)?
- Are all Obstacles worded as conditions?
- Are all IOs connected by arrows to other IOs (not to Obstacles)?
- Check the PRT with the modified CLR (Figure 7.32)

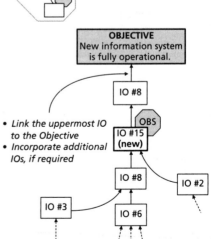

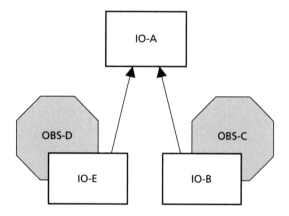

1. *Entity Existence:* Does **C** really exist?
2. *Causality Existence:* Does **C** really prevent **A**?
3. *Causality Existence:* Does **B** really overcome **C**?
4. *Cause Sufficiency:* Is **B** alone enough to overcome **C**?
5. *Additional Cause:* Will anything else (i.e., **D**) prevent **A**?
6. *Additional Cause:* Is **B** enough to overcome **D**, too, or is something else (i.e., **E**) needed?

Figure 7.32   Prerequisite Tree self-scrutiny checklist.

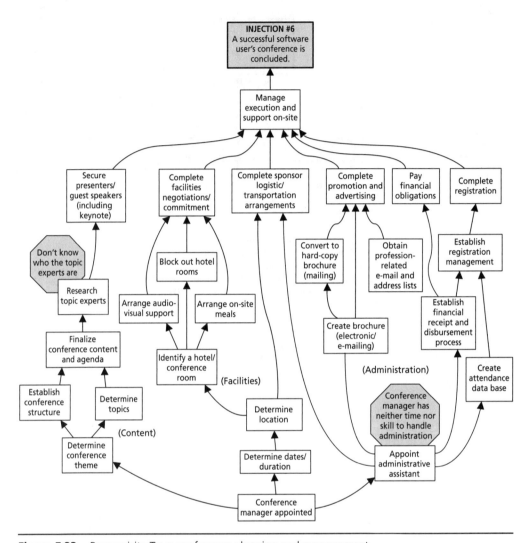

Figure 7.33   Prerequisite Tree: conference planning and management.

The desire to do something good doesn't get it done.

—Unknown

ENDNOTES

1. Covey, Stephen R. *The Seven Habits of Highly Effective People: Powerful Lessons in Personal Change.* NY: Simon & Schuster (Fireside), 1989.
2. Dettmer, H. William. *Brainpower Networking Using the Crawford Slip Method.* Victoria, BC (Canada): Trafford Publishing, 2003.
3. Leach, Lawrence P. *Critical Chain Project Management.* Boston, MA: Artech House, 2000.
4. _____. *Lean Project Management: Eight Principles for Success.* Boise, ID: Advanced Projects Institute, 2005.
5. Levine, Harvey A. *Project Portfolio Management.* San Francisco, CA: Jossey-Bass, 2005.
6. Morris, Peter W.G., and Jeffrey Pinto. *The Wiley Guide to Managing Projects.* Hoboken, New Jersey: John Wiley and Sons, 2004.
7. Newbold, Robert C. *Project Management in the Fast Lane: Applying the Theory of Constraints.* Boca Raton, FL: The St. Lucie Press, 1998.
8. Project Management Institute. *A Guide to the Project Management Body of Knowledge* (3rd ed.). Newtown Square, PA: Project Management Institute, 2003

8

Changing the Status Quo

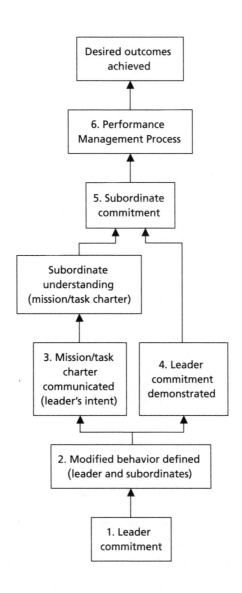

Nothing is more difficult to carry out, nor more doubtful of success, nor more dangerous to handle than to initiate a new order of things.

—Niccolò Machiavelli

PURPOSE

In this chapter we'll address the most frustrating problem attending organizational change: getting the members of the organization, from the very top to the bottom, to modify their behavior so as to ensure the highest possible probability of successful change.

This is not an easy thing to do. In most organizations, the drivers of human behavior are poorly understood, if their importance is recognized at all. An even more pervasive issue is the fact that behavior lies in the realm of psychologists, and psychology is anything but an exact science. Different psychologists have their own opinions about what motivates behavior and how to deal with it. Unlike the laws of physics, "it depends" applies much more in psychology.

There isn't enough room in this chapter to delve into the behavioral issue to the depth that it deserves, nor is that the purpose of this book. All that I can hope to achieve here is to impress upon you the importance of the psychological aspect of organizational change and to suggest a general approach for dealing with it. Deming insisted that psychology was one of the four pillars of profound knowledge.[7:96] He cautioned that system improvement efforts would fail without a functional understanding of it. Deming was right. I would go even farther: an inadequate understanding of human psychology (and lack of a strategy for dealing with it) is the single most frequent cause of system failure in most organizations.*

There are other resources to expand your education on human behavior. The endnotes at the conclusion of this chapter include some good places to start. If this discussion does no more than stimulate your awareness that you have a critical psychological component to address in your change efforts, it will have served its basic purpose. If it provides you even a rudimentary strategy for incorporating behavioral modification and reinforcement into your technical solutions, it will have been fully successful.

Here's where we're going in this chapter. The first part will cover some of the basics of human motivation—why people behave the way they do. While the behavior management process itself doesn't really depend on understanding why, the selection of "reinforcers" used to sustain desired behavior certainly does. We'll explore the role of leadership in organizational change. Then we'll discuss some of the basics of behavioral change—how to get individuals to behave the way the organization needs them to. Finally, we'll integrate these two topics with some general prescriptions you might consider in effecting your own organizational change. Just keep in mind that the old organizational excuse "But we're different!" has some elements of truth to it. We'll be talking about general principles and approaches here, but these will have to be customized for your individual situation.

ASSUMPTIONS

- The success of organizational improvement depends on multiple factors, not all of which are technical or economic.

- The most critical and least understood factors in organizational change are human factors.

---

* "The fault, dear Brutus, is not in our stars, but in ourselves, that we are underlings." Julius Caesar, Act I, scene 1, line 134.

- Most change agents ignore or give short shrift to the human element.

- Human behavior is rooted in motivation.

- Motivation results from unsatisfied needs.

- An effective change strategy fully integrates tactics for changing human behavior and sustaining such changes.

- The most critical component of organizational change is firm, conscientious leadership.

HOW TO USE THIS CHAPTER

- Read the first part of the chapter on the role of need satisfaction and leadership in human behavior.

- Decide which aspects of need theory and leadership warrant more detailed study later.

- Read the second part of the chapter on behavior modification.

- Decide which behavior modification resources to consult in greater detail later.

- Read "Prescriptions for Directing and Reinforcing Behavior Change."

- Decide how to modify or customize and apply the prescriptions presented here to suit your organizational environment.

> *It's a poor craftsman who blames his tools.*
> —Unknown

> *It's not the sword, it's the swordsman.*
> —Unknown

THE KEY TO SYSTEM IMPROVEMENT

Changing the status quo is the key to improving any system. If you always do what you've always done, you'll always get what you've always gotten. Many improvement methodologies— not just the theory of constraints but others as well, such as total quality management, business process reengineering, Lean, and Six Sigma—present a logical technical case for their use. Proponents typically argue how conscientious application of their methods will inevitably lead to the promised benefits. They presume that the logic of their case alone will be sufficient to inspire committed action by those who would realize such benefits. In other words, "As soon as they understand our logic, they're bound to agree with it and be eager to apply the method."

Understand the logic? Perhaps. Agree with it? Not necessarily. Eager to apply it? Maybe not even likely.

The Elements of System Improvement

The problem is that neither the benefits nor the behavior changes needed to realize them are inevitable, even if the technical solution is compelling. John Kotter, a well-known Harvard Business School professor, maintains that changing people's behavior is the most important challenge for business trying to compete in a turbulent world:

> *The central issue is never strategy, structure, culture, or systems. The core of the matter is always about changing the behavior of people.*[9:54]

Take a look at Figure 8.1. From our knowledge of sufficiency in cause and effect, the message of this tree should be obvious. System improvement results from three equally important and mutually dependent factors:

- Effective methods
- The potential to apply them
- The self-discipline to act using the methods

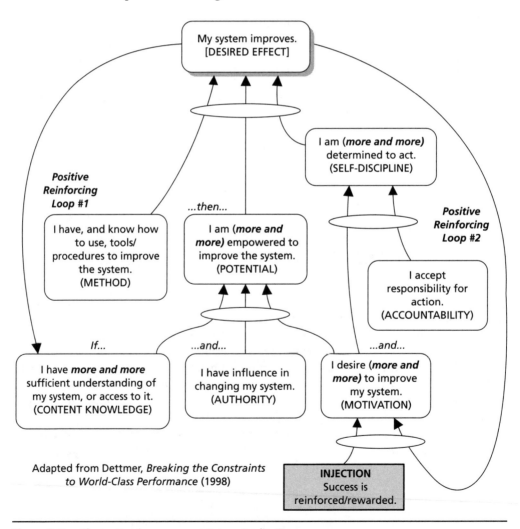

Figure 8.1 The system improvement Future Reality Tree.

Two of these three factors—potential and self-discipline—in turn, depend on:

- The state of our knowledge about our system
- Authority (including resources) to do something about it
- Motivation to improve
- Willingness to accept accountability for action

Successful system improvement then positively reinforces two causes lower in the tree. It enhances both system knowledge (technical) and motivation (psychological). The latter, however, requires an added leadership injection to effect the reinforcement.

Notice that the availability of an effective method doesn't depend on any of these causal elements. But the absence of any one of five contributors—method, content knowledge of the system, authority, motivation, and accountability...all entry points into this FRT—is enough to frustrate the achievement of system improvement.

Now, as we look more closely at these five contributors, we can see that two of them come from the system itself or from outside of it: method and authority. Another of the contributors, content knowledge of the system, is a product of both the system in place and our conscientious efforts to understand how it works. The last two—motivation and accountability—are very much internal personal characteristics. We must want to improve and we must be willing to accept accountability for our actions before any action will ever occur. And conversely, without that personal behavior (and its motivation), system improvement will *never* occur.

Reinforcement

There's an additional factor that's implicit in the motivation and self-discipline blocks in Figure 8.1 but which isn't specifically emphasized: the issue of *reinforcement*. As we'll see later, behavior changes require reinforcement to be effective and lasting.

HUMAN BEHAVIOR

Technical or economic solutions are not enough. The world is full of great ideas that failed through no deficiency in their merits. Rather, for most substantial changes the failure lies in the execution, not the technical or economic merit of the solution—or the methodology used to create it.

How many times have you heard people say, "We tried that...it didn't work"? And in many cases they say this in the face of other comparable situations in which the solution did work. The rejoinder that naturally follows when this is pointed out is, invariably, "Yes, but *we're different*," implying that what worked somewhere else won't work here. Well, if that were true, then nothing new would ever be adopted and human progress would stop—and we know that doesn't happen. Change failure usually happens in two modes: active resistance and passive resistance.

Active Resistance

As the term implies, active resistance is overt "pushback." There's no difficulty detecting it. People will object to a proposed change verbally, but their objections will almost always be based on challenges to technical or economic feasibility (that is, whether the change would work or how much it might cost). In some cases, they might cite political resistance (not their own, of course!).

Passive Resistance

Two critical mistakes many change agents make are assuming that logical solutions are enough to motivate people to apply them and equating intellectual commitment with appropriate action. A logical defense of a proposed change may be sufficient to persuade people intellectually; it is not sufficient to prompt the required action (behavior) to execute the change:

Intellectual commitment ≠ *Appropriate action*

Is Behavior Logical?

In the old *Star Trek* television series, the character Spock routinely observed that "humans are not logical." In some ways, undesirable behavior in the face of persuasive logic to the contrary would seem illogical. Yet it happens every day. People logically understand that they shouldn't smoke, or consume high-calorie, fatty foods, or engage in other kinds of high-risk behavior. But they do so anyway, in the face of that logic. They may even *acknowledge* the validity of the logic, then behave otherwise anyway. So maybe Spock was right.

Or was he? With a thorough understanding of why people behave as they do—or fail to behave as we think they should—it might be possible to anticipate their behavior or even predict it. And the ability to do this would make their behavior eminently logical.

In all cases—bar none—successful improvement of system operation is a function of *real* changes in people's behavior. Not only is this not an easy thing to achieve, it's probably the most critical part of executing a breakthrough solution to a problem. One might even say that the single *constraint* to system improvement, the ultimate determinant of success or failure, is changing people's behavior.

Changing Minds, or Changing Behavior?

For more than 50 years, psychologists have argued about what makes people act the way they do. There are two schools of thought on the subject: *behavioral* and *cognitive*.

The behavioral school contends that people's behavior is motivated by the promise of reward and the avoidance of punishment (or adverse consequences), and the way to channel behavior in desired directions is by the reasonable application of rewards and punishment (or withholding of rewards).

The cognitive school suggests that this doesn't explain behavior that seems to fly in the face of reward-punishment logic: people who behave in ways that they can reasonably expect will get them punished or who consciously forego behavior changes that will garner them apparent rewards. Cognitive proponents believe that a deeper internalization of the need for, and advisability of, change must occur before changed behavior will be sustained.[10:58-59] In other words, according to this school behavior modification techniques don't result in sustained new behavior because real cognition of the rationale for change hasn't taken place. In other words, like Pavlov's dog, people are only behaving to achieve short-term reinforcement, they don't actually *believe* in the new behavior. Thus, any failing or inconsistency in the reinforcement scheme will permit conditions for the original behavior to re-emerge.*

---

* Think about your own experiences. How many times have you seen mandated changes in "the way things are done," eventually followed by reversion to "the old way of doing things"? Could it be that the new way was not consistently reinforced?

The debate (and the divide) between the behaviorists and cognitionists continues with no indication of definitive resolution anytime soon. Nor would this book be the place for a detailed discussion of the issue. Suffice it to say that there is a cognitive basis for behavior and that issue should be addressed. But at some point all change agents must also deal with measurable behavior and its reinforcers.

It's worth understanding the role that the behavioral and cognitive philosophies play. For practitioners—the ultimate target audience of this book—our ultimate purpose is to articulate some general prescriptions for maximizing the probability of succeeding at, and sustaining, change.

Why Do People Resist Change?

We should note at the outset that resistance to change, per se, is not necessarily always bad. In fact, medical research indicates that there is some neurological foundation for it.[5] So there may be some evolutionary basis for "doing things the same old way."

Some level of resistance to change can be beneficial to preclude chaos from reigning in an organization. Unrestricted freedom to change at any time undermines structure and standardization, two characteristics that instill a degree of confidence and comfort in those who are part of any organization. So a level of resistance to change that at the very least demands rational justification for it is desirable. The real problem arises when the resistance to change becomes pathological, frustrating even beneficial change. Unfortunately, the demarcation between "good" resistance and "bad" is anything but clear.

Resistance to change, whether passive or active, is a type of behavior. Behavior is accepted by most psychologists as fundamentally motivated by unfulfilled needs. We're hungry, so we go to the refrigerator to look for something to eat. We don't feel safe on the streets at night, so we retreat to the comfort of our homes. We're lonely, so we look to others for company. We're bored, so we look for something engaging to do. The list goes on and on.

If we accept that behavior is motivated by unfulfilled needs, then the next logical question is what are those needs? What needs would people be satisfying by behaving in ways that we would consider resistance to change? In other words, "What's in it for me?"

Needs theory is a well-studied component of psychology. Among the earliest researchers in this area was Abraham Maslow. He was by no means the only student of motivation and behavior,* but his hierarchy of needs (see Figure 8.2)[19] is generally accepted—at least among practitioners, if not among all academics—as the basis for individuals' behavior in the real world.

Closely related to Maslow's theory are those of Herzberg, McClelland, and Adams. Each of these is described in slightly more detail in Appendix H. For the purposes of this discussion, we'll consider only the "interfaces"—the points at which these various theories seem to converge or overlap and their relevance to overcoming people's resistance to change.

Maslow

The majority of people in most organizations are functioning in levels 3 and 4 of Maslow's hierarchy. (See Figure 8.2.) Yes, it's true that in tough economic times more will revert to level 2 (security) because of concern about their jobs. On the other hand, very few people—possibly only executives, and perhaps not even they—routinely function at level 5 (self-actualization) for much of the time. This majority at levels 3 and 4 is likely to include most middle- and upper-level managers. They're most concerned about their status

---

* Others include Herzberg, Alderfer, McClelland, Adams, Skinner, Vroom, and Locke.

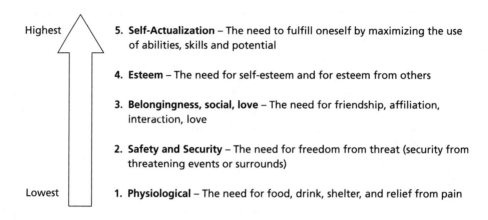

Highest

5. **Self-Actualization** – The need to fulfill oneself by maximizing the use of abilities, skills and potential

4. **Esteem** – The need for self-esteem and for esteem from others

3. **Belongingness, social, love** – The need for friendship, affiliation, interaction, love

2. **Safety and Security** – The need for freedom from threat (security from threatening events or surrounds)

Lowest

1. **Physiological** – The need for food, drink, shelter, and relief from pain

Figure 8.2 Maslow's hierarchy of needs.

within the organization, which is related to affiliation and esteem needs. Anything that might compromise their acceptance by others or their image in the eyes of others is something to be wary of.

Herzberg

After B.F. Skinner, perhaps no other theorist has been so roundly criticized in organizational circles as Herzberg. Without getting into the specifics of his "hygiene-motivation" theory, the most relevant part of it for our purposes concerns the satisfaction of extrinsic and intrinsic needs. He maintained that satisfaction of extrinsic needs could prevent people from being de-motivated, but unless intrinsic needs were satisfied they wouldn't be truly motivated.[11:109] Herzberg suggested that the usual features of organizational compensation plans satisfy primarily extrinsic needs—those lowest in Maslow's hierarchy (levels 1 and 2). The intrinsic needs, which are operative primarily at Maslow's levels 3 and higher, are largely satisfied from within the individual. The best that an organization can do to satisfy them is provide individuals the *opportunity* to do so. (Ever heard the shibboleth "Only you are responsible for your own happiness"?)

McClelland

McClelland suggested that many needs are acquired or learned from the culture of a society.[11:112] Among these are the need for affiliation, achievement, and power. Affiliation would certainly relate to Maslow's level 3 (social, love). Achievement would likely be on level 4 (esteem of self and others), and power* is almost certainly a level 5 (self-actualization) candidate.

Adams

J. Stacey Adams, a research psychologist at General Electric Corporation in New York in the early 1960s, developed and tested an equity theory of motivation.[10:152-156] He found that people compared their efforts and rewards with those of others. As long as that comparison is equivalent (ratio of outputs to inputs), they're satisfied. However, when they perceive that they have to work harder than others for the same or less pay, they're not. Or if others work the same or less for more pay, they're dissatisfied, too. The driver of their dissatisfaction is the perceived inequity.

---

* "It's *good* to be da king!" (Mel Brooks, as King Louis XVI, in *History of the World, Part 1*)

Someone with higher responsibility, or who works longer hours, may be paid more. People aren't concerned about that, because they can convince themselves that the person earns it. The problems arise when someone receives disproportionately greater reward (either in extrinsic compensation or adulation) than another equivalent person receives. For example, a middle manager may see the chief executive making 15 times as much as he or she does and not be bothered by it. But if that same CEO makes 400 times the middle manager's compensation (not an unusual circumstance in America between 1995 and 2007), it seems inequitable to the manager.

Feelings of inequity directly threaten levels 3 and 4 in Maslow's hierarchy. Members of an organization don't feel appreciated (level 4) by superiors and they may feel jealous of or estranged from contemporaries (level 3).

Figure 8.3 illustrates the relationship between the theories of Maslow, Herzberg, McClelland, and Adams. In one way or another, all of the effects described above conspire to push people out of their "comfort zones."

Anaclitic Depression Blues

Emotional connections with others and our own ideas are an important part of motivation. Harvey has described the phenomenon of "separation anxiety," whether it's estrangement from other people or even being forced out of one's comfort zone by new ways of doing things, as *anaclitic depression*. Specifically, it's

> *...melancholia that we often experience when the individuals, organizations, or belief systems that we lean on or [depend] on for emotional support are withdrawn from us.*[12:112-113]

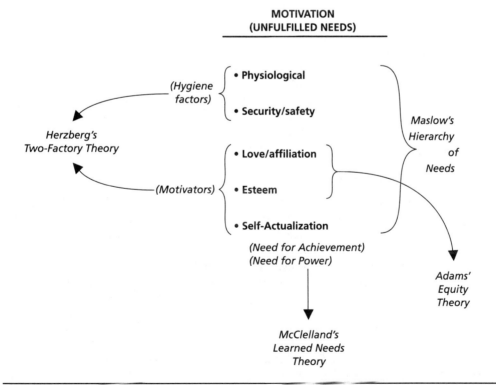

Figure 8.3 Elements of motivation.

Everybody suffers it—or has suffered from it—at one time or another. It's not a pleasant feeling. It manifests itself as a general feeling of discouragement—the "blues." It may not be as debilitating as clinical depression, but it's an unpleasant experience nonetheless. Everybody who has experienced it (and who has not?) wants to avoid it in the future, even if they don't fully understand what it is or what's causing it.

In organizations, separation anxiety results not so much from the failure to satisfy the various needs described above. It's *fear of the threat* that a new way of doing things might somehow eventually separate us from the people, organization structure, assumptions, or ways of doing things that we've grown accustomed to, or comfortable with. In other words, it affects Maslow's levels 2 and 3. Never mind that the fears may be logically unfounded (Harvey refers to these as "negative fantasies").[13:22] The anaclitic depression blues have little to do with logic and everything to do with emotions. And it's purely instinctive for people to avoid them.

Security or Satisfaction?

Here's another way to look at it. In the early 1990s, a young psychology student in Israel, Efrat Goldratt, postulated that people universally sought to be happy in their lives. The achievement of this goal depended on satisfying two necessary conditions: achieving security and achieving satisfaction.[8:117-119]

Goldratt specified particular definitions for security and satisfaction. People felt secure, she said, when they had *confidence in the predictability of events* in their lives. She offered no value judgment on the desirability of any such events. Rather it's the confidence in predictability that engenders a sense of security. Goldratt defined satisfaction as the positive feeling one obtains after *realizing a particularly difficult objective*, one in which the outcome was in doubt.* The tougher the objective, the more satisfaction accrues when one actually accomplishes it. Winning a world or Olympic championship might be an example.

What are Goldratt's definitions of security and satisfaction but elements of Maslow's hierarchy of needs? Security might encompass levels 1 through 3 (physiological, safety/security, and love/affiliation needs). Satisfaction would clearly reside in levels 4 and 5 (esteem and self-actualization).

Goldratt went on to propose that people's drive to satisfy these needs and realize the ultimate objective of happiness was the root of the elemental personal conflict that everybody faces in their lives: Don't change and protect the status quo (preserve security) or embrace change and achieve great things (achieve satisfaction). (See Figure 8.4)

The Impact on Solutions

In consolidating the theories of Maslow, Herzberg, McClelland, Adams, and Harvey, it's fairly clear that their common intersection occurs primarily at levels 3 and 4 of Maslow's hierarchy: the social and esteem needs that all people share. And Efrat Goldratt's conflict gets at the heart of the dilemma that a big change—in the form of sweeping modifications to the way businesses operate—poses for individuals. This dilemma (resist change or embrace change) mires people in indecision, the result of which is that they often don't act

---

* I once asked a fighter pilot friend of mine which airplane he preferred flying, the older F-4 Phantom or the newer F-16 Fighting Falcon. Without hesitation, he replied, "I prefer flying the F-4. It's a tougher airplane to fly, and it'll 'bite' you if you don't stay on top of it at all times. It takes a really good pilot to do that. Not everybody's equal to the task. There's no virtue in doing something that just anybody can do." That, to me, is the essence of Goldratt's definition of satisfaction: being able to do what few others can do.

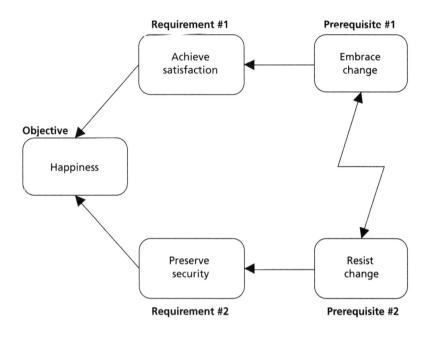

SOURCE: Dettmer, *Strategic Navigation* (2003)

Figure 8.4   How to achieve happiness: Efrat's Cloud.

at all, either to resist or to embrace. Instead they do nothing, waiting to see how things shake out. When asked, they may express positive words about the proposed changes, but their action (or inaction) tells a different story about how they think.

For change agents, this dichotomy between what people do and what they say is particularly vexing. It's called *behavioral incongruence.*[1] When a person's espoused behavior (what they say they do) differs from what they actually do, their behavior is incongruent with their statements about it. Think about your own experiences in organizations. Have you seen situations where people say they typically do one thing, but actually do something completely different? Or *say* that they are going to act in one way, but then don't actually do so? If so, you've encountered this phenomenon.

Overcoming the dilemma of Efrat's Cloud (Figure 8.4) demands effective leadership. And leaders of organizations tend to have a lot of things on their minds. It's ironic that executives spend more time reviewing financial issues than they do attending to the psyches and behaviors of their employees. Given the time delay between human behavior and quarterly reports, that's akin to driving your car down the freeway by reference only to the rear-view mirror.

> *Consider how hard it is to change yourself, and you'll understand what little chance you have of trying to change others.*
>
> —Jacob M. Braude

LEADERSHIP

Have you seen them? Which way did they go? I must be after them, for I am their leader!

—Unknown

Leadership is almost a hackneyed term. People use the term interchangeably with *management*. The two are not the same. They're not even close. And one reason why many organizations are in such trouble is that there is a surfeit of management at the top and a simultaneous dearth of leadership.

What is leadership? Unfortunately, there are almost as many definitions as there are people. Decades of academic analysis have given us more than 350 definitions of leadership[2:4] and almost all differ in some respect. People may have difficulty agreeing on a definition, but most will agree that they know it when they see it. Let's consider a few definitions and see if we can distill a common, simple one.

A former student of mine (a U.S. Marine) once provided me the Marine Corps distinction between leadership and management: "You lead *people*; you manage *things*." At the time that, too, sounded hackneyed to me, but the more I've thought about leadership and studied it, the more I've come to recognize that the Marines are right. Unfortunately, though, in almost every modern organization the nominal leaders spend more time and energy on paperwork, financials, and other things than they do leading *people*.

Narrowly and organizationally (the context most of us are likely to be concerned with), leadership has been defined as "the ability of an individual to influence, motivate, and enable others to contribute toward the effectiveness and success of the organizations of which they are members."[14]

Elliott Jaques defines leadership as a process…

> *…in which one person sets the purpose or direction for one or more other persons and gets them to move along together with him and with each other with competence and full commitment.*[16:4]

These few definitions of leadership "circle around" the concise definition I believe will suffice for our purposes: *Leadership, at its highest, consists of getting people to do what you want them to do when they are under no obligation to do so.* Or, as the line goes in "The Impossible Dream" *(Man of LaMancha)*: "To be willing to march into hell for that heavenly cause…"*

How many organizational leaders do you know for whom their followers would march into hell?

Leadership Is About People

Harvey maintains that real leadership requires you to be emotionally bonded, attached, connected, or linked with those whom you lead. And it also requires that you ensure that your followers are similarly bonded with one another. In the absence of these bonds, you may be able to coerce people into doing what you want them to do—to *drive* them—but you can't *lead* them.[11:135]

---

* "The Impossible Dream," music by Mitch Leigh, lyrics by Joe Darion.

Think about how this relates to the last major organizational change you witnessed. Does the kind of emotional connection Harvey describes exist in your organization? Was the kind of loyalty and commitment to a larger group purpose instilled or preserved? Would members of the team have "marched into hell for a heavenly cause"? Would your organizational shepherd have left 99 sheep to find the one lost?* Is it any wonder, then, that people exert only half-hearted effort, while watching the clock for quitting time?

Leadership and the *Blitzkrieg*

If you're in charge of an organization, how do you practice the kind of leadership required to complete effective change? How can you ensure that your followers act "with competence and full commitment" to do what you would want them to do, even when you're not there to guide or direct them? It's instructive to consider the infamous *blitzkrieg* of World War II.

The German word translates to English as "lightning war." It was used to characterize the previously unseen concept of rapid-maneuver warfare, using smaller, fast-moving units to effect damage to the enemy far out of proportion to their numbers before opponents even knew what was happening. Surprise was, of course, a big element in the success of the *blitzkrieg*. But the well-coordinated actions of autonomous units were perhaps an even greater contributor to its success.**

The flexibility and maneuverability of German armored units owed itself to four basic principles, all of which are relevant to true leadership (as defined above) in *any* organization. These principles are: *mutual trust, personal professional skill, a moral contract,* and *focus*.[21:52-59] Figure 8.5 summarizes the *blitzkrieg* principles.

Mutual Trust

The German word for this is *einheit*. It refers to the certain knowledge of what to expect from one another that leaders and followers develop after repeatedly working together, time and time again. This trust is earned over time through two-way communication, training, practice, and patience. It can't be imposed; it must be earned. But when it exists, leaders need not check up on their subordinates—they know exactly what to expect from them, and subordinates know that their leaders will support them when they exercise their own initiative.

Personal Professional Skill

The Germans called this *fingerspitzengefühl*, which translates literally as "fingertip feel." It refers to the consummate skill craftsmen exercise when they do their work. They make even the most difficult, complicated tasks seem fluid and simple, smooth and effortless. Fingertip feel comes only with experience and repetition, which also is a function of time. Someone learning to ride a horse doesn't do so with the fingertip feel of a professional rodeo cowboy or competitive show rider. The mutual trust discussed above results from the confidence a leader has that his or her subordinates have this fingertip feel about their work—and vice-versa.

---

* Matthew 18: 10-14

** I hope that readers can separate in their minds the brilliance of the military tactics practiced by German panzer divisions from the ignoble purposes of the German regime for which they were used. The fact that I abhor everything that Nazi Germany stood for in no way changes the fact that the military tactics of the *blitzkrieg* were brilliantly conceived and executed by extraordinary military leaders.

Einheit (mutual trust): The confidence among one another that develops from shared experiences over a long period of time (i.e., not just a few discrete events). Mutual trust results in the ability to know what to expect from others in a variety of circumstances and the willingness to assume that others will do what is expected of them at the appropriate time without the need for continual checking.

Fingerspitzengefühl (personal professional skill): Literally, "fingertip feel." Intuitive skill or knowledge born of years of experience, practice, and self-discipline. Permits instinctive action (the sword is an extension of the arm).

Auftragstaktik (moral contract): A mutual agreement between leaders and followers wherein the followers voluntarily assume responsibility for an assignment from leaders with the implicit understanding that leaders will not ask the followers to do something beyond their capability or endanger them without an important strategic reason. Once concluded, leaders allow and expect followers to exercise initiative in deciding how the mission is accomplished, within broad parameters specified by the leaders. Followers are expected to challenge the request if they believe they don't have the resources to complete the mission or if they perceive the directed task to be ill-advised. But once concluded, leaders can assume that the task will be accomplished. An effective moral contract depends on prior establishment of einheit and fingerspitzengefühl.

Schwerpunkt (focus point): Any device or concept that gives focus to efforts; the main effort which all other activities of an organization must support (and know they must support it). Subordinates are expected to use their own initiative and set aside previously-issued orders whenever they can advance the focusing-and-directing mission. Effective schwerpunkt effort depends on the establishment of auftragstaktik and einheit.

Adapted from Richards, Certain to Win (2004)

Figure 8.5   Elements of the *Blitzkrieg*.

Moral Contract

The German word for this is *auftragstaktik*. It's a mutual agreement between leader and follower that implies: "I (the leader) know what you're capable of, and I trust you to do it if you agree to it. You trust me not to ask you to do something you cannot do or that will endanger you for no important strategic reason."[21:56] This moral contract, combined with mutual trust and an abiding confidence in the subordinate's personal professional skill, implies that subordinates can exercise initiative in situations when no specific guidance has previously been provided, and they won't be chastised for it afterward, even if things go awry. In fact, the exercise of such initiative is expected and encouraged.

When mutual trust, personal professional skill, and a moral contract are all in play, leaders can lead by *intent*, not just by specific direction.* They can describe the mission objective in broad strokes and say, "Go make it happen," with confidence that their subordinates understand what the leader wants and would act as the leader would have them do when the unexpected happens. They do so with full confidence that the outcome will meet with the leader's approval.

Focus

The final component of the *blitzkrieg* is a focus point, or in the German, *schwerpunkt*, which translates literally as "hard or difficult point." The real meaning is closer to "center of gravity or emphasis." One could also call it "direction." Or a system constraint. However you refer to it, it's the objective that all members of the organization bend efforts to attain. The leader is responsible for setting this direction and communicating it clearly to everyone. Without this single-minded purpose, the mutual trust, fingertip feel, and moral

---

* "The only thing worse than an employee who won't do what he's told is one that will do *only* what he's told."

contract won't be effective. In many organizations, it's referred to as "the vision thing."* People with vision are a surprisingly rare commodity. If you have it and can articulate it effectively, you can actually inspire people to follow you. Consider the immortal words of Dr. Martin Luther King: "I have a dream…" And think of the cultural revolution it mobilized in America. Now, *that's* focus!

Whether you call it focus or vision, it contributes to inspiration, which in turn is an indispensable component of leadership—the heavenly cause for which followers willingly march into hell.

These four principles—mutual trust, personal professional skill, a moral contract, and focus—are the bedrock of real leadership. Of persuading people to do what you want them to do when they are under no obligation to do so. Figure 8.6 shows the relationship of some components of effective leadership. The *blitzkrieg* factors are shaded.

Level 5 Leadership

Perhaps the true test of an effective hypothesis is the ability to find independent data to confirm it. Where leadership is concerned, that's not especially difficult to do. In his book *Good to Great*, Jim Collins made the following observations:

> *The good-to-great executives were all cut from the same cloth. It didn't matter whether the company was consumer or industrial, in crisis or steady state, offered services or products. It didn't matter when the transition took place or how big the company. All the good-to-great companies had Level 5 leadership at the time of transition. Furthermore, the absence of Level 5 leadership showed up as a consistent pattern in the comparison companies.*[4:21-22]

Collins described Level 5 leadership as "[building] enduring greatness through a paradoxical blend of personal humility and professional will."[4] Unfortunately, Collins offers no concrete prescriptions about how to become a Level 5 leader. In fact, he points out that his discussion of "Level 5" is about what they are and the kinds of things they do, not a roadmap for how to become such a leader.[4:37-38] (It's important to avoid confusion here. Collins' Level 5 leadership is not the same as Elliott Jaques' Level 5 organization structure, or Maslow's Level 5 needs. It is interesting to note, however, that organizations with Jaques' concept of Level 5 leaders would exhibit remarkably similar characteristics to Collins' Level 5 leaders.)

Personally, I don't believe that it's practical to lay down any discrete list of do's and don'ts for leaders. However, I do think that the four *blitzkrieg* principles line up pretty well with Collins' Level 5 leader concept. And they provide a framework to guide leader behavior that is generic enough to apply to all kinds and sizes of organization.

LEADERSHIP AND BEHAVIOR

The most important contributing factor to the behavior of people in organizations, and thus to the success of organizational change, is the quality of leadership. By "quality of leadership," I intentionally imply a double meaning.

The first meaning of quality is *characteristic,* and the first meaning of leadership relates to the *concept*. The second meaning of quality is *fineness* or *excellence,* and the second meaning of leadership is the *specific people* who occupy positions of authority. In other words, are the people in charge *really* leading, and how good are they at it? The success of any

---

* George H.W. Bush, 1987.

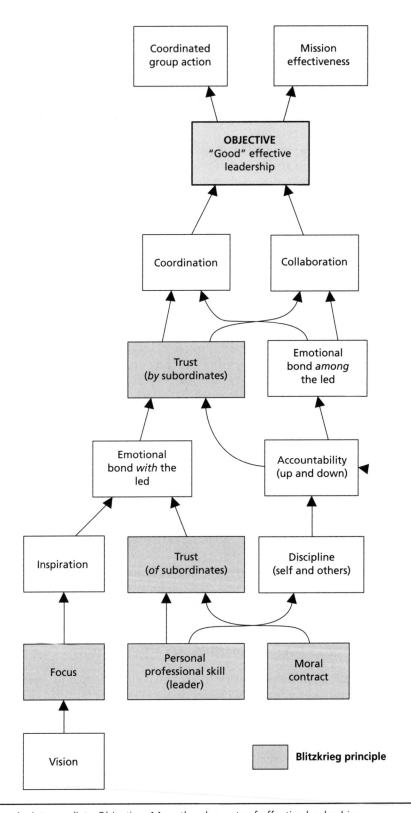

Figure 8.6   An Intermediate Objectives Map: the elements of effective leadership.

organizational change is a function of the people leading the organization and their skill in leading others to execute it—inspiring them "to march into hell for that heavenly cause."

The implications for the success of change are profound. If it's to succeed, change can't be driven from the middle of an organization. It must be driven from the top. The intended outcome of the change constitutes the *vision* we discussed earlier. Establishing that vision is solely the leader's responsibility. Leaders must *own* that vision themselves before they can inspire others to pursue it.

The *idea* for change can originate from anywhere, within the organization or without. But unless leaders embrace it publicly and repeatedly, and demonstrate (communicate) their commitment to it repeatedly with their own visible behavior, "it ain't a-gonna happen."

The story has been told about W. Edwards Deming's first visit to Ford Motor Company in 1979. Donald Peterson, chairman and CEO of Ford, convened Ford's vice presidents—some 400 of them—in the company auditorium and introduced Deming, admonishing them to pay close attention to what the quality guru had to say. Peterson then exited the auditorium and returned to his office (presumably to review financials and read paperwork!). When he turned around, he found Deming standing there in his office with him. Deming's explanation for why he followed Peterson: "Where you are, I am." It was a particularly persuasive way of communicating to Peterson that he needed to personally demonstrate by being there his commitment to what Deming would say to the people of Ford.* All I would add to that message is the word repeatedly. So let's say it once again to make it unmistakably clear:

> If the organization's leaders are not committed to a change and don't visibly demonstrate that commitment repeatedly, it will fail.

The Leader's Behavior

As suggested above, leaders communicate by their behavior as much as by their words. Actions speak louder than words, and people pay attention to that kind of communication. But the behavior of leaders is no less motivated by the satisfaction of needs than anyone else's. People do what they do to "scratch an itch." It's just that for leaders, those needs are usually higher in Maslow's hierarchy than the first three levels (physiological, security, and affiliation). They're almost always concentrated at levels 4 and 5 (esteem and self-actualization). And more specifically, those facets of level five that McClelland best articulated as needs for achievement and power.

At the same time, however, leaders are also security conscious. They're gratified with their position, their responsibilities, their authority, and perhaps even their compensation. They're aware that their decisions can have wide-ranging impacts on the success and health of the organization, and, not coincidentally, on their own job security. They perceive that they have a lot to lose by a wrong decision.

A study of executive compensation published in *The Economist* found that one reason for very large compensation packages for chief executives in particular was their relatively short longevity in the job.[29] Because boards of directors are looking for share-value results quickly, the average CEO isn't given a particularly long time to show results and boards are quick to offer them their severance packages. The Jack Welchs of the world, who stay in the position for a decade or more, are few and far between. Thus, there usually isn't time to recover from a misstep. This kind of thinking can make executives highly "security conscious."

---

* It's worth mentioning that Peterson reportedly cleared out his schedule for the rest of the day and returned to the auditorium with Deming. The ultimate result was "Quality is Job 1."

An early step in enlisting the commitment of leaders is for them to see how the successful implementation of the proposed change will help satisfy their needs—and persuade them emotionally that the idea is a good one. If this is done, the odds improve that the leader's behavior will match his or her words to subordinates about it.

Subordinates' Behavior

Unlike leaders, subordinates are less likely to be operating at Maslow's level 5. It's more likely that they're at level 3 (social, affiliation needs) and reaching for level 4 (esteem). However, in the turbulent, uncertain world of globalization and outsourcing, a great many subordinates have been forced down into concern about level 2 (security). Fear of the anaclitic depression blues affects leaders, too, but it's considerably more pronounced in the middle and lower levels of an organization, where employees don't have "golden parachutes."*

Subordinates take their cue about how to behave from a leader's behavior. Deming insisted that Peterson be with him so as to demonstrate that he was committed to what Deming would be telling the vice presidents. Whether they're aware of it or not, leaders are communicating a message with their body language and non-verbal feedback. And subordinates pick up these messages, whether they're conscious of it or not. Leaders' less than active commitment for a change is obvious to those observing them. And subordinates' behavior becomes a reflection of the leader's behavior. It's a rare subordinate who will try to "get inside the head" of the leader, anticipate what the leader intends, and take initiative to provide it without being specifically directed. And when subordinates do venture to exercise such initiative, they're very sensitive to the leader's reaction.

> *A new idea is delicate. It can be killed by a sneer or a yawn; it can be stabbed to death by a quip, and worried to death by a frown on the right person's brow.*

CREATING AND SUSTAINING DESIRED BEHAVIORS

From the preceding discussion of human motivation and leadership and their relationship to behavior, it should be clear that the challenge of changing behavior isn't a simple thing. It certainly involves more than constructing a logical solution, presenting it to people, expecting enlightenment to dawn, and anticipating immediate commitment to new behaviors to occur. In fact, it should be obvious that a logic-only approach to change is doomed to fail.

Antonio Damasio, a prominent neurologist, has made a persuasive, testable case for the idea that reason and emotion are inseparable and joined by the neurology of the brain.[4:xii] Moreover, he has concluded that not only does a purely logical mind not exist, but reasoning not based on an emotional foundation is pathologically prone to error. If this hypothesis is valid, then contrary to Descartes' philosophy, reasoning can't be separated from emotion, as people have popularly believed since the 1600s.

What does this signify for change management? Simply that effecting successful change requires far more than creating a logical solution and expecting people to embrace it or be persuaded by its logic. If, as Damasio contends, beliefs and behaviors are embedded in the brain's neural structures, changing minds has a biological component as well as a logical one. Behavior changes may then be Darwinian to some degree. This implies that simply standing up with a PowerPoint presentation to win people over, then expecting new behavior to be self-directed, is wishful thinking.

---

* It was really tough for most people to feel sorry for Carly Fiorina when the Hewlett-Packard board of directors terminated her as CEO with a $21.4 million severance package. (http://money.cnn.com/2005/02/12/news/newsmakers/fiorina_severance/)

But neither organizational leaders nor system owners have the patience to wait for evolutionary change to occur. For timely effectiveness, some kind of robust intervention is required or we may see the next ice age before it occurs naturally. This brings us to the question of how to direct and control the behaviors required to initiate and sustain the changes demanded by new ideas and solutions to system problems.

> *It's a wonderful feeling when you discover some logic to substantiate your beliefs.*
>
> —Unknown

> *If you work with people, sometimes logic has to take a back seat to understanding.*
>
> — Akio Morita, former CEO Sony Corp.

Behavior Change is a Leadership Function

At the outset, let's make one thing clear: In an organizational setting, initiating and sustaining behavioral change is primarily the responsibility of leaders. Subordinates *do*, leaders *direct*. And directing implies much more than just telling people what to do. In changing behavior, it means *to channel or focus toward a given result, object, or end*.[14:8] The leader is responsible for defining the object or end (in *blitzkrieg* parlance, this would be the *schwerpunkt*, or focus point).

The act of channeling or focusing is the function that leaders are supposed to perform. Moreover, subordinates are constantly looking to leaders for some kind of clue as to how they should behave. How do leaders do this?

A Behavioral Approach to Change

In most organizations, behavior is directed by the "carrot-or-stick" approach. In psychology circles, it's referred to as reinforcement theory.

Grossly oversimplified, reinforcement theory suggests that some policy, directive or "the boss's decree" (called an antecedent) prompts some kind of behavior. The behavior produces some outcome for the one doing the behavior (called a consequence). The degree to which that consequence is pleasing or displeasing to the person behaving determines the reinforcement, or repetition effectiveness, of that behavior.[6:8-9]

Reinforcement can be either positive or negative. If the kind of behavior you're trying to achieve is someone not doing something, applying a negative consequence (for example, punishment) is typically a good way to do it. But if you're trying to get people to affirmatively *do* something, positive reinforcement (for example, providing a pleasurable consequence) is much more effective. Daniels contends that *behavior is a function of its consequences.* Figure 8.7 illustrates how reinforcement of behavior works.

Notice that in Figure 8.7, of the four kinds consequences, three of them relate to unfavorable possibilities. The threat of punishment and penalty drives avoidance behavior, which is essentially passive—something *doesn't* happen. Negative reinforcement may produce some affirmative activity, but it doesn't prompt maximum performance, only the minimum level required to escape or avoid an unpleasant consequence. (The threat of being arrested for driving faster than the speed limit doesn't make you eagerly strive to stay 5 miles per hour below the limit, or even more eager to stay 10 below it. It prompts you to slow down just enough to get you below the value that will result in arrest and penalty.)

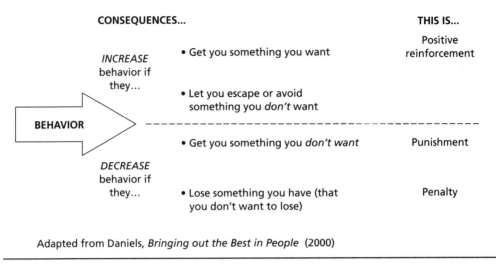

Adapted from Daniels, *Bringing out the Best in People* (2000)

Figure 8.7   Behavior, consequences, and reinforcement.

The problem lies in the fact that most organizations are really good at the negatives—if they're seriously concerned about reinforcing behavior at all. They're usually unaware that negative reinforcement secures a level of performance that is just enough to get by. If you want to maximize performance, you have to reinforce in a positive way.[6:43] But even those that strive to positively reinforce behavior are largely clueless on how to do it or don't do it very well.

Rewards or Reinforcement?
One reason leaders are often disappointed when their efforts at positive reinforcement don't give them the results they expect is that they fail to distinguish between *rewards* and *reinforcement*. Basically, rewards are typically delayed in time after the completion of the behavior. Reinforcers are immediate. Rewards may be intended as reinforcers, but they don't always achieve that expectation.

The corporate bonus at the end of the year is a reward and everybody looks forward to receiving it. But it's ineffective as a behavior reinforcer; it comes too long after the behavior that produced the results that generated the profits that enabled the chief financial officer to calculate how big the bonus should be. However, it comes just long enough after the behavior to take on the characteristics of an "entitlement" in many people's minds. Or worse—a demotivator: "I didn't get as big a bonus this year as I did last year...but those executives sure got theirs!" (Adams' equity theory at work again!)

The application of positive reinforcement often doesn't take place for three possible reasons. First, leaders assume that rewards (delayed) are behavior reinforcers, and sufficient ones, at that. ("We gave them a bonus. What more do they expect?") Second, they don't really know what kinds of things positively reinforce behavior (immediately). The third reason is that for many people in positions of authority, the whole business of giving positive reinforcement seems tedious and time consuming. And many managers don't see that as one of their important responsibilities.* My reaction to that draws on the

---

* Dr. Jerry Harvey related an exchange he had with an MBA student in one of his classes. The student walked out of his classroom near the beginning of the hour, clearly intending to drop the course after what he'd heard. His parting comment to Dr. Harvey was: "I took this class to learn how to be a manager. I don't want to waste my time worrying about anyone other than myself." [12:165]

observation my Marine student: You might be well suited to manage *things*, but never to lead *people*.

The lesson here is that successful change requires effective leadership. Effective leadership is first and foremost about people. Leading people—getting them to do what you want them to do when they are under no obligation to do so—demands deft skill in directing their behavior. This, in turn requires the sometimes tedious practice of positive reinforcement.

The astute reader will notice that I avoided a detailed discussion on what kinds of things represent positive reinforcers. For one thing, these will differ from one organization to another and from one person to another, and it's beyond the scope of this book to do that. For another, there are other sources specifically and entirely devoted to addressing this issue. One is Aubrey Daniels' book. (See endnotes for citation.) Two others that put reinforcement in a much broader system context are *Social Power and the CEO* and *The Requisite Organization*, both by Elliott Jaques.[17,18] Anyone searching for "an epiphany on the road to Damascus" is encouraged to read the latter two.

A GENERAL STRATEGY FOR IMPLEMENTING CHANGE

It's time to tie together everything we've explored so far. I call what follows a general strategy, because it's not practical to provide "cookbook directions." For one thing, that's beyond the scope of this book. For another, each organizational situation will differ enough from others that discrete step-by-step instructions wouldn't apply in many circumstances.

A Common Scenario

Though organizations may differ, most have some elemental factors pertaining to change in common. The creation of a flexible framework that can apply to different kinds of organizations requires a common set of assumptions and a scenario for how change is typically introduced.

Assumptions

Here are some change-related underlying assumptions common to most, if not all, human organizations:

- Organizations are hierarchical.

- Final authority is concentrated in the hands of one leader, that is, everybody knows where "the buck stops." (You may not always know who's right, but you always know who's in charge!)

- No significant change happens in any organization without the active commitment of its leader. Passive support is not enough.

- The organization's leader is Change Agent-in-Chief. Even if most of the "heavy lifting" is delegated, for change to succeed the leader must drive it.

- Leaders and subordinates alike behave in ways they perceive will satisfy their internal needs.

How Change "Gets In"

Any sort of new idea, methodology, or other change enters most organizations in one of two ways: either it comes from the leader, or some subordinate within the organization suggests it. If the impetus for change originates with the leader, it could come from "divine inspiration" or from some source outside the organization. Typical external sources might include media articles, journals, professional societies, conferences or symposia, or even networking with other leaders. If the initial impetus comes from a subordinate, it's likely the subordinate learned about it from some external source, too.

It's always better if leaders discover the idea for themselves. If they do, their interest in it is already established. Maybe they've even persuaded themselves already that it could satisfy their need. This isn't usually the case if the idea comes up through the organization.* Leaders may have to be persuaded that it's a good thing to do before they embrace it. Executive persuasion adds a prerequisite to the change, one that carries with it some other uncertain variables. Yet "filtering up" from within is how many organizations have been introduced to new ways of doing things, such as total quality management, business process re-engineering, lean, Six Sigma, and so forth.

The Leader as Change Agent-in-Chief

Regardless of how the idea for change enters the organization, it's almost axiomatic that if the leader doesn't want it, it won't happen. But the converse is not necessarily true, either. Just because a leader *does* want a change to happen doesn't mean that it will. Leaders must clearly and visibly demonstrate—by deeds as well as words—their commitment to seeing the change happen. In other words, they must *lead the change themselves*. This is not the same as day-to-day hands-on management. Leaders may delegate detailed change management to some trusted subordinate, but they can't put it on autopilot and say, "Report to me when it's done." The concept of positive reinforcement mentioned earlier applies here and it requires regular, repeated application.

Subordinates notice their leaders' behavior—and take their cues from it—even if they're not saying anything. They can tell very quickly if a task or initiative isn't high on the leader's agenda, or whether leaders' behavior is incongruent with their pronouncements. And they'll behave with the same sense of urgency (or lack of it) themselves. Leaders lead by their own example, whether they're conscious of it or not. And they have to get involved and stay involved.

It's almost a given that the high rate of failure of change initiatives—perhaps 80 percent by some estimates—occurs primarily because of human behavior, not because the change is technically or economically ineffective. Remember our discussions of human needs and the *blitzkrieg* principles from earlier in the chapter? It's time to see how these fit into the change formula. (See Figure 8.8.)

Increasing the odds of successful change begins with the leader's perception of what will satisfy his or her unfulfilled needs (the left side of Figure 8.8). Satisfaction of the leader's needs normally results from the effective discharge of the organization's mission (the top-center of Figure 8.8). This, in turn, is the outcome of the coordinated, effectively directed behavior of the leader's subordinates, from the top of the organization to the bottom. Let's call this *desired behavior* (upper right of Figure 8.8). But subordinates' behavior is the outcome of the perception that their needs will be satisfied by doing what the leader wants them to do (the right side of Figure 8.8).

The *blitzkrieg* principles represent a bridge of trust between the leader's needs and the subordinates' needs. To satisfy his or her needs, the leader *does* the four elements of

---

* Sometimes in this circumstance the leader's "defensive antennae" pop up.

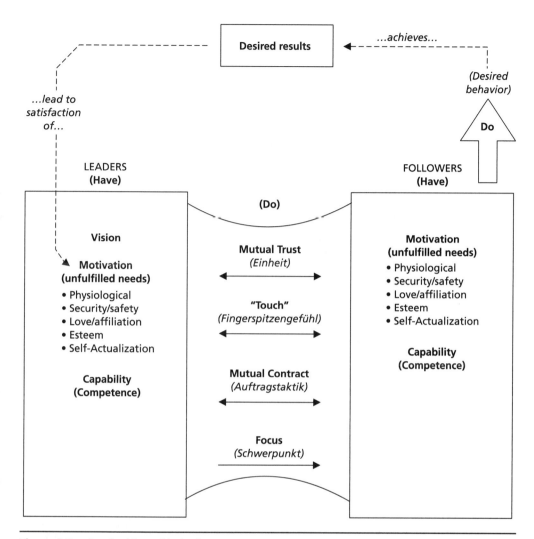

Figure 8.8   Leadership and behavior.

the *blitzkrieg*, which satisfy the needs of subordinates. The subordinates in turn *do* the behavior that the leader asks them to do, which both expect will produce the results that ultimately satisfy the leader's needs.

A Model for Implementing Change

Using the output of a Logical Thinking Process analysis (the topic of the first seven chapters of this book) as the "idea for change," let's see how a workable change process might unfold. For our purposes, the Thinking Process analysis may have been completed by either by an internal problem-solving team commissioned by an executive, or by an external facilitator with input from the organization. Figure 8.9 shows a notional model for this process.*

---

* Figure 8.9 is intended to be a flow chart, not a logic tree.

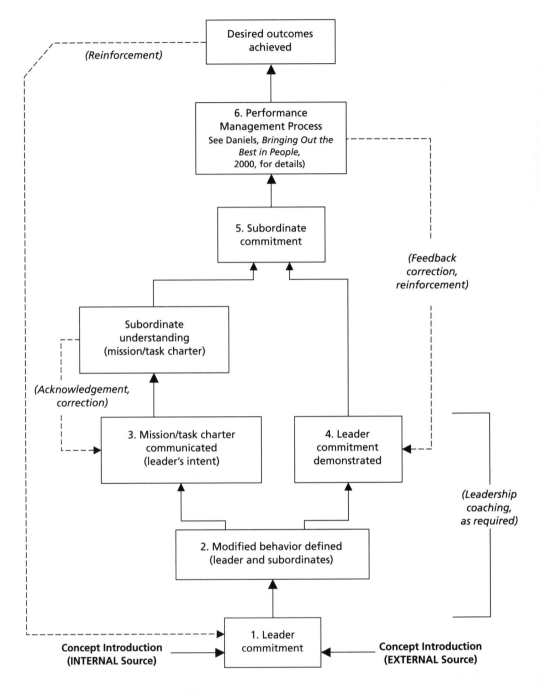

(Reinforcement)

Desired outcomes
achieved

6. Performance
Management Process
See Daniels, *Bringing Out the
Best in People,*
2000, for details)

5. Subordinate
commitment

*(Feedback
correction,
reinforcement)*

Subordinate
understanding
(mission/task charter)

*(Acknowledgement,
correction)*

3. Mission/task charter
communicated
(leader's intent)

4. Leader
commitment
demonstrated

*(Leadership
coaching,
as required)*

2. Modified behavior defined
(leader and subordinates)

1. Leader
commitment

**Concept Introduction
(INTERNAL Source)**

**Concept Introduction
(EXTERNAL Source)**

ASSUMPTIONS:
- *Introducer understands leader's needs*
- *Concept tailored to fulfill leader's needs*
- *Introducer demonstrates leader's need fulfillment*

Figure 8.9   A change implementation model.

1. Leader Commitment

As discussed above, if the organizational leader is not actively committed to the change, it won't happen. For the leaders to commit themselves three things must happen:

- Whoever introduces the leader to the new idea must understand the leader's needs, both their needs as leaders and their personal, emotional needs. Leaders probably have an intuitive understanding of their own needs, so if they discover the concept on their own, they should be able to make a direct connection between the benefits it offers and the needs it satisfies.

- The concept must fit the leader's needs. If it's introduced by someone else, either inside or outside the organization, that person must tailor the concept to emphasize the leader's needs. If the leader discovers the concept personally, he or she will either see its benefits immediately, or not.

- If the leader is introduced to the concept by someone else, that person must clearly demonstrate how the benefits will satisfy the leader's needs.

If these three conditions are met, the leader will likely be prepared to press ahead with implementation. But personal commitment alone isn't sufficient to get the job done.

2. Modified Behavior Defined

Once leaders are intellectually and emotionally committed to the new concept, they must have a clear picture of their responsibilities as Change Agents-in-Chief. This can often require external coaching by experts in the new concept, masters of behavioral change psychology, or both. The important thing to remember is that an authoritarian approach is not a good idea. Maximizing the odds of long-term success requires *blitzkrieg*-type mutual trust and moral contracts.

Before issuing the change charter to the organization, it's important to know exactly which leader and subordinate behaviors must change and how. The concept expert is probably in the best position to identify and quantify these behaviors and suggest measurements that can confirm effective behavioral change.

3. Mission/Task Charter Communicated

Once the new behaviors of both leaders and subordinates have been defined, the time has come for the leader to notify the organization of the change. Often, as in the Ford Motors example cited earlier in this chapter, the leader will delegate that to an expert, as Peterson did with Deming. But if at all possible, leaders should themselves brief the change in operational procedures and behaviors. It sets a better example because it demonstrates that the leader has internalized the concept well enough to convey it to others as his or her own.

An indispensable part of any communication process is "message received and understood." After delivering the new charter, leaders must confirm that all subordinates heard and understood what the leader expects. Just asking "Are there any questions?" at the end of the presentation of the mission may not be sufficient. It might be advisable for leaders to independently meet with key subordinates and opinion leaders to ascertain whether they truly understand what is being asked of them and agree to do it. This constitutes the moral contract step explained in Figure 8.5.

This step is where a *blitzkrieg*-competent organization (that is, one for which the four principles described in Figure 8.5 are second nature) has a decided advantage. Changes in direction cause no consternation in such organizations because these principles are the bedrock of maneuver warfare and maneuver automatically implies rapid change. Moreover, if the *blitzkrieg* principles have been effectively embedded within the organization, the leader's job of issuing the charter is significantly simplified: he or she can establish the *intent* alone, with complete confidence that subordinates will move heaven and earth to make the leader's wish their command.

4. Leader Commitment Demonstrated

In a *blitzkrieg*-type organization, this commitment is already inherent in the leader-subordinate relationship. Unfortunately, most organizations don't practice *blitzkrieg* principles. Consequently, the leader standing up and delivering the mission charter isn't likely to be sufficient. Building on the leader and subordinate behaviors defined in Step 2, leaders must make it clear that they will continue to be interested in progress on the change and they will expect periodic updates. Even more, they should plan to personally visit the subordinates' work place periodically to ask pointed questions about progress on the change. Positive verbal reinforcement on such occasions always helps.

5. Subordinate Commitment

If leaders complete the first four steps of this process, the probability of subordinate commitment improves dramatically. It's not necessarily guaranteed. The more authoritarian an organization is, the less trust has been established, the more likely it is that subordinates will do the minimum necessary to keep pressure off themselves and will not be personally committed to successful change.

This is likely to be the case in most organizations, since very few actually have such trust established. For this reason, the next step is required.

6. Performance Management Process

This is a subject worthy of a separate book all its own. In fact, such a book already exists: *Bringing Out the Best in People,* by Aubrey C. Daniels.[6] It explains "everything you always wanted to know but were afraid to ask" about how to positively reinforce desirable behavior to improve organizational performance. The ultimate result, however, is that the desired behaviors should be realized and sustained, and the desired outcomes achieved.

A Last Thought about Ensuring Effective Change

To bring this discussion of organizational change to conclusion, let me offer one other practical tool that leaders can use to ensure the change they've chartered will actually happen the way they want it to. This tool is a four-component process called the O-O-D-A loop (pronounced OOH-dah). It was conceived by John Boyd, who derived it from his experiences as a fighter pilot and from his study of military strategy going back to Sun Tzu. Boyd's theories inspired the battlefield strategy that defeated the Iraqi Army in Kuwait in just 96 hours back in 1991, and today they form the basis of the Marine Corps' maneuver warfare doctrine and many of the tactics used by modern special operations forces. (See Figure 8.10)

O-O-D-A stands for observe, orient, decide, and act. Somewhat similar to the Shewhart Cycle recommended by Deming, the O-O-D-A loop is designed to facilitate rapid, effective decision making.* Leaders who oversee their organizations with the O-O-D-A loop are not only concerned with shaping or even driving changes in the

---

* It must be emphasized, however, that Boyd was adamantly opposed to treating the O-O-D-A loop as a rigid cycle. He meant the arrows coming out of the orient stage to imply that one could go anywhere from there: skip over decision directly to action, or feed back to observe. It is a loop, because at some point all paths lead back to observe. But its objective is speed in completing multiple iterations of the loop, not to drive people through the kind of pedagogical cycle that the Shewhart Cycle represents.

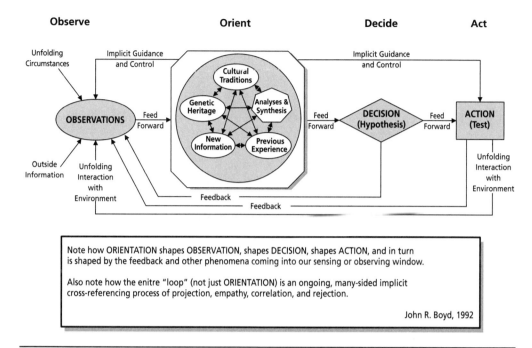

Observe	Orient	Decide	Act

Note how ORIENTATION shapes OBSERVATION, shapes DECISION, shapes ACTION, and in turn is shaped by the feedback and other phenomena coming into our sensing or observing window.

Also note how the enitre "loop" (not just ORIENTATION) is an ongoing, many-sided implicit cross-referencing process of projection, empathy, correlation, and rejection.

John R. Boyd, 1992

Figure 8.10   The O-O-D-A Loop.

environment that may affect organizational success, they're also ready to react with "course corrections" well before any deterioration to the tactical situation can occur. The O-O-D-A loop is an ideal tool for leaders to use in sustaining the inertia of change. However, as with human behavior and needs theory, there are better sources than this book for more information on this valuable tool. (See Richards, *Certain to Win*, 2004, and Osinga, *Science, Strategy, and War*, 2006).[21;20]

SUMMARY

If you take nothing else away from this chapter, internalize this:

- Logic is not enough. Emotional commitment is required as well.

- Creating a solution is not the most challenging part of problem solving; changing the status quo is.

- No change of any consequence happens without the unswerving participation of a leader who not only provides the organization its focus and direction but who also has the formal and moral authority to lead the change.

- Leaders and subordinates alike are motivated by the satisfaction of personal needs. The apparent "altruism" of dedication to an organization's mission is actually connected in some way to the satisfaction of personal needs.

- Personal needs can be the realization of something positive (esteem, self-actualization) or the avoidance of something negative (loss of security, affiliation—the anaclitic depression blues).

- Successful, sustained implementation of change depends on a combination of Level 5/*blitzkrieg*-type leadership and a rational system of positive reinforcement that satisfies the needs of leaders and subordinates alike.

- Consistent, effective application of reinforcement is not a one-time thing; it requires time and continuing personal discipline by leaders.

- If you don't have leadership commitment *a priori*, you're wasting your time trying to implement the change. If you don't have consistent, regular positive reinforcement that satisfies individual needs, no change can be sustained for long.

You can buy a man's time; you can buy his physical presence at a given place; you can even buy a measured number of his skilled muscular motions per hour. But you cannot buy his enthusiasm...you cannot buy loyalty...you cannot buy the devotion of hearts, minds, or souls. You must earn these.

—Clarence Francis

ENDNOTES

1. Argyris, Chris. *On Organizational Learning.* Oxford: Blackwell, 1992.
2. "A Special Report on Executive Pay," *The Economist*, January 20-26, 2007.
3. Bennis, Warren, and Burt Nanus. *Leaders: The Strategies for Taking Charge.* New York: Harper & Row, 1985.
4. Collins, Jim. *Good to Great: Why Some Companies Make the Leap…and Others Don't.* NY: Random House Business Books, 2001.
5. Damasio, Antonio R. *Descartes' Error: Emotion, Reason and the Human Brain.* NY: G.P. Putnam's Sons, 1994.
6. Daniels, Aubrey C. *Bringing Out the Best in People: How to Apply the Astonishing Power of Positive Reinforcement.* NY: McGraw-Hill, 2000.
7. Deming, W. Edwards. *The New Economics for Industry, Government, Education.* Cambridge, MA: MIT Center for Advanced Engineering Study, 1993.
8. Dettmer, H.W. *Strategic Navigation: A Systems Approach to Business Strategy.* Milwaukee, WI: ASQ Quality Press, 2003.
9. Deutschman, Alan. "Change or Die," *Fast Company*, May 2005, p.53
10. Gardner, Howard. *Changing Minds: The Art and Science of Changing Our Own and Other People's Minds.* Boston, MA: Harvard Business School Press, 2004.
11. Gibson, James L.; J. Ivancevich; J. Donnelly. *Organizations: Behavior, Structure, Processes* (7th ed.). Homewood, IL: Richard D. Irwin Inc., 1991.
12. Harvey, Jerry B. *How Come When I Get Stabbed in the Back My Fingerprints are Always on the Knife? And Other Meditations on Management.* San Francisco: Jossey-Bass, 1999.
13. _____. *The Abilene Paradox and Other Meditations on Management.* San Francisco: Lexington Books, 1988.
14. House, Robert J. *Culture, Leadership, and Organizations: The GLOBE Study of 62 Societies.* Thousand Oaks, CA: SAGE Publications, 2004.
15. http://dictionary.reference.com/browse/direct
16. Jaques, E. and S. Clement. *Executive Leadership.* Arlington, VA: Cason Hall, 1991.
17. _____. *Social Power and the CEO.* Westport, CT: Quorum Books, 2002.
18. _____. *The Requisite Organization* (rev. 2d. ed.). Arlington, VA: Cason Hall & Co., 1998.
19. Maslow, Abraham. "A Theory of Human Motivation," *Psychological Review*, July 1943, pp. 370-396.
20. Osinga, Frans P.B. *Science, Strategy, and War: The Strategic Theory of John Boyd.* London: Routledge, 2006.
21. Richards, Chet. *Certain to Win.* Xlibris, 2004.

Epilogue

We're at the end. There's considerably more "richness" to the Thinking Process than we can address in this book, both in applications and permutations and combinations of ways the logic trees can be used. The appendices that follow contain real-world examples of logic trees and discussions of topics too detailed to include in individual chapters.

In closing, I would leave you with some final thoughts:

- Everything that happens in this world is subject to cause and effect.

- The rules of cause and effect (Categories of Legitimate Reservation) are universally applicable to any logic-based situation.

- An Intermediate Objectives Map can provide a benchmark for desirable performance.

- A Current Reality Tree can reveal the interdependent cause-and-effect relationships behind deviations from desired performance.

- Evaporating Clouds can help resolve apparently intractable dilemmas, which often perpetuate critical root causes of undesirable effects.

- A Future Reality Tree can provide a robust "bench test" of proposed solutions, complete with consideration of potentially undesirable outcomes—unintended consequences—that might be associated with them.

- Prerequisite Trees are the bridge between logically constructed solutions and their implementation.

- Using the Thinking Process, you can start with an ill-defined problem and end with an implementation plan for a solution that offers a high probability of success.

- Logical solutions are not enough. Implementation requires effective leadership and careful consideration of human psychology.

From here on, it's up to you to decide what you do with the Thinking Process. After you've taken opportunities to practice and apply the trees, individually or in concert, I urge you to reread selected chapters, particularly Chapter 3 (Intermediate Objective Map) and Chapter 4 (Current Reality Tree). I think you'll find that what you read earlier will take on new meaning as you reread it through the clarifying lens of experience. And ultimately, your subsequent efforts will be more rewarding for doing so.

In closing, let me remind you of the message implicit in the O-O-D-A loop (Figure 8.10): Even good solutions deteriorate over time as the external environment and circumstances change. Or, as an anonymous farmer once said…

> *The hardest thing about milking cows is that they never stay milked.*
>
> —Anonymous

> *Reasonable people do everything to adjust to the world. Unreasonable people never give up trying to adjust the world to themselves. Therefore, all progress depends on unreasonable people.*
>
> —George Bernard Shaw

Appendix A
Strategic Intermediate Objective Map

The Intermediate Objectives Map that follows was created to be more than a problem-solving tool. It was conceived as the foundation for the strategy of a not-for-profit foundation formed in 2005. The Sam Spady Foundation (http://www.samspadyfoundation.org) was created by Samantha Spady's parents following her tragic death by alcohol poisoning at Colorado State University in Fort Collins, Colorado, in September 2004. The Spadys were determined that they would do everything they possibly could to prevent other young people from losing their lives in this way—and spare other parents from the inconsolable grief that they endured.

The Sam Spady Foundation Strategic Intermediate Objectives Map is actually more detailed than the one shown here, which has been abbreviated for illustration purposes. The original is actually two pages long and runs to about four levels of necessary conditions below the critical success factors. Not every IO Map needs to be that detailed, but because this was a start-up organization, the extra detail gave the Spadys a greater sense of confidence that they had all the required bases covered. If anything, this is an excellent example of the flexibility of the IO Map—it can incorporate as much or as little detail as the user needs.

It should be clear from reading the content of this IO Map that the goal, critical success factors, and necessary conditions for an educational foundation differ dramatically from those one would see in the IO Map of a commercial company or government agency. Each type of organization can expect to have an IO Map of different structure. And within similar types of organizations, content will differ, reflecting the unique characteristics of each foundation, company, or agency.

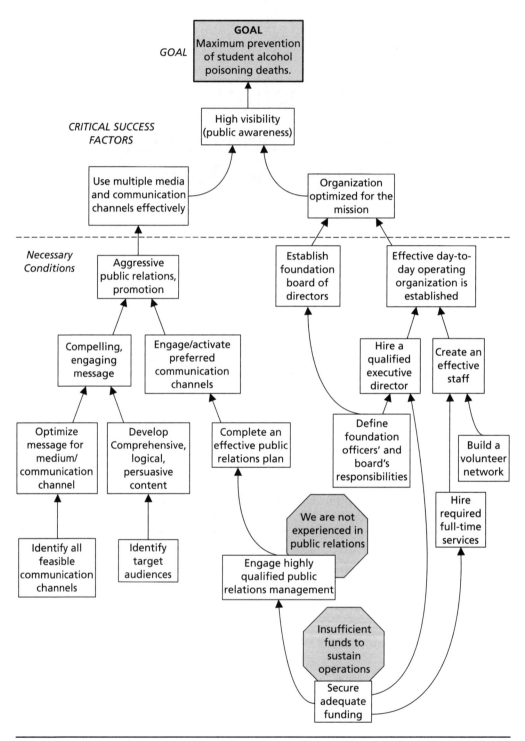

Figure A.1 Sam Spady Foundation strategic Intermediate Objectives Map.

Appendix B
Executive Summary Trees

Ever since Goldratt conceived the Thinking Process, practitioners have experienced a problem, particularly with the Current Reality and Future Reality Trees: *communicating the logic of problem definitions and solutions in a concise but effective manner.*

People build these trees to solve problems, but in most cases the critical root causes are outside their spans of control. This normally means that they need help from other people to resolve them, normally in the form of decision authority or influence. These "helpers" must often be persuaded of the need to help. It would seem natural to show these people the trees we've constructed to make a logical case for what we need them to do and why.

If you haven't already experienced it, you'll soon find that problem analysis and solution can often be quite complex. Some of these logic trees we've learned to construct can become very detailed. And those whom we need to persuade to help implement the solution may have neither the time nor the patience to "walk through" each layer of cause-and-effect logic all the way from the critical root cause to the undesirable effects, or from the injections to the desired effects. Yet they may need convincing about the validity of the logic before deciding (favorably) to help. In other words, it's quite possible to "bore to death" with details the very people whose help we need.

THE EXECUTIVE SUMMARY TREE

Since executives are usually the final authority for decisions that mandate major system change, they're the potential audience for Executive Summary Trees. Since most people don't have direct access to executives for decision authority, they're obligated to pass their analysis through some intermediate levels of management authority before even showing it to senior executives. At both levels, time is at a premium, and someone seeking a decision is required to get "on stage," present a succinct message, and get off in minimum time, often 30 minutes or less.*

One solution to this challenge is an Executive Summary Tree, designed exclusively to communicate parts of the Thinking Process analysis succinctly. This type of tree is *not a substitute* for a thorough, logical system analysis. In fact, such an analysis is the single

---

* It's been said that executives have the attention span of a five-year-old. If you can't get your message across quickly, you've lost them.

entering argument for the Executive Summary Tree. This type of tree is the second step in the process of obtaining a decision. The entire sequence is:

1. Complete the detailed logical system analysis

2. Compress the most critical issues into an Executive Summary Tree

3. Present the summary tree without excessive explanation, and allow the decision maker to ask questions for which he or she wants answers

The first step is time consuming but not difficult to do. The procedures in the eight chapters of this book explain how to do it. The second and third steps are the subject of this appendix.

PROCEDURES FOR CONSTRUCTING EXECUTIVE SUMMARY TREES

There are ten steps to this process. Each of them is explained below with supporting illustrations. It's best to do this with a piece of flip-chart paper and Post-it Notes first, then transfer the final results to digital form later as required. This will be the draft version of your Executive Summary Tree.

1. Complete Your Current/Future Reality Tree

You can't start an Executive Summary Tree without a completed sufficiency tree. Normally, decision makers are more interested in *what the problem is* and *what the recommended solution is.* They may be less interested in how you plan to implement the solution—at least until you've convinced them that the problem is real and that your proposed solution has potential for solving it. The trees that do this, of course, are the Current and Future Reality Trees. These are also the ones that are likely to pose the biggest challenge to present in a short time. Make certain that your CRT and/or FRT are as logically sound as you can make them. (See Figure B.1.)

2. Isolate the Undesirable Effects or Desired Effects Most Important to the Executive

If you've followed the approach recommended in this book, you will have only a limited number of UDEs or DEs, all of them equally critical to the attainment of the system goal. Even so, your targeted executive may only be really interested in a few of these. Use your judgment about which UDEs/DEs to include in the Summary Tree based on your own knowledge of the executive's personality and priorities.

If the number of UDEs/DEs is small, you may decide to show them all. If not, you can usually obtain decision approval based on a smaller number. *You* know that the other UDEs/DEs are there, and you can explain them if asked, but it might not be necessary to do so to achieve the approval you seek.

Replicate these UDEs/DEs on a blank page near the top.

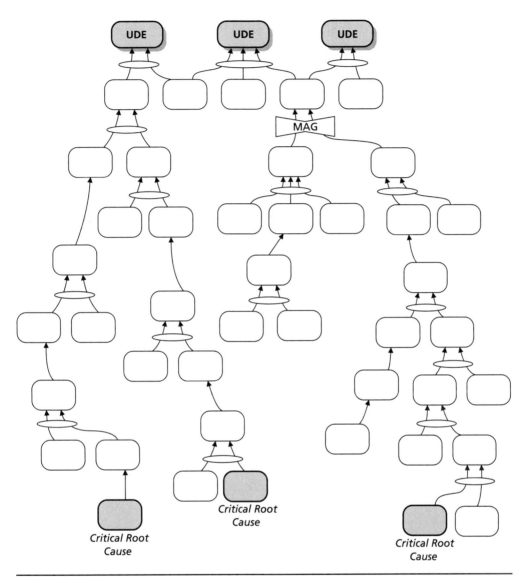

Figure B.1 Complete your Current or Future Reality Tree.

3. Identify the Critical Root Causes or Injections Producing the UDEs/DEs

From your full CRT or FRT, locate the critical root causes or injections that will lead to the UDEs/DEs you plan to present. Replicate these root causes or injections on the same page near the bottom.

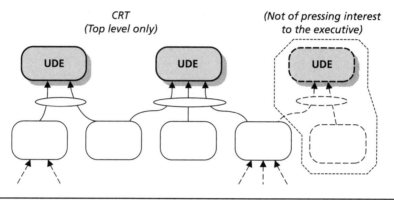

Figure B.2   Isolate the most important UDEs/DEs to the executive.

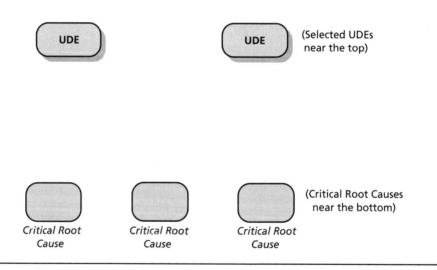

Figure B.3   Replicate the UDEs and Critical Root Causes on a Blank Sheet.

4. Identify the Major Paths Between the Root Causes/Injections and UDEs/DEs

Refer to your full CRT or FRT. By eye, trace the path of causality from the critical root causes you want to fix or the injections you want to implement to the UDEs/DEs. (See Figure B.4.)

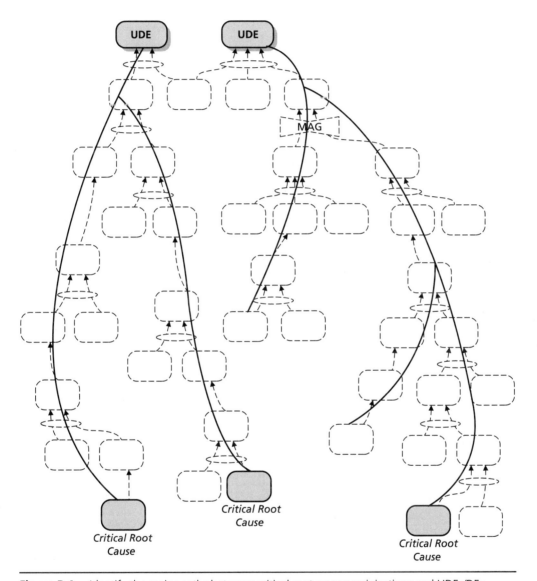

Figure B.4   Identify the major paths between critical root causes or injections and UDEs/DEs.

5. Replicate the Causal Paths on the Executive Summary Tree

In pencil, replicate these paths as smooth lines on the flip-chart paper. Connect the lines to the UDEs/DEs and critical root causes/injections. (See Figure B.5.)

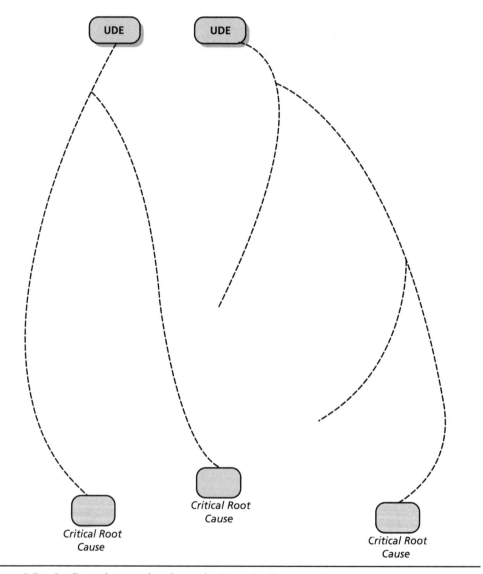

Figure B.5   Replicate the causal paths on the Executive Summary Tree.

6. Transfer Convergence/Divergence Entities from the CRT/FRT to the Executive Summary Tree

On the original CRT/FRT, identify the entities where major branches either converge or diverge. Replicate these entities in the Executive Summary Tree, and position them at the appropriate positions on the lines. (See Figure B.6.)

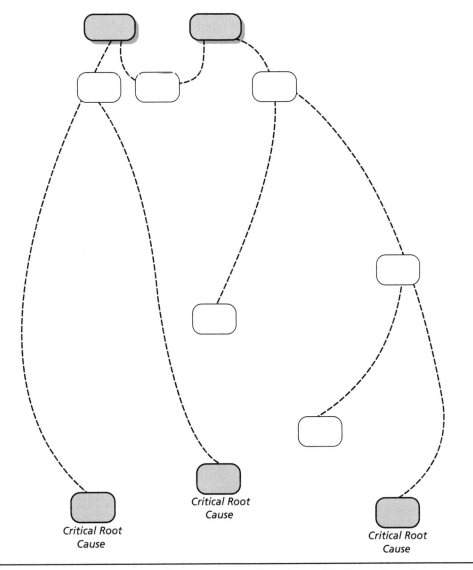

Critical Root Cause

Critical Root Cause

Critical Root Cause

Figure B.6   Transfer convergence/divergence entities from the CRT/FRT to the Executive Summary Tree.

7. Identify Key Intermediate Entities in Each Branch of the CRT/FRT

In Chapters 4 and 6, I exerted considerable effort to convince you to *avoid* logically "long" arrows. Now I'm going to ask you to do just the opposite: *create* them! How long (logically) to make these arrows will be a judgment call on your part. You must take your decision-maker's understanding of the system into consideration. If he or she is thoroughly familiar with all the detailed workings of the system, you can make longer leaps of logic. If not, you'll have to make shorter leaps.

When you have a sense for how much your executive knows about the situation, examine your original CRT/FRT carefully for key entities. These will be intermediate effects lying between the critical root causes/injections and the UDEs/DEs. You must ask yourself, "If I include only these intermediate entities, will the executive be able to follow,

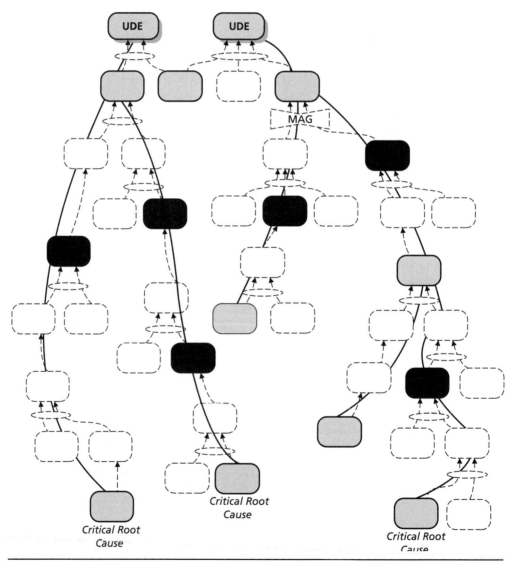

Figure B.7   Identify key intermediate entities in each branch of the CRT/FRT.

and accept, my causality logic?" *You* can make that leap personally, because you have the tree builder's intimate knowledge of all those causal layers in between. The real question you must answer is how much of a leap the executive can make with you. You're holding their hands (figuratively) on this journey, so shorten your stride to match theirs as necessary. (See Figure B.7.)

8. Replicate the Intermediate Entities in the Executive Summary Tree

Once you're certain you've identified enough "stepping stones" for the decision maker, replicate these intermediate entities in their respective positions in the Executive Summary Tree. (See Figure B.8.)

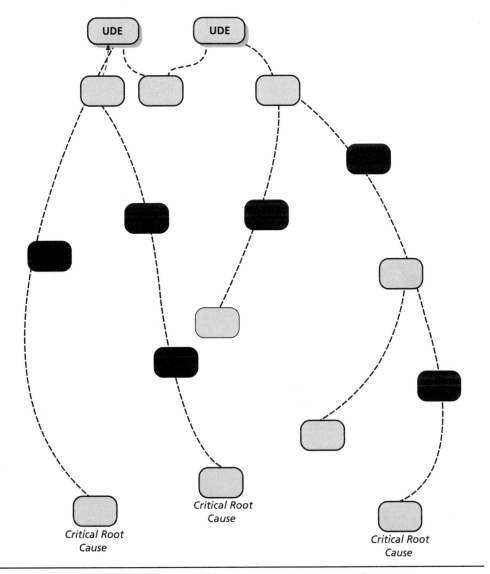

Figure B.8   Replicate the intermediate entities in the Executive Summary Tree.

9. Finalize the Executive Summary Tree

On the Executive Summary Tree, replace "soft" or dotted pencil lines with "hard" connections (arrows). *Don't* include ellipses. *Do* include magnitudinal "AND" symbols as required. The tree is now ready to be converted to digital format. When you do so, try to retain the smooth configuration, or tree shape, of the original CRT or FRT. You'll find that this is easier for your audience to absorb visually. (See Figure B.9.)

10. Divide Both Trees into Page-Sized Segments

Partition both your original CRT/FRT and your Executive Summary Tree into page-sized "bites." Your CRT or FRT may already be segmented that way, but if not, now is a good time to do it. The size of the segments for the Executive Summary Tree should be determined by how many entities of the original CRT/FRT you can comfortably fit on

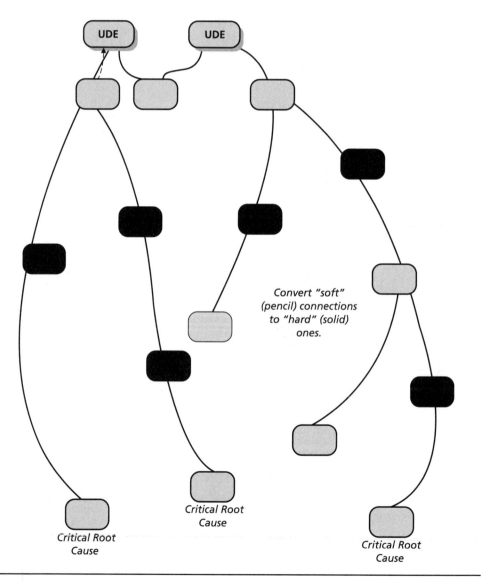

Figure B.9 Finalize the Executive Summary Tree.

one presentation page (paper copy or digital projection). It's your choice whether or not you show these segment divisions on the Executive Summary Tree you present to the decision maker. However, it would be advisable for you to have a paper copy of the Summary Tree with these dividing lines shown. (See Figure B.10.)

Why should you do this? Remember that you will be presenting a very streamlined tree. You do not want to force feed anymore detail than is required for executives to "make the logical leap" with you. But if you've guessed wrong and your executives want to know how you made that leap, you need to be prepared to walk them through the step-by-step CRT/FRT logic—but *only* for that particular segment that represents the "leap." If a question like this arises in the middle of your presentation, you want to be able to

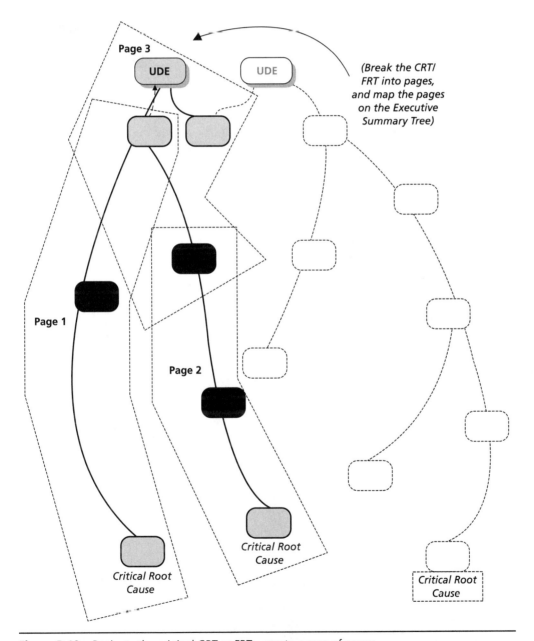

Figure B.10   Paginate the original CRT or FRT—create a map of pages.

display only that part of the CRT/FRT that answers that particular question. Having the CRT/FRT paginated for quick reference makes responding to challenges smoother. (See Figure B.11.)

Once you've answered the decision maker's question satisfactorily with step-by-step logic, go back to the Executive Summary Tree with its "long arrows."

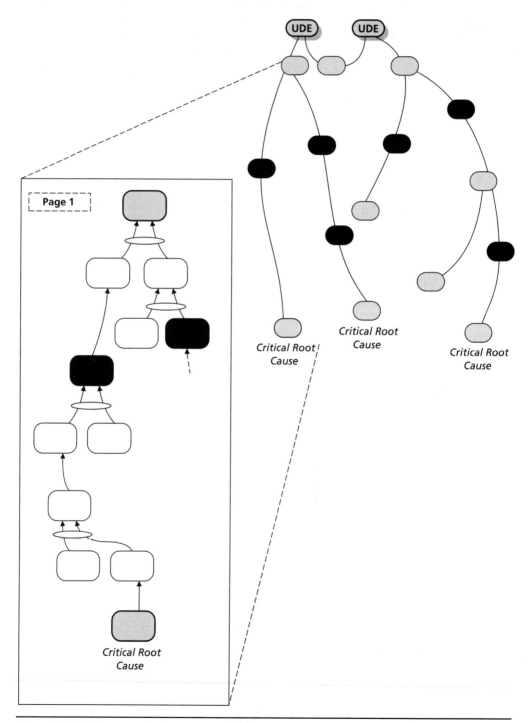

Figure B.11   Bring out only the segments required.

If you're challenged on your step-by-step cause-and-effect logic at all, it won't happen more than about twice before the decision maker accepts that you can answer any challenge. (Of course, this depends on the prior construction of an air-tight logical CRT or FRT.)

Presenting Your Executive Summary Tree

Now you're ready to present your case. You have a finished version of your Executive Summary Tree, either printed neatly on plotter-sized paper or in a digitally-projected presentation. Ideally, you'll have your digital version on no more than two slides. The paper version can be on one page.

You also have your complete CRT or FRT paginated on standard bond paper and arranged in a numbered sequence. You may even have an overall "map" on the cover page. The easiest way to prepare for questions is to have this completed CRT or FRT printed in enough copies for the executive and key staff members. I suggest not handing out these copies until and unless you are challenged about the step-by-step logic. In my experience, if you give people something they can hold in their hand, they will be busy reading it and not paying attention to you. That's something to be avoided as much as possible.

If you are challenged and find that you must hand out these paper copies of the full tree, when you've answered to question to the decision-maker's satisfaction, make a point of drawing attention back to your Executive Summary Tree when you've answered the question to the decision-maker's satisfaction: "If there are no more questions about that particular segment, let's return to this summary tree…"

Appendix C
Current Reality Tree Exercise

For Want of a Nail

For want of a nail, the shoe was lost.
For want of a shoe, the horse was lost.
For want of a horse, the rider was lost.
For want of a rider, the message was lost.
For want of a message, the battle was lost.
For want of a battle, the war was lost.
For want of a victory, the nation was lost.
All for want of a horseshoe nail.

The poem above is believed to date to the time of the American Revolution. It clearly reflects a worst-case scenario involving cause and effect. Consider it an expression of an actual situation. Obviously, there would be much more to this scenario than the poem indicates—details such as organizational relationships, tactical and strategic situations, resource availability, leadership, and so forth. Use your imagination to flesh out some of the details of the circumstances under which this poem might have been written. Using the guidelines you have for building trees and the Categories of Legitimate Reservation:

- Decide on the goal and critical success factors.

- Identify the undesirable effect(s) inherent in this situation, based on your determination of the goal and CSF.

- Using the procedures outlined in Figure 4.45, build a Current Reality Tree that accurately reflects the situation, and from it identify critical root causes.

- Use your imagination. You may make any assumptions necessary about the situation in order to fill in gaps and develop entities for your tree.

Appendix D
Evaporating Cloud Exercise

The Evaporating Cloud is one of the Thinking Process tools you are most likely to find daily uses for. Use this exercise to polish your skill at it.

THE SITUATION

Assume that you're employed by a corporation. You've been with the company for years, you're good at your job, and you've developed valuable skills. But you're dissatisfied. You have the nagging feeling that you could achieve more and go higher in the organization than you're currently allowed to do. Your "inner cowboy needs to yodel."

You recently began to think about leaving your company and going into business for yourself. The idea of being your own boss and letting your creativity flow appeals to you, but you have some trepidation about leaving the "warm, fuzzy" security of your current job. In a word, you feel conflicted.

YOUR ASSIGNMENT

Use this new conflict-resolution tool, the Evaporating Cloud, to work out your Hamlet-like dilemma. Consider the following questions:

- What are the opposing positions (actions) about which you feel conflicted?
- Why does each side appeal to you? What "itch" will you be scratching by following each path?
- What's your overall goal?
- What assumptions are you making (whether consciously or not) about each path?
- What can you do to relieve yourself of all "itches?"

CREATE AN EVAPORATING CLOUD

When you've thought about these questions for a while, proceed with your Evaporating Cloud:

1. State your opposing prerequisites.

2. State the non-negotiable requirements each prerequisite satisfies for you.

3. State the common objective of those requirements.

4. Identify all the assumptions that underlie each arrow in the Evaporating Cloud.

5. Create one or more injections to resolve the conflict.

Appendix E
The 3-UDE Cloud

A t some point in your experience with the Thinking Process, some of you will undoubtedly encounter a way of attacking the problem-solving phase known as the 3-UDE Cloud, sometimes called the Core Problem Cloud. Some of you reading this book may have elsewhere learned this as the preferred way of doing problem analysis. In both cases, it's worth exploring the differences between the 3-UDE Cloud method and the way described in this book—what I call the modified traditional approach. As the name implies, the traditional approach preceded the 3-UDE Cloud method by about six years.

THE BASIC DIFFERENCES

The differences between the two approaches (traditional and 3-UDE Cloud) can be summarized this way:

Traditional

The traditional approach follows the scientific method: identify the problem, develop possible solutions, test the candidates, and select the best one. In applying the Thinking Process to the challenge of problem solving in complex systems, we start with the IO Map to determine the standards of required system performance, then prepare a Current Reality Tree to define the root causes of deviations in real-world performance, resolve any possible change dilemmas with an Evaporating Cloud, and finally move on to the Future Reality Tree to design and logically test the solution.

3-UDE Cloud

The 3-UDE Cloud approach assumes that *all* system problems are the result of an underlying core conflict. This method seeks to ferret out that conflict *first* (that is, without actually establishing the causal connections), then uses that conflict to construct a "core" or "communication" Current Reality Tree to show how this conflict leads to the observed systemic undesirable effects.

Why Are There Two Methods?

The astute observer might well ask, "Why are there two methods? Why isn't the traditional approach enough?" It would seem logical to assume that if something is working the way it was intended, it shouldn't need to be changed. In fact, W. Edwards Deming saved some of his most critical comments for those who tampered with a stable process without proper understanding of what they were doing and why.[2] It would seem reasonable to ask what was wrong with the traditional approach that caused some people to move away from it.

Since we'd prefer not to speculate or resort to hearsay, its reasonable to look for some kind of documented history. Unfortunately, not much is available in the public domain. Documentation is limited to three sources: a paper in conference proceedings by Button,[1] a book published later the same year by Lepore and Cohen,[4] and a book by Scheinkopf.[5] We'll examine all three.

Why Replace the Traditional Approach?

Lepore and Cohen don't provide a rationale for jettisoning the traditional method, but Button does.

> Experience with CRTs has uncovered two undesirable elements. One is that the core problem often reflects poorly on management practices. When a CRT is presented to those responsible for the core problem, this tends to immediately activate their defense mechanism. Further productive dialogue may be very difficult.
>
> The other is that in my experience, a CRT that is well constructed can take from 5 to 10 hours to develop. Few individuals have the stamina to undertake this effort on a regular basis.[1:31]

If I interpret this line of reasoning correctly, Button finds two faults with traditional CRTs. The first is that management is frequently too insecure to "swallow the medicine" (that is, bad news that may be their responsibility). The second is that traditional CRTs are "too tough to do" in most people's attention span. In other words, it might actually take up to 10 hours to identify a particularly challenging problem, and complex problems with profound system-level impact should be definable in much less time.

Core Problems and Core Conflicts

Both Button and Lepore and Cohen explain the 3-UDE approach in some detail, though there are some minor procedural differences between the two. (Scheinkopf addresses "communication" Current Reality Trees, but doesn't mention the 3-UDE Cloud idea.) Button's explanation is also more pedagogical while Lepore's and Cohen's is more conceptual. Lepore and Cohen begin with the introduction of something called the Core Problem Cloud. The presumption in their discussion of the CRT[4:124] is that a Core Problem Cloud can be used to explain the existence of the UDEs in a CRT:

> One of the popular ways to construct a CRT is to base it on the Core CRT that is using the Core Problem Cloud.[4:124]

Now we have two apparently different terms: CRT and *core* CRT. Unfortunately, Lepore and Cohen don't make clear the distinction between the two. They do, however, address the concept of a *Core Problem Cloud* in some detail.[4:122-124] According to Lepore and Cohen:

> The Core Problem Cloud describes the conflict that prevents us from finding a solution to the core problem. There are three major types of Core Problem Clouds:
>
> 1. Conflict with the "rules" of the system
>
> 2. Personal dilemma of the leader
>
> 3. Conflict between functions, management levels, or individuals (chronic conflict)

There are a couple of unstated assumptions that require examination, and an interesting implication of Lepore's and Cohen's perspective on systems that follows from it. The first assumption, which I have personally heard Goldratt express, is that conflict underlies *all* core problems. And the second is that a large majority of a system's undesirable effects (Goldratt has said 70 percent or more) are accounted for by this core problem. The implication for Lepore's and Cohen's system perspective is that all possible conflicts perpetuating core problems are reducible to one of these three categories: rules, personal leadership dilemmas, or functional/management/personal conflict. In other words, no allowance is made for core problems resulting from incomplete knowledge (ignorance of causal connections), insufficient resources, or factors external to the system itself.

The second is even more interesting: that a large majority of a system's undesirable effects result from a core problem. This idea is somewhat easier to accept when we consider that since its inception (and until this second edition), an undesirable effect has been imprecisely defined as just about anything that's happening in your system that you or others don't like. Because that opens the door to virtually everything, it's easy to see how a single core problem might cause a large percentage of UDEs, maybe even a large majority. Lepore and Cohen confirm this:

> These UDEs cover a fairly large span; they originate from different sources and have different "weights."[4:124]

This represents an important and fundamental difference between the modified traditional approach to the Thinking Process described in this book and the Core Problem Cloud method. The latter suggests that not all UDEs are created equal, and that there are a lot of them in any system. The modified traditional method described in this book suggests that there are relatively few real UDEs in a system, and that they are clearly identifiable with respect to the system's goal and critical success factors—of which there are probably no more than three to five. And because each of these critical success factors is, by definition, a necessary condition to attaining the system goal, the absence of any one compromises goal attainment. This makes the few real UDEs any system might experience relatively equal in weight, and not a matter of one person's opinion versus another's.

To summarize briefly, the 3-UDE Cloud method, or Core Problem Cloud (as Lepore and Cohen refer to it), is based on the following assumptions:

- UDEs are subjectively determined
- Most system UDEs result from a single core problem
- Conflict underlies all core problems
- Core-problem conflicts fall into only three archetypes (Boy, that sure makes complex problem identification easy!)

On the other hand, the modified traditional approach to the Thinking Process is based on the following assumptions:

- All UDEs are objectively defined with respect to non-negotiable, system-critical success factors (refer to Chapter 3)
- There are relatively few real UDEs in any system
- All UDEs result from a few critical root causes (true core problems are relatively rare)
- Critical root causes are not limited to a few common archetypes ("generic")

Basics of the 3-UDE/Core Problem Cloud

The 3-UDE, or Core Problem Cloud, works essentially like this. First, you identify an UDE pertaining to the system. (Remember, almost anything you don't like can qualify as an UDE.) Then you determine its opposite condition—a corresponding *desired* effect. Repeat this process two more times, so that you have three UDEs and matching opposite desired effects. These pairs become the conflicting prerequisites in three different Evaporating Clouds.[1,4]

To construct the rest of the cloud, the usual right-to-left procedure is employed (refer to Chapter 5). In each case, however, the requirements and objective are established by determining the direct and immediate reason for existence—what outcome each conflicting prerequisite (the UDE and the desired effect) is aimed at achieving. The overall objective is then determined as some overarching condition that both requirements are intended to satisfy.

Clearly, the product of this part of the process is three discrete Evaporating Clouds, the only common thread of which may be that they are inherently part of the same larger system. These three clouds are then consolidated into a single "generic" cloud.[*7]

The process of consolidation, as described both by Button and by Lepore and Cohen, is purely *inductive* in that it attempts to reach a "general rule" conclusion from three component elements. And therein lies one of the logical fallacies with the 3-UDE/Core Problem Cloud method.

Inductive Reasoning

Why is a conclusion arrived at inductively not logically sound? The answer lies in the nature of inductive reasoning itself.

---

* "Generic," in its intended use here, is a bit of a misnomer. A thesaurus lists the following synonyms for the word: all-encompassing, blanket, collective, comprehensive, general, inclusive, nonexclusive, sweeping, universal, wide. The more appropriate term in this circumstance would be "inductive."

Induction or inductive reasoning, sometimes called inductive logic, is the process of reasoning in which the premises of an argument are *believed* to support the conclusion but do not ensure it. It's used to ascribe properties or relations to broader types based on tokens (that is, on one or a small number of observations or experiences), or to formulate laws based on limited observations of recurring phenomenal patterns.[3] Basically, it induces the universal from the particular. However, the conclusion is far from certain.

What, then, is the process of "genericizing" three discrete clouds into a single consolidated one, inducing a universal conclusion from particular details? It's *inductive reasoning*. And why is this a problem? The answer is that conclusions drawn in this manner are usually over-generalizations. Consider, for example:

> I always hang pictures on nails; therefore, all pictures hang from nails.

or

> Teenagers are given many speeding tickets; therefore, all teenagers speed.[3]

As mentioned earlier, Lepore and Cohen don't offer any specific examples, only conceptual directions. But Button does. Here's an example of generic cloud elements (in this case, the conflicting prerequisites) induced from particular, specific ones:[1]

	P1 (or D)	P2 (or D')
Specific cloud #1	Don't work overtime.	Work overtime.
Specific cloud #2	Buy a component.	Make a component.
Specific cloud #3	Build only on demand.	Build to stock.
Generic cloud	Take action for good department performance.	Take action for good system performance.

It's not obvious how any of these components produces its respective conclusion, and in some cases an argument could be made that the conclusion could actually require an opposite component. (For example, taking action for the good of a department might actually require working overtime.) Without beating this particular example to death, the other "UDE Cloud" elements constitute equally weak inductions.[3]

The Fundamental Problem with Inductive Reasoning

Formal logic, as most people learn it, is deductive rather than inductive. Some philosophers claim to have created systems of inductive logic, but it's a matter of some controversy whether a logic of induction is even possible. Karl Popper adamantly maintains that it is not.[6]

In contrast to deductive reasoning, conclusions arrived at by inductive reasoning do not necessarily have the same degree of certainty as the initial premises. For example, a conclusion that all swans are white is false, but may have been thought true in Europe until the settlement of Australia. Inductive arguments are *never binding*, but they may be cogent. (Let's not even go into cogency!)

Inductive reasoning is deductively invalid. (An argument in formal logic is valid if, and only if, it's not possible for the premises of the argument to be true while the conclusion is false.) In induction, there are always *many conclusions* that can reasonably be related to certain premises. Inductions are open; deductions are closed. Here's an example (somewhat ludicrous, perhaps, but the extreme case clearly demonstrates the potential invalidity of inductive reasoning):

A group of men regularly took birth control pills for three years.

None of the men got pregnant.

Therefore, birth control pills are effective at keeping men from getting pregnant.[6:38]

What's the problem with this, logically speaking? It's the proposed conclusion (the "therefore" part)—it's not valid. Because this is not a *deductive* statement, the conclusion a) doesn't have the same degree of certainty as the two initial premises, and b) it is only one of several possible conclusions that may be drawn. By accident or by design, the risk is higher of drawing an erroneous conclusion with inductive reasoning.

It is possible, however, to derive a true statement using inductive reasoning *if you already know the conclusion*. (This has implications for what is typically *done* with the generic cloud later.)

The only way to have an efficient argument by induction is if the known conclusion is true only when an unstated external conclusion (in Thinking Process parlance, an additional predicted effect) is also true. That external conclusion has certain criteria to be met in order to be true (separate from the primary conclusion). By substitution of one conclusion for the other, you can inductively find out what evidence you need in order for your induction to be true.

For example, let's say you have a window that opens only one way, but not the other. Assuming that you know that the only way for that to happen is that the hinges are faulty, inductively you can postulate that the only way for that condition to change would be to fix the window (that is, apply oil, or whatever will fix the unstated conclusion). From there on you can successfully build your case. However, if your unstated conclusion is false (which can only be proven by deductive reasoning!), then your whole argument by induction collapses. Thus, ultimately, pure inductive reasoning does not exist.[3]

Transitioning to the CRT

Setting aside for a moment the argument about whether the inductive (generic) cloud is valid or not, let's move ahead to what practitioners of the 3-UDE/Core Problem Cloud do with it.

Since one of the underlying assumptions behind the 3-UDE/Core Problem Cloud is that a core conflict underlies all UDEs—in other words, the idea that an ultimate root cause of an UDE might *not* have a conflict associated with it is excluded—a conflict of some kind, no matter how logically supportable, *must* be incorporated somewhere in the bottom of the CRT.

The procedure described by both Lepore and Cohen and Button calls for the generic Evaporating Cloud elements to be rotated 90 degrees counterclockwise, placing the objective of the cloud at the bottom and the conflicting prerequisites at the top. The arrows are then reversed, the wording is modified to support an "if-then" (sufficiency) verbalization, and additional entities (assumptions) are incorporated with ellipses to translate the former generic cloud into the bottom portion of a CRT.*

Additional layers of cause-and-effect are then extrapolated upward from there until broader system-level UDEs are reached. (Remember, though, that consistent with one of

---

* Lepore and Cohen describe this process only in conceptual terms, using no examples. Button provides an example of a CCRT (call it "core" or "communication," it's your choice..."You say po-TAY-to, I say po-TAH-to...") that makes understanding the process considerably easier. Unfortunately, that particular CRT is logically deficient to the point that its content is not persuasive.

the assumptions underlying the 3-UDE Cloud method, UDE determination is highly subjective.)[1,4]

Bottom-Up Versus Top-Down

There's another difference between the traditional CRT approach and the 3-UDE/Core Problem Cloud methods. In the traditional method, the CRT is constructed from the top down, like peeling the layers of an onion. Each lower layer of causality is hypothesized and then checked for validity using the Categories of Legitimate Reservation. This is inherently a *deductive* process, which is able to establish validity.

The 3-UDE/Core Problem Cloud method, on the other hand, builds *upward* from the presumed core conflict to the undesirable effects. In other words, it starts from a presumed (not validated by deductive logic) cause to a preconceived conclusion. Now, think back to the preceding discussion on inductive reasoning.[3] *Inductions are open; deductions are closed. It is, however, possible to derive a true statement using inductive reasoning if you already know the conclusion...The only way to have an efficient argument by induction is if the known conclusion is true only when an unstated external conclusion is also true...By substitution of one conclusion for the other, you can inductively find out what evidence you need in order for your induction to be true.*

There's another way to express this: When you start from a point you arbitrarily determine, build toward a predetermined destination, and know what supporting evidence you need to get there, it's almost amazing how often the cause-and-effect will turn out to be exactly what's needed to reach that destination.

What's more, building upward deliberately excludes the search for additional causes (the fourth of the Categories of Legitimate Reservation)—a pitfall of inductive logic that's avoided with deductive logic.

Why the Change? (Redux)

A substantial percentage of Thinking Process users have switched *away from* a method that is deductive and sound and that separates the resolution of conflict from the logically supportable determination of cause and effect. They've gone instead to a method that muddles the line between problem definition and conflict resolution, that doesn't offer the same degree of logical certainty, and that can't be evaluated for soundness. Why would anyone deliberately choose to do this?

I believe the answer lies in the rationale offered by Button—concern for defensiveness on the part of those in authority and ease of CRT construction.

At about the time the 3-UDE Cloud made its appearance, Goldratt was much involved with the idea of resistance to change. Some Thinking Process practitioners observed seemingly irrational behavior by decision makers: in the face of persuasive CRT logic, they denied or ignored the analysis of the identified core problem. Recognizing that *presenting* the logic in palatable way wasn't the same as *constructing it,* Goldratt conceived of the idea of a "communication" Current Reality Tree.* In her book, *Thinking for a Change,* Scheinkopf devotes a whole chapter to the idea.

---

* Goldratt published nothing about this rationale, but in 1999 Scheinkopf did.

> What if the party to whom you need to communicate the content of the current reality tree is someone who is, or thinks he is, directly responsible for the environment described in the current reality tree? How do you go about communicating the issues to him without putting him on the defensive?...The communication current reality tree (CCRT) combines the Evaporating Cloud with the current reality tree in a way that avoids the defensive response.[5:235]

In other words, the CCRT is a way of avoiding a negative reaction to "bad news" by a decision maker. But a little farther on, Scheinkopf provides an equally important but conveniently overlooked prescription:

> When you begin to create the communication current reality tree, you have *already completed a current reality tree and Evaporating Cloud.* (Emphasis added).[5:235]

This distinction is important, and it's relevant to what apparently happened later. It implies that the use of a CCRT for persuasion does not relieve one of the responsibility to conclude a thorough, deductively logical analysis *first* by the traditional approach: a CRT followed by an Evaporating Cloud. The use of the CCRT comes afterward, only when the traditional analysis is complete, and only for the purpose of making that analysis persuasive and non-threatening. In a video tape in 1995 (no longer widely available), Goldratt himself confirms this line of thinking.

So the second half of the 3-UDE/Core Problem Cloud method has a firm basis in rationality. As originally conceived, it applied the only aspect of inductive logic that is admitted to be valid: *It is, however, possible to derive a true statement using inductive reasoning if you already know the conclusion...*[3] The CCRT, as originally conceived, does this, that is, it operates from an already known conclusion. The traditional CRT and Evaporating Cloud on which it *should be* based were developed using sound deductive logic; thus, the conclusion is known in advance. And this is not only okay, it's *required* for efficient inductive reasoning!

The disconnect came later, when someone decided that the traditional CRT and Evaporating Cloud could be dispensed with. Instead the process could be "short-cut" by inducing a generic cloud from three discrete ones. Then using that generic cloud as the basis for a CCRT would be a good idea. In other words, they eliminated the only thing that made the bottom-to-top logical construction of the CCRT a logically robust process!

From our earlier examination, we know that the 3-UDE Cloud part of this process is fatally flawed because it depends on inductive reasoning for the analysis in the first place, rather than having the induction follow from a verified, validated deductive analysis. Button's second observation above (takes too long and too much effort) provides a clue to why this "shortcut" was adopted. Why would someone seek a shortcut in the first place? Two possible reasons:

- They aren't adept enough at constructing the deductive logic of the CRT to do it any faster. This could be a deficiency in teaching or just intellectual laziness.

- The traditional method wasn't complete or logically "tight" enough to be easily translatable to the real world by most people—in other words, a deficient method.

The latter difficulty is an acknowledged problem with the original method of constructing a CRT as initially taught by the A.Y. Goldratt Institute. I encountered the problem with clients of my own repeatedly over the first six years of applying the Thinking Process. The CRT was difficult to construct well and expeditiously. But that isn't the case anymore. Readers of this book know that Chapters 3 and 4 explain in detail how to construct a sound, logical CRT by starting with an Intermediate Objective Map first. CRTs may have taken up to 10 hours when Button and others first learned them. There's no reason that most of them should take longer than about four hours now.

Unfortunately, rather than refining and perfecting the traditional method of CRT construction, people looked for an easy way out. A general deterioration in the quality of CRTs and problem analyses has resulted. Yes, there are those who would say that they have been successful using the 3-UDE/Core Problem Cloud approach. I don't deny this. Rather I would observe that even a blind pig finds an acorn once in a while. Even with a faulty method, some level of success can be expected, though it may not be consistent or always optimal.

PREDETERMINED CAUSES TO PRECONCEIVED PROBLEMS

How many times have you heard the expression, "When your only tool is a hammer, all problems tend to look like nails"? This is an indication of an insidious trap that many people fall into. Whether your "hammer" is the Theory of Constraints, Six Sigma, Lean, or any number of other worthy methodologies, if you have an emotional or intellectual commitment to it, there is a real risk of partitioning and arranging reality to fit the tool. This is especially true when one assumes that most underlying problems fall into a limited number of archetypes.[4:122] How easy it becomes to say, "The reason must be *this*, because it fits our model so nicely!"

Because there is so much "semantic maneuvering room" in the inductive process of 3-UDE/Core Problem Cloud, it's so easy to make the presumed problem fit the details of the situation. And with no provision (or even thought) to validate the induction with deductive verification, the induced conclusion becomes the problem, in spite of the known deficiencies inherent in inductive reasoning. *Why bother with a deductive Thinking Process when you already know what the problem is?*

The insidious part of the Thinking Process is that it can be used to justify the existence of a preconceived cause—*if* (and only if) the Categories of Legitimate Reservation are not conscientiously applied. *All* of them, including additional cause. The reason the CLR safeguard against subversion of the Thinking Process is that they are part of a *deductive* reasoning routine, not *inductive*.

Yet in spite of the fallacies of inductive reasoning, the kind of "communication" current reality tree described by Scheinkopf[5:235] makes perfect sense—for presentation and persuasion, but not for logical analysis. Thus, as Scheinkopf recommends, the traditional (deductive) CRT should be the basis for—and the only logical justification for—the inductive "communication" CRT. And the 3-UDE/Core Problem Cloud does no more than exacerbate the inductions in a "communication" CRT.

SUMMARY AND CONCLUSION

As Lepore and Cohen said, the 3-UDE/Core Problem Cloud is one of the popular ways of constructing a CRT. The other one is the traditional method, as originally conceived by Goldratt and modified in this book.

The traditional method:

- Starts with a few objectively determined system-level UDEs

- Is deductive, and therefore its validity is logically verified

- Terminates in a few actionable critical root causes not confined to a few arbitrary archetypes

- Accommodates whatever valid additional causes might occur

The 3-UDE/Core Problem Cloud method:

- Starts with three subjectively chosen random data points (perceived localized UDEs)

- Uses inductive reasoning (less certain, not binding) to generalize (really, speculate—unlike in a traditional CRT, no attempt is made at verification using the CLR) five elements of an Evaporating Cloud

- Uses the inductively developed cloud as a starting point for a cause-effect journey to a predetermined conclusion (subjective system-level UDEs)

- Ignores potential valid additional causes

Of course, you're free to use whichever method you choose. Which one *would* you choose?

ENDNOTES

1. Button, Scott. "Genesis of a Communication Current Reality Tree: The Three-Cloud Process," *1999 Constraints Management Symposium Proceedings,* APICS, March 22-23, 1999.
2. http://www.qualityamerica.com/knowledgecenter/articles/CQEIVH3f.html
3. http://en.wikipedia.org/wiki/Inductive_reasoning
4. Lepore, Domenico, and Oded Cohen. *Deming and Goldratt: The Theory of Constraints and the System of Profound Knowledge.* Great Barrington, MA: The North River Press, 1999.
5. Scheinkopf, Lisa. *Thinking for a Change: Putting the TOC Thinking Processes to Work.* Boca Raton, FL: St. Lucie Press, 1999.
6. Stokes, Geoff. *Popper: Philosophy, Politics and Scientific Method.* Malden, MA: Blackwell Publishers, 1998.
7. Thesaurus.com.: "generic." *Roget's New Millennium? Thesaurus, First Edition (v 1.3.1),* Lexico Publishing Group, LLC. (http://thesaurus.reference.com/browse/generic) Accessed: November 05, 2006).

Appendix F
The Challenger Conflict

BACKGROUND

In 1972, the National Aeronautics and Space Administration (NASA) put into motion a series of events that would culminate fourteen years later with the explosion of the Space Shuttle Challenger 72 seconds after launch from Cape Canaveral. The exhaustive analysis of that accident by a blue-ribbon commission revealed the 14-year chain of cause-and-effect that led to that disaster.[1:233-241]

It's public knowledge that ill-fitting O-rings in the Space Shuttle solid rocket boosters (SRB), combined with low air temperatures prior to the scheduled launch time, precipitated the actual explosion. While the critical root cause of the accident could be logically attributed to acquisition policies that awarded the booster contract to the lowest bidder, a critical dilemma that developed during the engineering development phase of the program in 1976 presented a then-unrecognized opportunity to create a win-win resolution that would have prevented the Challenger accident and saved seven lives.

Morton-Thiokol Corporation (MTC) had been awarded the Space Shuttle SRB contract based largely on the fact that they were the lowest bidder by a significant margin. MTC felt confident in their low bid because they envisioned the Space Shuttle SRB as merely a scaled-up version of their highly reliable Titan-IIIB SRB. What they did not anticipate were the problems associated with fabricating a substantially larger booster of the same basic configuration.

The Titan-IIIB SRBs were narrower in diameter and assembled vertically in segments. The vertical assembly was done to ensure the integrity of the perfectly round cross section of the cylindrical booster segments. The joining of the booster segments was effected with a clevis-and-tang design, secured with neoprene O-rings to produce a seal between segments that could withstand the pressures of combustion during launch.

The Space Shuttle boosters were twice the diameter of the Titan-IIIB boosters and nearly twice the height, yet the booster skin was nearly the same thickness. Because of the height of the assembled boosters, the Space Shuttle SRBs could not be assembled vertically, as the Titan-IIB boosters had been. MTC decided to assemble the Space Shuttle SRBs horizontally. The completed booster, with propellant installed, would then be shipped by rail from MTC's facility in Utah to Cape Canaveral for assembly with the Space Shuttle main tank and orbiter vehicle.

In 1976, during SRB development, MTC encountered an unanticipated problem. The larger diameter of the Space Shuttle SRB, coupled with the weight of each of the four casing segments, caused distortion of the intended round shape when the booster segments were laid horizontally. Because the clevis ends were slightly more rigid than the tang ends, they didn't distend as much. The tolerance between the clevis and tang was very tight. The net result was that the tang of one segment would not fit into the clevis of its mated segment.

THE CRITICAL DILEMMA

MTC was faced with a dilemma: redesign the assembly equipment so that the boosters could be assembled vertically (like the Titan-IIB), or do design trade-offs to make the assembly work horizontally. The business decision trumped the engineering recommendation. Rather than invest the money to build the huge assembly tower required to assemble the 120-foot SRBs—which, besides incurring substantial cost, would cause unacceptable delays to the project—MTC and NASA program managers opted to trade off the design.

MTC engineers increased the space between the inner and outer parts of the clevis to accommodate the slightly-out-of-round distortion of the tang and allow the segments to fit together. But as Eric Sevareid once observed, "The chief cause of problems is solutions." MTC discovered the problem this solution created when they conducted hydrostatic tests to simulate launch pressures inside the booster casing. They pumped water into a sealed booster and increased the hydraulic pressure. At a pressure considerably less than projected launch conditions would produce, the mated segments leaked like a sieve. MTC's solution, approved by NASA, was to specify a larger O-ring to seal the offending segments. In addition, 180 shims had to be wedged around the circumference of the lower booster segment to ensure an adequate seal after the space had been enlarged. A sealing paste of potassium chromate was used to protect the O-rings from burning during rocket motor operation, and this appeared to do the trick.

Unfortunately, it was later determined that low ambient temperature stiffened the O-rings, making them inflexible during the vibrations of launch. A succession of events and management decisions that relaxed safety precautions but did nothing to change the functional safety of the system eventually led to the Challenger accident.

APPLYING AN EVAPORATING CLOUD TO THE PROBLEM

The Logical Thinking Process did not exist when MTC experienced their SRB design dilemma. In fact, the Challenger accident itself predated the creation of the Thinking Process by more than five years. But it's interesting to consider how history might have changed had the MTC personnel been able to apply an Evaporating Cloud to their engineering dilemma. With the luxury of hindsight, we can do that now.*

Construction of an Evaporating Cloud actually begins with the articulation of the two conflicting prerequisites. In the case of the Space Shuttle SRB design, these two prerequisites would be *completely redesign the SRB* versus *don't redesign the SRB*. Remember that MTC management foreclosed the option of assembling the booster vertically. (See Figure F.1.)

Once the opposing sides are stated, the requirements each side is intended to satisfy are determined. In the SRB situation, one requirement was to assure functionality and safety. The other was to adhere to the NASA budget. Notice that there is no inherent conflict between these two requirements. (See Figure F.2.)

---

* Application of the Thinking Process to the Challenger accident was the subject of a paper delivered at the APICS Constraints Management Special Interest Group Symposium in 1999.[2]

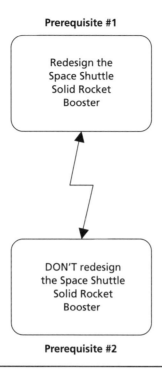

Figure F.1   Articulate the conflict.

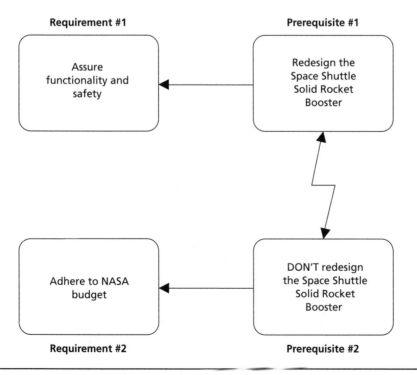

Figure F.2   Determine the requirements.

After the requirements are established, the common objective both requirements support must be formulated. For the SRB, that is a cost-effective space transportation system, where "effectiveness" implies safe to use. (See Figure F.3) The result is a completed Evaporating Cloud.

EXPOSING UNDERLYING ASSUMPTIONS

After the Evaporating Cloud is constructed, the next step is to develop the assumptions underlying each arrow in the cloud. Figure F.4 shows some assumptions for this cloud. There undoubtedly were more assumptions than we've shown here.

It's interesting to note that at first glance most of these assumptions appear to be valid. Only one assumption on each side seems to be invalid. But in the Space Shuttle case, political power was on the side of not redesigning the system.

Whether one side is weaker or not won't be a factor in this situation. In fact, as we saw in Chapter 5, it's possible to find that no invalid assumptions are obvious. Yet we can still "evaporate" the conflict by rendering one or more of the assumptions non-relevant. That's what we'll do in this case.

CREATING INJECTIONS

This particular conflict is clearly an engineering challenge as much as it is a political or financial one. It boils down to how to solve a technical problem within financial constraints. The injection stated in Figure F.5 characterizes the solution to this challenge.

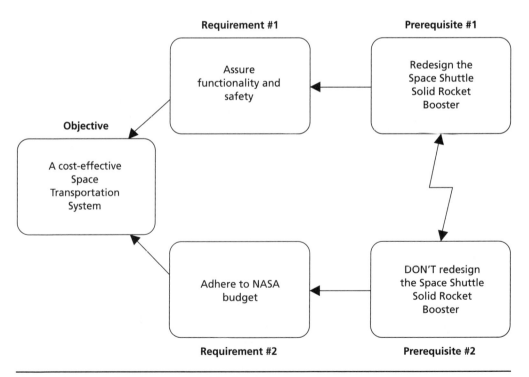

Figure F.3 Formulate the common objective.

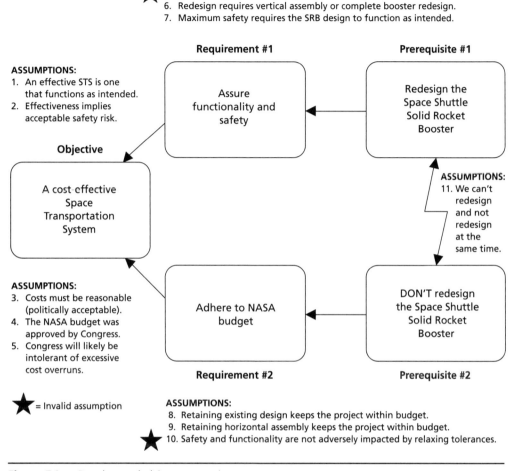

ASSUMPTIONS:
5. SRB redesign is the only way to assure safety and functionality.
6. Redesign requires vertical assembly or complete booster redesign.
7. Maximum safety requires the SRB design to function as intended.

ASSUMPTIONS:
1. An effective STS is one that functions as intended.
2. Effectiveness implies acceptable safety risk.

ASSUMPTIONS:
3. Costs must be reasonable (politically acceptable).
4. The NASA budget was approved by Congress.
5. Congress will likely be intolerant of excessive cost overruns.

ASSUMPTIONS:
11. We can't redesign and not redesign at the same time.

★ = Invalid assumption

ASSUMPTIONS:
8. Retaining existing design keeps the project within budget.
9. Retaining horizontal assembly keeps the project within budget.
10. Safety and functionality are not adversely impacted by relaxing tolerances.

Figure F.4   Develop underlying assumptions.

Remember that in Chapter 5 we learned that sometimes when we're not sure how to do something, we write the injection as an outcome condition we want to achieve. Our injection in Figure F.5 is just such a statement: *Maintain the circular integrity of the two booster segments in a horizontal orientation while they're being mated.*

Fortunately, there are a number of ways to generate creative ideas for solutions. One that particularly lends itself to the engineering environment is TRIZ (a Russian acronym for the *theory of inventive problem solving*). One of the precepts of TRIZ is to start by defining the ideal final result, the IFR. Our injection is such a statement.

As an exercise at a conference in 1999, TRIZ was demonstrated as an "idea generator" to resolve the Space Shuttle SRB conflict.[2:12] Two components of TRIZ are a set of 40 principles of problem solving and a contradiction matrix.[3] The contradiction matrix suggests a number of different possible principles to apply, depending on what you're trying to achieve (the entering arguments of the matrix). Not all principles suggested will

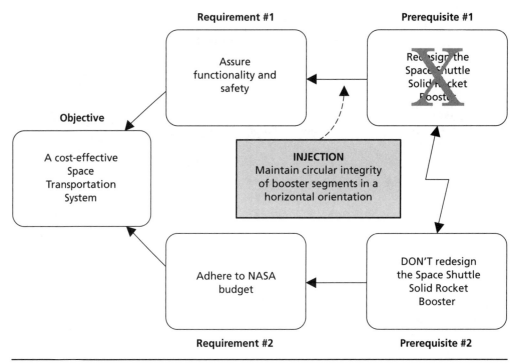

Figure F.5   Create injections.

apply to every situation, but they represent things to consider first. Two did help preserve shape and ease of manufacture when trying to hold cross-sectional area constant:

Principle 24
Use a mediator (an intermediary object to transfer or carry out action) that can be temporarily connected and removed easily.

Principle 34
After it has completed its function, remove an element of an object.

The creative result of these principles was the jig arrangement depicted in Figure F.6. It's one of several solutions proposed by exercise participants at the 1999 conference, and it's a powerful demonstration of the potential to integrate other tools with the Thinking Process.

Unfortunately, TRIZ was not known in the United States in 1976, and the Evaporating Cloud as a conflict resolution tool didn't exist. Ultimately, MTC and NASA jointly decided to trade off clevis-tang tolerances in the interest of making booster assembly of the existing design work. They accepted the degradation that came with it, applied "band-aid" solutions (bigger O-rings, shims, and zinc chromate), and the rest, as they say, is history.

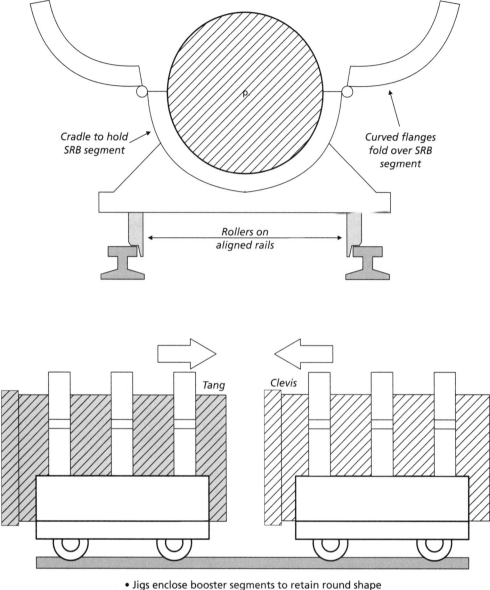

Figure F.6 An engineered solution.

ENDNOTES

1. Dettmer, H. William. *Breaking the Constraints to World-Class Performance*. Milwaukee, WI: ASQ Quality Press, 1998.
2. Domb, Ellen, and H. William Dettmer. "Breakthrough Innovation in Conflict Resolution: Marrying TRIZ and the TOC Thinking Process." *Proceedings*, Constraints Management Symposium. Alexandria, VA : APICS, 1999.
3. http://www.triz-journal.com/archives/contradiction_matrix/

Appendix G
Correlation vs. Cause and Effect

Baked bread may be a health hazard. Research shows that...

- More than 98 percent of convicted felons are bread eaters.
- Fully *half* of all children who grow up in bread-consuming households score below average on standardized tests.
- In the 18th century, when virtually all bread was baked in the home, the average life expectancy was less than 50 years; infant mortality rates were unacceptably high; many women died in childbirth; and diseases such as typhoid, yellow fever, and influenza ravaged whole nations.
- More than 90 percent of violent crimes are committed within 24 hours of eating bread.
- Bread is made from a substance called "dough." It has been proven that as little as one pound of dough can be used to suffocate a mouse. The average person eats more bread than that in one month!
- Primitive tribal societies that have no bread exhibit a low occurrence of cancer, Alzheimer's disease, Parkinson's disease, and osteoporosis.
- Bread has been proven to be addictive. Subjects deprived of bread and given only water actually begged for bread after only two days.
- Bread is often a "gateway" food item, leading the user to harder items such as butter, jelly, peanut butter, and even cold cuts.
- Bread has been proven to absorb water. Since the human body is more than 90 percent water, it follows that eating bread could lead to your body being taken over by this absorptive food product, turning you into a soggy, gooey, bread-pudding person.
- Newborn babies can choke on bread.
- Bread is baked at temperatures as high as 400 degrees Fahrenheit! That kind of heat can kill an adult in less than one minute.

And, most significant of all...

...most bread eaters are utterly unable to distinguish between significant scientific fact and meaningless statistical correlation!

Appendix H
Theories of Motivation

MASLOW'S NEEDS HIERARCHY

Abraham Maslow theorized that human needs described a hierarchy from the basic physiological to high-level self-actualization. There are five levels in Maslow's hierarchy:[1:102-105]

1. *Physiological.* The need for food, drink, shelter, and relief from pain.

2. *Safety and security.* The need for freedom from threat, or security from threatening events or surroundings.

3. *Belongingness, social, and love.* The need for friendship, affiliation, interaction, and love.

4. *Esteem.* The need for self-esteem and the esteem of others.

5. *Self-actualization.* The need to fulfill oneself by maximizing the use of abilities, skills, and potential.

Maslow assumed that people's behavior would be focused on the more basic needs to some level of satisfaction before diverting much of their attention to the higher-level needs. Maslow theorized that a satisfied need ceases to motivate. For example, when a person decides that he or she is earning enough money (how much is "enough" is a personal determination), money loses its power to motivate.

Since many companies provide a comfortable living wage, members of such organizations tend not to worry about where their next meal is coming from, how they'll make their next mortgage payment, or whether they can obtain aspirin to relieve their pain (level 1). They may even be able to live in a safe place, away from the threat of natural disaster or crime (level 2). While they never lose their concern for the things at these two levels, the preponderance of their behavior is likely to be directed toward things like affection and acceptance from others (level 3), or their admiration (level 4). Once they're reasonably well satisfied in these areas, many people's behaviors are more motivated by the need to create something, or to accomplish something noteworthy for their own internal satisfaction, separate from the esteem of others (level 5).

Abraham Maslow conceived of his hierarchy of human needs in the 1940s. It's worth noting that before he died, he repudiated his needs hierarchy and expressed dismay that people made so much of it. Apparently, that message didn't get out as widely as the needs hierarchy did, and people today still subscribe to it.

Notwithstanding the fact that Maslow changed his mind about his own construct, many people—this author included—still find merit in it. While psychologists may differ, practitioners have observed elements of the hierarchy of needs operating in the real world on an almost daily basis. Have you ever heard this saying: "When you're up to your waist in alligators, it's difficult to remember that your original objective was to drain the swamp"? There's an implication of Maslow's hierarchy to be drawn here. Maslow originally suggested that people would only begin operating at the higher levels—3, 4, and 5—after levels 1 and 2 were largely (not necessarily completely) satisfied. Most laymen would agree that it's possible to be operating on multiple levels simultaneously, but not likely on 1 and 5 at the same time, and not to the same degree. Maslow's hierarchy does give some rationale for why some people don't seem to be focused on the level we believe they should be.

In the final analysis, Maslow's theory hasn't been supported by field research studies. While it does explain aspects of human behavior in society, it's probably not smart to depend on it to explain individual-level behavior.[1:105]

HERZBERG'S TWO-FACTOR THEORY

In the late 1950s, Frederick Herzberg theorized that all factors that could motivate human behavior fell into one of two categories: they were either *satisfiers* or *dissatisfiers*. These two factors are also variously referred to as hygiene factors and motivators, or extrinsic and intrinsic factors.

For Herzberg, dissatisfiers included those things that were largely outside the individual, thus their characterization as extrinsic. These factors included:[1:109-111]

- Salary or pay (tangible rewards)
- Job security
- Working conditions
- Status
- Company procedures
- Quality of supervision
- Quality of interpersonal relations among peers, with superiors, and with subordinates

The reason these all seem to be work related is that Herzberg's research was done exclusively in the work place. Herzberg identified these factors as dissatisfiers because their absence (or unfulfillment) could demotivate people but their presence would not positively motivate them. However, some level of fulfillment is necessary to keep people from being demotivated.

As satisfiers, Herzberg identified the following factors:[1:110]

- Achievement
- Recognition
- Responsibility
- Advancement
- The nature of the work itself
- The possibility of growth

These are often referred to as *intrinsic* because they arise from within the individual, rather than from without. Their presence will positively motivate people, but their absence won't necessarily cause dissatisfaction or demotivation.

Herzberg's research on these factors was limited to a small sample (200) of engineers and accountants. For this reason, his theory is often criticized as not representative of a large enough cross-section of society to be validated.

The important lesson to be learned from Herzberg's theory is the concept that positive motivation comes from factors that may be more intellectual than tangible. In other words, they play to the psyche or the mind. Herzberg believed that the best that most organizations could do would be to clear the work place of the factors that would demotivate people (the so-called hygiene factors) and provide opportunities for people to realize the internal satisfaction that would actually motivate them.

McCLELLAND'S LEARNED NEEDS THEORY

David C. McClelland's learned-needs theory, much like Maslow's and Herzberg's theories, has the underlying assumption that people with strong needs will be motivated to use appropriate behaviors to satisfy their needs. McClelland goes further, however, in proposing that a person's needs are learned from the culture of a society.[1:112-117]

McClelland was less concerned with the base needs that comprise Maslow's two lower levels. Rather, he focused on three needs at the higher levels, which he defined as needs for *achievement, affiliation,* and *power*. McClelland[2]

Achievement

People with a high need for achievement (nAch) seek to excel and thus tend to avoid both low-risk and high-risk situations. Achievers avoid low-risk situations because the easily attained success is not a genuine achievement. In high-risk projects, achievers see the outcome as one of chance rather than one's own effort. High-nAch individuals prefer work that has a moderate probability of success, ideally a 50 percent chance. Achievers need regular feedback in order to monitor the progress of their achievements. They prefer either to work alone or with other high achievers.

Affiliation

Those with a high need for affiliation (nAff) need harmonious relationships with other people and need to feel accepted by other people. They tend to conform to the norms of their work group. High-nAff individuals prefer work that provides significant personal interaction. They perform well in customer-service and client-interaction situations.

Power

A person's need for power (nPow) can be one of two types: personal or institutional. Those who need personal power want to direct others, and this need often is perceived as undesirable. Persons who need institutional power (also known as social power) want to organize the efforts of others to further the goals of the organization. Managers with a high need for institutional power tend to be more effective than those with a high need for personal power.

Obviously, people with different needs are motivated differently. People with a high need for achievement seek challenging projects with reachable goals. They need frequent feedback. While money is not an important motivator, it can be an effective form of feedback. Others with a high affiliation need perform best in a cooperative environment. And those with a high need for power seek the opportunity to direct others. All three of these needs are clearly related to cultural mores and societal interactions.

McClelland's learned-needs theory is relevant to the kind of organizational and behavioral change contemplated in a logical Thinking Process analysis. People with high nAch needs are likely to be avid supporters of change—provided they were involved in the change design process (that is, the Thinking Process analysis). To the extent that someone else completed the Thinking Process analysis, nAch types may be interested or eager to participate if they perceive that the logically developed change affords them the opportunity for personal achievement.

People with a high need for affiliation are likely to be eager participants in a change process if it affords them the opportunity to work cooperatively with their valued contemporaries—in other words, a team effort. To some degree, their enthusiasm for change may be reinforced or tempered by the enthusiasm of those they work with.

People with a high need for power are the biggest question mark. A high-nPow type is likely to be a "type A" personality, a take-charge type, and may be a natural leader. This can be both good and bad. If high-nPow individuals are involved in the Thinking Process solution development, they are likely to want to take the lead. If not, they (often with extroverted personalities) would likely support behavior changes if they perceive that these changes will advance their own power agendas.

ADAMS' EQUITY THEORY

Unlike the theories of Maslow and McClelland (but like Herzberg), J. Stacey Adams' equity theory of motivation pertains exclusively to a work place. Equity theory is based on the assumption that people in a hierarchical work environment want to be treated equitably. To the extent that this assumption is valid, they'll compare their efforts and rewards with the efforts and rewards of others.[1:152-156] For Adams, the important issue was the comparative ratio, not the absolute values.

Adams actually summarized equity theory in a simple equation:

$$\frac{OP}{IP} = \frac{ORP}{IRP}$$

In this equation, the left side represents the outcomes of the individual doing the perceiving divided by the inputs of that same person. The right side of the equation represents the same outcomes and inputs for some reference person selected by the perceiving person. As long as the ratio of the observing or perceiving person remains relatively comparable to that of the person observed, the original observer perceives equity and no adverse behavioral consequence results. However, when a person observes that someone else realizes more or better outcomes with equal or less effort than they themselves expend, inequity is perceived. Adams then assumes that if the inequity persists over time, rewards are based on favoritism, luck, or some factor other that individual merit or effort. Basic behavioral theory (positive/negative motivation, reward, punishment, and so on) suggests that over time, motivation to do more than the minimum necessary to avoid adverse consequences will be extinguished.

Adams suggested that if management identifies the perceived inequity, they can act to restore equity by changing inputs, outcomes, or attitudes. However, if management does not identify the perceived inequity (and most probably don't), the observing person will act to change his or her inputs, outcomes, or attitudes. Changing inputs may be indicated by putting in less time or effort, having less concern for reliability, cooperating less with others, losing their sense of initiative, or having less inclination to accept responsibility. Changing outputs might show up as a direct confrontation with a boss asking for a raise in pay, more time off, or better assignments. A change in attitude may show itself as an individual deciding for himself or herself "I've put in enough time."

Most research on equity theory has focused on pay as the basic outcome. Some people assigned to high-status jobs actually increased their performance (in response to a perceived overpayment inequity). But it's not always clear who the comparison *others* are that people use for their equity assessments. There are other uncertainties associated with equity theory for which there is no definitive research, such as the impact of equities on decision making.

In summary, though, the concept of equity in organizational change—whether a Thinking Process analysis eliminates it or creates it—is a possible contributor to either support for a change or resistance to it. Consequently, it should be considered when scrutinizing Current and Future Reality Trees.

SUMMARY

As it relates to Chapter 8, "Changing the Status Quo," this appendix is no more than a "quick hit" on the subject of human motivation. And like Chapter 8, it can't substitute for an in-depth knowledge of why people behave as they do, or don't behave as we would have them do.

Nevertheless, human motivation and behavior remains the most influential determinant of success in solving complex system problems. If you fail to consider it adequately in your solutions, don't be surprised to see them fail.

ENDNOTES

1. Gibson, James L., John M. Ivancevich, and James H. Donnelly, Jr. *Organizations: Behavior, Structure, Processes* (7th ed.). Homewood, IL: Richard D. Irwin Publishers, 1991.
2. http://en.wikipedia.org/wiki/David_McClelland

Appendix I
Legal Application of the Thinking Process

This appendix describes the application of the Logical Thinking Process to preparation for litigation. The example used here was an actual case before a state court. Attorneys for the defendant applied the Thinking Process to the facts of the case and the law.

BACKGROUND

In 1993, Marston Oil brought suit against John Wilson, a former employee, for violation of the state's Uniform Trade Secrets Act.

Wilson had been employed by Marston Oil as a trader (sales representative) for their products, which included a variety of grades of petroleum products for industrial purposes. Marston Oil was a local distributor for large industrial oil producers such as Chevron. As such, they were the link between the producer and the end user, much as a retail store links manufacturers with consumers. This chief difference was that sales of Marston's products were usually concluded in very large volumes, for example, thousands of gallons of fuel oil or lubricants. Sales were referred to as "deals" because price and volume were negotiated on each one. Wilson was compensated by commission on these deals, and he was good at his job. In fact, Marston Oil had hired him away from another company because of his sales record. His specialty was the most lucrative of Marston's product lines, transmix, fuel, and heavy oils (abbreviated TF&H).

Marston Oil was a small family-owned company run by Alan and Geoffrey Hickman. Alan was the CEO and majority stockholder. Geoffrey was vice president. In 1992, Alan decided to run for U.S. Congress in his district. He expended substantial amounts of money on his (ultimately unsuccessful) political campaign, much of which came from Marston Oil's revenues. Expenditures on Hickman's campaign exceeded his expectations and severely reduced the company's cash reserves. Because Marston Oil's suppliers demanded full payment prior to delivery, Marston needed either cash or credit to buy the oil it would resell. Without cash reserves, Marston had to depend on its credit line, which was quickly fully committed.

Wilson found himself unable to capitalize on sales opportunities because there was insufficient cash or credit to purchase TF&H for resale. Lost opportunities meant lost commissions for him. Eventually, in March 1993, Wilson gave his notice and left Marston Oil, hired by another distributor to do the same work.

Marston Oil hired Rick Benson to replace Wilson. Benson was both less experienced in TF&H sales and had less cash/credit to work with than Wilson had before him. Marston Oil's financial difficulties continued.

In mid-1993, Alan Hickman brought suit against John Wilson, claiming Wilson had taken Martson's proprietary information (client lists, contacts, bidding formulae, and so on) with him when he left to go to one of Marston's competitors. Wilson hired a law firm to represent him in the suit.

PREREQUISITE TREE: THE LEGAL SITUATION

The attorney representing Wilson knew he had to prepare for courtroom litigation in the event that the lawsuit could not be settled out of court. Because the case was technically complex, he needed to organize the facts of the case and the provisions of the law in a way that a jury could easily understand. The Logical Thinking Process provided the means to convert the provisions of the state's Uniform Trade Secrets Act (UTSA) into an easily understood necessary-condition hierarchy and the facts of the case into a straightforward sequence of cause-and-effect.

The UTSA defined trade secrets and the circumstances under which it would be considered violated. The defendant's attorney and a Thinking Process facilitator structured the provisions of the law into a Prerequisite Tree (Figure I.1).

Each of the key definitions and provisions of the law was converted into a PRT entity. The actual structure of the text of the law governed the relationships among the necessary conditions. The law identified the standards for confidential information to be considered a trade secret and the standards of protection required. It also detailed the allowable circumstances under which protection of confidential information could be considered breached. And finally, it defined the provable elements for damages.

In the context of the Thinking Process, the relationship among these elements is necessity based. This means that for each successively higher level in the PRT to apply, all lower elements must verifiably apply. Thus, in reading the PRT, the plaintiff must prove that entities 108, 109, 110, 112, 114, and 116-118 happened. The defendant, on the other hand, must demonstrate the failure of proof that any of these happened.

According to the defendant's attorney, the PRT would prove most useful in closing arguments, after the facts of the case had been brought out, to summarize for the jury the failures of the plaintiff to make a case for the presence of those key entities.

FACTS OF THE CASE: THE CURRENT REALITY TREE

As with any legal case, the actual circumstances of the situation hold the evidence to support or refute the complaint. There are two sources of case facts: pre-trial depositions and courtroom testimony. In the Marston v. Wilson case, the depositions were voluminous. From deposition summaries, the defendant's attorney and the Thinking Process facilitator constructed a "story of the case" in the form of a Current Reality Tree. (See Figure I.2a though I.2h)

The CRT provides a concise, logical organization of the facts of the case and their implications. It links disparate facts into meaningful conclusions. And it provides several valuable benefits to an attorney preparing to go to trial.

Unified Picture of Events

The CRT provides a complete, systemic picture of what actually happened. It shows the whole "big picture" and how the various elements tie together.

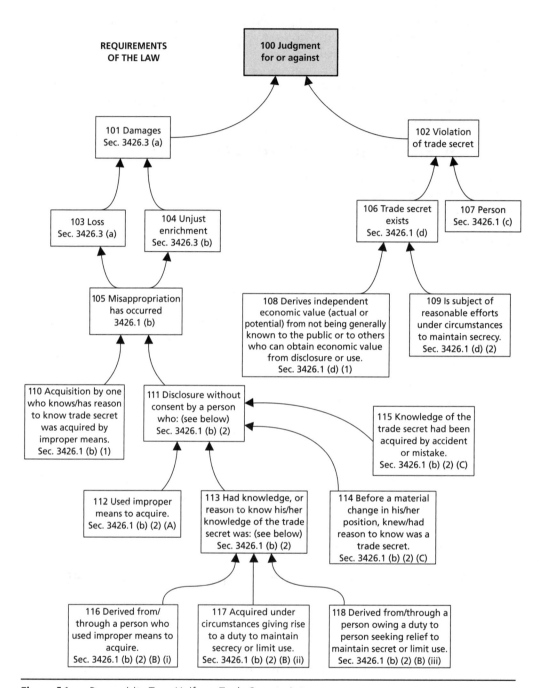

Figure I.1   Prerequisite Tree: Uniform Trade Secrets Act.

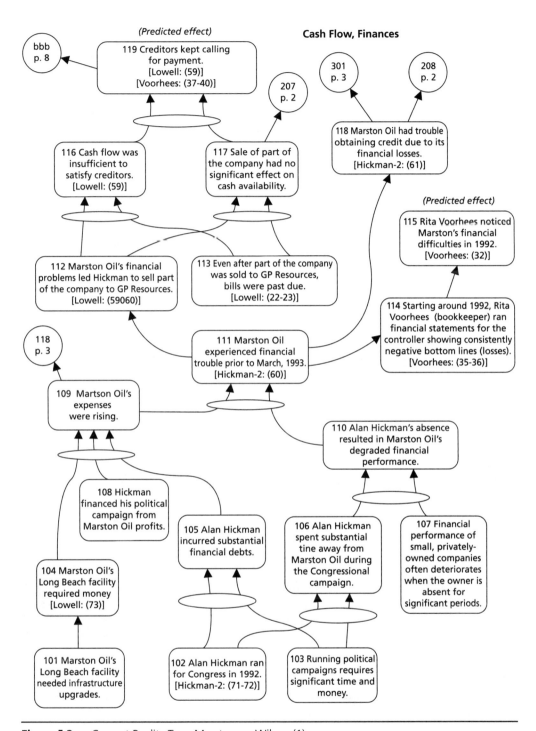

Figure I.2a Current Reality Tree: Marston vs. Wilson (1)

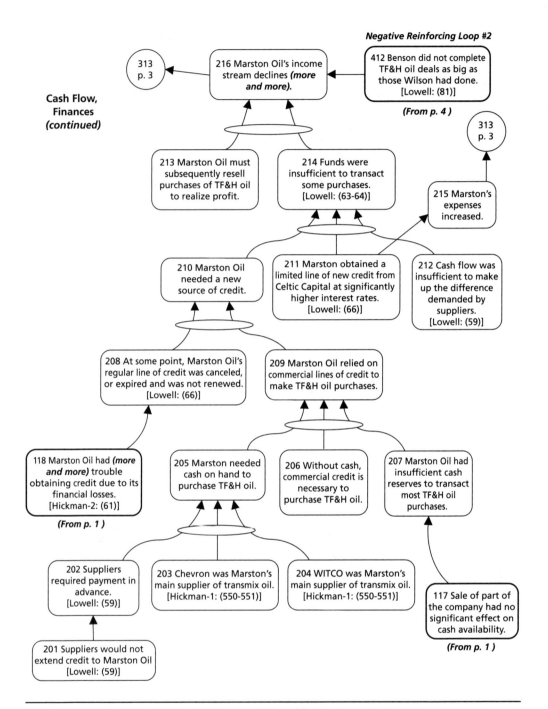

Figure I.2b   Current Reality Tree: Marston vs. Wilson (2)

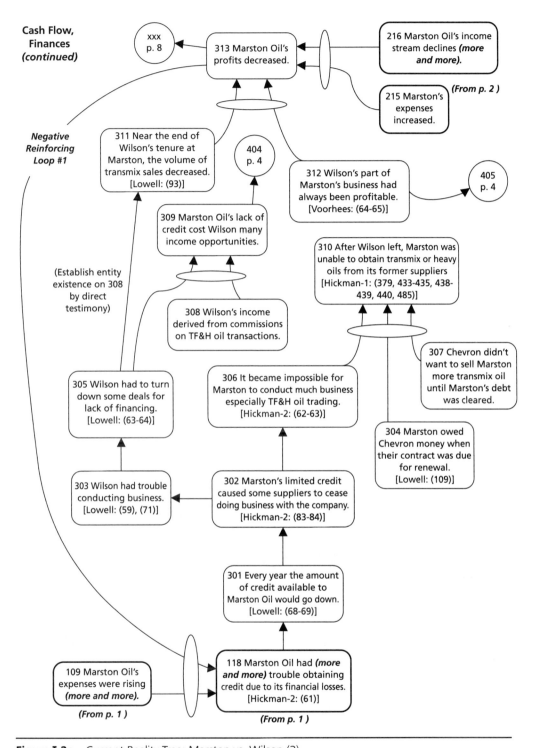

Figure I.2c   Current Reality Tree: Marston vs. Wilson (3)

Wilson's Departure

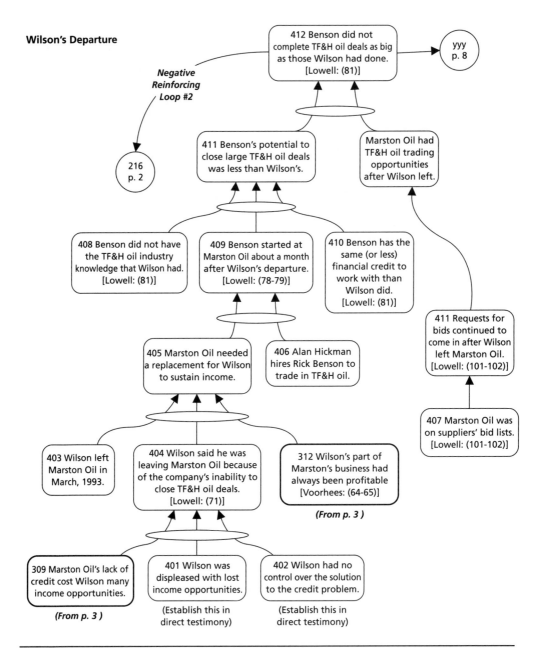

Figure I.2d Current Reality Tree: Marston vs. Wilson (4)

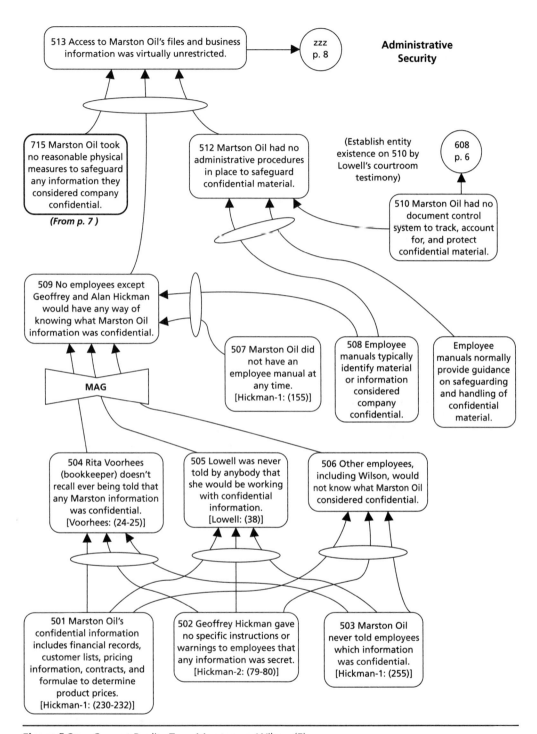

Figure I.2e   Current Reality Tree: Marston vs. Wilson (5)

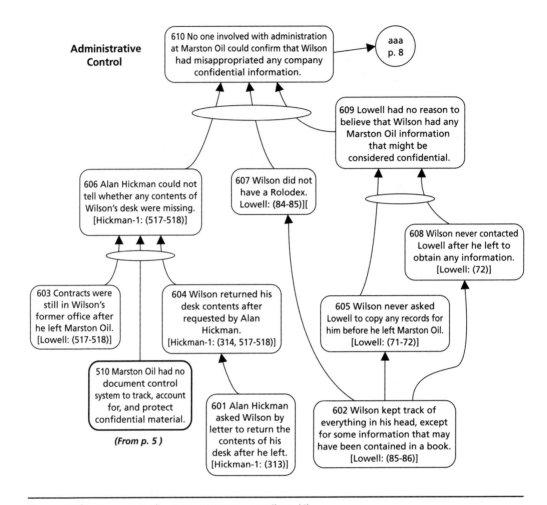

Administrative Control

610 No one involved with administration at Marston Oil could confirm that Wilson had misappropriated any company confidential information.

aaa p. 8

609 Lowell had no reason to believe that Wilson had any Marston Oil information that might be considered confidential.

606 Alan Hickman could not tell whether any contents of Wilson's desk were missing. [Hickman-1: (517-518)]

607 Wilson did not have a Rolodex. Lowell: (84-85)][

608 Wilson never contacted Lowell after he left to obtain any information. [Lowell: (72)]

603 Contracts were still in Wilson's former office after he left Marston Oil. [Lowell: (517-518)]

604 Wilson returned his desk contents after requested by Alan Hickman. [Hickman-1: (314, 517-518)]

605 Wilson never asked Lowell to copy any records for him before he left Marston Oil. [Lowell: (71-72)]

510 Marston Oil had no document control system to track, account for, and protect confidential material.

(From p. 5)

601 Alan Hickman asked Wilson by letter to return the contents of his desk after he left. [Hickman-1: (313)]

602 Wilson kept track of everything in his head, except for some information that may have been contained in a book. [Lowell: (85-86)]

Figure I.2f   Current Reality Tree: Marston vs. Wilson (6)

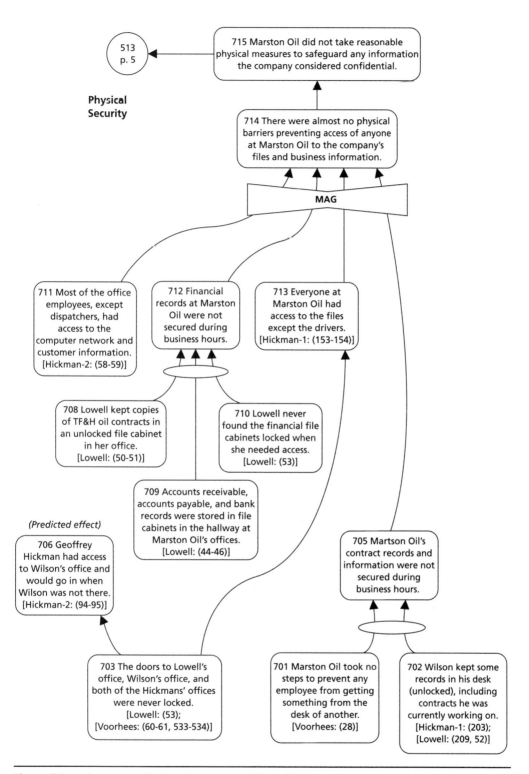

513
p. 5

715 Marston Oil did not take reasonable physical measures to safeguard any information the company considered confidential.

Physical Security

714 There were almost no physical barriers preventing access of anyone at Marston Oil to the company's files and business information.

MAG

711 Most of the office employees, except dispatchers, had access to the computer network and customer information.
[Hickman-2: (58-59)]

712 Financial records at Marston Oil were not secured during business hours.

713 Everyone at Marston Oil had access to the files except the drivers.
[Hickman-1: (153-154)]

708 Lowell kept copies of TF&H oil contracts in an unlocked file cabinet in her office.
[Lowell: (50-51)]

710 Lowell never found the financial file cabinets locked when she needed access.
[Lowell: (53)]

709 Accounts receivable, accounts payable, and bank records were stored in file cabinets in the hallway at Marston Oil's offices.
[Lowell: (44-46)]

(Predicted effect)

706 Geoffrey Hickman had access to Wilson's office and would go in when Wilson was not there.
[Hickman-2: (94-95)]

705 Marston Oil's contract records and information were not secured during business hours.

703 The doors to Lowell's office, Wilson's office, and both of the Hickmans' offices were never locked.
[Lowell: (53); [Voorhees: (60-61, 533-534)]

701 Marston Oil took no steps to prevent any employee from getting something from the desk of another.
[Voorhees: (28)]

702 Wilson kept some records in his desk (unlocked), including contracts he was currently working on.
[Hickman-1: (203); [Lowell: (209, 52)]

Figure I.2g Current Reality Tree: Marston vs. Wilson (7)

Summary

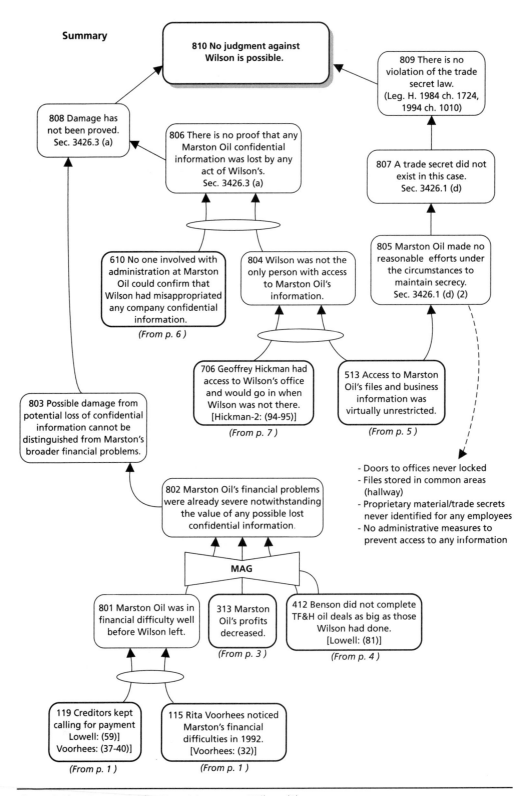

Figure I.2h   Current Reality Tree: Marston vs. Wilson (8)

Highlights Gaps

Perhaps the most valuable contribution the CRT makes is to point out insufficiencies in cause and effect. Using a CRT, it becomes easy for an attorney to identify effects that are missing significant contributing (dependent) causes. A CRT that is begun with deposition statements can quickly reveal what additional information is needed for sufficient cause and effect. This additional information must be obtained during courtroom examination or cross examination. (The CRT in Figure I.2 has such needs indicated.)

Organizes Courtroom Strategy

Testimony in court typically includes having witnesses confirm statements they made under oath in pre-trial depositions and answer other questions not previously addressed in depositions but for which proper foundation has been laid. These represent the additional information needed to demonstrate sufficient cause and effect. All of this information can be functionally organized, as indicated in Figure I.2.

Notice that the first three pages all address Marston Oil's financial situation and how it got to be so bad. The fourth page describes the circumstances that led to Wilson's departure from the company. The fifth, sixth, and seventh pages address the steps the plaintiff took (or, in this case failed to take) to ensure administrative and physical security of the information the company considered confidential. And the final page lays out how the financial, personnel, and information-security facts all combine with the provisions of the law to demonstrate that Wilson is not culpable.

With this kind of outline, the trial attorney can organize the sequence of witnesses and nail down the information that must be elicited or confirmed from each one.

Structures Closing Argument

The last step before a judge's instructions to a jury is the attorney's closing argument. In this phase, the attorney is permitted to do something than isn't allowed in earlier phases: educate the jury on the requirements of the law. The attorney then relates those requirements to evidence that either satisfies those requirements or demonstrates that the requirements have not been satisfied. A Prerequisite Tree such as the one in Figure I.1 can be a useful visual aid for explaining to a jury the necessary conditions specified by the law. And the summary page of the CRT can be a useful visual aid to demonstrate how the facts of the case either satisfy or fail to satisfy the requirements of the law.

> **NOTE:** It would not be prudent for attorneys to show a jury the entire CRT. In most cases, it would only confuse the jury, to the possible detriment of both the attorney and his or her client.

Outcome of Marston Oil v. Wilson

For those who are interested, the Marston Oil v. Wilson case dragged on through a succession of postponements for several years. It never went to trial. Using the facts of the case and the provisions of the law, as structured using the Thinking Process, the defendant's attorney persuaded the plaintiff's attorney that the plaintiff had no sustainable case. Moreover, the evidence was so plainly lacking on the plaintiff's part that the defendant intended to demur. The plaintiff's attorney persuaded the plaintiff to drop the case.

Appendix J
Transformation Logic Tree Software

Included with this book is a unique software application—the Transformation Logic Tree v.1.0 (TLT) for personal computers (PCs). It's the first software application designed specifically to build the trees of the Logical Thinking Process explained in this book. See Figure J.1 for a screen shot.

Developed by Professor Mark Van Oyen, University of Michigan College of Engineering, and his partners at Transformation Logic Tree, Inc., the TLT was created to make it easier for people to use the Logical Thinking Process and capture the results in an easily stored, easily printed form that can also be readily introduced into presentation programs such as Microsoft PowerPoint.

FEATURES OF THE TLT SOFTWARE

Here are some of the handy features of the TLT included on the accompanying disk:

- Fast installation (approximately a minute).

- Can be run from the CD itself, without installation (how many applications do you know that can do *that?*).

- Facilitates classroom teaching by Thinking Process instructors and exchange of trees for review and scrutiny.

- Full featured (not a time-limited or function-limited "trial" or demonstration version). The license has no expiration.

- Create and print worksheet pages of any size (plotter or standard-sized printer).

- Print whole trees on plotter-sized paper, or paginated trees on individual sheets of paper).

- Use with off-page connections, or lay out an entire tree on a multi-page workspace (can be tile-printed and pages taped together).

- Print directly from TLT or copy-and-paste into another standard application, if desired.

- Logic tree entities and symbols standardized to the conventions used in this book.

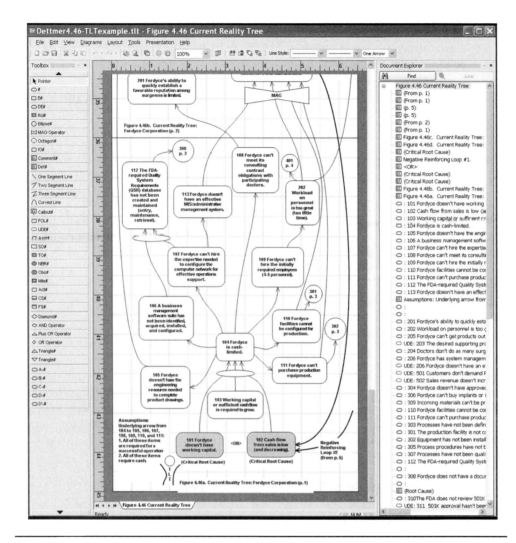

Figure J.1 TLT software – screen shot.

- Automatically generated glossary and list of all entities used in a worksheet/ workbook. You can even put a "story" behind each entity.

- Provides a "document explorer" with hyperlink ("jump to") capability.

- Tutorials included on the CD (in PowerPoint form) and on the TLT website for users without access to PowerPoint.

- Full user manual (on the CD and on the web site).

- Database driven. The same entity can appear on multiple pages, all of them linked. Make one change to the original, and it changes all copies throughout the document.

- "User friendly." Designed to minimize the number of mouse-clicks and knowledge of software details needed to create effective diagrams quickly.

- Auto-numbering and customizable labels.

- Automatic sizing of entities, based on content.

- Customize your connection lines. Select a default for line boldness, solid or dashed, or number of arrowheads (selected values will be applied to all newly created connectors). Double-clicking existing lines allows their style to be changed. Supported Lines: One Segment Line, Two Segment Line, Three Segment Line, Bezier Curve.

- Shade an entity, or several entities simultaneously.

These are only a few of the features of this new Thinking Process application program.

LEARNING SUPPORT

Three progressive tutorials are included on this CD. They are PowerPoint files linked to .TLT files that accompany them. Once you've installed the software, the tutorials automatically take you through the learning process by creating actual .TLT diagrams.

If you don't have PowerPoint installed on your computer, you can operate the tutorials on line. The TLT web site (http://transformation-logictree.com/Dettmer) contains the same tutorials and a full user manual as well as other supporting material, examples, and a helpful frequently-asked-questions (FAQ) page.

UPDATES

The full-featured Version 1.0 is included at no extra cost on the CD accompanying this book. There is no expiration on this version. By 2008, the same version will be offered for sale on the TLT web site to users who have not purchased this book. Check periodically for newer-generation expanded and enhanced versions. Procedures and cost for users of Version 1.0 to update their software are still being determined. (See http://transformation-logictree.com/Dettmer)

DIRECTIONS FOR INSTALLATION

1. Read the "README" file on the CD.

2. Insert the CD into the CD player of your computer running Windows XP or later.

3. Follow the instructions.

4. In the event that you encounter problems, contact the software authors at http://www.transformation-logictree.com/

FOR MORE INFORMATION ON
TRANSFORMATION LOGICTREE SOFTWARE

http://www.transformation-logictree.com/

Glossary of
Thinking Process Terms

action—Something performed. In logic trees, an action is something done by someone, as opposed to a condition of reality, which is a state of being or an outcome. An action is an entering argument (for example, "I wash the dishes"). In contrast, a condition is a resulting effect (for example, "The dishes are clean"). In logic trees, certain entities are phrased as actions, rather than conditions. Example: In the Evaporating Cloud (EC), conflicting prerequisites may be worded as actions (for example, "Do this/Don't do this"). Some injections in a Future Reality Tree and intermediate objectives in a Prerequisite Tree may also be worded as actions. All specific actions in a Transition Tree are phrased as actions.

assumption—A statement or condition accepted as valid without substantiation or proof. Assumptions sometimes are used because proof is not possible or available. Frequently based in tradition rather than logic. Represented by cause-and-effect arrows in all logic trees. The primary targets for refutation in searching for an idea (injection) to break through the conflict between Evaporating Cloud (EC) prerequisites. Invalidation of one or more assumptions in an EC "evaporates" the cloud and its attendant conflict.

categories of legitimate reservation (CLR)—Eight rational tests of a stated cause-effect relationship in a tree. A non-confrontational way of expressing non-acceptance of cause and effect. The eight categories are: Clarity, Entity Existence, Causality Existence, Cause Insufficiency, Additional Cause, Cause-Effect Reversal, Predicted Effect Existence, and Tautology (circular logic).

cause-and-effect arrow—An element of all logic trees that indicates a cause-effect relationship. The visual depiction (→) connects the cause (tail) with the effect (head). Expressed verbally as "If [statement at tail], then [statement at head]."

condition—A state of nature or being. A statement about existing or future reality (for example, "The light is on"). Different from an action, which implies that somebody does something (for example, "I turn the light on"). Conditions can be results of actions or, in a Current or Future Reality Tree, existing environmental reality. In a Future Reality Tree, an effect you're trying to achieve would be worded as a condition. So would the obstacles in a Prerequisite Tree. In an Evaporating Cloud (EC), the requirements and objective are worded as conditions.

constraint—Any element of a system or its environment that limits the output of the system. Analogous to the weak link in a chain. The entity that will ultimately prevent increases in Throughput regardless of improvements made to any other part of the system. Physical constraints (equipment, facilities, and so forth) are usually the result of some policy. If the capability of the system is not constrained internally (such as by physical means or policy), the constraint may lie outside the system, in the environment (for example, market demand).

core problem (CP)—Originally, a single underlying root cause of a majority (that is, approximately 70 percent) of Undesirable Effects (UDEs). The core problem, when effectively solved, automatically eliminates all resulting (downstream) UDEs. The prime target of improvement efforts. (See **critical root cause.**)

correlation—A close relationship in time between two variables. Correlation is the observation that one thing changes in concert with the changes in something else. Differs from cause and effect because no causality is rigorously and logically established. Example: "The team has a winning record; attendance is higher." No cause-effect relationship is established.

critical root cause (CRC)—A critical root cause is a policy, practice, or prevalent behavior that constitutes the lowest level of causality in existing reality lying within someone's sphere of influence to change. All Undesirable Effects (UDE) in a system result from a few critical root causes. One of the minimum number (usually more than one) of root causes in a Current Reality Tree (CRT) that must be neutralized to eliminate all UDEs in the CRT. **NOTE:** Supersedes the concept of a Core Problem (CP).

critical success factor (CSF)—A limited set (usually no more than three to five) of high-level requirements or necessary conditions that must be satisfied for a system to realize its goal. "Show-stoppers"—that is, if they aren't all satisfied, the goal can't be attained. Terminal outcomes in attaining the goal.

current reality tree (CRT)—A visual depiction of current cause and effect. Beginning with Undesirable Effects (UDEs), the Current Reality Tree (CRT) integrates UDEs, necessary conditions, and intermediate statements until all UDEs are linked and root causes and core problems are identified. A diagram that, through the bonds of cause and effect, connects all of the existing UDEs to a few critical root causes (CRC). Answers the question, "What are the critical root causes?"

desirable effect (DE)—A result or outcome that is, in and of itself, positive, desirable, or beneficial with respect to the system's Goal (G) or Critical Success Factors (CSF). The direct or indirect result of an injection. The opposite of an undesirable effect (UDE).

entity—A collective term referring to graphical blocks in a logic tree. Any statement of condition or action enclosed in a geometric figure is an entity. Effects, causes, actions, conditions, injections, intermediate objectives, and obstacles are all entities.

expected effect—A new condition, not previously existing in current reality, resulting from an injection. Depicted as a reality entity (round-cornered rectangle) because it is an outcome of an artificially constructed condition (injection).

Evaporating Cloud (EC)—A logical technique for identifying conflicts and opposing assumptions that underlie core problems and objectives. Composed of an objective (a statement of the system Goal or a Critical Success Factor), requirements (necessary conditions essential to obtaining the objective), and prerequisites (mutually exclusive actions that define the conflicting requirements).

future reality tree (FRT)—A visual depiction of future cause and effect. A means to logically test the efficacy and validity of proposed solutions (Injections) before embarking on implementation. Answers the question, "Does the proposed injection take us where we want to go?"

goal (G)—The ultimate purpose or outcome for which the system is created. A "final destination"; the single result or achievement toward which all system efforts are expended. The goal is determined solely by the owner(s) of the system. Any other influence exerted by internal or external forces other than the system's owners may be considered necessary conditions, but they will not be the goal.

injection—A new or not-yet-existing condition that must be created in order for future reality to unfold in the desired manner. A breakthrough idea that neutralizes conflict. A means of converting Undesirable Effects (UDEs) into Desired Effects (DEs) through a chain of cause and effect. A primary element of the Evaporating Cloud (EC) and the Future Reality Tree (FRT). May also reflect the culmination of a Prerequisite Tree (PRT). An action or condition that invalidates assumptions underlying the requirements and prerequisites of an EC.

intermediate objective (IO)—A lower-level necessary condition or requirement that must be accomplished to realize some higher-level necessary condition. An element of the Prerequisite Tree (PRT) and the Intermediate Objectives (IO) Map.

intermediate objectives (IO) map—A system-level logic tree based on necessary condition relationships. Identifies the system Goal (G), the limited set of Critical Success Factors (CSF), and supporting Necessary Conditions (NC) required to realize the Goal.

intuition—The ability to recognize and understand patterns and interactions of a system. The ability to see or connect patterns out of a few data points. Not "flying by the seat of your pants." Rather, the convergence of knowledge and experience.

inventory (I)—All the money a system invests in things it intends to sell. Includes raw materials, but also includes items traditionally considered assets, such as facilities, equipment, land, and so forth (things that can depreciate). Inventory is not really an asset. Inventory is not subject to value added (no value is added to inventory until the moment of sale).

necessary condition (NC)—A circumstance indispensable to some result, or that upon which everything is contingent. A condition or state of nature that must be satisfied in order to satisfy a Critical Success Factor and realize a system's Goal. Necessary conditions are imposed by the laws of physics or nature, and by power groups, both internal and external to the system. Without satisfying the necessary condition, the system will fail to realize its goal. Example: The goal may be to make more money, but necessary conditions may be product quality, customer satisfaction, regulatory compliance, production safety, and so on.

negative branch (NB)— An undesirable or unfavorable development in a Future Reality Tree (FRT) that results from an injection. May be a side effect deleterious to realizing desired effects (DEs), or may be a significant negative outcome that compromises the intended effects of a proposed problem solution (Injection). Requires an additional injection at the point where the tree branch starts turning negative in order to trim the branch.

objective (O)—The focus of an Evaporating Cloud (EC). The outcome that an injection is designed to achieve. Usually the Goal (G) or a Critical Success Factor (CSF) of a system.

obstacle (OBS)—A condition or opposing reaction that may prevent successful application of an Injection. An element of a Prerequisite Tree (PRT). Usually conceived or brainstormed by tree builders to anticipate possible complications in implementing the injection. Requires the creation of an Intermediate Objective (IO) to neutralize.

operating expense (OE)—All the money the system spends turning Inventory (I) into Throughput (T). A system-level measurement, not an individual product unit cost allocation. As Inventory is depreciated, it becomes an Operating Expense.

power group—An individual or group, internal or external to the system, exerting influence on realization of the system's goal by imposing necessary conditions. Examples are unions, government regulatory agencies, Congress, special interests, and so on.

prerequisite (P)—An element of Evaporating Clouds (EC) and Prerequisite Trees (PRT). In the EC, one of two mutually exclusive actions or apparent compulsions embodying a conflict. In the EC, a prerequisite is considered a "want" rather than a "need." In the PRT, the prerequisite is called an intermediate objective and constitutes the condition or action, not yet existing, necessary to overcome an obstacle.

prerequisite tree (PRT)—A logic tree used to identify all the component tasks necessary to the realization of an Injection. Also helps identify potential obstacles to proposed solutions (Injections) and ways to overcome them (Intermediate Objectives).

requirement (R)—An element in an Evaporating Cloud (EC). A non-negotiable need that must be satisfied to realize the objective of an EC. A necessary condition.

reservation—A non-confrontational means of qualifying acceptance of a cause-effect statement represented by a cause-effect arrow. Indicates that the cause-effect relationship, as depicted, is insufficiently clear to the observer. A request for more information. Expressed verbally as, "I have a reservation . . ." Must be followed by citing one of seven reasons (see **categories of legitimate reservation**).

root cause (RC)—An original cause, through a chain of cause and effect, of an undesirable effect (UDE). Any statement in a Current Reality Tree (CRT) that does not derive from another statement. An entry point into a CRT. Depicted as an entity from which cause-effect arrows lead away but do not enter. (See **critical root cause.**)

subject matter (SM)—The information content pertaining to an issue. In logic trees, the topic about which the tree pertains, as differentiated from the logic process itself.

throughput (T)—The rate at which the system generates money through sales (profit-making systems). Throughput (T) does not occur with the transfer of money internally (within the company). It can only occur through the infusion of new money from outside the system. Throughput and sales are not synonymous; T is concerned with the rate at which money is generated through sales. In not-for-profit systems, T may be reflected in some non-monetary metric that indicates progress toward the system's Goal.

transition tree (TT)—A logic tree for "fleshing out" detailed step-by-step implementation activities. A more detailed variety of Future Reality Tree (FRT). In essence, an implementation plan that structures management action to achieve FRT Injections.

undesirable effect (UDE)—A visible symptom of a deeper, underlying Critical Root Cause (CRC). An effect that is negative or undesirable with respect to the system's Goal or a Critical Success Factor (CRC). A terminal entity in a Current Reality Tree (CRT).

Bibliography

Books and Periodicals

Argyris, Chris. *On Organizational Learning*. Oxford: Blackwell, 1992.

"A Special Report on Executive Pay," *The Economist*, January 20-26, 2007.

Bennis, Warren, and Burt Nanus. *Leaders: Strategies for Taking Charge*. NY: Harper-Row Publishing Group, 1985.

Bragg, Steven M. *Throughput Accounting: A Guide to Constraint Management*. Hoboken, NJ: John Wiley and Sons, 2007.

Button, Scott. "Genesis of a Communication Current Reality Tree: The Three-Cloud Process," *1999 Constraints Management Symposium Proceedings*, APICS, March 22-23, 1999.

Caspari, John A., and Pamela Caspari. *Management Dynamics: Merging Constraints Accounting to Drive Improvement*. NJ: John Wiley and Sons, 2004.

Cilliers, Paul. *Complexity and Postmodernism: Understanding Complex Systems*. NY: Routledge (Taylor and Francis Group), 1998.

Collins, Jim. *Good to Great: Why Some Companies Make the Leap...and Others Don't*. NY: Random House Business Books, 2001.

Covey, Stephen R. *The Seven Habits of Highly Effective People: Powerful Lessons in Personal Change*. NY: Simon and Schuster, 1989.

Cox, James F., III, and Michael S. Spencer. *The Constraints Management Handbook*, Boca Raton, FL: The St. Lucie Press, 1998.

Damasio, Antonio R. *Descartes' Error: Emotion, Reason and the Human Brain*. NY: G.P. Putnam's Sons, 1994.

Daniels, Aubrey C. *Bringing Out the Best in People: How to Apply the Astonishing Power of Positive Reinforcement*. NY: McGraw-Hill, 2000.

Deming, W. Edwards. *Out of the Crisis.* Cambridge, Mass.: MIT Center for Advanced Engineering Study, 1986.

_____. *The New Economics for Industry, Government, Education.* Cambridge, Mass.: MIT Center for Advanced Engineering Study, 1993.

Dettmer, H. William. *Brainpower Networking Using the Crawford Slip Method.* Victoria, BC (Canada): Trafford Publishing, 2003.

_____. *Breaking the Constraints to World-Class Performance.* Milwaukee, WI: ASQ Quality Press, 1998.

_____. *Strategic Navigation: A Systems Approach to Business Strategy.* Milwaukee, WI: ASQ Quality Press, 2003.

Deutschman, Alan. "Change or Die," *Fast Company,* May 2005, p.53

Domb, Ellen, Ph.D., and H. William Dettmer. "Breakthrough Innovation in Conflict Resolution: Marrying TRIZ and the TOC Thinking Process." *Proceedings, Constraints Management SIG Symposium,* APICS, 1999.

Domb, Ellen, Ph.D., and Kalevi Rantanen. *Simplified TRIZ: New Problem-Solving Applications for Engineers and Manufacturing Professionals.* Boca Raton. FL: St. Lucie Press (2002).

Gardner, Howard. *Changing Minds: The Art and Science of Changing Our Own and Other People's Minds.* Boston, MA: Harvard Business School Press, 2004.

Gibson, James L.; J. Ivancevich; J. Donnelly. *Organizations: Behavior, Structure, Processes* (7th ed.). Homewood, IL: Richard D. Irwin Inc., 1991.

Goldratt, Eliyahu M. *Critical Chain,* Great Barrington, MA: North River Press, 1997.

_____. *It's Not Luck,* Great Barrington, MA: North River Press, 1994.

_____. *The Goal,* 2nd ed. Great Barrington, MA: North River Press, 1992.

_____. *The Haystack Syndrome* (Croton-on-Hudson, NY: North River Press, 1990).

_____ and Robert E. Fox. *The Race,* Croton-on-Hudson, NY: North River Press, 1987.

Harvey, Jerry B. *How Come When I Get Stabbed in the Back My Fingerprints are Always on the Knife? And Other Meditations on Management.* San Francisco: Jossey-Bass, 1999.

_____. *The Abilene Paradox and Other Meditations on Management.* San Francisco: Lexington Books, 1988.

House, Robert J. *Culture, Leadership, and Organizations: The GLOBE Study of 62 Societies.* Thousand Oaks, CA: SAGE Publications, 2004.

Jaques, Elliott. *Social Power and the CEO.* Westport, CT: Quorum Books, 2002.

_____. *The Requisite Organization* (rev. 2d. ed.). Arlington, VA:Cason Hall & Co., 1998.

Jaques, Elliott. and S. Clement. *Executive Leadership.* Arlington, VA: Cason Hall, 1991.

Kaufman, Stephen F. *Musashi's Book of Five Rings.* Boston, MA: Tuttle Publishing, 1994.

Leach, Lawrence P. *Critical Chain Project Management,* Boston, MA: Artech House, 2000. 14.

_____. *Lean Project Management: Eight Principles for Success.* Boise, ID: Advanced Projects Institute, 2005.

Lepore, Domenico, and Oded Cohen. *Deming and Goldratt: The Theory of Constraints and the System of Profound Knowledge.* Great Barrington, MA: The North River Press, 1999.

Levine, Harvey A. *Project Portfolio Management.* San Francisco, CA: Jossey-Bass, 2005.

Maslow, Abraham. "A Theory of Human Motivation," *Psychological Review,* July 1943, pp. 370-396.

Morris, Peter W.G., and Jeffrey Pinto. *The Wiley Guide to Managing Projects.* Hoboken, New Jersey: John Wiley and Sons, 2004.

Newbold, Robert C. *Project Management in the Fast Lane: Applying the Theory of Constraints.* Boca Raton, FL: The St. Lucie Press, 1998.

Osinga, Frans P. B. *Science, Strategy, and War: The Strategic Theory of John Boyd.* London: Routledge, 2006.

Project Management Institute. *A Guide to the Project Management Body of Knowledge* (3rd ed.). Newtown Square, PA: Project Management Institute, 2003

Richards, Chet. *Certain to Win.* Xlibris, 2004.

Roadman, Charles M., et.al. *Proceedings, Constraints Management SIG Symposium,* APICS, 1995.

Scheinkopf, Lisa. *Thinking for a Change: Putting the TOC Thinking Processes to Work.* Boca Raton, FL: St. Lucie Press, 1999.

Schragenheim, Eli, and H. William Dettmer. *Manufacturing at Warp Speed,* Boca Raton, FL: The St. Lucie Press, 2000.

Stokes, Geoff. *Popper: Philosophy, Politics and Scientific Method.* Malden, MA: Blackwell Publishers, 1998.

Terninko, John, Alla Zusman, and Boris Zlotin. *Systematic Innovation: An Introduction to TRIZ.* Boca Raton. FL: St. Lucie Press (1998).

University of Southern California. *Trojan Family Magazine,* Spring 2001, p.36

Internet

http://dictionary.reference.com/browse/direct

http://dictionary.reference.com/browse/goal

http://en.wikipedia.org/wiki/Big_Dig

http://en.wikipedia.org/wiki/David_McClelland

http://en.wikipedia.org/wiki/Inductive_reasoning

http://www.qualityamerica.com/knowledgecenter/articles/CQEIVH3f.html

http://www.sover.net/~devstar/define.htm

http://thesaurus.reference.com/browse/generic Thesaurus.com.: "generic." *Roget's New Millennium Thesaurus, First Edition (v 1.3.1)*, Lexico Publishing Group, LLC.

http://www.triz-journal.com/archives/contradiction_matrix/

Message posted to the TOC-L Internet Discussion List, July 19, 1995, SUBJ: "T, I, and OE in Not-For-Profit Organizations," summarizing a conversation between Dr. Eliyahu M. Goldratt and the author on July 16, 1995, and posted at Dr. Goldratt's request.

http://www.worldofquotes.com/author/Proverb/50/index.html

Index

Page numbers in *italics* refer to tables
or illustrations.

V

v-shaped connections, 105–106, *106*
validity, entity existence, 38, *38*
value, money as measure of, 19–20
Van Oyen, Mark, 394
verbalization
    assumptions, 183
    categories of legitimate reservation, 149
    Current Reality Tree, 111, 122–124
    Evaporating Cloud, 182–183, 185, 191
    negative reinforcing loops, 125–126
    of predicted effect existence, 54
    Prerequisite Tree, 276–278
    of underlying assumptions, 111
vertical systems hierarchy, *73*

W-Z

"wants" *vs.* "needs," 185–187
weakest links, 8–9, 12, 120. *See also* constraints
what to change, 15, 21, 23–29, 96, 219, 234, 294. *See also* Current Reality Tree (CRT)
what to change to, 15, 21, 23–29, 96, 219, 234, 294. *See also* conflict resolution diagram
Wilson, John, 382–393
win-win vs. win-lose, 163–164, 175
Wurtzburg Corporation, 203, *203*